Routledge Revivals

Transnational Party Co-operation and European Integration

In this book, first published in 1981, the authors trace and analyse the growth of transnational party co-operation and the factors important to it during the years before and immediately following direct elections. They recognise three major dimensions of transnational co-operation: the Euro-parliamentary groups; the new European party federations; and the national party frameworks in the member states. This title will be of interest to academics and students concerned with European affairs.

Transnational Party Co-operation and European Integration

The Process towards Direct Elections

Geoffrey Pridham
Pippa Pridham

Routledge
Taylor & Francis Group

First published in 1981
by George Allen & Unwin Ltd

This edition first published in 2016 by Routledge
2 Park Square, Milton Park, Abingdon, Oxon, OX14 4RN
and by Routledge
711 Third Avenue, New York, NY 10017

Routledge is an imprint of the Taylor & Francis Group, an informa business

© 1981 George Allen & Unwin (Publishers) Ltd

Publisher's Note
The publisher has gone to great lengths to ensure the quality of this reprint but points out that some imperfections in the original copies may be apparent.

Disclaimer
The publisher has made every effort to trace copyright holders and welcomes correspondence from those they have been unable to contact.

A Library of Congress record exists under LC control number: 80041479

ISBN 13: 978-1-138-95720-6 (hbk)
ISBN 13: 978-1-315-66524-5 (ebk)
ISBN 13: 978-1-138-95722-0 (pbk)

Transnational Party Co-operation and European Integration

GEOFFREY PRIDHAM
and
PIPPA PRIDHAM

London
GEORGE ALLEN & UNWIN
Boston   Sydney

First published in 1981

GEORGE ALLEN & UNWIN LTD
40 Museum Street, London WC1A 1LU

© George Allen & Unwin (Publishers) Ltd, 1981

British Library Cataloguing in Publication Data

Pridham, Geoffrey
    Transnational party co-operation and European
    integration.
    1. Political parties – European Economic
    Community countries
    I. Title   II. Pridham, Pippa
    329'.02'094   80-41479

    ISBN 0-04-329032-9

Set in 10 on 11 point Times by Grove Graphics
and printed in Great Britain
by Lowe & Brydone Limited. Thetford. Norfolk.

Contents

List of Tables

List of Abbreviations

EC	European Community
EP	European Parliament
MEP	Member of European Parliament
EPP	European People's Party
ELD	Federation of Liberal and Democratic Parties of the EC
CD	Christian Democratic group (group of the EPP) of the EP
Soc	Socialist group of the EP
Lib	Liberal and Democratic group of the EP
Con	European Conservative group of the EP
Comm	Communist and Allies group of the EP
DEP	European Progressive Democratic group of the EP
NI	*Non-inscrit* (independent) MEP
D	West Germany
I	Italy
Ire	Irish Republic
UK	Britain
Dk	Denmark
NL	Holland
B	Belgium
Lux	Luxemburg
F	France

Preface

The idea for this joint study arose from the authors' own co-operation in researching and writing two chapters on transnational party
co-operation in 1977 for Stanley Henig's *Political Parties in the
European Community*, at a time when this activity was already
acquiring a new importance with the prospect of direct elections to
the European Parliament. Their combined work on the subject in
fact began with this initial survey and continued from then on,
although Geoffrey Pridham had for many years previously during
the 1970s studied the growth of transnational party co-operation.

The method pursued in researching comprehensively what is,
apart from the background history of the Euro-parliamentary
groups, a relatively new area of European integration has been to
concentrate on extensive élite-level interviews with those involved in
transnational party activity which were substantiated by available
and relevant documentation from European Community and
national party sources. Interviews were conducted both at the
European level with MEPs and group secretariats, EP officials and
those working for the new party federations and in the national
capitals with party leaders, international secretaries and party
Euro-experts as well as national party officials and organisers. All
the national capitals were visited except for Rome and Dublin,
mainly because of time constraints, although this deficiency was in
part remedied by invitations to the party federation congresses
which proved an ideal location for contacts with party personnel
from the various EC countries all at the same time. Much further
information and material was gained by continuous and lengthy
correspondence with EC and national party contacts during 1978
and 1979.

Our greatest single debt is to the European Commission for providing us with one of their annual research grants in 1977. This
financed our many trips abroad which while undoubtedly bene-
ficial to the cause of academic hedonism allowed us the opportunity
to tap many fruitful and informative sources, open unexpected
doors to further investigation and also make several new friends.
Individual thanks must be recorded not only to all those mentioned
in the 'List of Interviews' at the end of this book who generously
gave us of their time, but also in particular to Michael Palmer and
David Millar (also for commenting on Chapter 2) of the EP
secretariat, David Blackman of the Socialist group secretariat for
showing a constant interest in our work and answering our tedious
requests for material, John Fitzmaurice for discussions on a subject

of mutual interest, Jay Blumler of Leeds University for reading Chapter 5, Schelto Patijn and Len Berghoef for making our visit to Holland so worthwhile and, last but not least, the Konnertz family, Fiona Macleod and Carol and Val Herman for their hospitality while working in Bonn, Luxemburg and The Hague respectively. Our main thanks in finishing the book go to Anne Merriman, without whose typing skills this work would have reached production in a much messier form. Although this Preface does not wish to end with a commercial, it has to be acknowledged that this study would have been less bearable at the writing stage without Nescafé and Kenya coffee supplies as well as Hamlet cigars, whose atmospheric effects were countered by the swinging-door relationship between the co-authors in the final months of the work. A final culinary thanks should be given to the staff of the Berkeley café, while much appreciation is felt for the countryside around Bristol where long rambles helped to clear our minds.

GEOFFREY PRIDHAM   *Bristol*
PIPPA PRIDHAM   *December 1979*

1

Political Parties and European Integration: The Historical Perspective

(a) The Party-Political Dimension of European Integration

The fundamental hypothesis of this analytical and empirical study of transnational party co-operation in the European Community (EC) during the 1970s is that party-political integration has for the first time come into its own as a serious prospect, even though it may trace its roots and history back to the pioneering years of European integration in the early 1950s. This is by way of describing in a shorthand manner a process of politicisation of transnational party activity in the EC – where this becomes less 'platonic' and begins to bear some relevance to party politics in general – deriving both from the more overt political nature of the EC itself in the 1970s as well as specifically from the important stimulus from direct elections to the European Parliament (EP). In the latter case, it was not only the event itself (first planned for May/June 1978, and later postponed to June 1979) which provided the momentum for more intensive European party co-operation – notably beyond the Parliament – but particularly the process itself towards, and preparations for, direct elections during the period 1974–9, that is from the time it was generally regarded as a realistic possibility, having been an object of pro-integration aspirations for well over twenty years. It should be remembered that this process was subsequent to, and simultaneous with, a refocusing of interest from the early 1970s in the institutional development and deficiences of the Community, notably with reference to the lack of democratic control over its increasing executive and bureaucratic orientation.

While the authors are sceptical about the broader possibility of altering or rectifying this imbalance even with a directly elected EP, there have nevertheless been recognisable and significant changes in the evolution of transnational party co-operation during the decade of the 1970s. As a working definition, 'transnational party co-operation' in the EC is the term applied to *the institutionalised co-ordination and promotion of common policy positions and other forms of European activity by political parties of the same ideological tendency from different member countries within the broad framework of the European Community.* In stressing the significance of its development in the third decade of European integration, the authors are comparing and contrasting with the essentially peripheral or 'passive' form of such co-operation during the preceding twenty years. The politicisation of such activity is furthermore likely to be long-term and incremental, depending on the future development of the European Community as a form of 'political system'.

The main element of this politicisation in the 1970s has been that transnational party co-operation has both affected its traditional Euro-parliamentary form and extended beyond it, assuming a new organisational and political importance in response to conscious initiatives, the move towards direct elections, in particular, and also the widening scope of European integration itself. Previously, the Euro-parliamentary dimension of such co-operation (the transnational party groups in the Common Assembly of the European Coal and Steel Community [ECSC] and later the EP) had existed as its sole formal expression largely in limbo with little, if any, influence on the EC executive institutions, not to mention the positions of individual political parties on European policy within the contexts of their own national political systems. Politicisation in the 1970s has entailed two significant changes in the nature of EC-wide transnational party co-operation: first, the introduction of a European party-organisational dimension with the establishment and promotion of three Community party federations by the Socialists, Liberals and Christian Democrats, representing an important departure from the loose consultative party associations like the traditional Internationals; secondly, a crystallisation process commencing with the growing interlinkage of the three dimensions of transnational party co-operation: the Euro-parliamentary, the transnational party-organisational and the national party frameworks. This has been accompanied by a growing inclination to express ideological differences in a European setting. The structure of this book is based substantially on an examination of these three dimensions of transnational party co-operation in the EC, as in Chapters 2, 3 and 4, with subsequent chapters concentrating on the importance of the event of direct elections for this process, in order to assess how the three dimensions have interrelated.

A major hypothesis of this study is that transnational party co-operation can no longer be considered purely at its horizontal level as a European exercise, but must also be examined vertically with respect to the impact of national party outlooks (not to mention differences within them) on such European-level activity as well as the possible influence of the latter on the former. Therefore, this book will take into account such factors emanating from the national party-political arena which have increasingly impinged on this co-operation. The obvious connecting factor between the European and national arenas of party activity – apart from executive institutional links – is the formulation of European policy in general, so that it is relevant to view individual parties' involvement in the transnational exercise in the light of their overall positions on Community policies. Background on these is provided in section (*b*) which follows, for it is instructive to look at the trend of party European policies as this should provide some key to the quality and degree of the national orientation of individual parties in relation to transnational activity. But how much can a correlation be established between the pro-integrationist ideology of parties and their receptivity to transnational involvement without the intervention of other factors? Whatever the answer, it is possible to begin to speak of an evolving party-political dimension to European integration even with all the necessary qualifications about the importance of this process in the 1970s.

From a different angle, the development of this transnational co-operation presents a certain unique opportunity for some new insights in the comparative study of West European political parties. Obviously, all parties engaging in this co-operation operate in the setting of like-minded or similar national political systems dominated by the concept and practice of 'party government', qualified in the case of France with its element of presidential government. This common denominator among EC countries is underlined by the explicit emphasis on the pluralism of political forces within democracy as a vital prerequisite for Community membership in the consideration of the post-dictatorship applications for EC entry from Greece, Spain and Portugal. However, the special contribution of transnational party co-operation in its more politicised form to comparative studies is precisely that this common activity reflects on the general problems of European party development and cannot be considered without reference to it. Transnational co-operation provides a location at which one can compare individual political parties *directly* in their relationship with each other for not only may their attitudes to European elections and transnational co-operation reflect on their wider approach to European integration, but also their behaviour in a transnational framework may touch, though sometimes only tangentially, on a variety of other factors such as national institutional procedures, political roles and political cultures – not to mention individual party traditions, identities and ideological motivations. These further aspects of party development have been brought more into play by the fact that, on the one hand, direct elections to the European Parliament have retained a supranational symbolism having been a federalist aspiration for so long, and hence have aroused divergent reactions from national parties, and, on the other hand, the practical process of preparations for these elections has required their involvement in a novel but concrete political exercise.

The previous lack of political impact and restricted scope of transnational party co-operation is illustrated by the nature or the very lack of literature on the subject of both this activity and political parties and European integration in general. The few scholarly studies that have appeared have concerned themselves solely with one or other of the three aforementioned dimensions in isolation. There is only a handful of pioneering works on the party groups in the European Parliament (EP), notably van Oudenhove on the period 1952–62 and Fitzmaurice on the years up to Community enlargement in 1973, although Haas had drawn attention to their potential importance as early as 1958.[1] More recently, Norbert Gresch has introduced discussion on a wider plane in a useful study devoted to both the EP party groups and the growth of transnational party organisation,[2] although the novelty of the latter dimension as a political exercise restricted to the Community has so far prevented detailed or elaborate accounts of the performance of the party federations.[3] The positions of parties in their national settings have inevitably received more attention, although there has still been a scarcity of studies focusing specifically on the development of their European policies. The few examples would include Criddle on the French Socialists during the 1950s, Marchal-van Belle on the Belgian Socialists during the period 1948–65, Paterson on the SPD from 1945 to 1973, and Walker on the Italian parties during the whole postwar period.[4]

The reasons for this shortage of surveys in the field are primarily connected with the development of European integration itself. While Haas had singled out political parties as well as interest groups as 'the significant carriers of values and ideologies whose opposition, identity or convergence determines the success or failure of a transnational ideology' in the development of European integration along the lines of a political community,[5] the actual course of integration over the past twenty years has emphasised the subordinate role of parties as such as 'actors' on the Community stage, compared with the dominance of executive institutions both national and European. Harrison noted in 1974: 'Key groups like parties and interest groups have not become *increasingly* involved at the Community level nor have they invested heavily in transnational organisation',[6] although events since have demanded some modification of his judgement. The low political profile or importance of parties directly in European integration has consequently not encouraged investigations of their performance and activity. With regard to the national party frameworks the problem has been more complicated for, as one researcher recently emphasised, 'up to the present it remains no easy task to assess the extent and significance of inter-party co-operation within single states on behalf of the European idea – the history of the various political parties has not yet been sufficiently investigated for that purpose'.[7] Academic interest in the field has inevitably begun to increase in the light of the first European elections and will probably continue in that direction afterwards, as those held in 1979 were the first of a permanent five-year cycle. Indeed, party-political integration as well as political parties *and* European integration has been something of a 'forgotten' aspect of Community studies. Paterson introduced his study of the SPD and European integration by stressing the neglected aspect of domestic political factors in the formulation of a party's European policy.[8] David Marquand summarises correctly the general problems which have faced an examination of this aspect of European integration:

> Most discussion about the Community, and particularly about its institutional structure, is based on the tacit assumption that its development and policies can be understood without reference to party; and, although that assumption has never been entirely accurate, it has contained an important element of truth. It would be impossible to write the history of the Community in the 1960s without paying at least some attention to the influence of Gaullist ideology on French policy-making, or the history of the Community since 1973 without paying similar attention to the ideological divisions within the British Labour Party. But, although the Community's development has been shaped, in part, by party pressures, these pressures have made themselves felt almost wholly at the national level.[9]

A variety of broad questions about the role of political parties in the European Community arise at this point. The development, performance and significance of transnational party co-operation cannot clearly be assessed outside the general institutional and political context within which it has operated, which in turn points to the problem of what kind of evolving 'political system' is represented by the EC. This underlines the conceptual risks associated with too narrow an approach to the subject by focusing exclusively on one dimension or the other. Viewed in a wide perspective, the development of transnational party co-operation easily leads to a consideration of such specific questions as the following. Does the relative politicisation of this process in the 1970s mark the pre-history or early stages of a future European party system? Are transnational party formations essentially dependent variables or also possible determinants of the integration process? Can it still be assumed in all certainty that the national arena of activity will remain the exclusive priority in the thinking of individual political parties, thus presenting a fundamental limitation on their willingness or ability to merge their sovereignty within the framework of party co-operation at the European level?

Because of the specialism of studies so far in this field there has been a lack of broader interpretative thought on the contextual role of political parties in European integration. Certain assertions have been made somewhat loosely about the form of transnational party development, which under more rigorous scrutiny show an analytical weakness. The most notable instance is that the most relevant model is provided by the US party system. Ernst Haas, who was the first to portray the responses of the political parties of the then six member states to the early efforts to create European institutions, stated in his *The Uniting of Europe* (1958) that 'the major indices of behaviour make ECSC parties quite similar to the American or Canadian prototypes'.[10] This assertion has been repeated since, sometimes rather unsystematically, for there is an initial attraction in the parallel because of the inevitably loose structure of any European party formations. Reference is made to a specific period in US history, as with Marquand, who draws an analogy with the American Whigs and Democrats of the 1830s and 1840s, although he does admit that the parallel 'should not be pushed too far'.[11]

One major weakness of the US analogy is that it offers no more than a 'still-life' model, for it attempts to compare non-comparables when viewed at the dynamic level. The authors would argue that European transnational co-operation can only be measured by the criteria of European party development, of which the political parties engaged in such transnational activity are themselves prime examples. In reference to the European party federations, it is already clear that, unlike modern US parties, they are not merely conceived of as only electoral organisations for they have already embarked on the business of policy formulation, despite the severe limitations imposed on this exercise by their operating on the basis of pre-existing national parties with their own histories and, in some cases, long traditions.[12] Furthermore, the US model is weakened fundamentally by the fact that the European Community has developed alongside, or in conjunction with, fully fledged nation-states, so that any presupposition about a European federal structure is inaccurate. There is, above all, no historical parallel for equating modern European nations with the pre-history of the USA up to the 1780s. The *sui generis* nature of the 'political system' of the EC demands approaching this investigation by using initially at least the criteria of European party development for reasons of historical background.

The ultimate reference point for any discussion of a possible 'European party system' arising from transnational party co-operation must clearly be the present and likely future form of the 'political system' of the EC as a whole. Such a long-term and open question relates to the potential role conceived for transnational party formations in acting as political infrastructures for the EC or as suprastructures for party harmonisation in the EC, or both. Yet, any discussion of a 'European party system' immediately encounters the problem of the lack of political weight and constitutional powers of the 'supranational' institutions of the EC, notably the European Parliament, which has provided the most important restriction on the scope and potential of transnational activity. Haas stressed this basic limitation in his pioneering survey of the party groups in the Common Assembly of the ECSC,[13] and it has been an unavoidable factor since. The same problem has been a subject of renewed political and academic debate during the 1970s as direct elections have drawn attention to the institutional deficiencies and the question of powers of the European Parliament.

There are three introductory points worth making about the political system of the EC, which have some general bearing on the long-term potential of transnational party co-operation. First, as Roy Jenkins, President of the European Commission, has remarked, 'the Community is rooted firmly in the principles of representative democracy and, while its means may be largely economic, its origins and objectives have always been political' (speech to the Dutch European Movement, April 1979). This was notably true of the Schuman Plan of 1950 and, while European integration has since then been more implicitly than explicitly political, there are significant ways in which this has been visible. The analogy of the Rome Treaty of 1957 with a national constitution has some relevance, but it in fact goes further in outlining the common policies to be pursued. The general aim of transferring relevant powers of economic policy-making from the national governments to the EEC obviously has important political implications. The relevance of all this for transnational party activity is that there exists and has developed a genuine arena at the European level for policy discussion and political engagement, the main problem being the structural channels for achieving this.

The second point concerning the EC's 'political system' is its unique nature. There are sufficient *sui generis* elements in the EC to make its 'system' unique for, as Roy Jenkins correctly asserts: 'I do not believe that what we shall achieve over the next generation will be directly comparable to any model of political scientists, whether federal or confederal.' It is essential not to overlook the principal feature of Community decision-making with the two interconnected levels of activity of the evolving European one and the traditional national, whereby each has consequences for the other without the outcome being recognisable in conventional, structural or political terms. This corresponds with the three-dimensional interpretation (two European and one national) of transnational party activity. The EP is itself unique, just as the EC differs from conventional and non-integrative (European) international organisations like the Council of Europe and the Western European Union, which have also boasted European assemblies.

Thirdly, the development of the EC as a form of 'political community' in a broad sense rather than just as an institutional structure has some relevance to the potential of transnational party co-operation, especially with a view to its possible role of consensus-formation and of mobilisation. This broader aspect of the political scope of Community development has in particular attracted the attention of integration theorists such as Karl Deutsch in his concentration on a 'social-psychological' form of political community (in his *Political Community and the North Atlantic Area*, 1957), though his later work tended to confirm the continuing hold of the nation-states (in *France, Germany and the Western Alliance: A Study of Élite Attitudes on European Integration and World Politics*, 1967). Ronald Inglehart similarly recorded the small evidence of any major shift of loyalties and expectations from the national to the European levels among the public opinions of the member countries, although there had developed a 'permissive consensus' about European integration and a more favourable attitude among the postwar than the earlier generations.[14] This would point to the very limited scope for the public effects of a more politicised form of transnational party co-operation and its 'exposure' with direct elections, although it is possible that some of Inglehart's conclusions might have to be revised a decade later.

In conclusion, general development of the European Community in the 1970s has promoted and conditioned the politicisation of transnational party co-operation. While the recent course of European integration has been described as following a more intergovernmental path than before, the full implications of this process cannot be confined to what is traditionally regarded as 'intergovernmental', because of its ever-enveloping character. The different member countries have over time become increasingly intermeshed economically and, to some extent, socially with the completion of the common customs union, the continuation of the common agricultural policy, new commercial policies and regional and social programmes as well as plans to establish EC monetary arrangements. The discussion or elaboration of 'second-generation' policies from 1969 has also created a broader, and sometimes more controversial, scope for Community policy activity, notably in the inclusion of more overt political areas such as foreign-policy co-ordination. Equally, embarking on European elections was un-doubtedly a political act, while the revived debate over European institutional powers is a reflection of the same trend. At the same time, EC enlargement in 1973 and projected further enlargement from the early 1980s have increased the international profile of the Community.

The EC has therefore been progressively outgrowing the lines of development introduced by the Rome Treaty. This move in a broader political direction has strengthened the argument for some kind of European-level party activity both to 'interpret' these trends and to offer a means of exposing, controlling and influencing policy decisions. Yet, parallel to all these developments has been a growing tendency to assert openly national interests in Community policy-making. This is partly logical as new areas of policy activity come closer to national sensitivities, but also environmental as the insta-bility of the international monetary system and the energy crisis, while underlining the interdependence of EC member states, have at the same time sharpened this national assertiveness. The econo-mic environment has in the 1970s been substantially different from that of the 1950s, when the Common Market was created in a period of sustained growth among the then member states. This accordingly raises doubts about the political cohesion of the EC as a whole with obvious implications for party co-operation. In other words, the European Community has in varying ways entered a new historical phase in the 1970s. This chapter will continue to look at the significance of these general changes for transnational party development by considering some of its thematic aspects within an historical perspective.

(b) The Evolution of the European Policies of Political Parties

In view of the proposition in the Introduction that there is some relationship between the positions of political parties on European integration in general and on transnational party co-operation in particular, this section focuses separately on the former aspect delineating the development of the European policies of individual parties and of the main ideological tendencies during the two decades up to the period on which this book concentrates, namely the 1970s. We shall therefore to some extent look towards the examination of the national party frameworks in Chapter 4.

Just as European integration has involved the dovetailing between national and *communautaire* positions, so it is legitimate to ask how much the politicisation of transnational party co-operation has furthered a two-way process of both an 'internalisation' of European questions and a 'Europeanisation' of national party positions. Here, the historical background of party European policies should throw light on the quality and degree of the national orientation of individual parties in relation to transnational activity. The historical perspective is, for instance, crucial in determining the nature and importance of party attitudes, traditions and identities and how these have been moulded by the national political environment. Can the ready consensus on direct elections in the mid- and later 1970s in countries such as West Germany, Italy and Belgium, and, by contrast, the divisions between and within parties on the same question in France, Britain and Denmark, be largely explained by history as against immediate circumstances? The historical dimension further allows a long-term view of parties' positions on European integration, thereby indicating their consistency, or lack of it, the imprint of their ideology and, above all, the influence of a variety of sometimes conflicting factors or 'inputs' and 'outputs' which characterise the formulation of party policies in general.

The potential for the above-mentioned two-way process of 'internalisation' and 'Europeanisation' depends ultimately on the impact of European integration as a factor in national politics, especially whether it has continued as one among many issue-areas in national politics or has increasingly benefited from a growing European dimension at the national level. The latter development would naturally reflect on the possibilities for, and effects of, the process of politicisation in the EC during the 1970s. Writing in the early 1970s with reference to national administrative procedures, Helen Wallace stated unambiguously that 'the weight of the evidence so far available suggests that the Communities have not penetrated dramatically into the national political scene, but have rather been confined predominantly within the executive (particularly within some departments) and within the sphere of certain national élites'.[15] She concluded that 'European issues have, in practice, tended to be regarded as one bundle of issues rather than as a new dimension pervading the political spectrum'.[16] However, this question does need reopening following the emergence of the party-political dimension of European integration in the course of the 1970s in order to see whether this largely confirms the predominance of élites and the compartmentalisation of European policy. What still emerges as the decisive overall determinant of trans-national party co-operation is the 'internal' or national party factor. Despite this, the general process of politicisation in the EC has compelled national parties to pay more attention to the need for their European co-operation. In addition, a distinction must be made between the various member countries, such as those regarded as having 'penetrated systems' such as Italy and West Germany – with their closer interlinkage of domestic and external (including European) politics – and others where European policy is viewed as an extension of foreign or diplomatic activity. However, even the latter have been affected by the 'overflow' of EC common policies into the domestic area of policy-making, notably in agriculture and increasingly in other sectors of economic and social policy.

One general trend is immediately apparent when looking at integration and the evolution of party European policies: a growing consensus about the basic value of European integration across the whole ideological spectrum of European politics, while at the same time there has emerged a more distinct tendency to differentiate within that consensus about how to interpret European integration in relation to actual or envisaged Community policies. One may, of course, chart the European positions of different political forces, but without resorting to too detailed a discussion of individual cases it is preferred here to select a number of key features of this development before categorising specific determinants which have motivated party European policies in the past.

It is a statement of the obvious, but relevant for this study, to observe that parties in the European Community (i.e. in the member states) are predominantly liberal-democratic in nature. By definition, they occupy a middle-of-the-road position on the axis between egalitarianism and inegalitarianism; they orientate towards liberalism as distinct from authoritarianism; and they base their philosophy on democracy rather than monocracy.[17] With a small margin for variation, this may be stated about all of them, whether they are labelled as Liberal, Conservative, Christian Democratic or Social Democratic. There are, however, important exceptions with the West European Communist parties and those parties of the moderate left, which should be termed Socialist rather than Social Democratic because they aim at radical changes in favour of equality.

This broad classification facilitates perception of the nature and development of the party-political consensus around European integration in the 1950s and 1960s. Originally, support for European projects was very narrowly liberal-democratic in party terms; or, more precisely, it came with the greatest conviction from the

Christian Democrats whose European credentials were established in the name of the Community founding fathers of Adenauer, De Gasperi and Schuman. These projects also had the backing of various centre-right and centre-left parties such as the German FDP (Free Democratic Party), the Belgian Liberals and a section of the French Radicals, as well as the French Socialist SFIO and the Italian Social Democrats. As Haas noted in his examination of party positions in the six member states of the early 1950s, Christian Democratic support alone did not suffice to establish European projects (especially the ECSC) but was dependent on the convergence of 'a sufficiently large number of separate national party positions'.[18] The fact that this 'European majority' was 'based on convergent rather than homogeneous motives and ideologies' and hence 'brittle' was amply demonstrated by the collapse of the project for a European Defence Community in the mid-1950s. Only in Holland was 'Europeanism' then accepted without dissent, while support from the Socialist/Social Democratic parties (with the Dutch and French as the main exceptions) was either tenuous or not forthcoming[19] – the German SPD being regarded as essentially Socialist until its revisionist course with the Godesberg Programme of 1959. The Communist parties were, of course, decisively negative then, including the Dutch one.

There followed two major stages in the enlargement of the integrationist consensus with the inclusion of virtually all Socialist/ Social Democratic parties and the solidification of support from the miscellaneous (and on the earlier occasion partially hesitant) centre-right parties by the late 1950s, with the notable exception of the French Gaullists; followed by the considered movement of the Communist parties, particularly the Italian PCI (Italian Communist Party), towards a positive acceptance of European integration during the 1960s, though belatedly and reluctantly on the part of the other major example, the French PCF (French Communist Party), during the 1970s. The extreme right, a fringe force in all member states, had not really featured in the integration debate, although in its most consistent form, in Italy, it had assumed a positive position already in the 1950s.

With the first stage, one begins to notice a pattern of differentiation appearing within pro-integration positions because the adoption of these by the Socialist/Social Democratic parties did not entail a full-scale ideological reorientation, although certain basic policy assumptions were changed, as in the two most relevant cases of the Italian PSI (Italian Socialist Party) and, more dramatically, the German SPD (German Social Democratic Party). In the latter instance, the SPD's historical change of programmatic direction made it more possible to accept the essence of the West

German CDU/CSU's European policy. Common, however, to both cases was the respective party's 'vocation for government', for with the PSI an espousal of European integration (as well as of the Atlantic Alliance) was regarded as an imperative touchstone of faith by the ruling Democrazia Cristiana (DC) before the conclusion of the centre-left alliance in Italy in the early 1960s. One feature which nevertheless still distinguished the moderate left from the Christian Democratic parties was that the former's internationalism was less Euro-centric. This voiced itself in a greater attention to the need for Community enlargement to include Britain and Scandinavia and later other countries from the Mediterranean, without forgetting the attention paid by these parties to a greater role for the EC in the Third World. It is also significant that their earlier reservations about European integration had focused on the belief that this would lead to the creation of a 'clerical' Europe. The fervent Christian Democratic motivation behind the early European projects had aroused anti-clerical suspicions and traditions among Socialists, whether they included parties already pro-integrationist, like the French SFIO[20] and the Belgian PSB (Belgian Socialist Party),[21] or those, like the SPD, which still took an intransigent line.[22] Behind such a concern on the part of the moderate left lay a latent or expressed desire to shape the future political course of European integration, a motive which was later to bear fruit in demands for a more activist pursuit of integration policies, especially with a social content, and ultimately to encourage a more politically binding form of transnational party co-operation in the 1960s.

From the preceding discussion there emerges a clear dividing line for the Social Democratic parties or the Social Democratic wings in Socialist parties were more conventionally pro-integrationist than were the Socialists. This distinction was underlined by the consequences of the programmatic transformation of the SPD, the continuing postwar divide between the Italian PSDI (Italian Social Democratic Party) and PSI over European policy and the general feature whereby Socialists were more committed than Social Democrats (as basically progressive pragmatists at heart) to the pursuit of their ideological aims which could run counter to the liberal-democratic ideological sympathies of the European projects at this stage.

A brief reference to individual cases shows, however, that this assumption, while containing much truth, nevertheless excludes other factors contributing to the 'conversion' of Socialist parties. Illustrating the above-mentioned distinction, Criddle claims that the SFIO's position was not really ideologically motivated on Europe[23] (i.e. Social Democratic?) and that 'there is no real evidence of the

SFIO pursuing what could be interpreted as specifically socialist economic goals'.[24] Similarly, Veenstra comments that the Dutch Labour Party (PvdA) placed European integration before the creation of a Socialist order in its priorities;[25] while, on the other hand, the SPD of the earlier 1950s emphasised among its integrationist reservations the need for British entry to strengthen the forces of the left in the incipient Community.[26] However, it should not be forgotten that, in the case of a strong national consensus on integration, as in the Netherlands, this inevitably affected the position of the party in question (the PvdA). The effects of government or opposition roles, or the desire for a role in government (as with the SPD in the 1960s, not to mention the PCI in the 1970s), could also help to mould a party's European policy for reasons of political convenience as well as programmatic conversion. As Marchal-van Belle has shown, intermittent governmental responsibility facilitated the assumption of pro-integrationist positions by the Belgian Socialist Party;[27] but more significant was the fact that by the later 1950s those groups in the PSB which had previously been hostile to abandoning national sovereignty were now demanding stronger EEC institutions and better organisation for the Socialist parties in the Six to make their ideas prevail in Europe.[28] Parties of the moderate left were, for instance, insistent on the need for a greater priority to be accorded social affairs in Community policy-making. This channelling of partisan commitments into a more activist integrationist course did, of course, find one major exception among the moderate left in the British Labour Party with its deep ideological antagonism to integration and an internationalist outlook resolutely linked to the concept of a 'wider world'.

The second stage of the enlargement of the pro-integrationist consensus among political forces with the partial inclusion of the Communists was even more significant because of its international implications. The USSR eventually assumed a position of *de facto* recognition of the European Community in 1972, but well before then the PCI as the most 'entrepreneurial' of the Communist parties in the member states had embarked on a revisionist course over European integration. It is perhaps relevant to note that the EEC was established when there was a general reorientation within the international communist movement, following the Hungarian crisis of 1956 and Khrushchev's rebuttal of Stalin the same year. The PCI was the first such party to start rethinking its own assumptions about integration, beginning in the early 1960s and evolving during the subsequent decade with the adoption of an activist position on integration, participation in the Community institutions (the European Parliament in 1969) and a reversal of the demand for the Italian withdrawal from NATO in 1974.[29]

It is worth summarising at this point the main reasons for the change in the PCI's European policy or, as it is more significantly called, its European 'strategy', because this case illustrates how much a non liberal-democratic party offered a distinctly different interpretation of European integration. First, this revisionist course must be intrinsically linked, on the one hand, to the party's own domestic strategy of the 'Italian road to socialism' and later the 'historic compromise' and, on the other, its overall international approach of taking an independent line towards Moscow. The latter's relevance for the PCI's revised position on integration is reflected, for instance, in the party's pronounced pan-European viewpoint on the Community's development with its espousal of further enlargement and continuing emphasis on the need to 'overcome' the two military blocs in postwar Europe.

Secondly, the PCI's move from a fundamentally negative stand on integration as the economic base of the Atlantic Alliance to a positive position did not mean a simple acceptance of the conventional values of the EC. The very fact that in changing course the PCI did not enter the liberal-democratic camp as a 'Social Democratic' force, but instead proclaimed the 'European road to socialism', enhanced qualitatively the scope for party-political differentiation within the framework of integration itself. The originality of this course derived from the party's need to marry its programmatic change on the EC with its long-term ideological orientation. This produced specific demands for 'positive integration' in the EC, that is a priority given to elaborating new policy alternatives which would create further areas of harmonisation. The PCI's espousal of 'positive integration' expressed itself in a number of ways – in demands for new regional and social policies, the insistence on breaking the dominance of monopolies and on 'restructuring' the European economy and regular advocacy of the democratisation of the EC's 'authoritarian' institutions. While its own pro-integrationist position contained a genuine recognition that many policy problems could no longer be solved by nation-states, as the PCI had discovered through its own experience the limitations of a purely national strategy,[30] its motivation was also decidedly national in seeking to enhance its own legitimacy as a political force by means of the European stage.

The principal remaining point of divergence on integration among the major political forces throughout the EC was the retention of traditional ideological reservations towards integration by the French PCF and smaller Communist parties, unable, as they were, to relinquish completely their negative outlook concerning the cold war origins of European unification. This reluctance to adopt a pro-integrationist course was in the case of the PCF undoubtedly linked to and determined by its more sectarian approach in domestic politics (compared with the PCI) and the imprint of French political values as in its insistence on national 'independence'. Not until after the union of the left with French Socialists and its entry to the EP in 1973 did the PCF evidence some willingness to conform to the pro-integrationist consensus, but even then it maintained many contrary positions to the PCI and did not essentially abandon its negative attitude to the EC. With regard to the smaller Communist parties in member states which have remained negative or sectarian over European integration, it is useful to note that they have been much less subject than the two major cases to electoral or other domestic political pressures, which have certainly been an influential factor in motivating both the latter's conversion and the general growth of the pro-integrationist consensus during the 1950s and 1960s.

In concluding the historical evolution of party European policies, some further comments enlarge on the problems of their formulation. First, it is the view of the authors that the terms 'pro-European' and 'anti-European' are misleading and essentially outdated, particularly with reference to the development of party positions. These terms have, of course, been widely used in public debate and, while possibly applicable to individual groups within parties at different times (notably with proposed Community membership), they are not viable analytical tools. Preferable terms are 'pro-integrationist' and 'anti-integrationist', allowing for variations of degree, since it is quite legitimate to participate in the Community process and yet take a restrictionist line about future development.

Secondly, there was a distinct absence of concrete party European programmes as distinct from European policy forming a subsection of general party programmes during the period under discussion. The Socialist parties of the Six did formulate a common European action programme in 1962,[31] at a time when direct elections to the EP were temporarily under discussion, but instances of individual national parties drawing up comprehensive European programmes as such were very rare. One such exception was the European manifesto of the Dutch Christian Democratic parties of May 1962 and another the programme for Europe outlined by the newly established Giscardian Independent Republicans (FNRI) in October 1966, although their prime motivation was to promote a separate profile from the dominant Gaullists. This clear absence of conscious programmatic initiatives on Europe by political parties revealed how little European integration had percolated downwards as a real source of contentious debate, and confirmed the dominance of the integration process by the national executive institutions.

Thirdly, it is worth repeating that the formulation of European policies – and particularly changes of position on European integration – was determined by a variety of motives, including modifications of party strategy or alternation between government and opposition roles, general developments in international relations and the influence of economic factors as well as ideological or programmatic revisionism. These influences on party European policies will now be considered systematically with reference to three categories of determinants which lie primarily within the arena of the national party frameworks: the party-traditional factor, the political-functional factor and the socio-political factor. These determinants will provide the analytical basis in this study for assessing the form and degree of influence of national party politics on transnational co-operation and the scope for some merger between the two.

(i) *The party-traditional factor:* Features grouped in this category are the influence of individual party traditions (for example of an internationalist kind), particularly whether these promote a positive or negative attitude towards European integration or as such accord a high priority to European policy in relation to other international areas; the relevance of party ideology as either directly pro-integrationist, whereby 'Europe' has been built into the party's 'way of life', or secondary because the absence of a systematic ideology may have allowed a 'pragmatic' approach to European questions; and, finally, how much the very experience of Community membership may have modified traditional party outlooks. A background theme is the erosion of the traditional distinction between foreign and domestic politics as an evolving consequence of European integration.

The Christian Democratic parties have traditionally evidenced the most favourable attitude towards European positions. The German CDU has emphatically adhered to Adenauer's postwar 'European vocation' (in the words of its leader in the 1970s, Helmut Kohl, it is 'the classical party of European integration'), the former French Mouvement Républician Populaire (MRP) fully espoused the European cause, while the Italian DC under De Gasperi adopted European integration on distinctly political grounds, not to mention the pro-integrationist outlook of the respective parties in the Benelux states. In general, therefore, Christian Democracy, as essentially a new postwar movement, adopted European unity unreservedly as one of its principal tenets. Furthermore, pro-integrationist values were not just a privilege of their party élites but became an element in the 'belief system' of their activists.[32] Their attitude on Europe accordingly had an ideological character despite the 'pragmatic' reputation of these parties. However, their attachment to European unification did owe much to its indentification with their establishment after the Second World War as leading parties in government. This was reflected in the anti-communist beliefs of Christian Democrats for integration was launched during the Cold War, while it also allowed them to strengthen their claims as a force for postwar renewal. Their Euro-peanist convictions depended also on the personal role of their leaders then. The MRP did not become fully committed to a pro-integrationist course until Schuman's initiative with his Plan for the ECSC in 1950.[33] Similarly, the Italian DC expressed little interest in the first postwar years in the European option but eventually moved to a pro-integrationist position from 1948, when De Gasperi accepted its arguments on the grounds of international security and domestic political consolidation, hence involving as a consequence support for federalist solutions rather than vice versa.[34]

A common denominator among the different political forces of the member states has been some direct relationship between their sense of internationalist identity and their readiness to espouse a clear pro-integrationist position or otherwise. While the Christian Democrats were essentially Euro-centric for the reasons stated above, the oppo-site was true of the West European Communist parties, especially when they continued to follow a traditional path in their inter-nationalist orientation. Even their change towards a pro-integra-tionist stance required a fairly elaborate process of ideological justification, amply illustrated in the case of the PCI, resulting in a 'redefinition' rather than rejection of the cause of 'proletarian internationalism'. By comparison, the Socialist/Social Democratic parties have stood midway in varying degrees between the two extremities of Euro-centricity and broad internationalism. In the earlier postwar period the French SFIO was probably the closest to the former, as reflected in its popularising the idea of Socialist party co-operation within the framework of the Council of Europe,[35] but common to all the parties of the moderate left during the 1950s was their promotion of wider Community membership and in parti-cular their solicitation for British entry. The SPD was concerned primarily with the national preoccupation of German reunification during the first postwar decade, which helped to determine its reluctant attitude on integration; while at this time the British Labour Party's main tenets of its external policy, as developed during the period of the Attlee government (1945–51), were a principled preference for limited forms of intergovernmental co-operation rather than integration, and a priority accorded Common-wealth interests and the transatlantic relationship over the other 'circle' of Europe in the British foreign policy spectrum. These positions were to continue influencing Labour approaches to Euro-pean integration during the decades which followed. Hence, the pro-integrationism of different parties has been decisively influenced over time by ideological considerations (their internationalist traditions) and national considerations (traditional international concerns).

Another major point of reference for assessing the impact of the party-traditional factor on European policy is the general tendency of parties towards national sovereignty as against supranationality. Whilst most political parties in question have not been specifically located at one extremity or the other, this is nevertheless a useful analytical starting-point for comparative purposes. It is a reasonable assumption that a strong attachment to national sovereignty as a distinct value by a political party will entail a negative, or at least restrictive, position on integration, if only because this involves a long-term acceptance of ever closer union between different member states, which is likely to touch on ideological outlooks.

It is possible to chart the general positions of individual parties within this ideological spectrum, though with the necessary qualifications made for changes of position over time, the degree of attachment to one preference or the other and internal party differences. On the supranational side, the Christian Democratic parties would appear with only minor variations as those most ideologically receptive to a federal Europe. The Italian PCI could be included as having moved towards this side for very different reasons, as already seen. On the national-sovereignty side of the spectrum, the French Gaullists and Communists together with British Labour possessed a pronounced ideological bent with perhaps the addition at a later stage of certain left-wing Danish parties, like the Socialist People's Party (SF) or the Radikal Venstre, which voiced the concern about Danish entry that 'at longer range we could completely lose our sovereignty in a Community that could grow both political and military'.[36] Clearly, different motives lay behind such convergent positions within this spectrum for, whereas the Gaullists had expressed themselves most clearly in this respect in the 1950s over national control over the French army in the European Defence Community debate, and later adhered to de Gaulle's concept of a *Europe des patries*, the British Labour Party was motivated more by the desire to maintain national control over socio-economic policy-making and the idea of parliamentary sovereignty. Before its own conversion to British entry, the Conservative Party also revealed a concern about national sovereignty, though in a milder fashion.[37] Other political parties were located between the two extremities, often with shades of grey and some ambiguity. Paterson has commented that the SPD 'oscillated wildly' in its attitude to supranationalism in the 1950s,[38] just as Marchal-van Belle has shown conclusively that the Belgian Socialists retained a certain scepticism about abandoning sovereignty while accepting integration.[39] During the same period, the Dutch Labour Party was closer to the supranational side in supporting the transfer of sovereignty, though obviously it was reflecting the strong pro-integrationist consensus within the Netherlands. It is evident that national factors counted very strongly in applying this ideological spectrum as a test of basic party attitudes.

The party-traditional factor cannot be assessed fully without attention to internal party differences over integration, especially where these related to individual party traditions, for they were bound to affect the formulation of European policies. An early example was the moderate left French Radical Party, which during its governmental period in the Fourth Republic was often bitterly split over successive European projects with 'neo-Radicals' supporting them, even the EDC, and other internal groups taking an intransigent line because of anti-German or anti-Catholic attitudes.[40] It was the Socialist parties which otherwise featured the deepest divisions on integration, specifically the British and Danish cases, where the traditional left/right internal cleavages have provided the most reliable indicator of attitudes towards the Community for 'the further Left one is, the more likely one is to oppose the idea' of integration.[41] In the Dutch, Italian and German instances, the party left was usually consistently pro-integrationist, though not always uncritical of the policy direction taken by the EC.[42] Among the strongly pro-integrationist Christian Democratic parties internal divisions have at times appeared over European policy, notably during the mid-1960s when the CDU/CSU suffered bitter disputes in its Gaullist/Atlanticist controversy about the international orientation of its EEC policy, which threatened to undermine the careful cohesion it had established after the war between its Catholic and Protestant elements.[43] A more continuous case has been the Italian DC with its internal system of *correnti*, whose traditional policy outlooks have included differences over European policy, ranging from the right, which most readily espoused the political cum Atlanticist arguments for integration, to the occasionally dissident position assumed by groups on the left whether for reasons of Christian internationalism, neutralism or a critical outlook on integration motivated by a concern for social reformism.[44]

All these shades of differentiation over integration both between and within political parties suggest that one cannot speak of party-traditional aspects with regard to Europe in too uniform a manner. The determinants of party European policies encompass a wide scope of different variables, but before turning to other domestic constraints or promotive factors it is important to note the influence of Community membership itself on the evolution of European policies. Some distinction must be drawn between the original six member states and those which entered the EC in 1973, in so far as adaptation to the basic principle of integration is more likely once membership and its after-effects have ceased to be a contentious issue. Both the Socialist and Communist parties have over time made such an adjustment, whereas the sceptical or anti-integrationists of the 1970s are (with the major exception of France) located in two of the three new member states. The adverse economic climate of the 1970s, compared with the growth of the 1950s, has affected attitudes since much electoral appeal is based on economic issues, but all the same the imprint of party traditions has continued to be felt, notably with the Labour Party even after the 1975 referendum confirmed decisively British membership, and also among the Danish left with its anti-capitalist concerns. The Irish Labour Party is, however, a pertinent example of a party adjusting directly to EC membership having opposed this prior to entry, although with the overwhelming 83 per cent 'Yes' vote in favour in the 1972 referendum it could hardly do otherwise.[45] The one significant exception to this pattern of greater adjustment to the EC among the Six (because there is more long-term evidence thereof) is the two French parties of the Gaullists and Communists. While different factors have been present in their cases, the most relevant one in this context is a certain rigidity of party traditions – ideological on the part of the PCF, and personalistic with the Gaullists because of their adamant adherence to de Gaulle's conception of Europe.

In conclusion, this discussion has shown that party traditions provide a regular and fundamental determinant of European policies, as with all other major policy areas. Much depends on the form of party identity, the priority accorded integration, and how strongly the motivation of a particular national party is ideological. Admittedly, ideological goals provide only a vague guide to a party's behaviour since, as demonstrated, party positions on European integration may over time be modified. Another result of looking at the party-traditional factor is to emphasise that European policies cannot be viewed without reference to the domestic arena of political parties, on which we now focus more concretely by considering this in an instrumental, rather than ideological, light.

(ii) *The political-functional factor:* This category combines a number of interrelated features emanating from domestic politics, including the very assumption about the primacy of national politics *vis-à-vis* European politics, the respective impact of government and opposition roles, the pull of domestic alliances with other political parties and the power structure within national parties as a constraint on policy-making, whether European or otherwise. All these determinants have at one time or other and in varying degrees conditioned the course, priority and content of party European policies. So far as any generalisation is possible, they underline the national focus of party activity because of the power-orientation of political parties, though whether this focus is an exclusive one remains to be seen as a pointer to possible politicisation in the field of European-level party activity.

The primacy of national politics is a truism but one of over-riding importance. Speaking at a conference on European trans-national relationships in 1968, Bonvicini concluded these were 'superficial' because 'in the parties' eyes real political life goes on exclusively in the national framework, consisting as it does of winning and controlling power, for it is only at the national level that they can participate in the exercise of power'.[46] Yet, the integration process over the past decade in particular makes it all the more necessary to analyse the specific reasons why individual parties may at different times act in different ways, for political behaviour can never be assumed to be one-dimensional. There are two consequences of this national primacy: the relentless demands of every-day politics in terms of expenditure and pressures of time, especially when parties are preoccupied in national office; national constraints inevitably impose short-term perspectives, whereas 'European' or 'supranational' decisions – such as support for the ECSC, EDC and EEC or the question of Community membership – have required a more intermediate or long-term approach. This conflict of priorities has occasioned ambiguities in the presentation of European policies for, as Marchal-van Belle noted in the case of the Belgian Socialist Party: 'It is difficult, if not impossible, to pursue for example a "patriotic" policy on energy, agriculture and economic and social expansion and a *communautaire* policy on the same object.'[47] Nevertheless, 'European' decisions were taken often for a variety of both long- and short-term motives so that already in the 1950s the weight of party-political *qua* governmental considerations were not all in one direction (i.e. exclusively nationally oriented as such), for arguments were accepted, as over the ECSC, that certain national interests were better served at the European level.

One crucial variable in estimating the national orientation of party activity is the government/opposition dimension. There are several points which must be taken into account when considering the influence of governmental responsibility on party European policy and notably where this has changed as a result – perception of the national interest, compelling economic pressures (which contributed to the reversal of Labour policy on British entry while in government during the 1966 Parliament), the mere need to establish relative policy priorities while in office and also the existence or not of national bipartisanship over European policy.

The salience of government/opposition roles has been most visible where trends of polarisation in national parliaments have affected European policy, or where there is a clear divide between the two roles. A change of, or discontent with, its role in the political system may affect the content as well as presentation of a party's European policy, which becomes subject to intransigent 'opposition politics', notably with the SPD in the earlier 1950s and the British Labour Party after its loss of the 1970 election and its antipathy to Heath's European policy, although a later or projected return to office may occasion acceptance of the *faits accomplis* of the meantime. On the other side, domestic polarisation can also strengthen the governing party's solidarity over European questions, as with Adenauer's CDU/CSU during the 1950s, which needed the foil offered by Schumacher's onslaughts to give final cohesion to its virtual unanimity over integration; and again with the British Conservatives, whose agnostics over EC entry became 'converts' in the face of Labour attacks on the Heath government. In other EC states, such as Holland with its traditional 'politics of accommodation' and Italy with its politics of convergence, such stark government/opposition contrasts have usually not arisen so that distinctions between different national parties over European policy have become somewhat blurred. Government/opposition roles may therefore affect European policy in divergent ways, depending not least on the priority given European positions in domestic politics. There is the additional problem of looking at parties in opposition that their exact positions on European policy may be less easily documented than those of governing parties where, as Paterson notes about the SPD in the 1950s, 'reference can be made to governmental actions to establish exactly what the policy is'.[48]

Closely related to the government/opposition dimension is the question of political alliances, for in nearly all EC countries coalitions have been the rule rather than exception and even oppositional alliances have sometimes operated. These alliances may condition or colour the positions assumed over integration – notably in the movement of the PSI from an oppositional co-operation with the PCI to a centre-left formation with the DC in government – thus indeed suggesting, from one point of view, an 'internalisation' of European policy positions. In the 1950s, as Criddle has observed, the French SFIO was at one time faced with a strategic dilemma over the EDC because of the vitriolic but successful campaign of the PCF against it, which was 'frustrating the SFIO's eternal hope of winning back working-class support from the Communists', and its concern to return to power in a coalition which, for reasons for parliamentary mathematics, would have had to include the pro-integrationist MRP.[19] Hence, European policy positions could be subject to inter-party considerations, although it is difficult to disentangle tactical positions from changes of substance in policy content. In more recent times, the Union of the Left in France (1972–7) required some compromise on both sides. The French Socialist PS, already reconstituted as a party ideologically more to the left than its predecessor, the SFIO, now dampened traditional French Socialist pro-integrationism in favour of a new emphasis on anti-capitalism in the EC and the multinationals issue and an agreement in the common programme on the unanimity rule in the Council of Ministers;[30] while the PCF adopted a marginally less intransigent approach to the EC in general.

Finally, the political-functional factor cannot exclude reference to the nature of internal power structures within national parties: how much the leadership or leader places a priority on European questions or not *per se*, and whether control over this area is exclusive or diffuse. This again touches on the government/opposition roles, for clearly the weight of government authority behind the leadership encourages a more concentrated approach, whereas in opposition the leadership might well be more vulnerable to internal party pressures, a classic example of both being the British Labour Party's 'somersaults' over Community membership.[51] To a large extent party policy is fairly indistinguishable from government policy when in office, but once more this depends on how far individual parties have been content with or preferred to question the policy assumptions of their leaders. Marchal-van Belle has similarly concluded in his study of the Belgian Socialists that Paul-Henri Spaak's personal authority over European questions was substantially enhanced once he became Foreign Minister, when he was allowed a relatively free hand *vis-à-vis* the party in this area despite remaining reservations in the latter over integration.[52] The British case further provides a useful illustration of a distinct difference between the power structures of the two main political parties with Labour's tradition of stronger influence by rank-and-file members in contrast with the Conservative Party's preferred habit of deference to the leadership, especially where external policies are concerned. This feature played a decisive part in the formulation of the respective parties' European policies. In the Conservative case, Kitzinger rightly stresses that 'whether it fully realised it or not' the party 'took its most decisive step towards British entry into the EEC eight years before 1973' with the election of the strongly committed pro-European Heath to the leadership in 1965.[53] In comparison, Wilson as Labour leader had much less room for manœuvre over EEC entry, motivated as he was by the primary consideration of maintaining party unity, as had Gaitskell been over the same issue in the early 1960s,[54] so that here control over European policy formulation was less exclusive. Among the older EC states, perhaps the best example of European policy being determined exclusively was the West German CDU during the earlier 1950s, when Adenauer imposed his own pro-integration convictions on his party, made this policy area a matter of personal loyalty to his leadership and was very reluctant to consult with his parliamentary supporters over the various European projects.

From this brief survey it is evident that, whereas a pro- or anti-integration ideology provides a direction or motivation for a particular party's policy course, there are many constraints and determinants in the domestic political arena with regard to actual policy options or priorities. However, the history of the 1950s and 1960s shows that not all party-political considerations were loaded in the one direction of the national focus of policy action.

(iii) *The socio-political factor:* This category is more heterogeneous and less easy to define than the other two, because it is really shorthand for a variety of influences deriving from the broader national political environment: public-political constraints on European policy, important structural changes in national party systems – such as those resulting from long-term, socio-political developments – and different influences which together may be termed 'political-cultural'.

The public-political aspect is relevant because it ultimately relates to the possibilities for politicisation in the field of European party politics. The willingness or reticence of a political party to promote its European policy has at least partly been determined by the extent to which the national public has been interested as such in 'Europe' and perceives itself as favourably affected by Community activity. This 'law' also applies where there has been a low salience of European questions in the eyes of the public. As Inglehart's researches up to 1970 showed, there were marked differences between the national publics in both respects, although there was only some evidence that public opinion in general was 'becoming increasingly important in relation to decisions concerning European integration',[55] by which he meant increasing public familiarity with European-level politics.

It is obvious that any growth of what Inglehart calls 'cognitive mobilisation' of the electorate over integration will condition a party's behaviour in this field, although integration has traditionally been an élite policy area. Prior to direct elections of the European Parliament in the late 1970s, there had been very few *direct* tests of national public attitudes over EC issues, if one discards national parliamentary elections. These few cases all occurred in the 1970s, being the referenda in France on enlargement (1972), in Denmark and Ireland (also Norway) in 1972 on prospective Community membership and in Britain on the renegotiated terms of membership (1975). In all instances, European integration was officially the sole theme of the electoral event, although, as in the interesting French case of 1972, separate domestic political calculations entered the scene: President Pompidou's all-too-transparent effort to use the referendum both to outflank the orthodox Gaullists over British entry and drive a wedge between the PS and PCF with their different approaches to integration rebounded severely on him with the high abstention rate of nearly 40 per cent.[36] The fact that referenda cannot be considered as a 'pure' exercise in testing popular opinion on the official European question was further underlined by the Danish referendum of 1972 acting as a spur to fragmentation in an already brittle party system, not to mention the even more critical case of the negative result in Norway. These few cases pointed to the likelihood of an intermixture of European and national politics in the event of further occasions of voting on the EC.

Before the 1970s there were no such direct tests of public reactions to the process of European integration. As an indirect and rather unique case in point, the French presidential election of 1965, which coincided with the highpoint of the EEC's 'constitutional crisis' following the French boycott of its institutions, witnessed public disapproval of de Gaulle's intransigence which helped to force him into a second ballot before being re-elected.[37] Again, as an earlier instance, German domestic polarisation over the EDC project encouraged the SPD opposition to mobilise support successfully for its rejection of rearmament in a series of Landtag elections during 1950–1.[38] What nevertheless emerges from looking at national parliamentary elections is that European integration has usually featured as a subordinate or peripheral aspect of party programmes. In countries where there has been a solid consensus of opinion around integration, parties have sometimes outlined clear aims (for example, the Dutch PvdA advocated a 'supranational Europe' in its 1956 electoral programme), but this very consensus has reduced the chances for politicisation over the issue based on party rivalry. Where there has been a trend of polarisation, as in the Federal Republic during the earlier 1950s, integration has predictably been sucked into the party-political battle, but in such an atmosphere of polemics it has been virtually impossible to disentangle the relative impact of different policy areas. In Italy, as Vannicelli noted in the earlier 1970s, 'the extent of a party's commitment to European unity seems to be of little relevance to the electorate; EEC issues are not an important aspect of electoral programmes . . . and have not played a significant role in the outcome of elections'.[59] In Britain, as a country noted for its public apathy about integration, the Common Market was, in the words of the Nuffield 1970 election study, 'the most recurrent of the issues that never really received any limelight',[60] although, judging by the two elections of 1974 and 1979, it seems that the EC has become one among several standard issues once entry was achieved. There is evidence of a similar trend in other new member states.

The question of major structural changes in national party systems is relevant where changes in the long-term political fortunes of distinctly pro- or anti-integrationist parties might accordingly modify the balance of European policy consensus within a member state, and hence affect the European policy positions of other national parties in turn. A few examples illustrate the possible impact on European policy of such developments. The important European project initiatives of 1950 owed much to the fact that Christian Democrats were dominant in most of the governments of the Six, while their decline in several cases – France in the 1951 elections, and Italy relatively in 1953 – directly contributed to the declining pressure for supranational proposals. With the Italian DC the loss of its absolute majority in 1953 and the subsequent retirement of De Gasperi meant that the party showed a lower interest in integration because of its other domestic preoccupations.[61] The virtual eclipse of the French MRP by the end of the Fourth Republic, with the later rise of the Gaullists as a political force under the General's tutelage, eventually produced a major shift in the country's European policy. A different, though related, aspect is that because parties are ultimately answerable to their electorates the particular socio-economic structure of their own voting support may condition their line on EC policy. For example, the different electorates of the Italian PSI (largely industrial and middle-class) and PCI (which aside from its working-class voters enjoys significant support from the agricultural proletariat) has motivated the latter in taking a far more critical position on the common agricultural policy (CAP).[62]

Lastly, 'political-cultural' influences contained in the national environment form a background to the presentation or implementation of European policies. These refer to national outlooks or sentiment towards other members of the EC, which have sometimes coloured the way European projects are received domestically. Perhaps the most pertinent example is the manner in which Franco-German reconciliation, as the kernel feature of European integration, has continued to be accompanied by anti-German sentiments with roots in the war experience and revived by the Federal Republic's growing role in the EC, sufficient to be exploited by parties of the left especially in France – continuously by the PCF, and on earlier occasions by the Socialists – while in other member states anti-German feeling has surfaced in party contests over European questions, such as during the Danish referendum on Community membership in 1972.[63] In so far as the politicisation of European party activity might acerbate national feelings as well as promote a greater sense of Community consciousness, such 'cultural' influences could bear upon the socio-political background of transnational party co-operation. Also relevant in this context is the way in which broad national outlooks – the sense of Scandinavian links in Denmark, the ubiquitous pro-European feeling in Italy – may affect the presentation of European policies by parties.

While the question of transnational party co-operation entered little into party-political considerations on European affairs during the 1950s and 1960s, patterns of European policy formulation and content provide different indicators about party behaviour in the event of a later politicisation of such co-operation. An historical discussion of party European policies offers several lessons for future European party activity, notably the potential for the intermeshing of national with European politics, the variety of different influences which come into play and the divergent approaches to integration between member states as well as competing ideological forces. While the experience of the 1950s and 1960 did not produce any marked European dimension in party politics, several useful conclusions may be drawn which do not suppose an exclusive preoccupation with national standpoints. First, the progress of the EC throughout its history – and particularly in the 1970s – reflects a gradual erosion of the traditional distinction between foreign and domestic politics in party-political considerations as well as in general. This must have implications for transnational party development, all the more as political parties in the member states have not failed to accept the increasing overlap of EC policy concerns into the domestic arena. Secondly, a European dimension involves both an 'internalisation' of European politics and a 'Europeanisation' of national politics at the same time. The former has occurred in several ways, either because the national political system in question is a 'penetrated' one, where the European arena provides one outlet for seeking legitimacy as a political force, or because of the priority given to European positions under the influence of traditional party outlooks. 'Europeanisation' is more difficult to measure, but, while it is understandable for parties to be nationally oriented, this does not exclude their acquiring an element of European 'thinking' or, indeed, promoting European solutions in the national context. Thirdly, the growing party-political consensus on European integration which developed during the first two decades of Community activity did significantly occasion a marked differentiation between, and also within, the various ideological tendencies about the purpose and priorities of European policy. This was probably the most relevant pointer to the possibilities of transnational party co-operation in a more politicised form.

(c)   The Historical Development of Transnational Party Co-operation

It remains before considering in full the greater emergence of transnational party co-operation to provide some historical focus for this process, both to establish patterns which might condition its later operation and to measure the extent to which transnational party activity has by comparison achieved more momentum and developed a dynamic of its own during the 1970s.

The question of a possible new departure in party-political harmonisation in the EC during the third decade of integration assumes the existence of distinguishable historical phases in its earlier development. It also follows from the introductory hypothesis about the integral relationship between party European policies and involvement in transnational co-operation, as well as the need to consider the latter's operation within the wider EC institutional framework, that any such historical phases must fall within similar periods of integration development as a whole.

So far as transnational party co-operation is concerned, there are problems in asserting the existence of historical phases because of its political marginality as a specific field of integration activity in the 1950s and 1960s. For this reason, a framework of historical phases more specifically geared to the area of transnational party activity which still takes account of the impact of Community development in general is preferable.

It is the basic argument of this study that transnational party co-operation has in the course of the 1970s, and particularly during the process towards direct elections of 1974–9, entered a new historical phase and one which is distinctly more important than any preceding one because of the politicisation of this activity and its greater claim as an area of European integration. This is because the focus in the third decade of Community history has been more on positive than negative integration, thus entailing the need for conscious political initiatives outside the guidelines of the Treaty of Rome. The new historical phase may be said to have commenced with The Hague Community summit of December 1969, which witnessed several important initiatives for future EC development along the lines of 'completion' (of the transition period), 'deepening' (the adoption of new policy areas such as economic and monetary union [EMU] and political co-ordination) and 'enlargement' with the agreement to open negotiations for EC entry with Britain, Ireland, Denmark and Norway. The final communiqué also stated that 'the Council of Ministers will continue to study the question of direct elections' and announced the intention to 'strengthen the budgetary powers of the European Parliament'. Despite the various setbacks which followed – the failure of EMU, the lack of any serious political initiative over direct elections until late 1974 – the Hague summit may be seen in retrospect as having inaugurated a new lease of life for Community development after the stagnation of the mid- and later 1960s (the EP's budgetary powers were increased, and Community enlargement was – minus Norway – negotiated). It is, of course, possible to make a distinction between the years 1969–74 and 1974–9 in view of the special impetus for transnational party development provided by the prospect of direct elections. The authors nevertheless prefer to see the years 1969–74 as a preliminary stage of the same historical phase because of the overall process of politicisation in the EC, which forms an essential background to the theme of this study.

Looking now at pre-1969 developments, it is viable to divide transnational party co-operation into three historical phases. The first phase, the period of the separate Common Assembly of the ECSC (1953–8), saw the beginning of transnational party activity with the formation and operation of ideologically, rather than nationally, based groups in that assembly. This period was distinctive also because it witnessed an element of partisan conflict with the tendency of the Socialist group to take an active oppositional line and challenge executive decisions by the ECSC's High Authority, while the Christian Democrats and Liberals were inclined to defend the latter.[14] This suggested that the creation of a new 'supranational' decision-making centre could have a catalysing effect on group relationships, although this development was conditioned by the then limited scope of integration (confined to certain fields of coal and steel policy).

The second historical phase, the birth of the Common Market, widened the prospects for European integration (1958–62), including discussion for the first time of direct elections to the newly constituted EP (as these were provided for in the Rome Treaty, Article 138) following the report presented by Fernand Dehousse, a Belgian Socialist and MEP, in 1960. This interest in direct elections had a mobilising effect on party co-operation within the EEC framework, notably among the Socialist parties of the Six, which

began to develop some common organisation confined to their
member states and oriented to their transnational parliamentary
group. Their co-operation went so far as to adopt a common action
programme on Community policy in 1962, though in the case of the
other political forces such transnational activity was far less marked
despite their general commitment to integration.

The third phase, the period of stagnation in European integration
(1962–9), had a stultifying effect on the role of transnational party
co-operation, for the sober atmosphere in the Community occasioned by the lapse in momentum and its 'constitutional crisis' of
1965–6 discouraged initiatives to strengthen such co-operation politically. In the EP there surfaced some element of 'partial opposition' with conflict over the values of the integration process between
the Gaullists and the other groups. This contributed to a more
diverse party-political picture in the Parliament, a development
further emphasised by the admission in 1969 of the Italian Communists with their own divergent outlook on integration. The end
of this phase of stagnation began with de Gaulle's retirement in the
spring of 1969 as a prelude to the new initiatives which came with
the Hague summit.

The period since 1969 has therefore amounted to the fourth phase
in transnational party co-operation. In order to assess further its
importance in relation to earlier development, some mention is
necessary of emerging patterns of transnational party co-operation
during the 1950s and 1960s with reference to the three dimensions
of the Euro-parliamentary, the transnational party-organisational
and the national party frameworks before concluding this discussion
of the historical background.

The transnational party groups in the EP were the most established feature in the earlier history of party co-operation within the
Community institutional framework. As both studies on pre-1970
developments by van Oudenhove and Fitzmaurice have shown, the
party groups succeeded rapidly in asserting and consolidating their
dominance over the procedural operation of the Common Assembly
and later the EP. This occurred despite the fact that the treaties of
Paris, 1951, and Rome, 1957, made no mention of, or provision for,
ideologically based parliamentary parties. In setting the precedent
for their constitution in the Common Assembly in the summer of
1953, the Assembly was drawing on its right under the ECSC
Treaty to 'fix its own rules of procedure' and in these it gave
official recognition to the transnational groups when it noted that
'the delegates may form groups according to political persuasion'.
The Rome Treaty of 1957 made no reference at all to the groups,
although by then they had already firmly established their presence.
Indeed, with some postwar exceptions political parties in Western

Europe have rarely been accorded recognition in national constitutions either.

On a political plane, van Oudenhove's assertion that 'ideological bonds were stronger than national ties' in the five years' operation of the Common Assembly, and that the success of the party groups 'was a major factor in the prestige acquired by the Assembly during its brief span',[65] was probably technically correct in the somewhat rarefied and isolated atmosphere of the Assembly full of committed Europeans, but his judgement still reflected the prevalent optimism of the period during which he was writing. In the light of developments since, a revised assessment is necessary, particularly with the acknowledgement of influential national subgroups in the transnational groups and the formation of quasi-national groups in the EP alongside the maintenance of old group identities. Even van Oudenhove, who was tempted to see in the transnational groups 'the starting-point for the development of specific European ideologies',[66] fully recognised the obstacles facing this possibility.[67] As Haas had foreseen in his analysis in the late 1950s of the transnational groups as possible 'federal parties', their actual and potential operation was effectively circumscribed by the institutional weaknesses of the Assembly.[68] This fundamental point was also applicable to the EP for nothing significant changed in its constitutional role during the 1960s. The result was the overall tendency among the transnational groups towards compromise rather than conflict in a common desire not to undermine the principal role of the Parliament then in acting as a form of pro-integrationist pressure group in institutional clothing. This low political profile in a wider sense of the transnational groups was underlined by their lack of any real public relations,[69] for they were essentially intra-parliamentary *Fraktionen*.

It was not only the absence of any effective institutional relationship with the executive powers in the Community which meant that the party groups as the Euro-parliamentary branch of transnational activity were politically isolated entities, but also they were neither responsible to an electorate nor subject to any form of extra-parliamentary organisational pressure. In this sense, a transnational party-organisational dimension was really lacking before the 1970s, although there were some signs of efforts in this direction during the preceding decade. The two essential characteristics of such a dimension had to be: a membership of such European-level party organisations strictly confined to member states of the EC in view of the distinctive nature of the integration process which makes it so different from other European organisations, such as the Council of Europe; and a commitment to an active pursuit of policy goals inside the Community. Inevitably, this entails the establishment of an institutional and integrated relationship with the respective transnational groups in the EP, for whatever new developments might occur in transnational party co-operation the Parliament remains its institutional focal point.

The main framework of non-parliamentary party organisational activity in European politics were the traditional Internationals: the Socialist International re-established after the Second World War in 1951, the Liberal International formed in 1947 and the European Union of Christian Democrats (EUCD) in 1965 as the successor of the Nouvelles Equipes Internationales (NEI) originally created in 1947. Although membership of the Internationals was based on the principle of political affinity, their political importance was, and is, no more than 'platonic' for they have remained no more than purely consultative bodies with minimal organisational links. Norbert Gresch has summarised aptly their limited form of political activity:

> Despite their fixed organisation of a permanent institutionalised basis, the Internationals lack the capacity for making concrete policy. Because of their global and stratified character co-operation among their component parties is restricted to the exchange of information and viewpoints and the passing of declarations on general problems of world politics of a non-binding character. Resolutions are without effect because there is no real point at which to direct them and because their organisation lacks power, either over their own members or over any political institution with the power of decision.[70]

Their lack of political 'punch' was predictably reflected in the Internationals' minimal structures with invariably a Bureau being the principal organ, consisting, as in the case of the Socialist one, of the national parties' international secretaries and other delegates meeting at irregular intervals. The Internationals could not in any sense be regarded as having an integrative potential, apart from the fact that they did not confine their deliberations to matters of Community policy.

However, the Internationals did eventually provide a form of umbrella organisation in association with which the first modest steps were taken towards Community-wide party organisations. As an extra-parliamentary version of transnational co-operation, this did not occur at all during the ECSC period of the 1950s. As van Oudenhove commented, any such contacts between the groups in the Assembly and outside bodies were 'of a purely informal character'.[71] But from the late 1950s various initiatives were taken to orientate European party-organisational activity specifically towards Community policies following the birth of the EEC, involving the cautious development of corresponding institutional links. By far the most advanced example was given by the Socialist parties of the Six, who in 1957 held a conference prepared by the secretariat of the Socialist group in the Common Assembly, and at this agreed on setting up a Liaison Bureau to facilitate communication between their group in the EP and the national parties.[72] Members of the Socialist group executive participated in its bureau, and its congresses were devoted to topics of EEC concern.[73] With their formulation of an agricultural policy for the EEC in 1960 and the common action programme of 1962 the Socialist parties of the Six started to tread the path of transnational policy; but it still lacked a binding character while the work of the Liaison Bureau suffered from the absence of financial backing and the tendency of national parties to leave routine participation in it to their own MEPs.[74]

The other political forces were much less ambitious, being less programmatically stimulated by the then heady pace of economic integration in the young EEC. Only the Christian Democrats showed signs of an awareness of the need to channel energies towards Community policies as such, though at first this was largely confined to conferences of leaders and secretaries-general of parties in the Six as from 1959 with some organisational basis in the NEI.[75] In 1965, the EUCD was formed, though its membership was not limited to EEC states and it professed no direct link with the fraternal group in the EP.[76] The European Liberals were at this stage reluctant to accept the idea of more active engagement in policy discussion, not to mention the necessary institutional followup, so that their only concession to this early move towards transnational party organisation was to institute *ad hoc* conferences of party leaders.[77]

This absence of a direct institutional as well as meaningful political link between the transnational groups in the European Parliament and corresponding transnational party-organisational entities was similarly reflected in the manner in which the former also lacked any integral relationship with the national parties. The only form of vertical relationship that had developed was transmitted solely through the national contingents in the transnational groups, though even here the tendency was for MEPs to act as individual parliamentarians rather than a means whereby national parties could exert an influence on the workings of the European Parliament. As Fitzmaurice observed, the relationship in general between the EP and the national parliaments was by the 1970s still only 'limited and patchy' for 'on both sides there have been reservations on closer involvement and inter-relationships',[78] although there had developed a practice in some member states of formal and informal reports by MEPs on sessions of the EP to their national parliaments.[79] Ultimately, the question reverted once more to the basic institutional and political weakness of the European Parliament. Henk Vredeling, himself an active MEP and later Dutch minister, pinpointed the problem succinctly in 1971:

> In the eyes of the national groups, members who sit in the European Parliament are of only limited importance. They are certainly of great help in shedding light on the obscure process of European integration. But they have no real say in policy-making. The result is that members of national political groups who play an important part in shaping domestic policy are practically never members of the European Parliament. The selection of representatives to the European Parliament is a negative process for two reasons. On the one hand, national groups tend to put forward only second-line politicians as candidates; and, on the other, if influential national parliamentarians become members of the European Parliament or if lesser known figures – as often happens – discharge their European parliamentary duties with devotion and zeal and in so doing acquire national recognition, the time inevitably comes when they are called upon to assume a responsible post in national politics, either in the national government or in opposition. This may be beneficial to the national groups, but the overall effect on the European Parliament is adverse. This phenomenon is due to the fact that the European Parliament has no political power.[80]

Vredeling's touch of optimism about the national political prospects of MEPs was more applicable in some countries than others, notably his own, where Dutch parliamentarians were elected on a list system and his own party, the PvdA, was noted for its readiness to allow some members to devote the major part of their time to European activity.[81] Generally, MEPs have more often suffered at their home base from their involvement as European 'actors', particularly as their choice of the EP has been motivated by or involved them in espousing attitudes on integration questions that may be divergent from those of their national party leaderships or parliamentarians.[82] Only rarely has a party's delegation to the EP been accorded a role of influence in the party structure, the main exception being the important contribution made by the PCI's MEPs from 1969 to the elaboration of its European policy,[83] although it should not be forgotten that their influence derived as much from their own national prominence in many cases as well as their credentials as European experts.

One likely agent of change in this general situation is a growing interest in the political potential of the EP as a Community institution. The speech made by Chancellor Willy Brandt before it in November 1973 – the first time the Parliament was addressed by a current head of government – urged that leading national parliamentarians should be allowed to take part in its debates.[84] Already by then the outlook for possible direct elections seemed brighter, and the agreement the following year to hold them was a decision by the national governments. Van Oudenhove had speculated in the early 1960s that direct elections with an extension of the EP's powers would mean that 'the European party struggle is likely to become keener';[85] while Vredeling commented more pointedly a decade later that 'the national political parties would be highly embarrassed if the governments took a positive decision'[86] in favour of European elections because they would be forced suddenly to take transnational co-operation seriously. Vredeling emphasised at the same time that the basic reason for the reluctance of national parties to form European parties was fear of the erosion of their power and authority.[87]

The history of transnational party co-operation in the 1950s and 1960s shows that political parties essentially failed to impose their views on the development of European integration, save through their institutional role in government. All the same, these first two decades indicated several pointers to possible politicisation at a later stage: the growth of ideological consensus on European integration being accompanied by party-political differentiation as to its purpose; the start of a two-way process with some mild 'Europeanisation' of national party politics as well as the 'internalisation' of European policy activity; the efforts in varying degrees of different political forces in the six member states in the 1960s to reorientate their international co-operation more distinctly towards Community policies, suggesting that the transnational harmonisation of their positions and activities had some future, given a more favourable political and institutional context; and, above all, the potential offered by the widening process of integration itself for party co-operation. With all due scepticism about the EC's 'political system', it should not be forgotten that the *raison d'être* of political parties in West European democracies is to respond and adapt to, if not promote or control, new political and socio-economic demands. One salient feature of this important fourth historical phase of transnational party co-operation during the 1970s is that the adjustment by political parties to the prospect of direct elections almost automatically brought with it a greater involvement by them in broader questions of the Community's progress.

Party-political co-ordination has for the first time seriously entered the scene of European integration, so that a number of key questions need to be discussed. Are the factors constraining and promoting party activity on transnational co-operation in general and direct elections in particular the same as those which have conditioned this process in the past, or have new ones appeared? How have the two poles of the national political environment and the European-level ideological orientation of parties related with the politicisation of transnational co-operation? In the light of the trends of positive integration in the Community, have transnational parties begun to emerge as possible determinants as well as dependent variables of the integration process? And, finally, does the development of transnational party co-operation in the EC in the 1970s constitute the early stages of some form of European party system?

Chapter 1: References

1 Guy van Oudenhove. *The Political Parties in the European Parliament* (1965); John Fitzmaurice. *The Party Groups in the European Parliament* (1975); Ernst B. Haas. *The Uniting of Europe: Political, Social and Economic Forces, 1950–1957* (1958). esp. ch. 11.

2 Norbert Gresch. *Transnationale Parteienzusammenarbeit in der EG* (1978).

3 Though see articles by G. and P. Pridham and R. Hrbek in the bibliography.

4 Byron Criddle. *Socialists and European Integration: A Study of the French Socialist Party* (1969); G. Marchal-van Belle. *Les Socialistes Belges et l'integration Européenne* (1968); William E. Paterson. *The SPD and European Integration* (1974); Richard Walker. *Dal confronto al consenso: i partiti politici italiani e l'integrazione europea* (1976).

5 Haas. op. cit., p. 5.

6 R. J. Harrison. *Europe in Question: Theories of Regional International Integration* (1974). p. 89.

7 C. L. Baljé. 'The influence of inter-party co-operation on the process of political integration'. paper to the TEPSA conference on European parties Amsterdam. April 1978. p. 3.

8 Paterson. *The SPD and European Integration*. p. ix.

9 David Marquand. *Parliament for Europe* (1979). p. 111.

10 Haas. op. cit., p. 437.

11 Marquand. op. cit., pp. 125–6.

12 For a development of this point with reference to the party federations. see G. and P. Pridham. 'The new European party federations and direct elections'. *The World Today*, vol. 35. no. 2 (February 1979). pp. 64–5.

13 Haas. op. cit., ch. 11. esp. pp. 437–8.

14 R. Inglehart. 'Public opinion and regional integration'. in M. Hodges (ed.). *European Integration: Selected Readings* (1972). esp. pp. 334–5.

15 Helen Wallace. 'The impact of the European Communities on national policy-making'. *Government and Opposition*, vol. 6. no. 4 (Autumn 1971). p. 552.

16 ibid., p. 538.

17 Jean Blondel. *Political Parties: A Genuine Case for Discontent?* (London: Wildwood House. 1978). p. 113.

18 Haas. op. cit., p. 154.

19   ibid., p. 153.
20   Criddle, op. cit.. pp. 52–4.
21   Marchal-van Belle, op. cit., pp. 90, 154 about the PSB's concern over the dominance of the political right in Community institutions.
22   R. Hrbek, *Die SPD – Deutschland und Europa: die Haltung der Sozial-demokratie zum Verhältnis von Deutschland-Politik und West-Integration, 1945–1957* (1972), ch. 6 *passim.*
23   Criddle, op. cit.. p. 95.
24   ibid., p. 93.
25   W. J. Veenstra, 'De Partij van de Arbeid en Europa', *Internationale Spectator* (April 1977), p. 247.
26   Paterson. *The SPD and European Integration*, pp. 65, 130.
27   Marchal-van Belle, op. cit.
28   ibid.. p. 156.
29   Donald Sassoon, 'The Italian Communist Party's European strategy', *Political Quarterly*, vol. 47 (July 1976). pp. 254 ff.
30   ibid.. p. 254.
31   van Oudenhove, op. cit.. pp. 234–5.
32   See R. E. M. Irving, *Christian Democracy in France* (1973), ch. 6. esp. pp. 168–71; Geoffrey Pridham. *Christian Democracy in Western Germany* (London: Croom Helm. 1977), ch. 2 *passim;* and R. E. M. Irving, *The Christian Democratic Parties of Western Europe* (1979), ch. 8 on the other Christian Democratic parties.
33   R. E. M. Irving, *Christian Democracy in France*, p. 159.
34   Walker, op. cit., pp. 29, 35.
35   Criddle. op. cit., p. 40.
36   The Radikal Venstre's foreign spokesman. quoted in *The Times* (26 April 1971).
37   Arthur Aughey, *Conservative Party Attitudes towards the Common Market,* Hull Paper in Politics. no. 2 (November 1978). p. 7; and Uwe Kitzinger, *Diplomacy and Persuasion: How Britain Joined the Common Market* (London: Thames & Hudson, 1973). p. 184.
38   Paterson, *The SPD and European Integration*, p. 130.
39   Marchal-van Belle, op. cit., p. 28.
40   Francis de Tarr, *The French Radical Party* (London: OUP, 1961), pp. 119–20 and 209–11.
41   W. E. Paterson and A. Thomas (eds), 'Social Democratic parties of the European Community', *Journal of Common Market Studies*, vol. XIII no. 4 (June 1975), p. 416; see also R. Bilski. 'The Common Market and the growing strength of Labour's left wing', *Government and Opposition*, vol. 12, no. 3 (Summer 1977).
42   Paterson and Thomas. 'Social Democratic parties of the European Community'. p. 416.
43   G. Pridham, op. cit.. pp. 150–3.
44   Primo Vannicelli. *Italy, NATO and the European Community* (1974), pp. 14–15 and 27; and Walker. op. cit.. pp. 33–4.
45   This became clear immediately after the Irish referendum; see report in *Irish Times* (12 May 1972).
46   At conference on political parties and European integration held by the Association des Instituts d'Etudes Européennes at Bruges, November 1968.
47   Marchal-van Belle. op. cit., p. 184.
48   Paterson, *The SPD and European Integration*, p. 129.
49   Criddle, op. cit., pp. 66–7.
50   David Bell, 'The Parti Socialiste in France'. *Journal of Common Market Studies*, vol. XIII, no. 4 (June 1975). pp. 428–30.

51 Kitzinger, op. cit., p. 278.
52 Marchal-van Belle. op. cit.. p. 129.
53 Kitzinger. op. cit.. p. 147.
54 M. Wheaton. 'The Labour Party and Europe. 1950–1971', in G. Ionescu (ed.). *The New Politics of European Integration* (1972). pp. 80–97.
55 Inglehart in Hodges. op. cit.. p. 346.
56 *The Times* (18 March 1972). and report in *Le Monde* (25 April 1972).
57 John Newhouse. *Collision in Brussels* (London: Faber. 1967). pp. 148–9.
58 F. Roy Willis. *France, Germany and the New Europe, 1945–1967* (1969). p. 152.
59 Vannicelli. op. cit.. p. 38.
60 D. Butler and M. Pinto-Duschinsky. *The British General Election of 1970* (London: Macmillan. 1971). p. 440.
61 Walker. op. cit.. pp. 46–7.
62 ibid.. pp. 60–1.
63 *The Times* (30 September 1972).
64 See Fitzmaurice. op. cit.. ch. 2.
65 van Oudenhove. op. cit.. pp. 117. 119.
66 ibid.. p. 59.
67 ibid.. pp. 59–61.
68 Haas, op. cit.. pp. 414–22 and 437–40.
69 See van Oudenhove. op. cit.. pp. 157–8.
70 Gresch. op. cit.. p. 31.
71 van Oudenhove. op. cit.. p. 153.
72 Gresch. op. cit.. p. 83.
73 ibid.. pp. 95, 97.
74 ibid., p. 98.
75 ibid., p. 84.
76 ibid.. pp. 98. 100.
77 ibid.. pp. 90–1.
78 Fitzmaurice. op. cit.. p. 191.
79 ibid.. p. 177.
80 H. Vredeling. 'The Common Market of political parties'. in G. Ionescu (ed.), *The New Politics of European Integration* (1972). pp. 125–6.
81 Fitzmaurice. op. cit., p. 185.
82 For example. Marchal-van Belle. op. cit.. p. 103. on the Belgian Socialist MEPs *vis-à-vis* the PSB ministers over the question of direct elections.
83 Walker. op. cit.. p. 97.
84 *The Times* (14 November 1973).
85 van Oudenhove. op. cit., p. 239.
86 Vredeling. in Ionescu. op. cit.. p. 131.
87 ibid., p. 129.

2

Transnational Party Co-operation in the European Parliament: the Euro-Parliamentary Groups and the Growth of Politicisation

(a)   The Party Groups and the European Parliament

The decade of the 1970s has witnessed a distinct growth in the politicisation of the party groups and their role in the European Parliament. In this context, politicisation has had two competitive characteristics: on the one hand, the emergence of an active political role and clearer profile of the groups; on the other, the increasing articulation of national interests and approaches and party-political pressures which more overtly challenged their unity and cohesion. The basis of this dual development has been the growing interlinkage between national and European politics arising from the greater political relevance of the Community as a whole. In the previous decades, the expression of party political differences had – apart from the Socialists for a time in the 1950s, and the Gaullists as a 'partial opposition' in the 1960s – been largely submerged in the Parliament's attempt to act as a unified motor for integration. In addition, such differences lacked immediacy due to the Parliament's isolation in terms of power and influence from other Community and national institutions.

As the oldest form of transnational party co-operation in the Community, the party groups cannot be considered without first some reference to their institutional context of the European Parliament.* An important background factor of the fourth historical phase of party co-operation in the EC since 1969 has been the increased constitutional power and political influence of the Parliament. Its evolution as an institution was summarised in the retrospective words of Simone Veil in her first speech as President of the EP to its inauguratory session after direct elections in July 1979:

---

*For full discussion of the European Parliament during the 1970s, see John Fitzmaurice. *The European Parliament* (1978); and Valentine Herman and Juliet Lodge. *The European Parliament and the European Community* (1978).

Its beginnings were modest and discreet, in keeping with the limited powers conferred on it by the Treaty of Rome, but, through the growing political influence it has gradually acquired, the European Parliament has consolidated its role among the institutions and in the building of the Community. It was this growing influence which led to the signing of the Treaties of 21 April 1970 and 22 July 1975 which strengthened the Assembly's budgetary powers. Furthermore, through a number of practical arrangements, the part played by the Assembly in the exercise of the Community's responsibilities has been given sharper form and wider scope.[1]

Although the Treaty of Rome provided for consultation of the Parliament on proposals for legislation on a wide range of subjects, the distinction between discretionary and obligatory consultation of the EP has in practice been largely abandoned[2] so that the Council of Ministers now normally invites an opinion from it on Commission proposals for Community legislation even where this is not actually required.[3] This reflects the growing tendency on the part of the EC executive institutions to recognise the Parliament's role as well as to participate in its proceedings.

As well as the wider interpretation of the limited powers of the Parliament, more procedures have been introduced into its functioning which have reinforced this development. In 1973 with enlargement, question time was introduced, which in 1975 was extended to the foreign ministers of the EC as well as the Commission. Other procedural reforms during the 1970s included the provision for oral questions followed by debate, the introduction of emergency debates and the adoption of a 'concertation' procedure not only in connection with the budget but on all proposals for legislation having financial consequences in which the EP and the Council of Ministers would meet as equal partners. As a measure of the effective use of such procedures, the number of written questions presented by MEPs increased from 659 in 1973 to 750 in 1975 and 1,300 in 1978; while the number of oral questions with or without debate grew from 1 in 1969 to 30 in 1975, 80 in 1977 and 125 in 1978. There have also been four motions to dismiss the Commission by the Parliament – all of these tabled since December 1972 – and an increasing number of conciliation meetings between delegations of the Parliament and the Council of Ministers. The political swansong of the indirectly elected Parliament over the 1979 Community budget illustrated its potential for interpreting and applying its existing powers more rigorously when it challenged the Council of Ministers outright over the regional fund allocation.[4]

This anticipated probable trends of the future. However, notwith-standing this relative increase in the political impact and visibility of the EP, it has continued to suffer as a result of its distance from the disparate centres of EC decision-making.

The transnational party groups as a whole have benefited from this upgrading of the EP as an institution, as well as being stimu-lated by the broader and more overt political area of policy discus-sion in the Community during the 1970s. This chapter will therefore discuss their activity and development in the context of these changes and the process towards direct elections. It will deal in turn with the two competitive characteristics of the politicisation of the party groups.

(b)   The Growth of the Political Role and Profile of the Party Groups

The potential for the party groups in the EP to develop into stronger political entities has always existed. Indeed, one of the EP's distinguishing characteristics in comparison with other inter-national assemblies is that its central component elements have been based not on national delegations but on European-wide ideologies. These ideological divisions were determined by those found in member national parliaments of the EC – especially the Socialist, Christian Democratic, Liberal and Communist – although in other cases they were somewhat artificial creations unique to the Euro-parliamentary level. Equally, the operation of the groups was based to a greater or lesser degree on the organisation and structure of national parliamentary parties in member states, just as the committee system in the EP followed the European model of parlia-mentary work. In the absence of the government/opposition dimen-sion in the Parliament, the possible competition from the commit-tees in terms of political influence within this institution was an additional stimulus to the consolidation of the groups' position in the EP during the 1970s.

While the increase in the political role and profile of the Euro-parliamentary groups was less spectacular than that of the party federations during this decade, it nevertheless represented a qualita-tive change, particularly with the disappearance of the broad tendency towards unanimity which had marked the previous period. This relative politicisation will be considered with reference to the organisational dominance of the party groups in the EP, the grow-ing importance attributed to the formation of majorities, the greater attention paid by them to internal cohesion, their more elaborate formulation of group policies, the role of group leadership and a new interest in their external relations.

(i) *The organisational dominance of the party groups:* The party groups have always formed the dominant political and organisational unit of the European Parliament and, as such, they enjoyed the first priority in the allocation of posts and finance. The groups: nominated and elected the President and the twelve Vice-Presidents of the Parliament; allocated members to committees (at the same time ensuring that no major imbalance occurred in national representation); agreed between themselves committee chairmanships, vice-chairmanships and rapporteurships, although the occupants of the first two posts were formally elected by the committees; had priority and longer speaking time for their spokesmen in debates than individuals or *non inscrit* (independent) members; and received EP finance in proportion to their overall size and their number of component nationalities. This allocation was for the operating funds of the secretariats (telephone calls, officials' travel expenses, etc.); for political activities to enable them to hold study sessions, meetings in various capitals and to carry out fact-finding missions; and in 1977 and 1978 the groups were given additional finance for the distribution of information on direct elections and funds to conduct their campaigns. In addition, places in the increasing number of parliamentary delegations, such as to the USA, Israel and Africa, were distributed on a group basis.

Individual groups have also gradually come to be associated with holding certain chairmanships of the Parliament's standing committees. The chairman – and, hence, indirectly the groups – may have a strong guiding influence over the work of their committees in directing discussion and working closely with the committees' secretariats in the production of reports. The Socialist group, being the largest group since 1975, held four of the twelve standing committee chairmanships, and established the precedent of holding those of the politically important economic and monetary affairs and the budget committees; while the Christian Democratic group has notably held that of the political affairs committee; the Liberal group has for years retained that of the agricultural committee; and the Conservative group has emphasised its tenure of the chair of the legal committee. This has illustrated the fact that 'this partisan representation is much more effective than the representation of nationality, where, for example (over the seven years up to 1979), Eire and Denmark have held only one chairman-year each, in this period, whereas France (18 chairman-years), Germany (16 chairman-years) and the Netherlands (13 chairman-years) are over represented'.[5] This priority of groups over nationalities has been part of a conscious attempt on the part of the former to reinforce their positions of dominance in relation to the standing committees.

The organisational dominance was further underlined by the *non inscrit* members being by contrast under-represented in all the parliamentary bodies and receiving no secretarial facilities or offices until 1977. Even though this discrimination was challenged in a filibuster in the first session of the directly elected Parliament in July 1979, led by the 'leader' of the *non inscrit* members, Marco Pannella (NI/I), they themselves formed a seventh group in the EP, so acknowledging group dominance. Winnie Ewing, a former independent, joined the Gaullist/Fianna Fail group (European Progressive Democrats, DEP) 'to ensure a seat for herself on the regional committee'.[6]

This organisational hegemony of the party groups provided the essential basis for their growing political role within the Parliament, the potential for which was apparent during the 1950s and 1960s, although it did not become open and consistent until the 1970s. As a feature of this process there was a progressive increase in the consolidation of power and influence of the chairmen of the groups *vis-à-vis* the official parliamentary organs during this decade. According to the parliamentary rules of procedure the Enlarged Bureau which comprises the Bureau (the EP President and twelve Vice-Presidents) and the chairmen of the party groups decides the agenda for plenary sessions. In practice, however, the agenda has come to be drawn up more and more by the groups' secretaries-general on behalf of their chairmen meeting together, and presented to the Enlarged Bureau for approval rather than discussion. In addition, in the two-year run up to direct elections it became increasingly apparent that the committees faced greater difficulties in getting their topics placed on the agenda, while proportionately more time was spent in the plenaries discussing resolutions and oral questions proposed directly by the political groups.

During the course of 1979 meetings between the group chairmen (and correspondingly the secretaries-general) grew more frequent as they attempted to formulate proposals ensuring the continuation of the dominant role of the established groups in the Parliament and the maintenance of influence in the hands of the chairmen, in view of the uncertainties posed by direct elections. In fact, these elections saw few personal changes in the leadership of the party groups with either previous leaders or influential former members as chairmen. Egon Klepsch (CD/D), Giorgio Amendola (Comm/I) and Christian de la Malène (DEP/F) remained as chairmen of their respective groups, while Ernest Glinne (Soc/B) new Socialist chairman, had been an MEP since 1968, Martin Bangemann (Lib/D) had played a major role as a vice-chairman in the Liberal group and James Scott-Hopkins (Con/UK) had for many months preceding the elections been 'chairman elect' of the group. This implies the directly elected Parliament is likely to see the maintenance of power and influence in the hands of the group chairmen, or at least strenuous efforts to ensure that there is no encroachment on it.

Direct elections clearly provided the immediate stimulus to this growing desire to control the work of the Parliament. However, it also was a reaction to the longer-term growth of the influence of the Parliament in respect to other Community institutions and the according need to ensure group dominance in this process.

(ii) *The formation of group-based majorities:* The new political role of the party groups has been significantly characterised by a growing importance attached to the concept and practice of forming majorities for votes in both plenaries and committees, on a regular basis. This has helped to strengthen the orientation of parliamentary roles around the groups, in particular the two main ones of the Socialists and Christian Democrats, with the others playing supporting roles of a temporary, intermittent or longer-term nature. This new way of thinking was underlined by the Liberal group secretary-general in reference to the effects of EC enlargement in 1973 on the EP: 'Following this, there has been political struggle around majority and minority. Majority and minority has, however, changed from time to time because there is no government . . . but this has led to the groups becoming politicised.'[7]

Relations between the groups have become more conflictual as the Parliament moved away from its traditional position of consensus as an institution generally promoting integration within the Community structure. As one prominent Socialist MEP observed:

My impression is that there is much more functioning as political groups and, secondly, that has led to a certain, not enormous, but a certain, polarisation within this Parliament. That is, a clearer division between groups, less unanimity. At the beginning every consultative assembly has a tendency to unanimity. But the experience of the last twenty years has been that it does not impress much, so that there is a kind of turn back to clearer political attitudes and that means also a bit more confrontation between groups, and that at the same time enhances this development of the recognisable profile of some groups; even if you have some odd groups, because they are national – Conservatives, Gaullists – which fall out of this pattern, because they do not have the problems of forming a European group.[8]

The Parliament has become a livelier forum of ideologically moti-vated exchanges between left and right, which not only promoted the internal cohesion of the main groups but in turn stimulated closer relations between groups on the right of the political spectrum – the Christian Democratic group and the European Conservatives – notably in reaction to the Socialists becoming the largest group in 1975. This development was forcefully explained by the Christian Democratic group in its report on activities for 1977–8.

> With the accession of three new Member States to the Com-munity in 1973 there began a period of radical change: the Socialist Group, strengthened after some considerable delay by the British Labour Members, became the largest group; the goal of harmony in the European Parliament, hitherto supported by the need for Parliament to hold its own against the other Com-munity institutions, was replaced by political confrontation. This led to an increasing number of debates on external matters which did not really fall within the Community's terms of reference, with the groups endeavouring to improve their political profile. With more and more frequent application of Article 235 of the EEC Treaty, new policies (e.g. regional, environmental, energy) were added to the Community's traditional policies. The strength-ening of Parliament's budgetary powers by the Treaties of 1970 and 1975 for the first time put it on a par (at least) with the Council of Ministers in a decisive area of Community policy. The substantial increase in the volume of the budget enabled the Community to increase its financial contribution in such important areas as regional policy, development aid policy, energy and research policy, etc.[9]

Thus, the development of relatively more partisan responses to the policies under discussion has been a consequence of the increasing scope of issues introduced into the Parliament. It also reflected the projection of national conflictual outlooks into the Euro-parlia-mentary forum, especially on the part of the influential German and British delegations to the main groups.

This process has occurred and promoted a sense of majority formation despite the absence of an institutional government and opposition dimension to the Parliament's operation. Nevertheless, the limited political position of the Parliament in the EC has meant that the formation of such majorities has been somewhat unreal with their lack of an institutional focus. For this reason, they have not developed to the level of formal alliances.

Bearing in mind this limitation, the closest relationship has developed between the Christian Democratic and Conservative groups. Officially the Conservatives have described these links as 'close but informal contacts at all levels',[10] but in fact this contact covers a multiplicity of relations and manœuvres. The question of a possible fusion was raised informally late in 1972 shortly before British EC entry, and was rejected for a variety of reasons. The majority of Christian Democrats were reluctant to be fully and openly associated with Conservatives because of the continuing impact of historically conditioned party labels and an unwillingness by the leadership to push the matter to the extent of affecting group unity. In a similar way, individual national party identity accounted partly for a lack of enthusiasm on the part of the British Conservatives also, for they wanted to avoid too close an association with parties which had predominantly a Catholic background. In addition, the Conservatives' position as a separate group granted them proportionately more influence – with the leadership enjoying a higher status – in the Parliament than they would have had as part of a larger group, a greater freedom of manœuvre and all the organisational advantages of separate facilities, staff and sources of income, as well as ease of communication in a fundamentally mono-linguistic group.

Organisationally the Christian Democrats would have gained by embracing the new Conservative members, for such a fusion would have ensured their role in the long term as the largest group in the Parliament with its accompanying status and political and financial advantages. However, the Christian Democrats and Conservatives as separate groups have developed patterns of co-operation, although they have not been consistently harmonious. The over-riding motive has been the desire to form a counterbalance to the growing Socialist influence, but it was limited by a lack of immediate legislative consequences of the Parliament's work. Much has also depended on the personal relations between the two group chairmen and in turn on relations between each of them and their own group members. For instance, co-operation in the form of joint group bureaux and full group meetings and a joint working party on agriculture occurred after the arrival of the British Conservatives in the European Parliament in 1973.[11] It declined during the chairmanship of Alfred Bertrand, a Belgian Christian Democrat, 1975–7, who did not take such an interest in this co-operation as his German predecessor, Hans-August Lücker (chairman of the Christian Democratic group, 1969–75) and successor, Egon Klepsch. As direct elections approached Egon Klepsch and James Scott-Hopkins, as prospective Conservative chairman, emphasised their willingness to work closely together in future,[12] although they were vague about the precise form that this co-operation would take in the new directly elected Parliament.

Following direct elections the European Conservative group formally acknowledged that the term 'Conservative', with its strong right-wing connotations in most other European countries, prevented a closer alliance of centre-right parties. In line with the Conservatives' transnational organisational link of the European Democratic Union (EDU) (see Chapter 3, Section *d*, pp. 164–8) the group changed its name to the European Democratic Group in July 1979. According to a close observer:

> By changing the name, and the rules of the group so as to enshrine the rights of smaller parties, the Tories are plainly hoping to pick up some of the two dozen or so non-aligned members. Some even nursed more ambitious thoughts about persuading some of the Giscardians to join the fold, and even some of the Liberals.[13]

Furthermore, 'the new name, it is argued, would also open the way for the right-wing parties in Greece, Spain and Portugal, which will be joining the EEC in the next few years, to unite their forces with the Conservatives'.[14]

Several points arise from this case. Although the change of name by the Conservative group does have a major symbolic importance with regard to a broader centre-right alliance, in practice those original factors which prevented the fusion of the two groups in the past are likely to continue to inhibit the formation of a longer term and more formal alliance. However, the two groups may well continue to hold regular common meetings and to appoint common spokesmen on an increasing number of issues and to develop practical forms of co-operation on an anti-left basis.

There was no corresponding growth of closer or systematic relations between the parties of the left to match those which were taking place on the right of the political spectrum. This derived from the lack of compulsion due to the relative majority status of the Socialist group and also from the repercussions which would have been felt in most national parties if the Socialist group had developed any close relationship with the Communists (particularly the dominant German SPD). Nevertheless, despite these problems of co-operation on the left, agreements of mutual support were arranged on an *ad hoc* and informal basis between committee members of the two groups and facilitated by negotiations between corresponding secretariat staff. Even these loose forms of co-operation were played down on the part of the Socialist group.

Within the Communist group thinking about the formation of majorities has strictly followed the pattern of national alliance strategies, and hence divergences have emerged between PCI and PCF MEPs. The flexible attitude of the PCI towards coalitions in Italy is reproduced at the European level, where it has been sensitive about the minority status of Communist forces and the possible danger of 'isolation'. This attitude was expressed by the party leader, Enrico Berlinguer, before his election to the EP, who said that the Communist Party must create a 'dialectic' between political forces which is wider than that which traditionally existed in national parliaments and

> this indeed is already taking place in the present [European] Parliament. On our part, we look and we will look for a union of all forces of the European Left and also with the Christian Democrats, or at least with those forces of the Christian Democrats who do not work on the basis of ideological preclusion.[15]

By contrast the PCF has not given serious consideration to European alliance possibilities because of its preoccupation with national concerns, including its own uneasy alliance with the French Socialists, and its reluctance based on its view of most member parties of the Socialist group as 'Social Democratic', particularly the dominant German SPD. One authoritative Socialist MEP commented on the experience of relations with the Communist group, during 1978, following the breakdown of the Union of the Left in France: 'This year it has been made manifestly clear in many instances that the Italian Communists have voted with the Socialists while the French Communists have so extreme attitudes that it is impossible to vote with them.'[16]

The Christian Democrats have attempted to gain political advantage out of even these minimal links between Socialists and Communists in the EP, arguing that: 'the Socialists' attempts to draw a line between themselves and the Communists are deceptive. In the pursuit of Left-wing objectives they at any rate join forces in the European Parliament',[17] and that as a consequence 'interest in the European Peoples' Party in particular is increasing ... growing out of the Socialist challenge that they [the centre-right] all face'.[18] Issues which have caused clear left-right ideological divisions have usually included such problems as multinationals, about whose power the Socialist group became increasingly concerned, and unemployment.

The Liberal group, as the third largest, has also become aware of the question of majority formation centred around the two major groups, since neither alone has been in a position of overall numerical dominance. While the Liberal parties have tended to coalesce either on the centre-right or centre-left in most EC countries, their common position in the EP not uninfluenced by this consideration has been characterised by flexibility, as illustrated by the Liberal group secretary-general:

> When our line on Europe coincides with that of the Socialists, we are with them. When it coincides with the Christian Democrats', we are with the Christian Democrats. For example, on defence policy we have voted with the Christian Democrats because the Socialists do not want it. In other analogous cases, such as on workers' participation in industry, we have been nearer the Socialists. Because there is no government and while there is no popular election of members, the majorities have been variable.[19]

Thus, as left-right polarisation has emerged the Liberals have begun increasingly to play a middling role in the Parliament, choosing 'coalition' partners according to issue. There has also been thinking among Liberal MEPs about their group's potential influence as a balancing factor in the future directly elected EP.[20]

There have, therefore, been two salient characteristics of the emergence of majority formation in the Parliament during the 1970s. First, a left-right polarisation has become manifest in response to the weakening of support for the idea of general unanimity within the EP, the effects of enlargement with the introduction of additional national MEPs and the growth of European problems under discussion. Secondly, around this polarisation there has developed a practice of floating or loose coalitions among the smaller groups.

While increasing importance has been attached to forming part of a majority *per se*, so reflecting politicisation in the EP despite the absence of a government/opposition focus, the closer relationship between national and European parliamentary politics has also inhibited the development of inter-group relations beyond those of *ad hoc* arrangements on policy consultation or action on the left, and prevented no more than tentative steps towards longer-term or more formal alliances on the right. By contrast with national parliaments, there have therefore been no permanent ideological majorities as such based on alternatively left-right, centre-left or centre-right formations, and only intermittent ones in so far as issues have become ideologically controversial. The greater interest shown by the groups in control of the EP presidency has also illustrated the same trend towards majority formation.

(iii)   *The election of the EP President: a case study of majorities:*
The election of the President of the EP is the biennial manifestation of the new importance of the formation of majorities among

the transnational groups. The President is the *primus inter pares* in the parliamentary bureau, and directs the activities of the plenary sessions. More importantly he/she speaks on behalf of the Parliament in relations with other Community institutions, particularly in its negotiations with the Council of Ministers, and also represents it externally at the national level within and outside the Community. This post has in the light of the upgraded role of the EP attracted more and more the attention of the party groups, so that it has moved in line with West European national traditions of political parliamentary presidents.

Until 1960 the President of the EP was nominated by acclamation. That year saw the first party political competition between a Christian Democratic and Liberal candidate representing the then two largest groups, with the former winning. From that time, there developed the principle that the party groups nominate the candidates, who by general consent should hold the post for two years, with the practice that the Christian Democrats nominated one candidate and the Socialists with the Liberals another.[21] During the 1960s, Christian Democratic candidates won the position five out of six times, which eventually stimulated a sense of party-political competition by the 1970s.

Thus, until 1971 there had been a tendency towards the control by the Christian Democrats over the presidency. For this reason, the Socialists, Liberals and Gaullists agreed between their groups in that year on an arrangement whereby they should elect a President from each of their groups in turn. A Socialist, Walter Behrendt, was duly elected in 1971 and, according to established tradition, re-elected unopposed in 1972. In 1973, when a Liberal was elected with the previously agreed support of the other co-operating groups, some disgruntlement was expressed by the Christian Democrats that the new Conservative group did not support their candidate to counter the success of this prearranged rota. In 1974, although the Liberal, Cornelis Berkhouwer, was re-elected, it was becoming increasingly apparent that the agreement between the three groups on the rotation of the presidency was beginning to disintegrate because of their own rivalries, so that in 1975 every group except the Liberals put forward candidates. Ultimately four ballots were required to elect the Socialist, Georges Spénale, as President. A new majority was in the process of formation with the Christian Democrats as the main proponent. In 1977 the Socialists proposed Spénale for a third year in the belief that direct elections would occur in 1978, making the intervening year a stop gap; however, Egon Klepsch, as Christian Democratic group chairman, demonstrated the dissolution of the previous rotation by gaining the support of the Liberals – with the vague promise of the presidency after direct elections – for the Christian Democratic candidate, Emilio Colombo. When the Socialist group appreciated that the Liberals were unlikely to renege on their support for the Christian Democrats, they made an agreement with the DEP group that, in return for support for the Socialist candidate in the first two rounds of the election, the Socialists would in turn vote for the Irish candidate, Senator Yeats, for the following ballots. After some wheeling and dealing and several ballots, the Christian Democratic candidate won the presidency with the support of the Christian Democrats, the European Conservatives and the Liberals, opposed by the Socialist group with some abstentions supporting the DEP candidate, Michael Yeats. This sequence of elections during the 1970s with the need to construct an overall majority and growing competition illustrated well the evolution of formations around the two main groups.

In 1977 and 1978 the 'election' of the Vice-Presidents of the EP was also given a new political twist, when Winifred Ewing (NI/UK) expressed her dissatisfaction with the convention whereby the twelve Vice-Presidents were automatically distributed among the party groups to ensure fair party and national representation by standing as a thirteenth candidate, so precipitating an election for the first time in 1977 and necessitating two ballots in 1978. Although instigated by an individual MEP, this further departure from unanimity set a new practice.

After direct elections in 1979, the presidential and vice-presidential elections confirmed the party-political trends which had been developing during the 1970s. As a result of the agreement in the old Parliament the Liberal group provided the candidate for the centre-right group majority, with the EPP (Christian Democratic) and Liberal groups supported by the European Democrats (Conservatives). Simone Veil (Lib/F) was not, however, unanimously supported by all members of the centre-right, because of internal group disaffection deriving mainly from national political considerations. Some members of the Liberal group would have preferred Gaston Thorn (Lib/Lux) in view of his strong European credentials; various Irish, Italian and Dutch Christian Democrats held ethical reservations about Simone Veil's role in promoting the French abortion law; while a small number of European Democratic MEPs objected to supporting a Liberal who was also a close ally of the President of France.[22] On the other hand, it was also argued among British Conservatives that supporting Simone Veil might improve Franco-British relations under Margaret Thatcher, the new British Prime Minister. In the event, Simone Veil did not gain an overall majority on the first ballot since for French domestic reasons the Gaullists produced a candidate; although in the second round, when the Gaullist and *non inscrit* candidates withdrew, she obtained 192 votes out of 377 cast, the Socialist candidate acquiring 138 votes. There were in addition three ballots for the twelve Vice-presidential posts with 14 candidates standing, with the result that the EEP group won 5 vice-presidential posts, the Socialists 4, the European Democrats 2, and the Communists 1.[23]

This discussion of the election of the President of the EP has generally demonstrated the growing politicisation within the Parliament in a variety of ways. It has above all underlined the entrenched role of the party groups and their determined control of political positions. It has further confirmed patterns of majority building with their likely continuation after direct elections, with, for example, the Liberal–Christian Democratic agreement being upheld in the new Parliament. Successive cases have nevertheless illustrated the special problems of securing an overall majority with the need to uphold the individual groups' cohesion and their interests in the face of inter-group bargaining. Also, by the late 1970s the closer relationship between national and European party politics had begun to intrude into this scenario more than before. Despite these problems, the limited power factor associated with the EP presidency had become an object of the evolving left-right polarisation, at the Euro-parliamentary level. This contest for the presidential post even became something of a general party-political issue before and during the direct elections campaign.

(iv) *The growing importance of cohesion:* Politicisation of activity in the EP, together with the new interest in majority formation, led in turn to greater attention being paid to the need for cohesion especially within the major groups. Before the 1970s, although groups had generally been more cohesive than national delegations, the question of individual group cohesion had been submerged in the overall tendency of unanimity in the Parliament.[24] While the Socialists had maintained a record of the strongest internal unity, the Christian Democrats and Liberals had been notably less cohesive. Cohesion was, of course, always regarded as giving validity and concrete backing to the existence of transnational parliamentary groups, thus reflecting the transference of national party-political norms to the European level, but now this question achieved more salience. This section will discuss methods of assessing this factor, the relative cohesion of the different groups and the ways they have attempted to ensure it.

In the search for an effective and meaningful measurement of cohesion, there has been a tendency to concentrate on roll-call votes. Gerda Zellentin even developed a 'cohesion index' for the groups in the first decade of the EP[25] based on this procedure. But roll-call votes have been relatively rare, and therefore an incomplete basis for judgement. For example, there were no roll-call votes between June 1966 and January 1975,[26] and of the 235 resolutions passed in the session 1975–6 only one vote was a roll-call, as they were used only in a limited number of cases and often arbitrarily for 'on certain votes it is not entirely clear why the roll-call was demanded (and it was probably not clear to observers at the time)'.[27] Therefore ideally, although statistically less satisfactory, it would be more politically valid to measure group cohesion by considering the divisions within groups as they appeared in plenary debates with, for example, the number of spokesmen per group, the frequency and nature of the dissenting speeches, the votes against the group line; and the extent of deviation by group representatives in parliamentary committees and the lack of consensus in group meetings. It would also give greater political depth to such an analysis to consider the strength of support within individual groups for inter-group agreements and the construction of majorities, in terms of reliability over a range of issues. For the purposes of this general comparative study, however this discussion will focus on the broad differences in behaviour between the groups.

The Socialist group has traditionally been regarded as the most cohesive transnational group. This is because the member parties have a strong common ideological background, as through their experience of working in the Socialist International, and a general practice of systematic internal discipline at the national level. Up to the time of EC enlargement, and more particularly until the arrival of the British Labour delegation in 1975, it was almost unanimous in its pro-integrationist support of progress in a supranational direction and of greater 'democratisation' of the Community as well as being active in fully exploiting the powers of the Parliament, asking questions and applying pressure in furthering their demands. Since enlargement, however, an increasing number of pressures associated with the closer relationship between national and Euro-parliamentary politics have been placed on the achievement of unity (see Chapter 2, Section C); but the group has nevertheless striven to maintain it in a number of political and organisational ways, in order to reinforce its numerical dominance in the Parliament and ensure the impact of its political weight.

Compared with the other groups, the Socialists have developed the most elaborate methods of achieving unity. The chairman from 1975 to 1979, Ludwig Fellermaier (SPD), and the secretary-general worked closely together in resolving national differences and divergencies of ideological interpretation within the group. Although effective, this approach eventually produced friction and a certain resentment at German disciplinary methods. However, until the arrival of the Labour delegation which questioned general acceptance of internal unity, the group had accepted a fairly strict rule of majority decisions binding on all its members. After July 1975 it had as a consequence to relax this somewhat, with the rules of procedure allowing the freedom for members to disagree;[28] but in practice behind-the-scenes pressure continued to be applied to ensure that ultimately the group's members supported its policy positions. If they failed to reach a suitable compromise, all efforts were made to prevent a public rupture within the group in the plenary vote where, for instance, members were encouraged to absent themselves to 'make some telephone calls during the vote', or to abstain rather than to speak or vote against the group. However, if such moves were obviously not going to succeed, then the group was allowed a free vote. Despite these growing problems the Socialist group nevertheless remained the relatively most cohesive of all in the Parliament.

The Christian Democrats had traditionally been less cohesive but they took steps to improve their internal process of working from the mid-1970s. The overriding common denominator among the Christian Democrats, applicable also to their own national parties in general, has always been their unquestionably strong ideological attachment to European integration, which outlook has provided them with their underlying basis for co-operation in the group. However, this broad commitment and the vague character of Christian Democratic ideology, with its emphasis on peace, freedom, humanity and solidarity, has not been sufficient to ensure group cohesion over policy issues, with problems stemming particularly from the fact that the group consists of parties which are ideologically related but which have their own national history and national structure. Unlike the Socialist group, they did not encounter any marked difficulties as a consequence of enlargement in absorbing new nationalities because their only addition was from the small pro-integration Irish Fine Gael.

Since enlargement, however, following the consequent loss of its position as the largest group in the EP, held since its founding in 1953, the Christian Democratic group has given increasing priority to the question of its own cohesion. In February 1975, it revised its rules of procedure in order to aid the achievement of this, although it had already refused entry to the group from the 'anti-tax' Progress Party member from Denmark because of incompatibility over this particular approach. After some delay the group came to terms with its loss of majority status and, with the election of Egon Klepsch as new chairman in 1977, gave increasing priority to developing the strength of its political profile and to this end integrating its different component elements.

Until EC enlargement, the Liberals were by far the least cohesive of the three older and major transnational groups because of the disparate ideological background and numerousness of their member parties (for example, their twenty-five MEPs represented thirteen parties in 1969). They were, all the same, broadly united on the progress of European integration, especially over institutional questions, with the exception (after enlargement) of the Danish Radikal Venstre member and the five French Republicans who were hesitant about the group's declared support of a 'federal system at the European level' and its readiness to accept a 'fair measure of supranational authority'.[29] During the 1970s the Liberal group became relatively more coherent ideologically. In 1972 the two extreme right-wing Italian party members – the neo-Fascist MSI (Italian Socialist Movement) and the monarchist PDIUM – were excluded and became *non inscrit*. On enlargement, the two new Danish parties and the British Liberals shifted the group's ideological balance marginally to the left.

The chairman and the secretary-general of the group began to place more importance on the possibilities open to an active and united group. However, one of the main recognised tenets of the Liberal outlook being freedom of the individual and the principle of diversity, there have remained basic limitations to cohesion. Accordingly, as one British MEP summarised, there are 'differences in terms of different technical solutions rather than objectives in principle'.[30] This pattern of behaviour was described by the Liberal secretary-general, who emphasised the group's unity on broader issues, although these do not generally predominate in the work of the Parliament:

> ... on the small problems we allow a certain autonomy, a certain independence. But on the elections of the directive organs of the European Parliament, on important policies, for example ... on defence, which was brought into the Parliament by Lord Gladwyn [Lib/UK], on regional policy, which interests Russell Johnston [Lib/UK], on these important problems obviously the group has to have a unified position... For, if we were not united on these problems, a Liberal ideology would not exist any more.[31]

Although over the 1970s the Liberal group has through its own efforts achieved some greater cohesion, it has continued to find compromises over specific and concrete issues difficult to obtain.

Of the remaining smaller groups, the Conservatives have also given priority to their own cohesion, which has been much easier to achieve because they are a quasi-national rather than a strictly transnational group (with only a few Danish MEPs), coupled with a British Conservative custom of maintaining outward solidarity. It was the strong importance which the Conservatives gave to their unity and discipline when they first arrived in the Parliament in January 1973, with the firm leadership of Peter Kirk and a strict whipping system, which helped to explain their immediate impact on the Parliament's work.[32] However, this impressive record of assiduity and regular voting presence of Conservative MEPs began to decline from the mid-1970s, once initial enthusiasm diminished and Kirk was replaced in 1977 by the less dynamic chairman, Geoffrey Rippon. Nevertheless, the group continued to be one of the most cohesive in the Parliament.

The other two cases – the DEP and the Communist group founded in July and October 1973 respectively – offered an example of structurally incohesive groups owing to fundamental internal differences over key matters of integration as well as some specific issues. The DEP, comprising French Gaullist and Irish Fianna Fail MEPs, was formed primarily to benefit from the organisational and financial facilities offered to official groups, which would not have been made available to them had they continued as *non inscrit* members. However, they have taken pains to stress what they regard as their common characteristics: their pragmatic approach to politics; their anxiety to preserve and defend their respective national interests and their common belief that the development towards a united Europe should be based on the 'reality of its member states coming together'.[33] The Irish, in addition, stressed particularly that the two parties were supported by similar electorates being predominantly Catholic and agricultural; that both parties had the same approach to 'life and tradition';[34] that they were united in their belief that the nation [state] is the basic unit of international affairs;[35] and both share a devotion to the 'father figures' of de Gaulle and De Valera respectively. At first, the two parties apparently worked harmoniously together in the group, accepting their differences over direct elections with the Irish fully supporting them while the Gaullists were strictly opposed, and offering each other passive support over issues which did not affect the national interests of the other. Tensions gradually emerged between the two parties, coming to a head in late 1978 after the French Gaullist party leader, Jacques Chirac, delivered a speech in Cork emphasising the Gaullists' sceptical and even hostile attitude to the EC contrary to prevailing Irish enthusiasm for it. Thus, while acknowledging the need for group unity, even the appearance of it became difficult to maintain.

A similarly incohesive group, based on divergent national party approaches to integration, characterised the Communists' work in the EP. The Italian Communists first joined the Parliament in 1969 forming an unofficial group, and became renowned for their assiduous attendance and hard work. On enlargement they were joined by a member of the Danish Socialist People's Party (SF) and soon after by the French Communists, which enabled them to form an official group, but at the cost of their previous cohesion.

Such national divergences as evident in the group do, however, accord with the principle of 'Eurocommunism' that each Western European Communist party should be free to pursue its own national approach. For the first few years after the formation of the group in 1973 the two national delegations and their respective secretariats apparently worked in comparative harmony. As the French Communists began to pursue aggressively a more nationalist line, internal group relations became strained, so that by the time of direct elections the group was effectively functioning as two separate national entities. Both, however, continued to stress their unity on the fundamental issues of defence of the workers, maintenance of jobs, the fight against unemployment, liberty and the rights of man, while at the same time French Communist MEPs took pride in emphasising that of all the parties in the EC they are 'probably the only party which does not have two politics – one at Paris and one at Strasbourg. Those things we defend here ... are exactly those we defend in Paris'[36] and justified the divisions in the Communist group on the grounds that:

> Each party has complete independence, and takes the initiative that it wants. When we have a common position and point of view, then we act together ... When we have a different point of view, we do not take a common stand ... We have different politics in different countries. The other groups take a supranational position which at times goes against the interests of a country, something which we could not accept.[37]

The French and Italian Communist MEPs most closely reflect and pursue their respective national party lines. Their members are in part selected from among the leaders of their own national parties, while their secretariats are not considered as separate or isolated European autonomous entities, as with the other groups, but as an extension of the national party organisational structure, so that the respective national party headquarters control and direct the appointment of staff.

The groups are, however, faced with the fundamental problem that the maintenance of discipline can only ultimately result from regular negotiation and informal agreements, more so than with national parliamentary parties, since there have been no strong sanctions associated with promotion and career prospects which can be imposed on members who break the 'party line': the Socialist group, for example, having particular problems with members from the Labour Party, when one Dutch member of the Socialist group felt that 'sometimes there is a premium on acting contrary to the advice of the chairman in order to be re-elected . . . in order to remain popular or become popular at home'.[38] Despite this problem of transnational co-ordination, however, it has been observed over the duration of the life of the Parliament, and particularly since enlargement brought in members who were either sceptical about the EC or anti-integrationist, that there has been a form of 'socialisation'. This behavioural pattern was first suggested and developed by Henry H. Kerr, in a study of the attitudes of French and German MEPs in 1967–8, who identified four factors influential in this respect: contact with foreign colleagues; new sources of information; acceptance of non-national roles; and the influence of group norms and discipline,[39] while Featherstone later argued that 'observations made by the Labour members suggest a further source of influence, not highlighted sufficiently by Kerr – that stemming from a new pattern of work inside the [relatively new] institution'[40] promoting interest and enthusiasm in it. The authors would argue that a more realistic determinant than this would be the recognition that, as Community decisions were made at the European level and becoming increasingly relevant at the national level, it was important to use all available methods to influence their formulation in view of the upgraded Parliament. Kerr argued that these factors of socialisation promoted a cognitive rather than affective change of outlook, so that members became more knowledgeable and more aware of the European situation. There is also some ground for suggesting affective change, taking the important example of British Labour anti-marketeers becoming more involved in the work of the Parliament and less opposed to it in principle.[41]

In general, cohesion has come to be recognised as a factor of political weight in the need to assert group influence in the more politicised Parliament. While all groups have recognised this consideration, they have differed markedly in their ability to achieve it in practice. Whereas the largest groups have shown the greatest success in maintaining or even increasing their cohesive force, the smaller groups have for reasons of internal structural or ideological divisions been unable to meet the increasing requirements for group unity. Accordingly, although size has still determined representative strength in parliamentary bodies, cohesion has gradually become an important determinant of the political impact of individual groups within the EP.

(v) *The process of policy formulation:* One obvious and major area for comparative analysis is the method and achievement of policy positions by the transnational groups, since this not only reveals their state of cohesion more specifically but also indicates through their degree of political commitment the nature of trans-national co-operation at the Euro-parliamentary level. In this section we shall consider this by looking selectively at statements produced by groups, the subject areas in which they have managed to reach a compromise and, equally significantly, those areas in which they have not. This is all the more interesting with the introduction of new (often more controversial) policy areas. We shall determine the extent to which the resulting policy positions have been simply expressions of belief and principle or rather definite proposals for action. Finally, we shall note the extent to which the groups have endeavoured to publicise their positions beyond the Parliament in an attempt to promote their political profile outside the somewhat isolated forum of the EP.

The development of policy stands by the groups has generally acquired more importance in the 1970s because of the widening scope of policy discussion in the European Community. In the words of one active MEP during this decade the breakdown of overall consensus owed much to this:

It has to do with the period we are in and integration. The first 15 years of the Common Market from 1958 to 1973, or 1970 let us say, were not very exciting as far as development [is concerned] because everybody wanted free trade: who's against free trade? It was foreseen in the Treaties that there should be an agricultural policy, so there was an agricultural policy. You could discuss techniques and measures of things like that. Everybody wanted enlargement of the powers of the Parliament, the budgetary powers... But now you have come to a situation where you have to plan: where shall we go? In a more planned direction or a more liberal direction...? It is the point of integration where you are... It is the issues which have politicised it... EMS, industrial policy, social policy, foreign policy. These are politicising things, not if the reduction of 10% of the internal tariffs should be on the 1st February 1962 or the 1st December 1962. Those were the problems of the first ten years – setting up a common market... but the politicisation is now due to the issues.[42]

One additional dimension of the general development of the Parliament during the 1970s is that, according to Coombes:

the Parliament has devoted an increasing proportion of its time to dealing with matters on its own initiative rather than at the invitation of the Commission or the Council in accordance with legislative or budgetary procedures, so that now normally nearly half of any normal sitting is spent in this way.[43]

Although many of these matters were concerned with technicalities, as with much policy discussion in member states' parliaments, some have been of such political significance that they have become a source of deep division between the groups. One prominent example was the Klepsch report on USA–Europe arms procurement, published in February 1979, following the appointment of the CD group chairman as rapporteur on the subject by the political affairs committee at the start of 1977. This took a strong stand in calling for co-operation in arms procurement as part of a common industrial policy run by the Brussels Commission and taking the view that Western Europe was not getting enough defence for its money. This was supported by the Christian Democrats, European Conservatives, the Liberals and Italian Communists (who saw an EC involvement here as a natural development of an EC industrial policy), but was attacked by the Socialists, the DEP and French Communists, who were unwilling to envisage any EC involvement in sectors impinging on defence policy.[44] The Parliament has also increasingly debated current controversial political issues such as the energy crisis, multinationals, unemployment, fishing, the outcome of the Camp David summit in October 1978 and the EMS (European Monetary System) in the following month.

All the groups have expressed their interest in human rights and deplore in common their violation. In July 1977, a meeting in London between delegates from the EP and the US Congress (a practice initiated in 1971) set up a procedure for more rapid consultations between the two parliaments on this question,[45] as a part of the developing close relations between the two bodies. However, this issue also became the subject of confrontation between the major political groups. The Socialists accused the 'conservative groups' of employing obstructive tactics to prevent holding an official parliamentary hearing in May 1978 on the violation of human rights in Argentina;[46] while the Christian Democratic group accused the Socialists of directing their wrath solely towards 'right-wing' regimes while the conduct of totalitarian left-wing regimes went uncensured.[47] Similar traditional ideological divisions have emerged between the groups over the Socialists' efforts to extend control over multinational companies, as the Christian Democratic group activities' report stressed:

The Socialists condemn the concentration of capital and the multinational companies, which they claim interfere with Socialist economic policy, although the distinction between desirable and undesirable transnational co-operation becomes blurred in the process. The non-Socialists weigh up the advantages and dis-advantages of multinationals and favour checks on fiscal, mone-tary and legal advantages wrongly derived from transfrontier activities.[48]

The Socialist group regarded it as one of its most significant objectives, 'the attempt to evolve a common Socialist view on all matters affecting the development of the Community' in order 'to contribute to the democratisaion of the European Community and to the shaping of a policy in favour of workers and consumers'.[49] It has drawn up group positions on such internally political contro-versial areas as the reform of the common agricultural policy,[50] energy policy,[51] the law of the sea[52] and social policy.[53] In order to overcome the internal national and ideological divisions (see below, Chapter 2, Section *b*, vi, p. 68), 'careful preparation and extensive consultation'[54] has taken place. This was aided institutionally by a multiplicity of group standing committees and *ad hoc* working par-ties of MEPs, supported by secretariat staff who drew up working documents for the group to discuss, and have sometimes involved investigative trips in order to appreciate the problems involved. These proposals were often considered during the regular (normally biannual) course of study days, such as that held in Newcastle in May 1976 on agricultural policy and regional policy.[55] Finally, although the Socialist group statements have tended to be the most specific of all the groups, they have contained much history of the relevant situation and current Community views and have in-cluded such general proposals as 'the Socialist Group recognises that the further development of nuclear power is necessary if the Community is to avoid an energy shortfall from the mid-1980s on-wards. Each member state must choose its preferred reactor type, but Community design and safety standards are to be encouraged',[56] emphasising that a Community Socialist approach to energy policy should not attempt to prescribe detailed action for each member state. In this manner the group was able to adopt unanimously this policy, despite the sharp differences in approach to nuclear energy between national parties. This new policy position formed the main feature and centre of discussion of the Socialist group's monthly publication, *Euso*, in November 1978.

The Christian Democratic group has also recognised the political importance of forming a united and coherent set of policy ap-proaches. Its unanimity on the principles of European integration has provided a point of reference for its positions on many issues, but, on policy matters which touch more closely on concrete national issues, the group has faced difficulties in being too specific: so that, for example, while *The Work of the Socialist Group in the European Parliament*,[57] prepared as a report to the 10th Congress of the Confederation of the Socialist Parties in Brussels in January 1979, devoted about thirty of its fifty pages to discussing the group's position on a broad range of specific Community policy areas, an equivalent document of the Christian Democratic group devoted only eleven out of forty-eight pages to policy stands, with proportionately more space given to the organisation, structure and activities of the group.[58] These policy stands involved broad allembracing commitments to the necessity for Community institutions to solve the current problems of energy supplies, inflation and the protection of the environment. However, their statements on the position of the group have tended to remain on the level of commentary on what had already been done, while there has been a growing tendency for the group to attack the positions taken by the Socialist group and the left in the Parliament.

The Christian Democratic group's structure for the preparation and formulation of policies was correspondingly not so highly developed and formal as that of the Socialist group, with its working groups tending to be established on an *ad hoc* basis. While the Socialists acknowledged that 'the more important the issue, the more difficult it often is to come to a common position; and it is even more difficult to follow up these positions when it comes to a vote on concrete proposals',[59] the Christian Democratic group was less willing to admit formally such difficulties, arguing that: 'In principle, political decisions which as a general rule are accepted and upheld by the members of the group are taken at plenary meetings of the group, and in general form the basis for obtaining a majority in Parliament itself.'[60] The group had a co-ordinator for each topic who was responsible for preparing the group's decisions. On important questions it also set up its own working groups, or, in the case of complex or controversial topics, additional *ad hoc* working parties.[61] The Christian Democrats emphasised the important role that the biannual study days played in discussing wideranging issues, clarifying controversial questions, and preparing for the plenary sessions. The number of group meetings has increased from sixty in 1972–3 to eighty in 1974–5.[62] The group publishes a *European Digest* with, for example, that of July 1978 devoted to individual reports including human rights and Lomé, which were discussed at the group's study meeting that month in Mandelieu – La Napoule.[63] The group also made efforts to publicise its positions beyond the Parliament, so that:

For the general public the group maintains a press service which disseminates the group's views on all important topics. In addition, at the end of each part-session, it publishes a report of the group's activities containing statements on the week's subjects together with an account of the work completed and the decisions taken during the preceding month. The *CD Europa Bulletin* is published approximately every six weeks in the [5] languages of the group. It also reports on the work of the EPP and the other international Christian-Democratic bodies.[64]

Like the Christian Democrats, the Liberal group has had even greater problems of drawing up unanimously supported specific policy proposals. Its members were united in their strong belief in human rights: the protection, promotion and freedom of the individual, equal opportunities for all and free competition of ideas and parties. Some firmly believed in 'private enterprise and free competition, in the right of ownership and the right to strike',[65] but the necessity of including all shades of economic opinion in the group meant that the group also had 'to make concessions over worker participation, public intervention and the redistribution of wealth'.[66] Similarly, although the group produced a statement on agriculture after study days in September 1976, it tended to be a rather vague compromise 'on the development of the Common Agricultural Policy in ways which both benefit consumers and encourage efficient farming'.[67]

One important consequence of the principles of freedom of the individual and belief in 'diversity', on which the Liberal outlook is based, is that the group has provided the backdrop for a number of members to pursue their own particular policies and issues which the larger groups for political and ideological reasons would be reluctant to do. The group has thus initiated ventures into such controversial fields as defence, which, once established as acceptable in the Parliament, was pursued by Klepsch and resulted in the Klepsch report.

The development of policy approaches in the Liberal group during the latter part of the 1970s was closely connected with the formulation of the ELD (Federation of Liberal and Democratic Parties of the European Community) Common Manifesto (see Chapter 3, Section *c*, pp. 148–9), which became a reference point for its line in the EP. The group has had no permanent committees for the development and formulation of policies. The bureau or the group meeting normally discussed the position its representatives should take in the Parliament's twelve standing committees on the basis of the recommendations of those members serving on them.[68] Study days, therefore, are the principal occasions when members have met to consider political attitudes and approaches[69] and when discussions ranged widely from education to mountain and hill farming. Because of the informality of policy formulation within the Liberal group, there was considerable scope for individuals to pursue their particular policy interests and be responsible for documents to be discussed by the group – such as Martin Bangemann's working document, 'Common Agricultural Policy: The Current Situation and Possible Reform Measures'[70] and Werner Zywietz's report on energy for the group meeting in Porticcio (Corsica) in May 1977.[71] The group does not have such extensive publicity of its policy approaches as the other groups, although it has published a regular information bulletin called *Présence Libérale*.

According to the Conservative group's rules of procedure the group chairman and four member bureau have had a central and determining role in the formulation and application of policies. However, like the Liberals, individuals in the Conservative group have tended to be responsible for specific policy areas, and each member of the secretariat covered a particular policy field or two and provided the necessary research and administrative assistance in the preparation of policy documents. Since late 1977, under the auspices of the group, a number of glossy publications authored by members of the group have been produced, with the proviso that 'the views expressed in this pamphlet are those of the author and do not necessarily commit the European Conservative Group'.[72] Subjects discussed in this manner have included a Community rural policy and shortly before direct elections one entitled *Energy for Europe*.[73] In addition, the group produced a number of official statements, particularly for the several regional conferences which were held around Britain in 1978 as part of the pre-election information campaign. These were not so much policy statements as background working papers and information documents which reflected the group's concern to create effective European agriculture, energy and regional policies. Although fairly autonomous, there were indications that the group was reluctant to take too different a stand from the party at home. It has tended to concentrate on its impact in institutional terms on the Parliament and lay emphasis on less controversial policies, such as the hall-marking of precious metals in 1977 and its amendment 'to the 1978 draft directive regulating contracts and conditions for door-to-door sales that ensured that Community rules would not apply to food and drink deliveries to the home'[74] or nationally distant policies such as the need for the EC to 'speak with one voice to the rest of the world' on human rights and the renegotiation of the Lomé Convention. The group has nevertheless evolved somewhat independent policy positions in specific areas, such as energy, which in particular was more advanced than that followed by the party at Westminster.

The European Progressive Democrats (DEP) have been assiduous in producing 'memoranda' or policy documents on a range of subjects from the CAP to consumer policy, tourism, and EC-Comecon trade policy, yet very selectively according to those areas of common agreement. These were drawn up by individual rapporteurs with the aid of a member of the secretariat who assisted or collaborated in the research and the production. The memoranda, containing much background information and views and few specific proposals, were then approved by the group at study meetings – such as that at Lyon in June/July 1977 on *Towards a European Consumer Policy* and *The Threat of Unbridled Competition: A Challenge to Europe*. On the question of *Integration or Enlargement?* in the same series, the pamphlet was however, sub-titled 'Reflections' in acknowledgement of the divisions within the group on such questions as the development of the Community.[75] The Gaullists prepared a synthesis of these policy positions for home consumption, entitled '20 Propositions for the Europe of Realities', with special emphasis on those positions which would be of interest to France. These policy statements did not include the subject of fishing since the differences between the two component parties have been irreconcilable.

The Communist group has made no equivalent attempt to produce common statements on policy for the reasons given earlier that the two major parties in the group have tended to reflect the line pursued at home. The Italians have published fairly extensive documentation on their participation in the work of the Parliament, while the French have published a bulletin entitled *Les Communistes Français et L'Europe*. There has been an interesting modification of the basis of their policy approach as their relations at the national level with the French Socialists became more strained. In 1977 they were emphasising in the editorial of their first bulletin that their action in the EP was 'inseparable from our struggle in France' on the basis of the common programme which they had with the Socialists[76] in 1977. In 1979, by contrast, their commitment to the construction of a Europe of the workers was reaffirmed, but the rest of the article was a description of the antagonism of the French Socialists towards them.[77]

In summary, all the groups, with the exception of the Communists, have attempted to produce a broad set of policy statements in as many fields as possible, including those which caused divisions within them on national and ideological grounds. The Socialist group was the most assiduous and the most successful in terms of the scope of areas and the definite manner in which they were treated. The Christian Democratic group also attempted to formulate a comprehensive set of policy positions but, like the Liberals, the wide differences of outlook internally led to their concentrating on broad statements of principle and, in the case of the Liberals, individual policy proposals. The smaller groups featured less elaborate mechanisms for policy discussion and less convincing examples of transnational policy positions. Also, these various examples illustrated different approaches to the exercise of policy formulation *per se*.

What significance has this activity had? The increasing attempts to develop policy approaches by the party groups is a measure of their response to the growing politicisation in the Community. It is also an essential feature of authenticating their claims to transnationality at the European level, as underlined by their attempts to promote their policy profile outside the EP. However, some reservations about the importance of this activity should be borne in mind, especially with the absence of the governmental focus in the Parliament, its non-legislative character and its distance from the political reality of the national parliaments. The statements are not equivalent to policy stands drawn up within national parliamentary parties for the transnational groups have had no direct means to promote their implementation. For these reasons, such statements do not have the same binding force as those adopted by parliamentary groups at the national level.

In view of the greater desire of most groups to produce a comprehensive set of policy proposals up to direct elections, several interesting questions arise for the future. To what extent will newly elected MEPs and their party groups regard these existing policies as a basis for their own activity, or will they feel the need to rewrite the policies in view of the new mandate? One limitation on the latter possibility will be that the secretariats have remained largely unchanged in composition and, as they continue to be responsible for much of the preparation of policy stands, they will provide a factor of continuity. A further question which arises is how the up-graded transnational groups will co-operate with their respective party federations, where applicable, over the formulation of common programmes for the second European elections.

(vi) *Group leadership: political role or transnational diplomacy?* The discussion so far has broadly referred to the responses of the groups to the growing politicisation of the 1970s, and their own contribution to it. It is necessary in this context to give some attention to the nature of leadership in the groups in order to determine the extent to which transnational party co-operation in the EP has owed its development to party élites. It is important to remember that such a discussion of the role of the chairmen must also include reference to the political influence of the group secretariats, since the former have increasingly had to delegate work to the latter as a consequence of the demands of the dual-mandate.

As already noted, the group chairmen have played a key role in consolidating the dominant position of the groups with regard to the organisation of the Parliament's activities. Leaders of the groups on the right of the political spectrum have played an important personal part in the development of the closer inter-group relations, while all the chairmen have played a very influential role in the formation of majorities for the election of the EP President. They have also been broadly responsible for the establishment of political priorities within their respective groups, but it is in this sphere that they have faced the most constraints as the ensuing discussion will reveal.

Formally, the work of the Socialist group is directed by the chairman and the bureau (including the several vice-chairmen) acting as the executive body taking decisions on its own authority, especially so because of the part-time work of ordinary MEPs up to direct elections. The leadership of the group became more prestigious when the Socialists became the largest force in the Parliament on the arrival of the Labour delegation in July 1975. At the same time internal leadership became more difficult, as some of the new Labour MEPs challenged the chairman's previously unquestioned position within the group, so that he 'was presented with a conciliatory role which he had not had to exercise before'.[78] This increased the necessity to devote more time and effort to maintaining harmonious relations, to co-ordination and to wider consultation, leading to the introduction of procedures for reporting back to the group on decisions taken on their behalf.[79] In order to absorb these pressures, however, the organisation of the secretariat was overhauled to ensure the more efficient co-ordination of group activities in committees, while informal negotiations and pressures normally applied by leaders and members of the secretariat to maintain the cohesion of the group and its political strength in the Parliament continued.

There has been similar attention paid to improving methods of internal leadership in the Christian Democratic group, especially in the interests of efficiency. In February 1975, there was a revision of the rules of procedure of the group. Its hierarchical structure became more streamlined so that, instead of having a chairman, seven vice-chairmen and nine additional members of the bureau, the group now had a chairman and two vice-chairmen (these three comprising the chairman's office), a small bureau taking into account national representation, and an enlarged bureau which comprised the ex-Presidents of the Parliament, committee chairmen and ex-group chairmen. In addition, the revision of the rules of procedure amended the method of election of the group organs and gave them more precise powers. These revisions, combined with the dynamic leadership of Egon Klepsch (chairman since May 1977), have improved the efficient running of the group and at the same time consolidated Klepsch's position within it. Klepsch has not faced any open challenge to his leadership as occurred in the Socialist group, particularly as there was no one collection of individuals strong enough to counter his weight. As with the Socialist and Liberal groups, much of the chairman's work has been delegated to the secretary-general of the group, with Klepsch keeping in daily telephone contact with the group secretariat in the EP. This contrasted with the previous chairman, Alfred Bertrand, who took an active interest in two or three issues rather than in all the problems facing the group.[80] Hence, although the group lost its position as the largest in the Parliament, reorganisation and a change of leadership gave it a new dynamism.

Most of the regular work of the Liberal group was also conducted by the chairman and the secretary-general, but there was sufficient scope for active individuals to have had an important influence on the activities of the group. According to one vice-chairman, the 'role of Liberal leader may be marginally more potent in that national groups within the group are smaller and therefore not so difficult to deal with'.[81] Among the other groups, the role of Conservative group chairman has undergone considerable modification since the group first joined the EP in 1973. Under Peter Kirk (1973–7) it not only performed a pioneering role but was also regarded as the spokesman for Britain in the absence of the Labour delegation, of which Kirk effectively took advantage. On the arrival of the Labour delegation, followed by the change of chairmanship to Geoffrey Rippon (1977–9), the leadership became less of a driving motive force within the group. With the DEP and the Communists' group the cohabitation of two independent member parties has meant that leadership as such has been less of a crucial factor.

Although the chairmen have enjoyed a relatively large amount of autonomy – particularly in their activities outside their groups – there were considerable constraints on their influence within them, depending on the group. These pressures will be discussed in more detail below (see Chapter 2, Section *c*), but broadly they arise from the institutional weakness of the Parliament itself. The leaders were to some extent generating their own politics in a political vacuum because no ultimate goal of the control of, or participation in, government existed. The direct consequence of this was that the chairmen had no effective sanctions to apply to recalcitrant members who did not 'toe the party line'. Instead they had to rely on other political skills such as conciliation and the art of convincing, if not less subtle pressures, such as exclusion from the more coveted delegation visits or placing in a less interesting committee. But even this was constrained by the need to take into account national considerations and balance. In the EP a chairman has had no influence on who his parliamentary colleagues will be. While in most EC national parliamentary parties leaders can influence their composition through control of the list system, in the Euro-parliamentary group this opportunity is not available since the choice of MEPs has usually been a consequence of decisions at the national level.

A final point to emerge from this discussion is the political role of the group secretariats. Norbert Gresch has argued that the secretariats have three functions:

(1)   The administrative and communications function.
(2)   External publicity and contacts.
(3)   Policy initiation in co-operation with group bureaux.[82]

This forms a fair summary of their work, but is too constitutional and does not sufficiently consider the basic differences between the groups, and notably the political nature of the work of the larger group secretariats.

As the Parliament's role increased and the political activities of the groups evolved, the secretaries-general assumed more of the functions normally associated with those of parliamentary party leaders.[83] This was partly by default since the Parliament was part-time and the chairmen had to delegate more of their responsibilities for running their groups than would usually be the case at the national level. This gradual accumulation of influence on the part of the secretariats, and specifically the secretaries-general, also reflected their own desire to ease the change from a mandated Parliament to an elected Parliament. Group secretaries-general gradually became responsible for allocating committee chairmanships, vice-chairmanships, rapporteurships, and some of the less arduous tasks such as the increasing number of parliamentary delegations. They were also expected to press for the most influential parliamentary posts on behalf of their groups and they developed a practice of their own common meetings before direct elections. With the exception of the Communist group, for reasons already explained, the secretariats were largely isolated from the national parties and were responsible for recruiting their own staff, so emphasising their autonomy. As parliamentary votes have become more controversial and majority formation more significant, the secretariats in the larger groups especially have played an influential role in arranging support from members of other groups as well as ensuring the support of their own groups. Although internally members of the secretariats have tended to work for their own nationals among the MEPs, they have played a part in easing relations among the different elements in their groups.

During the 1960s, most of the work of the then small group

secretariats had been technical and administrative. During the 1970s, the size of the secretariats increased rapidly to accord with their more political role, with, for example, that of the Socialist group increasing from six to thirty-seven from 1972 to 1979, 'roughly half of whom are "political advisers" to the group'.[84] The Christian Democratic group secretariat has also increased at a similar rate. Both groups have reorganised their bureaucratic structures in order to co-ordinate their work more effectively: so that, for example:

> To improve the position of Socialists in the committees, the group has brought in two innovations in the last few years. For each committee, the group now appoints a co-ordinator, usually a Socialist vice-chairman (or a leading member of the committee when a Socialist is chairman). The co-ordinator is responsible together with the relevant members of the group secretariat for preparing the meetings of the committee, co-ordinating as far as possible the views of the Socialist members on the day's committee business, and preparing Socialist initiatives in the fields covered by that committee. Before the committee meets, the Socialist members hold a short preparatory meeting chaired by the co-ordinator.[85]

As one Socialist MEP described it:

> Every day I get a little list from my group secretariat on how we shall vote on amendments and resolutions and so on . . . decided by the group . . . we thrash it out at group meetings. If it is small amendments we leave it to the spokesmen to tell us. On important amendments and resolutions we decide it in the group how we vote, what amendments we submit ourselves.[86]

The Christian Democratic group has also developed in the later 1970s a more comprehensive organisational structure in the secretariat. In the report of the group on its work from March 1978 to February 1979 the secretary-general described the work of the secretariat and his role in particular. According to him, out of 30 members, 16 were functionaries, 10 secretaries and 4 research assistants, of which the functionaries in particular followed the work of the committees in the Parliament, assisting their MEPs there with the preparation of information briefings on the most important points, background knowledge, the position of other groups, and other technical or statistical information. The secretary-general is also responsible for ensuring the presence of group members for a vote in committee.[87] The secretariats of the other groups played a similar role in principle, particularly the Liberals, but, in the case of the largely bi-national and quasi-national groups, their internal structures were less complicated and formal.

While the development during the 1970s has been in the direction of a more political role for the group leaderships rather than simply one of transnational diplomacy, the period after direct elections may well lead to a reinforcement of this trend. However, the new full-time status of MEPs could reduce the previous advantage enjoyed by group leaders of controlling regular work in the partial absence of their ordinary members. As to the future role of the group secretariats, changes in the status of both leaders and MEPs creates uncertainty about their continuing political influence.

(vii) *External relations of the party groups:* The development by the groups of relationships outside the EP has been a further feature of their growing political role and an obvious area for promoting their profile. This subject is discussed again below with reference to both the groups' links with their respective federations (see Chapter 3, Section *b*, pp. 129–34) and with their member national parties (see Chapter 4, Section *b*, pp. 220–3).

The Socialist group developed the most extensive contacts with fraternal parties outside the Community, in addition to relations with its own EC parties through the Socialist Confederation. Between 1976 and 1979, for example, it sent delegations to a number of EFTA countries including Norway, Sweden, Austria and Portugal. Of the several Mediterranean delegations over recent years, one included talks with Don Mintoff in Malta. The group also on several occasions used its funds to provide material and political assistance to other Socialist parties 'fighting to restore democracy' for their election campaigns, most notably the Portuguese Socialist Party (PSP) and the Spanish Socialist Workers' Party (PSOE). The bureau of the group met in Madrid and Lisbon in 1977, while several Spanish and Portuguese trainees spent periods working in the secretariat of the group.[88]

The Socialist group has the least developed relationship with its Commissioners. There was no regular formal or informal contact between the Commission and the group secretariat, with the complaint that the Socialist Commission under Roy Jenkins had made no attempt to establish any form of 'good will'. One source in the Socialist group judged the Jenkins Commission as that of 'an a-political President and a management team'. Some Socialist Commissioners occasionally went to group meetings, but relations with the Commission were not over emphasised. This may partly be due to the fact that until the end of the 1970s Socialist governmental leaders were dominant in the Council of Ministers, and therefore there was no pressing need to develop such institutional links.

The Christian Democratic group also developed contacts within the Community framework and outside it, placing particular importance on its relations with the European People's Party (EPP). The group saw itself as a focal point for the EC Christian Democratic parties: 'The CD group in the European Parliament is the natural link with national Christian-Democratic parliamentary groups in the Community. Its task is to act as intermediary in the dissemination of information and in conducting discussions on questions which need to be clarified.'[89] At the same time the group emphasised that 'there is close co-operation with the Christian-Democratic members of the Commission and with foreign associations of CD parties',[90] and Commissioner Davignon in particular had close contact with the Christian Democratic group and attended their study days. Thus, whereas the Socialist group tended to stress its broad international links, the CD group placed more emphasis on the building of close relations within the Community context reflecting the general approach towards its potential as the parliamentary group of a European political party.

Of the three major groups, the Liberals have had the least developed external contacts with parties either within or outside the Community. Instead, it has tended to emphasise its membership and participation in a number of governments of EC member states. The group has also stressed the close links that it had with its one Commissioner who took part in its meetings.

All the groups have been furthering their contacts towards the national level during the 1970s. There have been an increasing number of visits to the EP in general and to some of the groups in particular from trade union delegations, party activists and students, as well as exchange visits between groups and delegations from the applicant member countries of Greece, Spain and Portugal. Such visits began to increase after EC enlargement and there was a noticeable growth from the time that direct elections were announced until they took place.

The development of external relations by the groups within and outside the Community reflected especially their efforts to promote their own profiles. This area of activity applied almost exclusively to the three largest groups, due to the bi-national or quasi-national character of the other groups, whose links accordingly were usually transmitted through their respective national parties.

In conclusion, this survey of the role of the transnational party groups in the EP during the 1970s, and their response to political developments in the European Community, has illustrated their consolidation of organisational dominance of parliamentary work and greater readiness to assert a more overt party-political function, especially in the case of the three larger groups. This change has been evident in the growing importance attached to the formation of majorities between groups, the question of internal cohesion within these transnational bodies and the business of formulating common policy positions. While this development has derived from the broader scope of EC policy areas, the impact of enlargement and the prospect of direct elections, these new patterns of behaviour by the party groups have themselves contributed to the growing politicisation of the Parliament.

The most significant departure has been away from the EP as a united organ for integration towards an institution containing real political confrontation between the various groups along a left/right ideological divide. This qualitative change is most clearly evident when comparing with the EP of the 1950s and 1960s, rather than with present national parliaments. Although in earlier decades there were moments of political conflict in the EP, the unique characteristic of the more recent decade is that such conflicts have been more consistently present and influential on the part the groups have played. Undoubtedly, this growth in the political role and profile of the groups themselves within the EP has benefited from the absence of governmental constraints; on the other hand, the limited importance of the Parliament as a Community institution has restricted their wider political impact.

(c)　The Growing Influence of National and Party-Political Pressures at the Euro-parliamentary Level

The growth of politicisation of the party groups in the European Parliament has had two competitive facets. On the one hand, the growing inclination to express party-political differences at the European level has contributed to the strengthening and reinforcement of the groups, as already discussed. At the same time, the EP has become relatively less isolated than before. Its increasing approximation to the national political stage in terms of policies under discussion, the prospect of direct elections, and the growing interrelationship of the three dimensions of transnational party co-operation have resulted in a more consistent influence and expression of pressures and influences usually associated with national party politics. At the Euro-parliamentary level, the absence of the government/opposition dimension and its accompanying career structure and rewards of office, together with the limited political relevance of the EP, has meant that the emergence of such pressures has put correspondingly more strain on the cohesion of the party groups.

There have broadly been two distinguishable but interrelated sources of pressures on the unity of the party groups. The first is unique to the EP and derives from national loyalty as well as differences in national approach and interest, so presenting a challenge to the transnational ideological spectrum. On certain issues considered to be fundamental to a country's interests it has not been unknown for national delegations to vote across group loyalties. Similarly, within party groups this national solidarity has become more overtly expressed during the 1970s. Although it could be argued by those drawing parallels with the development of political parties in the USA that such national influences are similar to state loyalties there, the latter are in fact much weaker. While most state representatives are ultimately loyal to the USA and its sense of nationhood, the ultimate loyalty of all MEPs is to their own country and not to the European Community.

The second source of pressures is easily recognisable from the national party-political context. Although these may relate to the national differences mentioned above, they do not necessarily neatly coincide with them. Those pressures relevant to this discussion are the particular ideological orientation of national political parties as reflected in the EP (an aspect of the party-traditional factor); the national government/opposition situation (an aspect of the political-functional factor); and sectional and individual interests (an aspect of the socio-political factor).

Both the national and party-political pressures have been mildly present in the Parliament since it was established. During the 1950s and the 1960s on a few notably controversial issues one or several of these influences were articulated arbitrarily. As M. Forsyth has shown, these cross-group or internal group forces played 'an important part'[91] during this period, although he did not attempt to evaluate their relative importance, or analyse the real part they played in the operation of the groups. However, the study indicated that occasionally such pressures emerged on important national issues but with no apparent long-term direction or permanence. Fitzmaurice, in a later study, devoted more attention to the existence of these pressures within the groups, but tended to place the emphasis on national tendencies in terms of the general approach to certain issues, or policy specialisation by national members.[92] The implication of neglecting a thorough analysis of these pressures and underlying interests is that they were not considered sufficiently important to merit attention. This reflected the role the Parliament and its constituent groups assumed as an institutional pressure group for integration. This section will therefore give special attention to the different national and party-political pressures which have increasingly come into play in the operation of the transnational party groups.

(i) *Cross-group national pressures:* Nationality has always been in principle the most influential source of differences across party groups. Defence of national interests, as opposed to transnational group loyalty, has relatively increased since the 1960s, but has nevertheless continued to be rare and only temporary. This is because of the few occasions when national interests have conspicuously been under severe threat, the strong influence of party loyalty and, of course, the relative isolation of the EP from the centres of decision-making.

Cross-group national alliances have from time to time emerged in the EP both in the committees and in the plenaries. Research has shown that, while debates in committees may be 'heated and drawn out' as a result of ideological differences, 'in general, however, MEPs consider that issues are perceived in national terms in the first instance and party considerations are a close second in importance (perception of issues: National 30·8%; Ideological 26·2%; European 20·0%, N=43).[93] Thus, despite this national awareness, the actual behaviour of MEPs in practice has tended to confirm their effective loyalty to their party groups.

In plenaries *ad hoc* national alliances may be regarded as significantly more important when expressed, since the plenary is the public forum and the 'publicity arena' of the party groups. They may take the form of speakers from different groups, but from the same country, voicing support for a policy which has distinct national implications, or go so far as members from the same country voting in support of a policy across party group divisions and breaking party group discipline. A characteristic of the 1960s was that a national bloc would vote together 'usually with the party [group] that most favours their national interest, but sometimes forming a separate bloc of their own'.[94] Defence of national interests has most consistently emerged over agriculture, the most advanced of the Community common policies. The Dutch members, in whose country the agricultural prices were the lowest in the Community during the 1960s, tended to vote *en bloc* with the Socialists against the fixing of high Community prices.[95] Similarly, they formed a 'national opposition' over cereal prices in 1962, as did the Italian members over the Lulling Report on the application of the CAP to tobacco in July 1969.[96]

During the 1970s, the CAP has continued to be the most nationally divisive policy and has sometimes led to clear-cut national lines, so that, as Gwyneth Dunwoody (Soc/UK) observed:

At the moment all they [the people] hear is . . . that we are all good Europeans now and of course we are all working together, which is manifestly not true because as soon as you get to a specific thing like the Italians on wine or olive oil, or the French on something which concerns them or the Germans on brewing, you suddenly realise that people are extremely national in their approach.'[97]

Other policies which have developed during the 1970s have also called into play national differences and even caused deep national divisions within the Parliament. There are those which have been developed outside the specific reference of the Treaty of Rome, such as the regional and social policies, which form a part of the 'non-compulsory expenditure' over which the Parliament has considerably more say than, for example, the expenditure on CAP (viz. 1979 budget 'crisis' of the Parliament over regional policy). Thus, in these areas where MEPs can have a certain influence on policy expenditure, this has stimulated the greater awareness of national interests. These particular policies have been of special interest to the Italian and Irish members, for example, since in both countries there are regions which are economically in need of assistance. Although the Italians held a national delegation meeting of their MEPs from the various groups over the reform of the social fund in the June session, 1971, generally there is agreement in the Parliament between the groups that the regional and social funds should be increased.

However, this broad consensus on regional and social policy has contrasted with the persistent national divisions over fishing and energy policies in the later 1970s. All the groups have been divided on these matters, as each national political party has sought to defend closely the interests of its home country. Divisions on fishing, for example, are between those who believe that any EC country should be allowed to fish freely in Community waters, and those (UK and Ireland) who believe that there should be preferential zones of up to fifty miles surrounding their coasts. Although debates have been characterised by individuals putting forward support for their country's interests and there have been some votes where national delegations have voted together – with, on one occasion, the British and the Irish voting against the Germans, Dutch and Danes – the three major groups have attempted to draw up a common policy or approach which would reconcile conflicting interests, while, for example, the two countries' representatives in the DEP group have agreed that their interests in fishing are opposing and irreconcilable.

Although such nationally based *ad hoc* agreements have continued to emerge, they were relatively infrequent and unstable and tended to last no longer than the debate in question, dissolving immediately into the transnational party alignments. They have been rare for relatively few issues discussed touched on fundamental national interests. In addition, since all MEPs were mandated national parliamentarians, voting with long-standing national political rivals would not be considered except under extreme duress. Thus, these *ad hoc* arrangements have not been a major challenge to party group loyalty, which continued to be the main focus of attention and activity, buttressed by party traditions formed at the national level.

It is difficult to project whether national alliances across the party groups will become a more prominent feature of the new Parliament after direct elections. This is possible once the upgraded EP acquires more political clout. However, when, during the European campaign Giscard d'Estaing, President of France, suggested that all the French members form a national *ad hoc* inter-party consultative body, this was soundly rejected by the French parties.[98]

(ii)   *Intra-group national pressures:* Another major reason for the relative absence of cross-group national alliances has been the process of internal group compromise. This has been a significant feature of transnational party co-operation but the absorption of different and sometimes conflicting national demands by the groups has placed more stress on the maintenance of their cohesion. The influence of national outlooks and interests within the party groups has developed beyond that identified in the 1960s and early 1970s, of specialisation in, and approach to, certain policy fields, to the more frequent and more open defence of national and national party-political interests.

In the Socialist group, some of the national specialisations have included the Dutch Labour Party members pushing hard for the extension of development aid, for a Community employment policy and, hence, a common industrial policy and the control of economic power;[99] the German members continuing to show a special interest in the funding of Community projects; and the French members with their particular concern about wine-growing. The group has especially had to find a compromise between those whose electorates were partly agricultural, such as the French and notably the Irish, and those whose electorates were primarily consumer-based, particularly the German members and (after enlargement) the British Labour members, with the former anxious to raise agricultural prices and the latter to maintain lower ones. Despite these fundamental differences the group produced a document in October 1976 on the *Reform of the Common Agricultural Policy.* On the more recent controversial issue of energy, the group has also experienced divisions based on nationality. By way of summary, one member of the group secretariat assessed as follows: 'On 80% of the positions we have to take in the Socialist group, we arrive approximately at a compromise. 15 to 20% cause disagreement, with 10% on agriculture and the other 5% are on problems of the degree of integration for Europe'.[100]

While these broad lines have been apparent, it has not always been a straightforward case of having to absorb clear national demands because of internal national differences. A Dutch Socialist MEP elaborated on this in his answer:

The group as such is a compromise of different national tendencies, so there is never a very clear point of view, because one has always to merge different, sometimes very different, national views on how Socialist policies in Europe should develop.

Q: Are the strongest divisions on national lines?

A: I would say, in principle, yes. In practice, not always because, for instance, the Labour group is rather divided because of Marketeers and anti-Marketeers.

Q: So you have divisions within the national groups too?

A: You also see the same phenomenon in the SPD. I would say that the younger generation in the SPD are more Left-wing ... are more open to solutions of economic pressures in which the state plays a greater role that for the older generation in the SPD would not be acceptable ... [In the Low Countries] divisions there certainly are. It is difficult to say whether they are exactly according to generation division lines. I would say that it is more complicated than that. It is dependent on their [MEPs'] positions in the national parties, on specific fields of interest and so on. Some fields of interest never create divisions, others do. It is very complicated.[101]

This surfacing of internal national differences at the European level has become a more evident characteristic of transnational party cooperation, thus modifying the question of a national *v*. European perspective.

Similar specialisms have also been found in the Christian Democratic group, but its less intensive concern with specific policy formulation has muted national divergences. The German Christian Democrats have been particularly interested in agricultural policy and the Italian Christian Democrats in the regional fund, because of its benefit to the Mezzogiorno. As a whole, the group was generally able to find support for the Common Agricultural Policy, as a consequence of the large rural vote for Christian Democratic parties. However, differences have arisen within the group as a consequence of West Germany's being a source of finance for the CAP, with Italy and Ireland being beneficiaries. National divisions have also arisen within the group over energy policy, between the Dutch and the Germans, for example, as a result of the differing outlooks and needs on this question. The very concept of compromise has been central to internal group relations for, as one member commented, basic differences raised not so much problems as discussion and this nearly always produced a compromise.[102]

In the Liberal group, national specialisms have tended to coincide with the particular interests of individuals, due to the small number of representatives from each national party. However, 'you may get a tendency for the French to be interested in agriculture, and the Danes in fishing'.[103] The most important divisions in the Liberal group have been over the CAP[104] and fishing[105]. These differences have tended to be in 'terms of different technical solutions rather than objectives in principle'. The French MEPs have been reluctant to promote any major structural changes, tending to prefer assistance and the assurance of good prices for the French farmers, while the German, British and Dutch Liberals have preferred a pricing policy which is of benefit to the consumer. The group has therefore agreed on a rather vague compromise, discussed above, 'on the development of the Common Agricultural Policy in ways which both benefit consumers and encourage efficient farming'. Nevertheless, the group has always played a prominent part in the area of agricultural policy. The group has also been divided over energy policy with the French, the Dutch and Belgians being more for atomic energy and the Danes, Germans, British and Italians ranging from sceptical positions to a concern about the development of atomic power.

Although policy specialisms as such may not actively challenge the cohesion of the groups, they have been, as has been seen, inevitably linked to particular national interests. It is the more open defence of national interests which has given rise to divisions within the groups. In addition, there have formed at times *ad hoc* agreements between different nationalities for the protection of mutual interests. For instance, there have been temporary agreements between the members of the smaller countries to protect their interests against those of the larger or economically stronger countries, such as between the Belgians, Dutch and Luxemburgers, forming a common bloc with a 'quasi-identity' in the Christian Democratic group,[106] or the habit of individual smaller countries aligning with one of the larger countries over certain policies. For example, the Dutch and the British views on development aid and control of the multinationals in the Socialist group have been close, while in the Christian Democratic group Dutch interests have coincided with those of the West Germans on agriculture and with the Italian, French and Belgian interests on social policy.[107]

The two smaller bi-national groups, the Communists and the DEP, have been characterised by sharp and increasingly public divisions between their component nationalities, with the former in particular presenting two separate spokesmen in debates. By contrast, the larger groups have always attempted to accommodate differences of national approach and between national political parties within them. With the exception of the Gaullist defection from the Liberal group in 1963, there has been no serious threat of any other national party breaking away from any of the three major political groups.

In June 1975, before the British Labour members joined the Socialist group, they briefly discussed the possibility of forming an independent group because of their differences from other Socialists on European integration, agricultural and economic policy as well as the fear of being in the minority within the group.[108] In the larger groups all attempts are usually made to resolve national differences internally before debates in plenaries. However, it is less possible to say of all the groups in the EP, as it was in the 1960s, that:

National points of view play a more important role in the formation of the opinion of the political groups than in that of the plenary assembly. One can say that, before appearing in the plenary session, national elements have already been 'filtered' or 'arranged' through the exchange of views in the groups.[109]

The greatest problem in the 1970s has been for the Socialists. Since the Danes joined in 1973 and the British in 1975, there has been an increase in national differences internal to the group being aired in the plenaries: so that, for example:

. . . on several occasions a Danish Social Democrat has spoken in dissent from the group position [on matters of an institutional nature such as budgetary powers, political co-operation, European union, defence co-operation], making it clear that in doing so he also spoke in the name of the other Danish Social Democrats.[110]

The problem of expressing national differences in plenaries has not concerned the Christian Democrats or the Liberal groups so much, for the former have not contained any Danish or British members with their nationally pronounced reservations about membership. Similarly, a major characteristic of the Liberal group, already discussed, has been the greater conceptual acceptance of differences of national viewpoints.

Before leaving the discussion of the effects of national loyalties on the internal working of the groups, it is also important to record that they have influenced the closeness of co-operation and alliances formed between the groups. Reservations based on nationality in the Christian Democratic group, combined with similar nationally based reservations on the part of the British Conservatives, prevented a more formal alliance of the two groups. Closer relations between the parties on the left – the Socialists and the Communists – were prevented by national reservations on the part of influential members. For domestic electoral reasons the German Social Democrats could not condone closer formal relations with the Communist group, while the Italian Socialists, too, were aiming to disassociate themselves from the Communists at home. In the Communist group, the Italians would have been willing to extend co-operation, but the French Communists came to be entirely opposed as a consequence of the breakdown of the Union of the Left between the Communists and Socialists after the 1978 elections in France.

Finally, national differences are underlined on the technical level of communication. One of the bases for the major groups' claims to transnationality has been the large number of nationalities within them. Enlargement introduced two more working languages for the translation of documents. Problems of delay in interpretation, misunderstandings in communication and the necessity for instantaneous translation has emphasised national distinctions. These are also important as secretariat staff have tended to work for their own nationals. Such problems in communication and the language barriers have added an extra factor of complexity to the functioning of the party groups.

In conclusion, from the discussion of the direct influence of national approaches and interests, it has become apparent that such pressures were not sufficiently united or durable to provide a serious challenge to the dominance of the party groups. National delegations within the larger political groups have not been sufficiently united over a broad number of policy areas to challenge the basic structure and approach of the group. A corollary to this is that there has generally not been the continued dominance of one bloc of national interests over any other, so that the numerically smaller representation of the less populous countries has not meant that their interests were necessarily subordinate to those of the larger. Nevertheless, direct expression of national differences has continued to be an important influence in the functioning of the groups in general and has become more overt during the 1970s, with an increase in the number of bi- or quasi-national groups and their open manifestation of national differences. The greater ability of the larger groups to incorporate different approaches based on nationality has underlined the distinctions between them and the smaller groups. It has also become apparent from the discussion that it is difficult to attribute differences simply to nationality or defence of national interests, as distinct from other factors of complexity, except in certain policy fields such as the CAP and fishing.

(iii) *Party-political pressures: ideological:* The second aspect of the growing interlinkage during the 1970s between national and European party politics has been the more accurate reflection of pressures associated with national party politics in the EP. Due to the limited nature of the Parliament as an institution and the problems of ensuring group discipline, such pressures have placed certain strains on the cohesion of the groups, in particular the Socialists.

The 1970s saw a widening of the ideological spectrum within the Parliament as a whole, and increasing ideological debate both between and within the groups. The Parliament has therefore become more representative of all national ideological strands, with Communists being present from 1969, and the Conservatives from 1973. At the same time, the increase in ideological confrontation between the groups, chiefly between the Socialists and Christian Democrats, has reflected the transference of ideological conflict from the national to the European stage. Furthermore, there has been an increasing articulation of ideological differences within the party groups and, from the mid-1970s, the expression of ideological differences within national delegations. These have amounted to variations of ideological interpretation and their application to specific policy areas. It is relevant here to focus both on general attitudes to integration and on particular policy formulation.

From the early 1960s, the Socialist group had been united and persistent in its call for faster progress in integration. Since enlargement, however, the group has had to incorporate reluctant integrationists from Denmark and anti-integrationists from Britain, including such members as John Prescott, who openly expressed hostility to direct elections as 'a political step towards a federal Europe'.[111] Also, since that time some of the French Socialists have expressed reservations about the extent and speed of integration. There have all the same been divisions within these national delegations, with the British Labour contingent comprising just over half as pro-marketeers. Similarly, in the French Socialists:

Some are more integrationist than others. Some of them think that, even if Europe does not go sufficiently quickly towards the way of Socialism, the interest of the workers, etc., we must anyway participate in the activities in Europe. Some of us think that we must be more prudent and that we must carefully consider the approach, and that we must have the power in France as Socialists before we can take action in Europe, but that is a question of approach, not a difference. Socialists are not so nationalist as the Gaullists and the Communists, but obliged for electoral reasons to say that we must construct a Europe without defeating France.[112]

This illustrates the closer projection of the national ideological differences to the European level, and also the influence that a party's position in government or opposition may have on its attitude and activities in the EP.

One of the overriding approaches uniting the Christian Democrats has been their commitment to a federal Europe, which has remained unchallenged since enlargement. Similarly, one of the chief focal points of the Liberal group, too, has been its commitment to political unity, with the British Liberals as no exception. The Danish Radikal Venstre's reservations about European institutions, which caused them to withdraw from the Liberal Federation, posed no problems for the Liberal group since they had no members in it. Although the French Republicans also have had such reservations, these have been less for ideological reasons than domestic political exigencies.

The differences in the Socialist group over integration have not threatened its fundamental stability as much as introduced an extra dimension which has had to be incorporated in order to maintain its unity. This ability to absorb and compromise internal differences over integration has contrasted with the situation in the Communist and DEP groups. Such differences have been insuperable in the former since the PCF joined, with the Italians supporting and the French opposing an increase in the powers of the Parliament and further enlargement of the Community. Also a fundamental divide over integration has become a basis of contention within the DEP group between the French Gaullists and the Irish Fianna Fail, with the former hostile to direct elections. While previously they were able to accept their inability to agree over this issue, it became a matter of dispute between the two parties as the European campaign approached.

The second focus of ideological differences between national parties and within them has been apparent in the formulation of policy. Although such differences based on individual national party traditions and development have always been acknowledged to exist, they have emerged more regularly within the larger groups as the policies under discussion have come to be more relevant in national political terms.

The Socialist group has always contained parties with different grades of interpretation, whether Socialist or Social Democratic. Despite these fairly defined differences of emphasis within the group, John Fitzmaurice wrote in 1975: 'At times it may be difficult to differentiate Social Democracy from more Marxist positions, with which it maintains at times an uneasy co-existence, but nonetheless there can be said to be a distinctly Social Democratic outlook.'[113] This latter feature was due largely then to the German SPD's numerical dominance, its disciplined unity and assiduousness, as well as the smaller size and political weakness of other more 'left-wing' delegations – the Italian Socialists in particular – which could render no challenge to this dominance. During the 1970s, and since 1975 in particular, the group has developed stronger 'Socialist' tendencies, even though it still contained a large German Social Democratic element, and was led by a German chairman and secretary-general. This can be partly attributable to the arrival of the British Labour delegation in July 1975, for, as one Labour MEP said, even the Tories acknowledged that 'Labour put the cutting-edge into Socialist policy'[114] in the EP.

This development was not unwelcome to other national delegations, which had previously been unable to influence the direction of Socialist group policy as much as they would have liked. One of two further stimulants in this respect was the renewal of the French Socialist delegation, which reflected more strongly the differences within its own party at the national level, so that younger and more left-wing members came to the EP creating extra pressure for the adoption of a more 'Socialist' approach of the group. The second source was the increasing number of younger Dutch Socialists being sent to the Parliament, who equally represented growing pressures in their party for a more critical outlook on European integration. These developments during the latter half of the 1970s have caused problems not only over the general approach to the Community, but also in specific policy areas such as the inclusion of the thirty-five hour working week as Socialist group policy, which caused a major confrontation within a group meeting, since it was in fact already a part of the Confederation's policy, and some members did not know that.[115] It is important to add that, despite the comparatively more left-wing orientation of the British Labour Party, divisions existed within it, so that the British delegation did not act as an internal ideological opposition. Rather a few active members, such as John Prescott, challenged the ideological orientation of the group, demanding a reappraisal of its approach towards Community policies.

Differences have also existed ideologically among the Socialists over relations with the Communist group, both between nationalities and within them. Generally, it would be true to say the Germans have been opposed in principle to any form of liaison with the Communist group in the Parliament, while during the early 1970s the French Socialists, who had formed a common programme with the PCF at the national level, took a different line. However, closer inspection reveals that there were divisions within the German SPD delegation, with the older members tending to take a harder line against the Communists while the younger members continued to have their reservations, but were more open. There have also been similar divisions within the French Socialists, particularly since the Union of the Left collapsed, while there were evident differences between the Italian PSI and the PSDI. This discussion illustrates the increasing complexity of the functioning of the Socialist group, and how the gradual turnover of personnel in group membership has influenced its approach and activities; while at the same time indicating the more faithful reflection of variegation in national party positions within the EP.

The Christian Democratic group has also revealed differences of ideological approach between and within national delegations. Unlike the Socialist group, these have arisen not so much out of dispute over the ideological interpretation of the principles of Christian Democracy, with which all parties are in broad agreement, as the way in which different national parties have developed their own traditions, so that differences tend to arise more over approach to specific issues, such as most notably economic policy and relations with the left-wing parties in the Parliament. Although there has been a certain evolution of positions within the Christian Democratic group throughout the 1970s, this has not caused the same upheavals as within the Socialist group. Nevertheless, with the politicisation of the party groups, particularly with regard to the growing confrontation between the Socialist and Christian Democratic groups, the internal differences of approach to this within the group have caused some stress. The German CDU/CSU members took the most fundamental anti-Socialist line seeking outright confrontation. The influence of this line has been facilitated by their numerical dominance within the group. Reservations have been expressed by Christian Democrat MEPs from Belgium and Holland, for example, with their parties' coalitions with Socialists at the national level.

Different national outlooks have come to the fore over such economic problems as the code of conduct of multinationals, which has become an increasing point of controversy between the groups and caused difficulties for the Christian Democrats to form a coherent policy on it. The two numerically dominant parties – the German CDU/CSU and Italian DC – have different basic approaches to economic policy with the former standing for a free market economy and the latter supporting a significant element of state control. A unique aspect of Christian Democratic parties has been their confessional basis, with some of Catholic origin, some Protestant and others mixed. This has been more a background factor than one of policy because confessional or moral issues have seldom arisen in the EP, although it has coloured attitudes to social questions within the group. With the exception of these three areas, the Christian Democrats have not had the same difficulties of absorbing different ideological approaches within the group, particularly as these have not usually been forcefully articulated and the group has not tried to develop such a clear policy profile as the Socialist group.

The Liberal group has remained renowned for the multiplicity of ideological streams incorporated within it, ranging from the 'right-wing' Italian Liberal Party, through the more centrist Walloon wing of the Belgian Liberals and the German FDP, to the more progressive British Liberals. Reflecting the different streams of European Liberalism, there were, as of the late 1970s, 13 different parties from 8 member states, with 5 parties from France and 2 parties each from Italy and Belgium. With this mixed composition the group has continued to be the least cohesive of the three major ones ideologically, although it has become marginally more coherent during the 1970s. As with the other groups, there were differences within national parties, which emerged particularly in left-right divisions over economic issues, such as the control of multinationals with the older Benelux members being more open to big business than their younger members, with the left being more anti-big business than pro-state control.[116] All the same, the single-MEP representation from most parties has made ideological differences very relative.

In conclusion, national party ideological emphases and interpretations have intruded more into the Euro-parliamentary dimension of transnational party co-operation. This has caused particular problems for cohesion maintenance in the Socialist group and has resulted in open division within the Communist group with difficulties in specific areas for the Christian Democrats. There are, however, two important points worth emphasising. First, despite these increasing strains for the two major groups in particular, loyalty to the transnational groups has ultimately dominated. Therefore, it is ideologically irrelevant to observe, as some commentators have, that a Belgian Christian Democrat might vote SPD in Germany and Liberal in the UK. Secondly, although national and ideological divisions can be broadly identified and isolated for analytical purposes, they cannot be divorced from the growing impact of the role of a party in government or opposition at the national level on its delegation's activities in the Euro-parliamentary sphere.

(iv) *Party-political pressures: governmental/opposition influences:* In the studies of the party groups until now, the discussion of the influence that national governments have had on them has tended to be primarily restricted to its direct organisational effects: the size and composition of national delegations, and the special problems imposed by the dual mandate. The political influence of the government/opposition role on the method of work and approach of the MEPs has to a great extent been neglected, except with the open pursuit by the Gaullists of their governmental line. This is partly due to the fact that it has only during the 1970s come to play a recognised part in the positions which national delegations and MEPs may take within their groups in the Parliament.

National governments have had an important direct effect on the existence, composition, relative size and ideological representation of the groups. The French and Italian governments excluded the extreme left throughout the 1960s. It was only under pressure from the centre-left coalition that the latter included the Communists and a fairer representation of Socialists in their delegation, which correspondingly reduced the number of the Italian Christian Democrats and, hence, the size of the CD group from 45 per cent of the Parliament to 37 per cent.[117] The French method of the appointment of MEPs has tended to work against the strictly proportional representation of the opposition parties, so that the Communists (PCF) did not gain representation until July 1973, though this was partly because they themselves were opposed to participation until the early 1970s. Thus, governments have always had a strong direct and determining impact on the groups in this particular way.

The influence of the government/opposition positions of parties at home has had an important and increasing influence on the internal positions taken by national MEPs within the groups. This has been a reaction to the surfacing of ideological and nationally controversial policy areas under discussion in the Parliament, which has been directing more of its attention to influencing the Council of Ministers. Indeed, Manfred Michel, secretary-general of the Socialist group, argued that 'the most fundamental differences within the groups derive from whether a party is in power or not, whether it is in Government or Opposition. For when a party is small and in Opposition it claims solutions which would not be possible in Government or as a part of a coalition'.[118] Members of other political groups agreed that members whose parties were in opposition were freer to indulge a purist ideological stance, and without the constraints of governmental office had proportionally more time to devote to these interests at the Euro-parliamentary level. This has been true of the French Socialists with their radical stand within the group and their long-term oppositional role at home. Similarly, since the Dutch Labour Party went into opposition at the national level in 1977, its MEPs have tended to pursue a more left-wing stance, although, like the French Socialists, they have not been united on the extent to which such a position should be carried. The Italian Socialists, in national opposition, were also able to adopt a radical attitude within the Socialist group.

It was also agreed by interviewees that parties in government had to be more circumspect about the positions which their MEPs took at the Euro-parliamentary level. Considering again the Socialists, who have been most aware of the contrast between programmatic aims and governmental responsibility, Schelto Patijn (Soc/NL) observed that: 'The British and the Germans are very hesitant to deviate from official government policy within the Socialist group', for, as John Prescott (Soc/UK) also observed:

If the government takes a certain stand . . . the MEPs can't go back and be the ones that undermined the government stand in the European Parliament. They have to be elected so that they are much more likely to reflect the national interests. [Otherwise] they will be belonging to an institution that is undermining the national interest.

Such influences and factors are applicable to other groups, but have not had such a profound influence on them as on the Socialists. The most important influence among governing Christian Democratic parties is a reluctance to be associated with or supporting a policy which could be regarded as opposed to that pursued by their governments in the Council of Ministers. The effect of returning to opposition or being in opposition has not had such a profound effect for these parties since they have long traditions of pragmatism and also because loss of power has tended to precipitate a national change of leadership rather than deep ideological debates.

Liberal parties have formed subsidiary coalition partners in many EC countries. Thus, although constrained by governmental influences, their lack of ultimate responsibility, combined with their acknowledged 'Europeanness' and membership of a relatively small and disparate group, has meant that MEPs from such parties have been able to pursue more freely their own views on integration in the Parliament, without too much limitation imposed by coalition partnerships.

The government/opposition position of a national party has most greatly affected the Socialist group, although it has had varying degrees of influence on the other groups too. There is, however, no simple correlation between a party being in opposition and being more radical or extreme, as might be first supposed, since, as with the French Socialists and the Italian Communists, it may also depend on their prospects for becoming a part of a future government. But what has become apparent is the development of a closer correlation between the individual positions taken in the Parliament and the government/opposition dimension of a party.

(v) *Party-political pressures: sectional and individual interests:* Among socio-political influences emerging in the work of the EP, those of particular relevance here are sectional and individual interests. There has been some mild development of interest group awareness among MEPs, although fairly recently and predictably most of all in the area of agriculture. Farm prices have notably caused such divisions:

In March 1977, the Socialists and the Social Democrats in the current European Parliament were at sixes and sevens, with some members calling for a 7 per cent increase in farm prices and others advocating a freeze. The European Commission proposed a 3 per cent increase, while the Christian Democrats called for 5 per cent and the farmers' associations for 7½ per cent. The Council of Ministers ended up by deciding on a three and a half per cent average.[119]

In April 1978, in a debate on the Annual Farm Price Review, those representing the producers voted for a price increase and those representing the consumers, the urban MEPs, voted for a freeze on prices, right across the groups and across member states, which was the first major occasion when that happened.[120] Whether such behaviour will become more of a pattern after direct elections, extending into other policy areas, will depend on various factors as yet undeveloped during the 1970s: the degree to which MEPs view their role as in part representing sectional interests; the nature of any links they might cultivate with outside interest groups; and, of course, the structure of the future uniform European electoral system.

Individual MEPs have always played a proportionately more significant role in the EP than in national parliaments. Individual initiatives and pressures have formed a crucial part of the activities of the groups in the Parliament. For this reason, Altiero Spinelli (Comm/I) went so far as to assert that:

> The most important division in the Parliament which runs through all the countries and all traditional parties is between the Inno-vators – those who say we have implemented this and that Europe, but we must go on and reinforce policies and institutions – and the Immobilists, who say that they are against Europe, with the 'Uncertain Ones' between the two, with the first two fighting for their support.[121]

Coombes acknowledges the emergence of this division between the 'maximalists' and 'minimalists', but argues that it was blurred in budgetary proceedings 'by another division: that between supporters and opponents of the present Common Agricultural Policy',[122] but conceded that 'the proceedings on the 1979 budget, however, have turned out to be an exception and may indicate a change of attitude with the prospect of direct election'. Spinelli indicated further that the nature of the directly elected Parliament as a 'pushing force' or an 'accepting institution' would depend on whether the majority of MEPs comprised 'innovators' or 'immobilists' and the size of the 'uncertain ones'.

Such a distinction between individual MEPs was less applicable before the 1970s because of the Parliament's tendency towards broad unanimity. However, it is important to remember that the two or three categories into which MEPs could be fitted have no formal institutional basis, and that the 'innovators' in the various groups do not work together methodically. Thus, the classification provides more a framework of common motivations between individuals, rather than a structured and divisive challenge to the party groups. For instance, this has been most apparent in the habit of certain MEPs and their vociferous pursuit of particular subject fields: Henk Vredeling (Soc/NL) for his persistent questioning of the Commission in the 1960s as well as his specialism in agriculture, and John Prescott on multinational companies and fishing during the later 1970s. As John Fitzmaurice wrote: 'It is not that these individual specialisations in themselves decrease the cohesion of the group, but rather tend to decrease its importance, in that initiatives are taken by individuals rather than by groups, causing the groups to lose some of their co-ordinating role.'[123] Although this could still be said to apply to the Christian Democratic and Liberal groups, the Socialist group has tried to incorporate the interests of individuals as a part of its policy, so maintaining the pre-eminence of the group as a source of direction and control of the individual activities of its members.

In general, the scope for individual action in the EP has been relatively great because of the lack of disciplinary measures by the group leaderships and the emphasis instead on conciliation. However, with this qualification the transnational groups have remained the principal and ultimate focus of parliamentary behaviour.

This overall assessment of the various national and party-political pressures has illustrated the growing challenge to the cohesion and prevalent role of the party groups in the European Parliament during the course of the 1970s, in contrast to the relative harmony of the previous decade. This development has been a central feature of the growing interlinkage between national and transnational party politics, but it has not been a question simply of conflict between national approaches and interests on the one hand, and transnational group loyalty on the other. With politicisation, factors of complexity have at the same time entered the Euro-parliamentary arena, especially ideological diversity within national delegations, the intervention of governmental or oppositional influences, the emergence of sectional-interest considerations and also the particular scope for individual activity. Therefore the direct challenge to the groups from national influences in general has been considerably modified and counterbalanced by the growing impact of such pluralistic intra-national elements. The major groups have been largely successful in absorbing or channelling these different and potentially divisive pressures through their own integrative efforts, buttressed by their established organisational dominance of parliamentary work, and because national challenges have been neither united nor consistent.

(d)   Conclusion: Politicisation and the Potential of the Party Groups

This chapter has analysed the process of the politicisation of transnational party co-operation in the European Parliament, with special reference to the 1970s. This politicisation has taken two forms corresponding to the two major sections of the chapter. First, there has been an overall development of distinguishable ideological identities between the groups, giving a more political dimension to what were largely organisational units in the Parliament, which has led to relatively greater confrontation between them. Secondly, at the same time there has been a growth in the influence of diverse political pressures emanating from the national level which have united occasionally across the groups, and also within them, providing a greater challenge to the political and organisational dominance of the groups in the Parliament.

This chapter has sought to identify:

– the form and manifestation of this politicisation
– the extent to which it applied to each of the groups
– its rate of development in the 1970s, particularly in comparison with the 1960s
– its consequences for transnational party co-operation
– the possible impact of direct elections

by considering the groups in relation to the Parliament, the groups in relation to each other and the groups internally. It has taken into account the limitations and the unique features of the EP, and its development within the Community system, and considered the development of the party groups as a form of transnational party co-operation primarily in relation to itself but, where necessary, with reference to the West European national political systems of which the parties form a part.

There has emerged a growing distinction, on the one hand, between the Socialist and Christian Democratic and, to a lesser extent, the Liberal groups which have been developing political characteristics and patterns of behaviour associated with respective national parliamentary parties; and on the other hand, the remaining three groups whose common features have tended to be predominantly their national approaches and defence of national interests within the organisational framework of the party groups. Despite this distinction they all have certain common features.

During the 1950s and 1960s the Parliament was largely characterised by unanimity between the groups, while in the 1970s there has been an increasing number of political divisions within it, with the formation of parliamentary majorities becoming regarded as increasingly important. This has led to the development of closer relations between the parties of the centre-right – most notably the Christian Democratic and European Conservative groups – which has both promoted and reflected the ideological nature of the divisions within the Parliament including, but extending beyond, the election of the EP President.

As in national parties, the unity and cohesion of the groups continues to be stressed as an important political priority by all the groups. In the case of the larger groups, it supported their transnational claims and for the smaller ones it gave political cement to their organisational basis. There were distinct differences between the efforts which the various groups made in order to achieve this unity and their ability to do so. The Socialist group has regarded it as an essential prerequisite for its activities in the Parliament, while at the other extreme the Communist group felt that uncompromising loyalty to their respective national party positions was the most important priority.

Similar differences emerged over the formulation of policy. Broadly, the number of areas over which the groups have taken policy stands has widened considerably during the decade, from reacting to Commission proposals to preparing group positions on issues unrelated to the Rome treaties. All the groups (except the Communists) have developed common policy positions in a number of areas, the distinctions between the groups being over the depth of commitment and detail in them, and the organisational and political effort exerted in their formulation and for achieving compromise between the emergent pressures which have come to the fore in the 1970s. These have included ideological nuances found within national political parties; different national interests; the more regular effect of the government/opposition role on the activities of MEPs, and the more overt expression of sectional interests together with their alignment across the groups.

As a result of these developments, the leaders and the secretariats have acquired more political weight during the 1970s, particularly in the larger groups. The role of the leader has become more political in relation to the organisation of the Parliament as a whole, and in the larger ones developed into that of a political director as well as conciliator in order to maintain the cohesion of the group and promote its effectiveness.

There are five reasons for the overall growth of the politicisation of the party groups, both in terms of the promotion of political profiles and also its accompanying complexity:

(1) The advanced stage of the Community and the development of three types of policy areas: those directly deriving from the Rome treaties; those deriving indirectly from the treaties; and the development of policies in response to world and European political developments.
(2) The enlargement of the Community to include three more members, two of which included sceptical or anti-integrationists.
(3) The relative increase of the powers of the EP which has promoted its self-confidence and involvement in internal dissension and discussion combined with the realisation that a united Parliament did not automatically produce acknowledgement of its opinions.
(4) The prospect of direct elections.
(5) The response of the transnational party groups themselves to these developments combined with their increased political activities in order to assure their predominance in the Parliament.

These conclusions vindicate van Oudenhove's diagnosis that there would be no reason to expect any appreciable increase in 'political tension' and Euro-parliamentary politics as long as the powers of the Parliament remained limited, as long as MEPs were under the dual-mandate and as long as unanimity allowed 'centrifugal forces as little latitude as possible'.[124] For it is precisely developments in these three areas which have resulted in an increase in the political cutting-edge of the EP.

This chapter has also illustrated the uneven development of transnational party co-operation in the EP. Its level of intensity and its nature have varied according to the issues which have arisen, with some policy areas being the subject of ideologically based conflict, and others more closely and directly associated with the conflicts of national interests, while much of the subject matter remains politically non-controversial. It is therefore important to remember that the increase in politicisation is relative to itself, and with the absence of the government/opposition dimension in the EP the politicisation has lacked the immediacy and the political impact typical of national parliaments.

It is the relative weakness of the Parliament as an institution and the lack of a powerful and cohesive extra-parliamentary base for the party groups which will continue to impede the development of their activity. The absence of a supranational government or executive either responsible to the Parliament or drawn from it has reduced the sense of responsibility and commitment to the policy statements of the groups and been reflected in the lack of specificity of their policy proposals. Nevertheless, the development of politicisation has illustrated the growing correlation between national party positions and those taken by their representatives in the EP, and hence the scope for national-political influences, giving it a political impetus which had been largely lacking up to the decade of the 1970s.

An additional question which this chapter has sought to elucidate is the extent to which the party groups have been determinants of European integration or merely dependent variables. Their institutional focus here has been the EP, and it has been seen that within its limited framework the party groups or individuals within them have seized opportunities to give a stimulus to European integration; for example, pressing for increased powers of the Parliament, and initiating the discussion of new policy areas. The scope for the groups to develop as active determinants of integration has marginally increased with politicisation during the 1970s.

The final question arising in this chapter is the effect that direct elections might have on the development of transnational party co-operation in the EP. More specifically, will there be an increase and strengthening of the political and organisational structures of the party groups, or will the various national and party-political pressures become increasingly important and continue to challenge this development? Although this is in the realm of speculation, there is one indicator which will provide a guide to the longer-term role of the EP. Its relatively full-time nature will probably result in an increase in the overall activities of the groups and hence their socialising effects and organisational impact.

In this connection, a crucial determining factor in the development of transnational party co-operation in the EP will be the priorities which individual MEPs set themselves for their work in the Parliament, and where they see their loyalties lying:

- to national interests
- to an ideological stream, as interpreted in the Euro-parliamentary context or as interpreted in the national context and adhered to in the group
- to support of their respective governments
- to the accurate reflection of their national party attitudes and policies in the European context
- to regional interests
- to specific sectional interests.

Table 2.1 *Party Groups in the European Parliament (as of October 1978)*

Group	Socialists	Christian Democrats	Liberals	European Conservatives	European Progressive Democrats	Communists	Independents
Total number	66	52	23	18	17	18	3
Belgium	(5) Parti socialiste belge (PSB), 3; Belgische Socialistische Partij (BSP), 2	(7) Christelijke Volkspartij (CVP), 5; Parti social-chrétien (PSC), 2	(2) Partij voor vrijheid en vooruitgang (PVV), 1; Parti des reformes et de la liberté de Wallonie (PRLW) 1	—	—	—	—
Denmark	(4) Social-demokratiet (s)	—	(1) Venstre (v)	(2) Centrum-Demokraterne (CD), 1; Det konservative folkeparti (KF), 1	(2) Fremskridtspartiet (FRP)	(1) Socialistik folkeparti (SF)	—
West Germany	(15) Sozialdemokratische Partei Deutschlands (SPD)	(18) Christlich-Demokratische Union (CDU), 14; Christlich-Sozial Union (CSU), 4	(3) Freie Demokratische Partei (FDP)	—	—	—	—
France	(10) Parti socialiste (PS), 8; Mouvement des radicaux de gauche (MRG), 2	(2) Réformateurs et démocrates sociaux (RDS), 1; Union centriste des démocrates de progrès (UCDP), 1	(9) Parti républicain (PR), 5; Républicains independants d'action sociale (RIAS), 1; Union pour la Démocratie Française (UDF), 1;	—	(9) Rassemblement pour la République (RPR)	(5) Parti communiste français (PCF)	—

Ireland	(1) Labour Party (Lab)	(3) Fine Gael (FG)	Réformateurs et démocrates sociaux (RDS), 1; Mouvement des radicaux de gauche (MRG), 1	—	(6) Fianna Fáil (FF)	—	—
Italy	(5) Partito socialista italiano (PSI), 4; Partito socialista democratico italiano (PSDI), 1	(5) Democrazia Cristiana (DC), 13; Südtiroler Volkspartei (SVP), 2	(2) Partito liberale italiano (PLI), 1; Partito repubblicano (PRI), 1	—	—	(12) Partito comunista italiano (PCI), 10; Indipendente di Sinistra (Ind Sin), 2	(2) Movimento Sociale Italiano–Destra Nazionale (MSI–DN)
Luxemburg	(2) Parti ouvrier socialiste luxembourgeois (POSL)	(2) Parti chrétien social (PCS)	(2) Parti démocratique (PD)	—	—	—	—
Netherlands	(6) Partij van de Arbeid (PvdA)	(5) Christen Democratisch Appèl (CDA), 3; Katholieke Volkspartij (KVP), 2	(3) Volkspartij voor Vrijheid en Democratie (VVD)	—	—	—	—
United Kingdom	(18) Labour Party	—	(1) Liberal Party	(16) Conservative Party	—	—	(1) Scottish National Party (SNP)

This, in turn, will depend on the criteria by which they were originally chosen as candidates, the extent and form of their previous political experience and the application of this to the European context, their individual commitment to, and promotion of, European integration, their linguistic abilities, individual motives for the pursuit of a Euro-parliamentary career, their relationship with specific interest groups and the general importance they attribute to their work in the EP. Although MEPs are likely to have a greater freedom from national parliamentary party constraints than when they were all dual-mandated, since most are on a party list they are likely to be constrained by national party factors with the necessity of ensuring reselection and a safe place on the list.

The final unknown factors which will determine the nature of the development of the Parliament and its component party groups are the attitudes to the newly elected Parliament by other Community institutions and the national parliaments; the institutional relations and systems of accountability established at the European level after direct elections; and the development of the triangular relationship between the party groups, the party federations and the national parties. Despite these unknown factors there have, during the 1970s, been formed by the party groups ideological, political and organisational precedents, which will probably continue as the basis for the development of transnational party co-operation after direct elections, so that the 1970s have not only marked a new historical phase at the Euro-parliamentary level but also opened the way for its further development in the 1980s.

Chapter 2: References

1   European Parliament, *Speeches by Mrs. Louise Weiss, Oldest Member, and Mrs. Simone Veil, President, Strasbourg, 17 and 18 July 1979* (Luxembourg: EP. 1979). p. 14.
2   Robert Jackson and John Fitzmaurice. *The European Parliament: A Guide to Direct Elections* (1979), pp. 70–1.
3   David Coombes. *The Future of the European Parliament* (May 1979), p. 17.
4   For an account of this see *The Economist* (23 December 1978), pp. 34–6. and *The Economist* (31 March 1979), p. 38.
5   Martin Wing and Mark Hagger. 'Committees in the European Parliament', in Valentine Herman and Rinus van Schendelen (eds), *The European Parliament and the National Parliaments* (1979). p. 57.
6   *The Economist* (28 July 1979). p. 58.
7   Interview no. 40.
8   Interview no. 44.
9   Christian Democratic group, *Report on the Activities of the Christian Democratic Group of the European Parliament (Group of the European People's Party), 15.5.1977–15.5.1978* (May 1978), p. 48.

10   European Conservative group, *Conservatives in Europe* (1979), p. 12.
11   *The Times* (11 January 1973); *Financial Times* (29 June 1976).
12   *Observer* (29 April 1979).
13   *Financial Times* (16 July 1979).
14   *Guardian* (15 June 1979).
15   Segretariato del Gruppo comunista e Apparentati al Parlamento Europeo, Interview with Enrico Berlinguer for *Comuni D'Europa* (19 December 1977), in Communist group, *I Comunisti italiani e l'Europa: dichiarazioni documenti, interventi, 1977–1978*, pp. 14, 15.
16   Interview no. 44.
17   Christian Democratic group, op. cit., p. 51.
18   ibid.
19   Interview no. 40.
20   ibid.
21   Guy van Oudenhove, *The Political Parties in the European Parliament* (1965), pp. 147, 148.
22   *Financial Times* (16 July 1979).
23   European Parliament, *European Parliament – EP News* (17–20 July 1979).
24   John Fitzmaurice, *The Party Groups in the European Parliament* (1975), ch. 11.
25   See G. Zellentin, 'Form and function of the opposition in the European Communities', *Government and Opposition*, vol. 2, no. 3 (April–July 1967).
26   Material supplied to the authors by Karlheinz Neunreither, Director, Committees of Interparliamentary Delegations, European Parliament, letter of 18 June 1979.
27   Letter to the authors from Karlheinz Neunreither (18 June 1979).
28   Interview no. 13.
29   *Political Groups in the European Parliament, the Liberal and Allies Group*, Jean Durieux (Lib/F), Chairman, November 1975, in publicity brochure.
30   Letter to the authors from Russell Johnston (Lib/UK) (8 August 1979).
31   Interview no. 40.
32   See Geoffrey Pridham and Pippa Pridham, 'Transnational parties in the European Community I: the party groups in the European Parliament', in Stanley Henig (ed.), *Political Parties in the European Community* (1979), p. 265.
33   *Political Groups in the European Parliament, European Progressive Democrats*, Christian de la Malène (DEP/F), Chairman, November 1975, in publicity brochure.
34   Interview no. 11.
35   Fitzmaurice, *The Party Groups in the European Parliament*, p. 121.
36   Interview no. 50 – Jacques Eberhard (Comm/F).
37   Interview no. 50 – Jean-Claude Thomas.
38   Interview no. 44.
39   Henry H. Kerr, 'Changing attitudes through international participation: European parliamentarians and integration', *International Organisation*, vol. 27 (1973), pp. 45–83.
40   Kevin Featherstone, 'Labour in Europe: the work of a national party delegation to the European Parliament', in Herman and van Schendelen, op. cit., pp. 101, 102.
41   Featherstone in Herman and van Schendelen, op. cit., pp. 99–110.
42   Interview no. 49.
43   Coombes, op. cit., p. 19.
44   Directorate-General for Information and Public Relations, European

100 *Transnational Party Co-operation and European Integration*

Parliament, *The Week* 12–16 June 1978, p. 6 (13 June 1979).
45 European Parliament, *European Parliament Report*, no. 38 (August 1977).
46 Socialist group, Ludwig Fellermaier, *The Work of the Socialist Group in the European Parliament*. Report to the 10th Congress of the Confederation of the Socialist Parties of the European Community, p. 29.
47 Christian Democratic group, op. cit., p. 53.
48 ibid.
49 Socialist group, Fellermaier. op. cit., p. 3.
50 PE/GS/191/76 – October 1976.
51 PE/GS/48/78/ final – 'A Community Socialist Approach to the Energy Crisis', June 1978.
52 PE/GS/204/76 – October 1976.
53 PE/GS/194/78/rev/2 – 1979.
54 Socialist group, Fellermaier. op. cit., p. 13, with reference to overcoming 'the emerging differences between our parties' in the Socialist group's attempts 'to elaborate a comprehensive energy policy acceptable to the whole group'.
55 For a list of the Socialist group study days from 1969 to 1977, together with those of the Christian Democratic and Liberal groups, see Norbert Gresch, *Transnationale Parteienzusammenarbeit in der EG* (1978), pp. 53–6.
56 Socialist group, *'A community socialist approach to the energy crisis'* (8 June 1978), p. 7.
57 Socialist group Fellermaier, op. cit.
58 Christian Democratic group, *Relazione di attività del gruppo Democratico Cristiano (Gruppo del Partito Popolare Europeo) del Parlamento Europeo per il periodo interoorrente tra il 1° e il 11° Congresso del Partito Popolare Europeo, marzo 1978–febbraio 1979* (February 1979). This document was not published in English.
59 Labour Party, *Parliamentary Labour Party – Delegation to the European Parliament – Report March 1977–March 1978* (July 1978), p. 6.
60 Christian Democratic group, *Report on the Activities of the Christian Democratic Group of the European Parliament*, p. 6.
61 ibid., p. 7.
62 Gresch, op. cit., p. 47.
63 *European Digest*, no. 41 (July 1978), as well as other issues on different policy areas.
64 Christian Democratic group, *Report on the Activities of the Christian Democratic Group*, p. 8.
65 *Political Groups in the European Parliament, Liberal and Democratic group*, Jean-François Pintat (Lib/F), Chairman, June 1978, in publicity brochure.
66 Liberal and Democratic group, information sheets (21 November 1978), p. 5.
67 Stuttgart Declaration. March 1976.
68 Letter to the authors from Russell Johnston (Lib/UK) (8 August 1979).
69 ibid.
70 Liberal and Democratic group, 2201/78/3 – DC/CT (Luxemburg: 22 May 1978).
71 Liberal and Democratic group, *The International Aspects of Nuclear Energy Policy*, speech by Werner Zywietz (Lib/D), 2201/77/1.
72 See, for example, European Conservative group, Jim Scott-Hopkins (EC/UK), *Food for Thought towards a Better Common Agricultural Policy* (April 1978).
73 European Conservative group, The Earl of Bessborough (Con/UK), Tom

Normanton (Con/UK) and John H. Osborn (Con/UK), *Energy for Europe* (May 1979). Other policy publications are: Nicholas Bethell, Jim Scott-Hopkins and Jim Spicer, *Consumers in Europe, a Conservative View* (November 1977); Jim Scott-Hopkins and John Corrie, *Towards a Community Rural Policy* (February 1978).

74 European Conservative group, *Conservatives in Europe*, p. 11.
75 The following documents were published in the same series under the auspices of the DEP group: *Towards a European Agricultural Economy*, rapporteur Michel Coinat (DEP/F) (Luxemburg: 1975); *Towards a European Full Employment Policy*, rapporteur Alain Terrenoir (DEP/F) (Luxemburg: September 1975); *A Mediterranean Policy for the Community*, rapporteur Gabriel Kaspereit (DEP/F) (Luxemburg: May 1976); *Towards a European Anti-Inflationary Policy*, rapporteur Brian Lenihan (DEP/Ire) (Luxemburg: September 1976); *EEC Comecon Trade Policy*, rapporteur Kai Nyborg (DEP/Dk) (Luxemburg: September 1976); *The Threat of Unbridled Competition – a Challenge to Europe*, rapporteur Michel Inchauspe (DEP/F) (Luxemburg: June 1977); *Towards a European Consumer Policy*, rapporteur Pierre-Bernard Cousté (DEP/F) June 1977); *A Policy for Sea Transport and the Shipbuilding Industry in the European Community*, rapporteur Kai Nyborg (DEP/Dk) (October 1977); *Integration or Enlargement*, rapporteur Pierre Charles Krieg (DEP/F) (October 1977); *Towards a Regional Development Policy for the European Community*, rapporteur Sean Brosnan (DE/Ire) (Luxemburg: 1978); *Towards a European Economic and Monetary Union*, rapporteur Vincent Ansquer (DEP/F) (June 1978); *Towards a European Policy for the Trades and Professions*, rapporteur Amédée Bouquerel (DEP/F) (October 1978).
76 Editorial, *Les Communistes Français et l'Europe*, no. 1, p. 1.
77 *Les Communistes Français et l'Europe*, no. 3 (January 1979). p. 31.
78 Interview no. 13.
79 Interview no. 47.
80 Interview no. 66.
81 Letter to the authors from Russell Johnston (Lib/UK) (8 August 1979).
82 Gresch, op. cit., p. 57.
83 Interview no. 66 and interview no. 58.
84 Dick Gupwell, 'The Socialist group and the Labour Party', *Socialist Community*, journal of the Young European Left, no. 5 (March 1979), p. 8.
85 ibid.
86 Interview no. 49.
87 Christian Democratic group, *Relazione di attività del gruppo Democratico Cristiano*, p. 23.
88 Socialist group, Fellermaier, op. cit.. p. 39.
89 Christian Democratic group, *Report on the Activities of the Christian Democratic Group*, p. 5.
90 ibid.
91 M. Forsyth, 'European Assemblies', in Henig and Pinder, op. cit., pp. 492, 493.
92 Fitzmaurice, *The Party Groups in the European Parliament*, pp. 164, 165.
93 Martin Wing and Mark Hagger, 'Committees in the European Parliament and committees in the national parliaments', ECPR Paper (Grenoble: 1978), pp. 13, 17.
94 Henig and Pinder, op. cit.. p. 492.
95 ibid.
96 John Fitzmaurice, *The European Parliament and the Concept of Opposi-*

tion, UACES Conference (Bristol 1975), p. 10.
97 Radio 4 (19 May 1979).
98 Giscard d'Estaing. in a speech in Hoerdt (15 May 1979): see *Financial Times* (22 May 1979) and *Daily Telegraph* (5 June 1979) and *Le Monde dossiers et documents, Les Premières Elections européennes* (June 1979), for full text of speech.
99 Interview no. 49.
100 Interview no. 56.
101 Interview no. 44.
102 Interview no. 65.
103 Letter to the authors from Russell Johnston (Lib/UK) (8 August 1979).
104 Interview no. 10.
105 Letter to the authors from Russell Johnston (Lib/UK) (8 August 1979).
106 Interview no. 66.
107 Interview no. 65
108 Interview no. 13.
109 Karlheinz Neunreither, *Europa-Archiv*, no. 22 (1966), quoted in Henig and Pinder, op. cit.. p. 485.
110 Fitzmaurice. *The Party Groups in the European Parliament*, p. 88.
111 Interview no. 47.
112 Interview no. 56.
113 Fitzmaurice, *The Party Groups in the European Parliament*, p. 95.
114 Interview no. 47.
115 Meeting. February 1979.
116 Interview no. 5 (1977).
117 See Gresch, op. cit.. p. 39, for a comprehensive diagrammatic survey of comparative sizes of groups in percentage terms from 1953 to 1977.
118 Interview no. 58.
119 *German Tribune* (8 January 1978).
120 Interview no. 55; letter to the authors from David Millar, European Parliament, Directorate-General V (22 October 1979).
121 Interview no. 42.
122 Coombes. op. cit., p. 34.
123 Fitzmaurice, *The Party Groups in the European Parliament*, p. 165.
124 van Oudenhove, op. cit., pp. 238, 239.

3

The New Transnational Party Organisational Dimension and the Process Towards Direct Elections

(a) The Origins and Motivation of the Party Federations

Whereas the party groups in the European Parliament as the most established and for a long time the exclusive form of transnational party activity were affected and modified by the growth of politicisation in the EC; the party federations as representing the extra-parliamentary branch of that activity were essentially a product of that very politicisation in the 1970s. The demarcation here between the 1970s and the two preceding decades of integration development is underlined by the virtual absence during the latter of any significant developments in the area of transnational party organisation. The most serious efforts in this direction were made by the Socialist parties of the Six, but these were very limited in their integrative quality (see above, Chapter 1, Section *c*, pp. 30–1) for altogether there was lacking a general momentum behind any possible organisational harmonisation, which was not surprising in the context of the uncertain and later stagnant process of European integration in the 1960s. As noted aove, the Hague Community summit of 1969 marked the beginning of a fourth historical phase in transnational party co-operation (see above, Chapter 1, Section *c*, pp. 29–30) of which one major development was the introduction of the European extra-parliamentary party-organisational dimension (see above, Chapter 1, Section *a*, p. 2). Henceforth, this co-operation was no longer confined solely to the parliamentary arena of Luxemburg and Strasbourg.

Transnational party organisation has, of course, still been a relatively modest exercise during this phase of the 1970s, limited both by the short time span allowed before the advent of direct elections but, more significantly, by the restraints and limitations on transnational party harmonisation already apparent in the operation of the party groups in the EP. These restraints, especially those emanating from the national pary frameworks, have been more influential in the case of transnational organisations because they lack the direct circumference of an institution like the EP. Although there were various moves to establish EC-wide party organisations in the early 1970s, some of them abortive and others preparatory to developments during the process towards direct elections, the real 'take-off' point in transnational organisation occurred from the mid-1970s with the creation of three formal European-level party federations: the Confederation of Socialist Parties of the European Community in 1974, followed by the Federation of Liberal and Democratic Parties of the European Community (ELD) and the (Christian Democratic) European People's Party (EPP), both in 1976. The term 'federation', as applied in blanket fashion to the three party formations, is strictly speaking misleading, although for reference useful, not so much because each one has adopted a different nomenclature but rather as this term refers to the possible future potential of the federations rather than to their present state.

Despite their basically restricted nature, the federations have pursued various interesting and meaningful activities during the later 1970s, so that it is the intention of this chapter to examine closely their development during this period and assess their significance so far. During the period of the process towards direct elections (1974–9), on which this study concentrates, the development of the federations may be subdivided into three phases: their formation during 1974–6, their activity during the long pre-campaign time of 1976–9 and the actual campaign phase in the spring of 1979. Following an introductory discussion of the origins of the three federations, this chapter will largely concentrate on the second phase, while the role of the federations in the European campaign is discussed in Chapter 5. Attention in this chapter will be mainly confined to the three federations as the more formal, more structured and most developed form of transnational party organisation, although there will be some discussion at the end of the intensification of organisational contacts among other political forces, notably the Conservatives and Communists, for, while less structured, these also owe their inspiration to the same factors of politicisation. It is relevant here to note the necessary distinction between 'transnational' party activity (which is integrative both formally and in practice) and that which is 'multilateral' and 'bilateral' (which is not formally integrative and involves loose or *ad hoc* co-operation in practice). The intensification of these latter links involved an important additional contributory but subsidiary factor in the growth of transnational party co-operation in the Community framework, but, as they have not been transnationally organised, they will be considered in Chapter 4 in the discussion of national party approaches.

Before turning to the origins of the three party federations, one initial question must be raised as to their representing a new and qualitative departure from the traditional Internationals (see above, Chapter 1, Section *c*, p.33). From the outset they were predictably hailed by prominent figures involved in their creation as a radical initiative with major implications for European integration. The establishment of the EPP was described by its first president, Leo Tindemans, the Belgian Prime Minister, as 'a breakthrough of historical importance', while Hans-Dietrich Genscher, the FDP leader and West German Foreign Minister, used similar language to claim that the formation of the ELD amounted to 'a turning-point in the history of the Liberal movement'. Although rhetorical prognostications, these assertions were not devoid of meaning. Even during this initial period the relevance and potential importance of the federations for transnational party co-operation was clearly twofold, for they differed from the Internationals in their strict confinement to EC member states and to the Community institutional framework, and also in the quality of policy commitment which characterised their activities. In this sense, the federations were integrative, or potentially so, and the Internationals as purely consultative associations with a much wider geographical application were not.

The constitutional basis of the federations' relationship within the Community framework was well established in the period up to the 1979 European elections, subject naturally to further elaboration following them depending on the future course of integration and the growing role of the European Parliament. Externally, the federations have their institutional point of reference in the Parliament, to which they relate via their respective party groups. They also have a nominal relationship to European Commissioners of the relevant party-political affiliation (this being recognised in their respective statutes) and an informal and somewhat faint connection with members of the Council of Ministers of the same political persuasion, as well as with European-level pressure groups. Internally, the federations have elaborated many of the features commonly associated with European party development in general. In addition to their statutes or rules of procedure, which have created such familiar entities as a leadership structure, executive organs, congresses and secretariats, the federations have developed since their founding other relevant features such as auxiliary or professional organisations, party-political foundations or institutes for research, means of publicity and specialised working groups or conferences (notably in the case of the Socialists). More significantly, the federations' main focus of activity in the 1976–9 period was programmatic, with their formulation of electoral programmes or platforms, inspired as these were by the avowed aim to mould the future orientation and priorities of the EC's 'political system'.

These various features of European-level party activity arouse the question of methodological approaches. The comparative analysis of European party systems has some bearing here. Problems relevant to this approach are the definition of general ideological relationships or identity both positively within each federation and negatively with regard to the others as party-political competitors, the emergence of left/right tendencies between and within member parties in the federations on specific questions and, very interestingly, the reflection of common differences between Christian Democratic, Socialist and Liberal forces at the national level in the operation of the federations, especially over the quality of the programmatic exercise, structural relationships (notably the very concept of what entails a 'political party') and other forms of political behaviour. On the other hand, as indicated in Chapter 1, the yardsticks of European party development can only be applied to party co-operation to a restricted extent, after which the uniqueness of the transnational party area has to be examined on its own merits. This is not only because of the relatively low political profile of this form of co-operation – the federations are not really channels of promotion, power and patronage like national parties (reflecting in turn the lack of political weight of the EP), but also as there is one other broad approach of political analysis alongside the comparative-political, which is the integrative proper. The most fundamental question here is how to view the federations. Should they be considered potentially more as superstructures (albeit very loose ones) in relation to the national parties or as infrastructures in relation to the EC institutional framework – or as moving towards both at the same time? One relevant problem in the former case is that the federations cannot act as agents of social aggregation except indirectly and distantly through the means of their different national member parties. However, in outline at least, they do possess many obvious organisational features of political parties and in their response to the deadline of direct elections they have evidenced a capacity to engage in political activity.

An examination of the origins of the federations demands both an assessment of the reasons for their creation and a delineation of the main stages leading to their establishment. In looking first at the reasons, one has to beware of rhetorical or *ex post facto* explanations or justifications for the existence of the federations, but what does emerge is that the motivation behind their formation was distinctly political. The reasons for their establishment were broadly the following three: an awareness of the implications of growing politicisation in the European Community; the desire to meet the argument about the 'democratic deficit' in the evolving system of the EC; and the very pressures exerted in favour of closer European co-operation by prospective direct elections, the full mobilising effects of which on transnational activity were apparently not fore-seen by the governmental heads who initiated the process from 1974 and decided on a deadline. These motives applied together to all three federations with some differences of degree in each case.

First, politicisation in the EC was characterised by the broadening scope of policy discussion at the European level and a growing attention to the more complicated process of positive integration (constructing Community common policies) rather than simply negative integration (abolishing or levelling out national obstacles to policy harmonisation). Added to this was a greater sensitivity to the increasing overlap of domestic policy into the European arena as well as vice versa, and more attention to the impact of political trends or tendencies in member states for the Community's development. General events, such as the emergence of 'Euro-communism', and even discussion of a possible 'Eurosocialism', indicated how much a sense of ideological competition was being transmitted to the European level, just as the post-dictatorial appli-cations for EC membership from Greece, Spain and Portugal sharpened the awareness of the political importance of the EC in terms of strengthening Western liberal democracy – and in the transnational party context of the future balance of political forces in a further enlarged Community. The federations' work recognised early that there was a growing interdependence between national economies and hence closer interlinkage between European and national policy concerns. The draft programme of the Socialist Confederation presented in 1977, for instance, emphasised in its preamble that in reference to its aim of socio-economic structural changes within the EC 'each country is by itself too small today to be able to achieve this task alone'. In launching this draft pro-gramme at a news conference, the Confederation's president com-mented that such problems as unemployment were global and could not be solved merely at the national level.[1] There were, therefore, two effects of politicisation in the EC so far as transnational party co-operation was concerned – a heightened sense of national inter-dependence over policy problems, especially arising out of inter-national economic developments and a feeling of crisis in the EC system, and a greater acceptance of ideological challenge at the European level, involving the need to combine political efforts on the part of ideologically related national forces. This was most marked with the Christian Democrats and their fears about the political left in the EC, but the sense of ideological competition was also present among the Socialists and, to some extent, the Liberals.

Secondly, the question of the 'democratic deficit' in the Community, although no new theme, underwent revival from the early 1970s as a consequence of growing concern about the trend of bureaucratisation in the EC's institutional machinery and the accretion of executive decisions at the European level. Following the Hague Summit of 1969, with its promise of new progress in integration, the Socialist parties of the Six for the first time discussed the possibility of creating a European Socialist party,[2] just as the chairman of the Christian Democratic group in the EP urged after the summit that 'this revival of the European unification process demands a political reaction from the parties'.[3] A prominent *leitmotiv* in such demands for an upgraded European-level activity by parties was the absence of effective democratic control over the EC's executive institutions, a requirement that was by no means satisfied by the mainly inadequate scrutiny procedures of Community legislation in the national parliaments.[4] It was interesting that this point was pressed strongly by those politicians involved in transnational party co-operation despite the EP's very limited constitutional powers, therefore suggesting a long-term perspective. The motive for advocating effective EC-wide party organisations with an integrative purpose was in this context twofold: to provide an agent of control over the party groups outside the EP, and generally to promote the democratisation of the EC's institutional structure. This form of thinking was illustrated clearly by Martin Bangemann, the FDP leader and an active proponent of the Liberal Federation, in a speech at his own party congress in October 1975:

At the moment the situation is such that we have indeed a Liberal group in the European Parliament, but no party organisation which stands behind this Liberal group. That impedes the work of the group considerably. Sometimes it perhaps makes it easier, as one doesn't have to go along with party congress resolutions but rather one can formulate and define policy almost freely. In principle, the establishment of a Federation of Liberal parties of the Community is an act of democratisation of the existing institutions. For when we create such a federation as a common party of a European kind, then we will give it the competences which it will exercise *vis-à-vis* the group in the European Parliament and can use as an instrument of control over practical policy carried out in this group.[5]

It was generally agreed that the older Internationals were not capable of performing the necessary role, both programmatically of dealing with EC policy issues and institutionally of providing a mechanism of democratic control. Consequently, the arguments on the grounds of the 'democratic deficit' followed the concurrent lines of both functional necessity and principle.

Thirdly, the party-political pressures engendered by direct elections during the 1974–9 period followed a recognisable pattern simply because parties respond to electoral challenges in an almost Pavlovian way, even though, as here, the EP was not an important focus of political power. European elections did symbolise a certain supranational potential in the EC, a viewpoint that was more likely to count with the strongly pro-integration parties; but it is also important to realise there were distinct concrete steps to be taken in preparing for the first popular election of the EP, and that the desire to win seats and emerge within the strongest group in the Parliament impelled parties along this path. The very deadline of the elections, originally set for the spring of 1978 and later postponed for a year, automatically imposed a series of tasks on the federations and their member parties, not to mention the early recognition of the need for common European programmes and the acceptance of a trans-national organisational framework for the campaign following the precedent of Euro-parliamentary groups. Thus, direct elections had an undoubted crystallising effect on the transnational organisational dimension *per se*, a factor emphasised or acknowledged by virtually all the authors' interviewees whether engaged in European-level or national party politics. With the major exception of the British Labour Party, the stimulus of direct elections on transnational activity was also evident among parties with integrationist reservations. A leading activist of the Danish Social Democrats described the attitude of his party as

> not one of the motive forces behind [promoting] direct elections, but on the other hand as soon as it was put on the agenda we realised that it's in the treaty and it has to take place sooner or later, so we were not the ones to stop it . . . a lot of our members, a lot of our voters were against joining the EEC, but now we're in and the direct elections are not about being pro or anti. They are about exercising your influence in the EEC.[6]

Pressures operating on the individual parties from the European electoral deadline produced an unprecedented degree of readiness to co-operate with ideologically linked forces at the European level. The executive secretary of the European Union of Christian Demo-crats (EUCD) commented in 1977 that a major consideration in forming the EPP was the view that:

> He who is for the general direct election of the European Parlia-ment must be prepared and be in a position to enlist support for

his ideas in a European campaign. It is, however, unthinkable that eight or nine Christian Democratic parties in the member states should announce diverse aims for their European policy. Therefore, we need the European party and a common programme.[7]

Tindemans underlined this point when asserting at the time of the EPP's establishment that 'European parties only have a meaning when it comes to the point of European elections to the European Parliament'.[8] The intensification of transnational organisational links with direct elections in mind spread outside the three federations to other political forces, even fringe ones like the extreme right and the ecologists. It is important to realise that the sense of political competition behind the creation of the federations and other looser formations derived much motive force from the national level, for the prospect of European elections impinged directly on the individual parties.

These three broad motives promoted or encouraged a consensus among Euro-parliamentary circles and also national party élites on the need to institutionalise party organisational links within the EC structure. It is possible that, without the *immediate* stimulus and *practical* pressures from these elections, the *long-term* or *principled* arguments resulting from overall politicisation in the Community and relating to the democratising of its structure would not have sufficed to catalyse this party-political institutionalisation or certainly the degree to which it was taken from the mid-1970s. This supposition is underlined by looking at the limited success of initiatives in the earlier 1970s before direct elections became a realistic prospect from late 1974 onwards. Admittedly, the broader motives which inspired this new departure – notably the case for effective democratic control through European party organisations – seemed well beyond the capacity of the federations at the time of their creation, but this did not diminish the ultimate motivation for their existence. Within the consensus that emerged there were also differences within and between the ideological movements about the actual form this European institutionalisation of party co-operation should take. These various problems are appreciated more clearly by examining the process itself of founding the federations from the early 1970s.

Without discussing in detail the formation of the three federations,* it is useful here to select some aspects of this process which

---

*For this see Norbert Gresch. *Transnationale Parteienzusammenarbeit in der EG* (1978), ch. 4; Geoffrey Pridham and Pippa Pridham, 'The development of European party federations', ch. 12 in Stanley Henig (ed.). *Political Parties in the European Community* (1979).

cast further light on the motives behind their establishment, put their institutional relationship with the EC in a broader context and provide some background to their subsequent development. These aspects may be introduced as the following questions. Were the federations consciously viewed and created as essentially new structures by their promoters, or were they rather an extension of pre-existing transnational links with a new integrative purpose? What, therefore, was their institutional relationship with other party-political bodies inside and outside the EC structure? And what specific differences were evident between the three federations in their manner of establishment which might have significance for their future development?

As we have seen, the traditional Internationals provided an historical background to transnational organisation but they were qualitatively different from what now transpired (see above, Chapter 1, Section *c*, p. 33). The idea of deliberately creating a new party-political structure within the EC was voiced first of all by the Socialists at the time of the 1969 Hague summit; not surprisingly as they had made the most advance, albeit limited, towards trans-national organisation before that time (see above, Chapter 1, Section *c*, pp. 30–3). It came over the proposal from the Dutch MEP, Henk Vredeling, in that year for a Progressive European Party (PEP), which, ignoring the established national parties, should form its own separate structure from the base upwards, and so fill the political vacuum presented by the non-existence of a direct institutional link between the distant EC structures and the national publics. This proposal was debated by various Socialist parties with some favourable towards the principle of a Socialist party for the EC, but they and others eventually maintained practical reservations on the grounds that the idea was premature and because of the binding powers the PEP would have on the national parties.[9] There occurred during 1971–4 intermittent deliberation over the precise form a new EC-wide party-political formation should assume – with the setting up of a special working group on the 'Reform of the Liaison Bureau', further discussion of the question at the 1971 conference of the Socialist parties of the Six and the appearance of the Mozer report in 1973 advocating a closer and more politicised transnational organisation[10] – but the eventual outcome was modest in comparison with the original proposal. Because of the Socialists' earlier progress in adapting their transnational links to the EC framework through their Liaison Bureau of the Socialist Parties of the Six, the decision in April 1974 to convert this bureau into the Confederation of the Socialist Parties of the EC was more an evolutionary step than any radical new departure. The Confederation was never conceived of as involving a European Socialist party; indeed, its first president,

Wilhelm Dröscher, stressed at the time its limited structural importance:

> It must be quite clearly noted that the development of a 'European Socialist Party' is not a realistic possibility in the near future. This would create insuperable problems for the national parties. But it is essential that in this transition stage the member parties of the Confederation should be united in a 'family of parties', which in a spirit of mutual understanding, constant dialogue and common resolve sees to it that the policy of democratic socialism does not remain a dead letter in the European Community, but in a common spirit of valiant endeavour points the way to transnational progress on important questions.[11]

Despite this limited change the political significance of the Confederation's birth was underlined by the fact that the decision to proceed with it was ultimately prompted by the occurrence of EC enlargement in 1973, the now looming possibility of direct elections and competition from similar moves by European Christian Democrats and Liberals.[12]

In the case of these two other formations, the decision to create EC party federations was consciously seen as providing the basis for future European parties and, seen against their earlier absence of EC-wide transnational organisation, these two initiatives did involve a radical departure. A similar proposal to that of Vredeling had been made by the Dutch Christian Democrat, Westerterp, in 1970 for a European People's Party, which would break with the loose and unbinding 'inter-state' structure of the EUCD and form a constituent party of a European party system, but this produced no direct results as circumstances were not yet favourable enough. Both the EPP and the ELD were that much more (European) electorally motivated than the Socialist Confederation, their formation in 1976 and plans for them occurring within the period when direct elections were already a likely possibility. This electoral motivation was openly stated by various leaders of the ELD, notably Martin Bangemann, chairman of its programme commission, who commented at the time of its founding in March 1976 that it had been formed 'because we took the line in view of elections to the European Parliament that soon we would have to follow a common election campaign in the whole of the European Community in order to promote a Liberal policy'.[13] Secondly, these two federations differed from the Socialist one in that they both applied the federal principle to their own organisation. This was written into the EPP and ELD statutes, and as the deputy secretary-general of the EPP explained: 'He who credibly supports the federal order for the European Union must accept and want the same basic federative structure for the merger of national parties in a European party he should not be content with a confederal "cover association".[14] However, neither the EPP nor the ELD could claim to have arisen entirely out of an institutional vacuum, which leads us to the second question.

The institutional relationship of the federations with other party-political bodies both inside the EC structure (the Euro-parliamentary groups) and outside it (the Internationals or their equivalents) placed their establishment in a wider perspective. General differences were evident between the three cases, largely because of their different institutional starting-points. The crucial role in the creation of the Socialist Confederation was played by the individual national parties acting through the Liaison Bureau, with some auxiliary involvement by the EP group consistent with the Bureau's general purpose as a channel of communication between the group and the parties. In the case of the EPP, both the EP group and the EUCD played an equally important and direct part in preparing and inaugurating the new federation; while the Liberals followed a much less structured procedure with the Liberal International acting as a loose framework for consultation at the early stage and the standing conference of Liberal party leaders providing the decisive motive force with some assistance from individual MEPs.

In view of these variations, it is interesting to note the different relationships of the federations with the older transnational bodies once the former began to operate. The Socialist Confederation saw itself as a regional association, though distinctly not as a substructure, of the Socialist International. As its rules of procedure indicate in clause 1, the co-operation of its member parties is 'based on the provisions of the statutes of the Socialist International pertaining to regional co-operation between members'. As such it remained quite autonomous from the International, even though many of the same political leaders and officials continued to meet in both organisations which developed regular contacts between their secretariats and some co-ordination in exchanging working papers.[15] The International has, in practice, tended to leave EC matters to the work of the Confederation.

The relationship of the ELD to the Liberal International has been less intimate. The former's statutes specified that it 'will act within the framework of the Liberal International', but in practice this relationship has been less harmonious than in the Socialist case. This has arisen not so much from the fact that not all ELD parties are in the International (for example, the French Giscardians) as the very integrative purpose of the Federation which contrasts starkly with the weak consultative method of the International. A sense of independence on the part of the ELD surfaced at the start when its constituent congress in 1976 rejected the International's proposal governing ELD membership – that this should be open to parties in the EC which belonged to the International and adhered to the Oxford Manifesto of 1947 and the Oxford Declaration of 1967[16] – in favour of the revised version: 'membership of the Federation is open to all political parties of the EC who accept the statutes and the policy programmes adopted by the Congress of the Federation' (Article 3 of the ELD statutes). Since then, some concern has emerged among non-EC members of the Internationals about their loss of involvement in European affairs.[17]

The Christian Democrats have differed in so far as their equivalent International, the EUCD, was already confined to the European area (not just the EC) as a regional section of the Christian Democratic World Union, so that it is not surprising that there should be more of an integral relationship between the EUCD and the EPP. The EPP's institutional predecessors had developed organically out of the EUCD in the early 1970s: the standing conference of party chairmen of the EC parties formed in 1970, and the Political Committee of the EC parties (formally acknowledged in the EUCD statutes) in 1972. This integral relationship was maintained with the creation of the EPP itself, with the presidents of the EUCD and the EPP acting as vice-presidents of the other respectively, the setting up of some common auxiliary associations and the holding of common meetings of their executive organs. According to one Christian Democratic official:

> We meet together, and according to whether it is an EPP or rather EUCD meeting more themes are discussed which go beyond the EC, and when it sits as the Political Bureau of the EPP under the chairmanship of the EPP president more themes are dealt with which concern the EC. In principle, invitations are sent out to all members of both organisations under the heading 'Political Bureau of the EPP/EUCD'.[18]

However, in spite of these different institutional relationships between the three party federations and their respective Internationals, the institutional motive on the part of the former in relation to the EC internally was the same in each case: the aim of providing extra-parliamentary organisational support to the EP groups, and thereby specialising actively in the area of EC policies. This relationship, already demonstrated by the contributory part played by the groups in setting up the federations, will be discussed more fully in the next section.

The third question relating to the establishment of the federations may be answered quite briefly, as this involves largely a collation of

various preceding points. Certain significant differences, both institutional and political, between the federations were becoming clear
even during the preparatory period and the time of their founding.
These were the varying degree of electoral motivation behind them
(less pronounced within the Socialist Confederation than the EPP
and ELD); the acceptance or not of federalism as the principle of
internal organisation; and the related concept of what basically a
'political party' consisted in terms of its structural articulation,
binding character and political purpose. In all respects, the Socialist
Confederation tended to diverge significantly from the other two
because of the more conscious sense of national party autonomy
among its members and its greater reluctance to embrace integrationist norms in its own organisation. This divergence again
appeared during the discussion and formulation of common programmes for the European elections.

Finally, it is worth concluding here with some reference to the
prospective further development of the federations in the light of
their establishment. The comment of Kurt Biedenkopf, CDU
general-secretary, when the EPP was formed – that 'founding a
European party is almost as difficult as erecting a European confederation, for the latter will in part be anticipated in the party'[19] –
was instructive, as it drew attention to the fact that no transnational
party organisation could operate without being affected by the possibilities and constraints of the EC's structural framework. In particular, the federations soon faced the different problems which had
for long, and increasingly so during the 1970s, characterised the
work of the Euro-parliamentary groups. These problems included
the diversification of programmatic interpretation within the same
ideological schools, both between and within national parties, the
inevitable and predominant imprint of national interests and outlooks in policy priorities and the effects of domestic political situations on a willingness to engage in transnational party co-operation.
With the general EC-framework and the long-term approach of
transnational co-operation in mind, the authors have adopted the
following five criteria or stages by which to measure progress towards
party-political integration in the case of the federations: [20]

(1) The titular or cosmetic, in which the component member parties
    of a federation operate or fight European elections under a
    common banner or distinct label.
(2) The programmatic, involving the agreement on common
    programmes with some definition of the ideological orientation
    of the federation and a commitment to the policies outlined
    in them.
(3) The electoral-organisational, where the federations acquire some

central control over electoral procedures, notably the selection of European candidates and active co-ordination of national campaigns, more likely in the event of a uniform electoral system throughout the EC.

(4) The political-organisational, namely the creation of some form of integrated hierarchical structure devolving to the local level which is more than just a formality.

(5) The emergence of an acknowledged political power-structure of leadership at the European party level.

Above all, what stands out in this schema is whether the party federations in the EC remain as merely dependent variables of the integration process or begin to emerge also as one of its active determinants.

(b) The Constitutional Basis of the Federations and their Institutional Interlinkage within the European Community

The value of looking more closely at the formal structural nature of the federations is that it both throws pertinent light on the intentions and thinking of those engaged in transnational party activity, such as how they envisage a 'European party', and offers some indication of the federations' potential in so far as constitutional provisions outline a framework for future development. However, constitutional analysis of political parties cannot ignore the admixture of formal and informal procedures in their operation, for, as Maurice Duverger pointed out, the lesson to be drawn from party development in Western Europe is that informal procedures count strongly in how party formations evolve and shape themselves: 'The organisation of parties depends essentially on unwritten practice and habit . . . constitutions and rules never give more than a partial idea of what happens, if indeed they describe reality at all, for they are rarely strictly applied.'[21] Duverger's sceptical comment is perhaps somewhat less applicable to European-level party formations because of the fairly strict adherence to legal procedures in the operative methods of the EC, but the basic problem he raises is still relevant to the federations. A leading activist of one of the federations complained in an interview that 'the legal personalities of the federations are not clear at all',[22] meaning that with the pressure to found them the full implications of their overall role in the EC framework had not been worked out sufficiently. Consequently, any discussion of their constitutional position must include informal as well as formal procedures which have moulded their development.

Broadly speaking, the location of the federations within the structure of the EC was not without some points of reference, despite the fact that the Rome Treaty made no provision for a serious development of European-level party organisations. These included, of course, the federations' institutional interlinkage with the Euro-parliamentary groups and their general role of co-ordination between national parties. But within these broad 'constitutional' contours the federations were left to formulate their own rules and regulations, dependent naturally on the transnational willingness of individual member parties.

One aspect fundamental to the potential of the federations as effective bodies was the question of member party autonomy. The difference in this respect between the EPP and ELD, which adhered formally to the federal principle as the basis of their internal structures, and the Socialist Confederation, which did not, has already been mentioned. Among Socialists both national party and Confederation leaders tended to make a principle of the autonomy of individual parties. Wilhelm Dröscher, first president of the Confederation, commented soon after its inauguration that the Confederation thought of itself as 'an instrument for supporting co-operation' between the parties, who formed it on the basis of their own 'freedom of decision'.[23] At the level of principle, the Christian Democratic EPP stated in their statutes that 'the member parties and équipes shall retain their name, their identity and their freedom of action within the framework of their national responsibilities' (Article 2), for it assumed an integrative role only in the field of European policy, while the ELD followed a similar line of thinking. It seemed that the Christian Democrats, together with the Liberals, and the Socialists approached party-political harmonisation from different or opposite positions of principle, the former emphasising its future potential and the latter the present realities. A Dutch Christian Democratic European expert enlarged on this question:

There are no problems in accepting the principle [of federalism], but we are very realistic about this – it is a very far-reaching target and quite difficult to reach in a generation's time. But we think a far-reaching target is necessary as a basis with which to act now – a great difference between us and the Socialists is just this view on the target.[24]

Behind the formal adherence to different principles of operation and the transnational rhetoric were the actual problems of party-political harmonisation in effect the same for the EPP, the ELD and the Confederation alike?

It is interesting in this context to ask how much 'models' of party development might have consciously influenced those involved in promoting transnational party organisation, especially as they were élite-created and therefore somewhat artificial. In the experience of the authors there were a few – especially federation officials, invariably with political-science backgrounds – who thought deliberately in such conceptual terms or had the precedent of US federal parties in mind, whereas elsewhere reference to the US model, if any, was usually very unsystematic. What seemed to weigh far more heavily were the habits of mind, forms of behaviour and structural relationships common to the experience of political parties in Western Europe. There was admittedly the German federal system, but even here party development has acted as a cohesive force rather than a loosê framework. This predominance of European patterns of party behaviour is hardly surprising when one considers that the vast proportion of those active in the working of the federations – apart from federation officials – have been national party 'actors', albeit temporarily wearing their European hats. How have such patterns been reflected in the actual constitutional structure and forms of institutional relationship, both internal and external, of the federations?

Internally, the structures of the federations are defined by their respective statutes (called more modestly 'rules of procedure' in the case of the Socialist Confederation). There is in outline a similarity of formal types of structure between the three cases. Each has an executive organ (the Bureau in the Confederation, the Executive Committee in the ELD and the Political Bureau supplemented by the Executive Committee in the EPP), together with a hierarchy of leadership officials including a president and vice-presidents, a congress and an administrative organ called a secretariat.

The formal tasks allotted to the executive organs are not dramatically different between the three federations, although defined more specifically in some respects. They may be described as predominantly involving routine administration with a flavour of political guidance. Thus, Article 7 of the Socialist Confederation rules of procedure lists the following tasks of its Bureau: discussing matters arising in connection with the activities of the EC; making recommendations to the member parties; organising the exchange of information between member parties; convening congresses, fixing their agenda and deciding where they are to be held; executing the decisions of congress; calling extraordinary meetings; and approving the budget and fixing membership dues. It could be said that such administrative tasks are always open to a more political interpretation in the event of the Confederation's assuming eventually a greater role in transnational activity. Similarly, the EPP statutes

(Article 7*g*) list among the functions of the Political Bureau (the more important of its two executive organs) fairly routine matters like electing its officials, considering applications for membership and adopting the budget, although 'organisation and co-ordination of the European election campaign' does indicate a possible political function. The ELD statutes are less detailed about the tasks of its Executive Committee, although probably most significant is Article 17 alluding to a political role which is both representational and possibly one of influence:

> Between meetings of the Congress, the Committee will be empowered to speak and act on behalf of the Federation in all spheres of the latter's jurisdiction. When there are direct elections to the European Parliament, the list of approved candidates from each country will be drawn up by the national member parties after consultation with the Committee.

A better indication of the political implications behind these constitutional rules is offered by the provisions governing decision-making within the executive organs. Here, the federal structure of the EPP and ELD begins to emerge for both allow for majority decisions provided there is a quorum of representatives present. The Confederation does also allow for majority decisions, but this is hedged by the procedure under Article 13 whereby the Bureau must vote unanimously prior to the Congress adopting a decision by a two-thirds majority which is binding on member parties. This restricted role of the Confederation's Bureau *vis-à-vis* the national parties is further illustrated by the detail with which its public role is outlined (Article 10):

> The Bureau may publicly define its position on current matters falling within its field of competence. Positions so defined shall be submitted to the affiliated parties, and shall bind them only if subsequently approved by them. Positions to be published on behalf of the affiliated parties shall be submitted to them before publication. Amendments of the affiliated parties shall be forwarded to the Bureau, which shall take them into account.

In view of the generally unostentatious functions of the executive organs, it is significant that the leadership role, especially of the federation presidents, is left unclarified and could be seen as implicitly low-profile. Only the EPP statutes describe the presidential role and this is mainly representational: 'The President shall represent the Party both internally and externally, he shall preside over all the Party's organs', be responsible for relations with the EP group, EUCD and other political forces and 'he may delegate certain tasks to members of the Executive Committee and of the Political Bureau' (Article 9). In practice, Leo Tindemans of the EPP and Gaston Thorn of the ELD have performed this representational role actively lending their individual prestige to the task, although that has been distinctly less so with the first two presidents of the Socialist Confederation – Wilhelm Dröscher (1974–7), and his successor from early 1978, Robert Pontillon – this being a matter of both more bureaucratic personalities and the ethos of working methods in the Confederation.

It is necessary to consider the operation itself of the executive organs of the federations. One frequent point of complaint in federation circles, including those politicians strongly committed to the federations as a transnational vehicle, is the sparse attendance by prominent national party leaders, who usually appear at federation congresses but participate only intermittently in the regular executive deliberations. Despite obvious practical restrictions on national leaders, always heavily committed at home, this factor has been viewed as something of a test case of how the federations might acquire an upgraded political role. Sicco Mansholt, the Dutch Socialist and a firm advocate of a strong Confederation role, made this criticism of its predecessor, the Liaison Bureau, when the Confederation was formed: 'The party chairmen must participate regularly, otherwise it will not do' for so far they had only sent their international secretaries or other party functionaries.[25] At the conference of Socialist party leaders the following November it was resolved by them that 'the parties should send to the Bureau qualified and responsible representatives'.[26]

The federations' statutes do, of course, provide for national party representation in the executive bodies, although the specific choice of personnel is invariably left to each party in question. Only the EPP spells out that each national delegation 'normally consists of the president or political secretary, the secretaries-general and the chairmen of the national parliamentary groups' (Article 7). In practice, there has been some variation between the federations in this respect, depending on the individual time constraints of national politicians (notably whether in government or not), although generally confirming the impression that federation executive meetings are often regarded by busy politicians as something of a *Sonntags-vergnügen* ('Sunday outing') or side-interest. In the Socialist Confederation there has been a predominant attendance by international secretaries (or general secretaries in the case of small parties) with some differences between parties as to whether they have sent authoritative personnel (for example, the Dutch PvdA sent their party chairwoman, the SPD their foreign-policy spokesman, while there was usually confusion over the consistency of representation from the Italian PSI because of its own leadership upheaval from 1976).[27] In 1979, the British Labour Party replaced its international secretary and the reluctant participant, Ian Mikardo, by the prominent and active left-wing leader, Tony Benn, and another left-wing politician, reflecting possibly a more determined interest in the Confederation's proceedings.

In the case of the EPP and ELD there has been more participation by prestigious figures, although there has continued to be a marked difference, especially with parties from the major EC states, between the impressive list of official national representatives and those among them who attend regularly. Thus, during 1976–9 the Italian DC political secretary, Zaccagnini, was unable to attend EPP Political Bureau meetings (or even the two EPP congresses) because of the pressing demands of his country's ever-complicated politics, although his regular deputy was Luigi Granelli, head of the DC's external office and himself an active figure of the DC left. The two German parties were usually represented by their general-secretaries, while during these years Strauss and Kohl attended only a couple of meetings each. By contrast, the Dutch, Belgian and Irish party chairmen were frequent attenders. Tindemans, as EPP president, usually chaired these meetings, although until he ceased being Belgian Prime Minister in late 1978 he found it impossible otherwise to devote much regular time to the EPP.[28] With the ELD, national chairmen coming from smaller countries were often more ready participants, depending again on their governmental commitments. Gaston Thorn, Luxemburg Prime Minister and head of various ministries during this period, as well as being ELD president, normally chaired executive meetings, was effective in promoting national contacts for the ELD but was otherwise constrained by pressures of time.[29]

The problem of participation leads to the general question of what kind of political 'actors' are involved in the working of the federations' decision-bodies. These include an intermixture of full-time European personnel (for example, party Eurocrats, European Commissioners) and part-time (for example, MEPs with a dual-mandate) European-level personnel and full-time national personnel of varying importance, with a numerical predominance of the last category in the federations' organs. This composition reflects the closer dovetailing between the European and national levels in transnational party organisation, a point emphasised by one FDP leader at the ELD's constituent congress, when he said that its Executive Committee's composition 'ensures that national and European levels well and truly intermesh, and this will be particularly valuable when, after the direct elections, the European Parliament has genuine authority'.[30] Moreover, the greater and more regular involvement of national party politicians and functionaries has lent a new political weight to transnational organisation despite the preceding reservations about attendance by prominent figures. The general-secretary of the ELD commented that this had been facilitated by the European electoral deadline:

> We started out with a band of European enthusiasts. This has been changing of course, because we are approaching elections now. So it's really the [national] party workers and party officials who get involved in the working of the federation more nowadays.[31]

What emerges in the operation of the federations up to the 1979 direct elections at least is the active role played by national politicians specialising in European affairs – that is, those who have contemporaneously or consecutively taken a serious part in transnational activity as well as national politics. Some notable exceptions may be said to have pursued a triangular career – in the EP groups, the federations and national party politics – such as Egon Klepsch (chairman of the Christian Democratic EP group from 1977, and chairman of the CDU/CSU parliamentary group's committee on European policy in Bonn), and Martin Bangemann, one-time FDP general-secretary and regional chairman as well as vice-chairman of the Liberal group and a very active figure in the early development of the ELD. Other federation leaders had at one time been MEPs (for example, Gaston Thorn, 1959–69); while there was a third category who retained positions in the national party hierarchy while assuming a role in the federations – notably, the first two presidents of the Socialist Confederation, Dröscher (SPD treasurer and a former regional party chairman) and Robert Pontillon (international secretary of the French PS). Similar, though less prominent, cases of this category of European experts are found in the other federations.

One vital aspect of the federations' executive organs is whether their operation has involved a political as well as merely administrative exercise despite their limited official functions. In so far as political matters have arisen within them these have often touched on the sensitive question of different ideological tendencies among member parties, a problem acknowledged most openly by the Socialists. Writing in 1977, Wilhelm Dröscher elaborated on this problem referring to the two-thirds majority rule for Congress decisions:

> The Bureau can unanimously express resolutions of the nine parties which can afterwards be rejected by one or two of the parent parties at the congress. These resolutions then become

binding for the parties. But that is a very difficult procedure, because it throws up unheard-of problems if one wishes to make valid majority decisions in the present state of affairs. I believe that is the same problem in all the party groupings, and we would be dishonest if we didn't admit it . . . There is no instrument for making decisions prevail'.[32]

During the period up to the 1979 elections the Bureau meetings of the Confederation very largely confined their deliberations to technical matters, such as the financing and organisation of common meetings for the European campaign, although there occurred some political debate about the content of the 1978 Declaration and the 1979 Appeal.[33] The desire to avoid too much conflict played a part here. This lack of political muscle on the part of the Bureau was reflected in the content of press releases after its meetings, with their mixture of routine decisions and generalised political declarations. One communiqué in late 1977, for instance, announced the formation of a working party on unemployment, deplored the tardiness of the European Council in fixing a final date for direct elections and condemned international terrorism; while another several months later announced the creation of a Wilhelm Dröscher prize to commemorate its late president, mentioned a forthcoming conference of party leaders and deplored American 'interference' in Italian domestic affairs.[34]

In the EPP's Political Bureau political matters were certainly discussed in a manner of mutual information and consultation alongside routine administrative tasks (which, as with the Confederation, usually had to do with the management of the European campaign). A typical meeting was that held in Rome in September 1978 which dealt with elections to EPP offices, considered national and common activities as well as discussing involvement in the European campaign, expressed solidarity for the DC's domestic policy, condemned international terrorism and expressed concern over the situation of the Christian community in the Lebanon.[35] When there was stronger attendance from national party leaders, these meetings could develop into a series of consecutive monologues;[36] but there were also occasions when controversial matters arose and, departing from the general practice of unanimous support for Bureau statements, minority views could be outvoted in exceptional cases.[37] The purpose of the Executive Committee, the secondary organ of the EPP, included filtering the most divisive issues before sessions of the Political Bureau.[38] While the EPP's executive organ touched more frequently on political affairs than that of the Socialist Confederation, it could not be said that it exercised, as such, significantly more political muscle. With the ELD this same general conclusion applied, although Liberal parties were somewhat less reluctant to broach political issues.

Meetings of the executive organs tended to become more frequent as direct elections approached. Both the ELD and Confederation statutes specified that their executives should meet at least four times a year, but in 1978 the ELD Executive Committee met six or seven times and a further three times in the first three months of 1979;[39] while the Socialist Bureau had reached a level of ten times a year in the immediate period before the elections.[40] As a consequence of this pattern of activity there began to appear unmistakable socialising effects of common involvement in the federation organs, a factor which should not be underrated for its indirect influence on transnational party co-operation. The deputy secretary-general of the EPP claimed that:

> During the time in which I have been observing this, it has appeared that national politicians who attend the organs of the transnational party families have undergone a certain change of consciousness in the course of their closer acquaintanceship with representatives of other parties on the European level. They have broadened nationally confined outlooks towards the European horizon, and today they understand European arguments much better than they did two, three or four years ago. On the other hand, the greatest disadvantage that we face is precisely the strong absorption of time available by national commitments which prevents involvement in European politics to the extent necessary.[41]

One should add to this basic problem various technical difficulties which are peculiar to transnational activity: the question of distance and air flight costs for meetings (although some EPP Bureau sessions have rotated among national capitals) and naturally the question of language. The latter appeared sometimes as an additional difficulty in the formulation of common programmes, although Martin Bangemann once made light of the matter by commenting that in his experience as chairman of the ELD programme commission he had learned of the existence of 'committee English'! At executive meetings language is as much inhibiting as it has been in the Euro-parliamentary groups, especially for those not linguistically versatile. The international secretary of the British Labour Party drew attention to this factor:

> One of the bad things about the Confederation, inevitably bad, is the fact that you have simultaneous interpretation. I mean no criticism of the interpreters, but somehow that stultifies everything. I'll give you an example, the Appeal to the electors . . .

Well, when we were drawing that up we had a working group on that, and I was on it for the Labour Party. We started working on it one day in a Bureau meeting of the Confederation. And in two hours with interpreters we got through about two paragraphs. You know, arguing the toss over the amendments that everybody wanted and we got nowhere. It was very very slow, and we really got nowhere. So that we then said we must meet that evening after dinner. We met at nine o'clock without interpreters in the Dutch Labour Party's offices, and we worked through until 3.30 in the morning. But in six hours we got through the whole of the Appeal.[42]

Similar practical problems have arisen with the arrangements for federation congresses. The ELD secretary-general commented in the light of his own experience on the special difficulties in arranging these transnational occasions:

The European party federations all have a congress as their supreme body, but these congresses are somewhat difficult to convene. They require long and careful preparation, particularly because of the number of languages involved, and it is thus more difficult for them to fulfil the watchdog or brains-trust function carried out by national party congresses.[43]

Such management difficulties strengthen the need for prearranging congress business and this is reflected in the strict regulations in the various congress rules of procedure, such as in the arrangements for selecting national delegates, for organising motions and the distribution of speaking time. The last of these is tightly controlled, as with the EPP, which requires that 'the President shall as a rule allocate speaking time in the order in which requests to speak are received; he shall ensure that as far as possible speakers from different delegations and using different languages are heard in turn' (Item 10 of EPP congress rules of procedure).

As to congresses' functions and composition some specifications differ between the federations, but their broad role is similar. Their occurrence is envisaged as regular (annual in the case of the ELD; at least once every two years with the EPP and unspecified with the Confederation), while their political role is defined in the EPP's case as 'to decide on the main guidelines and the political programme; in particular, it shall agree on the electoral platform; it shall also decide on any amendments to the statute' (Article 6b). The ELD statutes go furthest in listing in detail the functions of the congress, which all involve a certain political exercise; for example, making decisions on all matters within EC competence, regarding political co-operation in the Community and on other matters 'which the members have unanimously recognised as falling within its competence'. The Confederation does not formally indicate the congress's functions and only stipulates that in its case the two-thirds majority rule requires preceding unanimous support from the Bureau, otherwise binding decisions become merely recommendations (Article 13). There are differences also in the composition of the congresses, with the EPP adopting the transnational principle that the number of delegates are distributed among national parties in proportion to their totals of MEPs in the CD group. By contrast, ELD delegates are chosen on the basis of their national parties' electoral strength, providing therefore for strong representation for the British Liberals, whose voting strength falls victim to the system of representation in the UK. The proceedings of the congresses are public unless they should decide to meet in closed session.

Some political role is therefore officially allowed the congresses, but have they developed into anything beyond political jamborees? Some national party congresses may indeed offer little more than occasions for demonstrations of party solidarity, opportunities for the verbal airing of political differences or events when the leadership is forced to take note of rank-and-file feeling, but with federation congresses the particular problems of transnational activity once again arise and restrict their effective democratic function. The ELD general-secretary remarked:

> Examining the three federations in turn, one comes to the inescapable conclusion that a predominant role has so far been played by the party élites. This may seem a remarkable fact since they were set up with the very purpose of mobilising the electorate and the party rank and file for direct elections. It is, however, completely understandable and in fact reflects the situation in the EC itself. When part of one's own sovereignty is transferred to a higher authority, one naturally wishes to be part of that authority oneself in order to keep this process under careful scrutiny.
>
> Since the composition of the three federations' executives and congresses are extremely small in proportion to total party membership, anything other than élite representation would be inconceivable. For example, the total number of participants at the Liberal congresses was 230, the largest delegation being that of the British Liberal Party, viz. 45 representatives for 235,000 members. Whereas half of the delegation was elected by all party members in a postal vote – thus those elected were hardly unknowns – the other half was naturally a pure élite representing the party executive, the parliamentary party and the regional executives.[44]

The procedure for selecting congress delegates is less elaborate in the case of the other two federations, for here delegates are selected and, with the member parties being usually large rather than small like the Liberals, the criticism of élitism is even more applicable.

The performance of the federation congresses in the years up to the 1979 elections – the ELD held three, the EPP two and the Confederation one* – showed them to be largely occasions for expressing fraternal solidarity supplemented by an element of political or programmatic proclamation. Several of these were so-called electoral congresses, such as the 1979 EPP congress, which formalised its electoral platform just as the main concrete outcome of the Confederation congress in January 1979 was its Appeal to the European electorate. Some were, however, strongly programmatic, notably the ELD congress of 1977 where there were elaborate and sometimes lively altercations over the many amendments to the draft programme. At its 1978 congress the ELD focused on a variety of specific issues on which it produced resolutions, such as enlargement, the European monetary system, transport and human rights.[45] Otherwise, the proceedings of the federation congresses were dominated by successive speeches by prominent national party leaders concentrating on policy themes of their own choice or drawing attention to matters of national concern for domestic consumption; for example, Helmut Kohl on the dangers of Euro-communism at the 1978 EPP congress, or David Steel on the discriminatory nature for his party of the British electoral system on various occasions. These congresses were also used as an opportunity for self-advertisement by individual parties. For example, at the 1979 EPP congress both German parties displayed their electoral wares on separate stands by the congress rostrum, including in the CSU's case several books on chairman Franz-Josef Strauss, and distributed stickers and glossy literature to delegates from other countries.

Finally, there were other features of the internal structures of the federations which deserve some mention. All three set up secretariats in Brussels well before direct elections, with the Confederation moving there to rent former shop premises in the summer of 1976, having previously depended exclusively on the facilities of the EP group secretariat; while the newly formed EPP could take advantage of the EUCD secretariat already located in Brussels. Both offices liaised with the EP group secretarial offices in Brussels round the corner, while the ELD secretariat, opened in 1977, was housed in

* Following its constituent congress at Stuttgart in March 1976, the ELD held its first three at The Hague (November 1976). Brussels (November 1977) and London (December 1978). The two EPP congresses were both held in Brussels in March 1978 and February 1979. The much-delayed 10th Congress of the Socialist Confederation (following the numeration of the nine congresses of the Liaison Bureau from 1957) was held in Brussels in January 1979.

the same building as the latter. Staffing has been minimal for obvious financial reasons, there being three persons including the deputy general-secretary manning the Confederation's office and a similar number in the other two cases. With the burden of work increasing in the run-up to direct elections, this imposed a heavy task on the individuals concerned who were usually dedicated and prepared to include much translation work in their daily routine.[46] In general, the role of the secretariats and of the secretaries-general in person was administrative, although the 'co-ordination' (specifically described as such in the EPP statutes) of party-political work also had its political implications. The minimal bureaucratic element in the federations nevertheless illustrated the very limited (or embryo) state of their development.

In addition, the various federations articulated during the 1976–9 period other subsidiary forms of structural relationships which may together be categorised as 'informal' in that they were not specified in the respective statutes but followed the practice of European political parties. For instance, these included the formation of auxiliary or professional associations, foundations or research institutes and, of course, the appointment of programme commissions and electoral committees to decide on the detailed arrangements for co-ordination in the European campaign. Auxiliary associations are a typical feature of Christian Democratic party organisation, which practice was carried over into the EPP whose rules of procedure (Item 6) provided for their formation. Five such associations have been formed, some of them in conjunction with the EUCD: a women's section of the EPP, the European Union of Young Christian Democrats, a local authorities' association, a European association for Christian trade unionists and a European union for middle-class interests. The other two federations have not ignored this aspect of party-political activity, but have not articulated it so fully. The ELD provides in its statutes for a youth branch, called LYMEC, which has the status equivalent to a member party in internal federation affairs; while attached to the Socialist Confederation with observer status are a women's section, a youth organisation and an association of Socialist teachers of the EC. The three party-political foundations – the Robert Schuman Foundation of the EPP (established in January 1977), the Jean Jaures Foundation of the Confederation (late in 1977), and the Jean Rey Foundation of the ELD (end of 1978) – are much alike in their purpose, tending to follow the model of the German party foundations. Thus, the Robert Schuman Foundation, established by the Executive Committee of the EPP, provides for the political instruction of members and representatives of the federation;[47] while the Jean Jaures Foundation, under the chairmanship of the Confederation president, aims to 'co-ordinate and promote Socialist studies and research on economic and social problems raised by the European Community'.[48] Much of their work takes the form of seminars or conferences, although the Jean Jaures Foundation did also indicate that it would con tribute to the information campaign for direct elections. Equally, the federations set up commissions or working groups for the formulation of common programmes with representatives from the national parties and at a later date committees of electoral experts from the parties to co-ordinate detailed aspects of the European campaign. The ELD committee met roughly every two months from June 1978, though more often from early 1979. The Socialist Con federation, illustrating the strong programmatic orientation of its member parties, has developed most the habit of specialised policy discussion. It set up working groups on unemployment, enlargement, human rights, migrant workers and women,[49] some of them perman ent, which were different from the four working groups formed for drafting the common programme, involved MEPs less than the latter and more delegates from the national parties.[50] The Confederation further arranged for special conferences in member countries and the proposals from these were regarded as providing 'useful material for the work of the Socialist group in the European Parliament which is to be elected on 7–10 June'.[51]

In general, the internal institutional relationships within the three party federations followed the specifications of their limited con stitutional roles. During the few years preceding the 1979 European elections this development had both directly, through common political activities and further institutional elaboration, and in directly, through the socialising effects of these links, nevertheless reinforced the EC-orientation of transnational party co-operation. Such a development was, of course, fundamentally limited by the distinct autonomy and the national preoccupations of individual member parties, with some variation here between the federations and also within them, as will be exemplified further in the discussion below of the formulation of common programmes. It could be said at this point that, whereas formally the internal structures of the federations differed significantly – with the Confederation markedly less integrative than the other two – an examination of the reality of their internal relationships demonstrated many common features between the three cases, as well as illustrating the complexities of their operation. This admixture of formal and informal aspects is all the more necessary when considering, as now, the external relation ships of the federations or their institutional interlinkage within the EC, if only because these are only briefly mentioned in the various statutes.

By far the most important of these external relationships are those between the federations and their respective groups in the EP. Following the traditions of European party development, the federations were regarded by both sides as the extra-parliamentary arm of the groups in terms of support, control and influence. The statutes or rules of procedure recognised this institutional relationship, with their provisions for group representation in the federation executive organs and at the congresses. It was stated most clearly in the ELD statutes, which declared that 'the Federation is represented in the European Parliament by the Liberal group' (Article 10) and that the Congress should 'receive reports' from the group and 'make recommendations' to it (Article 26). Already in a resolution of May 1975 the Liberal group had declared its intention of 'close co-operation' with the future federation.[52] In practice, the federation/group relationship has developed in similar fashion in all three cases and during the period up to direct elections became established politically as well as constitutionally. The formalisation of the relationship went so far as renaming two of the Euro-parliamentary groups to accord with the federations: the Liberal and Allies Group to Liberal and Democratic Group* in 1976, and the Christian Democratic Group to Christian Democratic Group (Group of the EPP) in March 1978 and finally to Group of the EPP after direct elections in the summer of 1979. This link has also developed with the Confederation, despite its own looser internal structure, although by comparison the Socialists have been less emphatic about it. According to Wilhelm Dröscher, the Confederation saw itself as 'the party-political basis' of the EP group,[53] although he later made the relevant qualification that the Socialist group

> does not stand yet in the same relationship to the Confederation of parties as a national parliamentary group to a national party. That lies – by the way, with all party groupings – in the indirect manner of designating the parliamentarians. They have to be 'nationally' responsible as they are tied to national parliamentary groups. Parallel with the development of the EP up to election day and afterwards the Confederation of Social Democratic parties will increase in weight, and then will be a powerful support for the directly elected parliamentarians of the same political colour and their group.[54]

---

* The ELD statutes demand that MEPs 'belonging to one of the member parties of the Federation will be members of the Liberal Group' (Article 10). This rule of compatibility between group and federation was applied in two cases, when the Italian PRI representative moved from the Socialist to the Liberal group after the ELD was established and one French Left Radical did the same a few years later.

The different roles of the federations and groups within their inter-relationship followed in many respects the distinction between long- and short-term political activities. In the Confederation's case this was described as:

> Whereas the Socialist group looks after the day-to-day work for Europe's interests and must concern itself with problems that are frequently of a technical nature, the problems occupying the Confederation are of a more long-term nature, even though all concerned realise quite clearly that much discussion is still needed before common basic positions in regard to the future of Europe are worked out.[55]

This was broadly true of the other two federations, although one should qualify this in that the preparations and conduct of direct elections imposed a number of routine and immediate tasks on the federations. (See below, Chapter 5, Section (a), on the role of the federations in the European campaign.) This interrelationship was firmly established as it had evolved out of the very origins of the federations, when the groups had played some part in facilitating their birth. The very precedent in the Euro-parliamentary groups of transnational party co-operation was influential, for with the Con-federation 'the valuable experiences gained in the Socialist Group have contributed largely to making institutionalised co-operation possible at the party level, and even today this is still an important factor'.[56]

The habit of co-ordination between the federations and groups has reinforced their institutional links because of the greater need for mutual influence in the light of politicisation in the EC. The inter-national secretary of the Belgian Socialist Party emphasised this reinforcement when he said:

> Take an instance: if one of the attitudes adopted by, say, a Dutch member can have some kind of influence on the Danish Socialists, then somewhere those Danish Socialists should be in a position to ask questions of that Dutch MEP. So there is a need for some kind of mechanism that will allow this kind of control of European parliamentarians. In other words, it's my feeling that a political party develops in accordance with power; and, if you can create somewhere a new power, and even if it's a power more in terms of influence than a direct competence, then neces-sarily you create a need for some kind of political party counter-acting that.[57]

This solidification of the interlinkage has appeared in a variety of practical ways, notably over personnel and common facilities. At the bureaucratic level, there has been interchange or sharing of staff deriving from the time before the opening of their own offices when the federations had relied on the group secretaries for any routine administration. The deputy general-secretary of the EPP (former executive secretary of the EUCD) is an ex-MEP, while the ELD general-secretary was previously secretary of the Liberal group and continued to receive his official salary from the group. The deputy general-secretary of the Confederation, who runs its Brussels office, worked on the staff of the group secretariat before his appointment, for indeed service in the group is considered a necessary advantage. On the Socialist side, the group/federation link has been underlined by the fact that they have had the same person as secretary-general, who is called on to take decisions of a more overall or political nature, while his deputy in Brussels is concerned with regular matters.[58] With the Christian Democrats, the group secretariat has employed two staff whose task is to promote the work of the EPP and EUCD.[59] The groups and federations also share the same publicity officers. One feature which developed during the two years before direct elections was growing coverage of federation activities in the group news magazines. A deliberate decision to do so was made by *Euso* at the start of 1978,[60] while both *CD – Europe* and *Présence Liberale* increasingly gave attention to their federations in the run-up to direct elections, especially when congresses were held.

Furthermore, and most importantly, the federations have depended on the groups for the lion's share of their financing. In the Confederation's case, there is a formal arrangement whereby the national member parties meet the cost of Bureau meetings outside Luxemburg and make an annual contribution according to their relative strength as represented at the congress.[61] This is in addition to financial support from the group. The EPP budget has derived its main income from the group, although requests have been made to the various national parties that the group should not bear the sole responsibility here.[62] In addition to their normal budgets, the federations received 90 per cent of their groups' share of the special election fund of 2 million units of account set aside by the EP for general information purposes before the start of the Euro-pean campaign. One should add here indirect means of subsidising the federations, such as in their dependence on the groups for interpreting facilities. As the deputy general-secretary of the EPP explained, the timing of the monthly meetings of the Political Bureau and Executive Committee was conditioned by this factor:

We have so arranged this monthly cycle that the Euro-Parlia-mentary group assigns us the Parliament's interpreters – we do not have the money to pay our own interpreters on a regular basis . . . Our group regularly gives us the interpreters and the room on the Monday, Tuesday and Wednesday, and then uses them for its own deliberations on the Thursday and Friday. And during these three days we regularly make use of these facilities for Bureau meetings and meetings of the commissions.[63]

This all helped to reinforce the working relationship between the federations and groups.

This working relationship has been further promoted by co-operation in various political activities. The convention has developed in all three cases that the Euro-parliamentary group makes an official report to the federation at its congress on its own performance. In introducing his report to the Confederation congress in January 1979, Ludwig Fellermaier, the Socialist group chairman, commented that his group 'is, by its own definition, the representative of the ideas and political standpoints of all the member parties of the Confederation; on this basis, we have endeavoured, over these last years, effectively to fulfil our commitment' even though this co-operation had not been full-scale for 'given that, in the past, the Confederation was able only to a limited extent to supply the Group with information and indicate political objectives relating to its work, the Socialist Group itself has had to pursue action in various sectors on its own initiative'.[64] Similarly, at the ELD congress in 1978 a written report of the Liberal group activities was available to delegates and was followed by a policy speech from Pintat, the group chairman, with questions and answers.[65] There has also been a certain degree of programmatic interplay, above all in the formulation of common programmes where the federations drew on the expertise of some MEPs. Such policy consultation has also been evident on other occasions, as the deputy general secretary of the EPP noted:

The Political Bureau pays much heed to the proposals which representatives of the Group make in the Bureau, because they know better the internal circumstances from their special experience. Also, conversely, the Group asks the EPP, in the Bureau, if it would undertake certain initiatives – How does the EPP stand on this matter? Will you go along with this? Will you assume co-responsibility if we go public on this question? The system becomes established in practice, and this will develop more strongly when we have direct elections behind us. Altogether, we are on the course where a strong mutual influence in two directions is becoming evident.[66]

One important question relating to the future inter-relationship is how much the federation programmes or programmatic declarations become a serious basis for group activity. This cannot be judged until after direct elections, although the generalised diction of most of these documents cannot provide anything more than a vague guideline. Of course, good intentions have been expressed in this respect; for instance, by Egon Klepsch, who asserted in his speech to the 1979 EPP congress that his group had since the first congress a year before let its work be 'shaped according to the political programme of the EPP then finalised'. Similarly, Gaston Thorn proclaimed in his presidential address to the ELD congress in 1978: 'It is as a Federation that we have adopted a programme for Europe which binds us all; it is this programme which will guide the actions of the Liberal and Democratic Group for the next five years.'[67] There does not, of course, exist a formal common programme of the Socialist Confederation, so that in this case the nominal requirement to follow official guidelines does not apply. However, as shown in Chapter 2, the experience of formulating common group policy standpoints is, in any case, a complicated business and is unlikely to change substantially in this respect after direct elections, whether or not there is a federation programme.

The other established external institutional link of the federations, although a somewhat tenuous one, is with the relevant European Commissioners. This is really a nominal or symbolic link and can hardly be described as political. However, it does mean that the party-political affiliation of individual Commissioners becomes more openly recognised as a consequence. Roy Jenkins, as the new Commission President, said after taking office in 1977 that he would give the lead in relations with the EC's parliamentary arm and further 'close links' with the political groups.[68] The federation statutes formalise this link by providing for the representation of Commissioners on their executive organs and allowing for their right to speak at congresses. In practice, there has been some variation according to the particular interest of individual Commissioners. Guido Brunner, the one Liberal member of the Commission, was an enthusiastic supporter of the establishment of the ELD, has been an active participant at its congresses, has often been present at Executive Committee meetings and, for instance, helped with the setting up of the Jean Rey Foundation.[69] With the Confederation, the Socialist Commissioners have generally not played a visible role, although there has developed a practice of more frequent informal dinners with federation leaders to discuss both federation policies and those of the Commission.[70] On the Christian Democratic side, the Commissioners have played an interested, though not active, role in line with statutory procedures, including on occasions writing articles in the magazine *CD – Europe*.

This link might become closer as a by-effect of greater responsibility by the Commission to the EP in the future; but the Commission is by far the weaker of the EC's two executive institutions and it is difficult, at least so far, to discern any party-political *leitmotiv* in the Commission's work. With the Council of Ministers there has been virtually no link on the part of the federations, although national governmental leaders have spoken before federation congresses usually in some official capacity as a federation office holder. The ELD, however, has tended to emphasise its contacts with Liberal members of the Council (notably Thorn and Genscher). At the April 1979 rally of the ELD, Martin Bangemann went so far as to boast that: 'It is true that we Liberals have many ministers in the Council; in the Council of Foreign Ministers, with our five members, we even have an absolute majority, and many of these ministers, including our President, are here today, and have confirmed that they will collaborate with us in reducing the powers of this Council.'[71]

One further external institutional link is worth a mention, mainly because of its possible potential should transnational party co-operation enter a new qualitative stage after direct elections. This is the relationship between the federations and European-level interest groups. In the period up to 1979, there was very little sign of developments in this direction, which accords with the scarce interest shown by interest groups in the EP as such, except where this has some recognised influence on decision-making.[72] One obvious area for interlinkage is between European trade unions, notably the ETUC, and the Socialist Confederation, in which various prominent interviewees expressed an interest. The Confederation's Political Declaration of 1978 reflected this line of thinking by elaborating on the need for 'close co-operation with all trade union organisations, particularly the ETUC', in economic affairs in the EC, but no active steps were taken before the 1979 elections. The other two federations have also not developed any official links to interest groups, and only informally where individual MEPs might have good contacts, although it is always possible that federation auxiliary organisations might in future act as a point of co-operation. Should there be any development of this kind, it would be considered the most important field of 'informal' external relationships for the federations.

By way of conclusion, the institutional role and organisational articulation of the federations have shown much similarity to familiar patterns of European party development. The internal and external structural relationships of the federations evolved sufficiently in both formal and informal respects during the first years of their existence up to direct elections in 1979 that it is possible to speak of their having some validity as party-political formations, even though very limited in their political impact. Hence, comparative-political yardsticks are applicable to some extent in analysing their operation both conceptually and for estimating special similarities and differences between the three examples. But, as noted earlier, this approach cannot explain completely the institutional role of the federations without recourse also to the unique characteristics of European integration. It is evident from the foregoing analysis of the federations' structures that various problems inherent in transnational party activity, as already seen in the EP, have emerged to condition their operation. These include technical and organisational difficulties of co-ordination at the European level, but also other institutional problems arising from the new exercise in transnational party organisation, of which the most significant is likely to be the role of the federations in performing as an agent of effective control over their respective Euro-parliamentary groups, while remaining at the same time very dependent on the co-operation of national member parties.

There is, furthermore, the still open and unclarified question of the federations' position as superstructures and/or infrastructures. Here, their infrastructural role in relation to the EP groups is that which is most developed institutionally, while their infrastructural position in relation to the executive in the EC has hardly acquired any particular importance. The federations' superstructural role as organs of co-ordination for their national member parties is the other major feature of their institutional interlinkage within the Community and, as essentially a political question, will be discussed in the following section: while the federations' presence at the lower sub-European level is a likely matter of dispute. Only the EPP has so far provided for possible membership by individual persons, but this has remained a dead letter.[73] Above all, it is the independence of the national parties – whether Socialist, Christian Democratic or Liberal – that will remain the fundamental obstacle to a stronger institutional role for the federations.

(c) The Political Role and Programmatic Function of the Party Federations

Speaking of a political role for the party federations does seem pretentious in view of their peripheral position so far in the European Community. Such scepticism is correct in view of the limited constitutional position of the federations and natural regarding the predominance of the national arena of politics in general party activity. Nevertheless, it is still valid to consider how far they may have embarked on a political role during the period up to the 1979 elections, bearing in mind that they owed their existence to a growth of politicisation in the EC in the 1970s and that their pursuit of particular political goals would, with the experience of co-ordination within the federations, not to mention the pressures operating from the process towards direct elections, have some effects on their member parties.

The federations and their component parties acknowledged and sought to promote as their broad aim a more political emphasis in the European Community. The Socialist draft programme, for instance, stressed in its preamble:

> The construction of Europe should lead through the development of a uniform economic zone to a political community. This expectation has not been sufficiently fulfilled. Up to now the Europe of commerce has been too much in the foreground and not enough the Europe of the workers, of political tendencies, of the rights of citizens, of economic and social rights and of democratic rights.

Despite their own political differences, the federations and other transnational groupings all agreed in common that the EC had not evolved enough to a political stage.[74] They saw their role as distinctly political and not merely as that of electoral vehicles for the European campaign – although that latter role should not itself be underrated politically particularly as the 1979 elections were not merely a unique event but the first of a five-yearly series, thus establishing a permanent political focus of action.

This broad political purpose is indicated officially in the federation statutes. The ELD statutes (Article 2) specify three aims: to seek a common position on all the important problems affecting the Community; to undertake to support elections to the EP by universal suffrage, with a view to strengthening the democratic character of the EC; and to inform the public and involve it in the construction of a united and liberal Europe. Federation leaders or officials have since not hesitated to underline the political importance of their activities. When the ELD was founded, Gaston Thorn, as its newly elected president, declared that the Federation was 'the Liberal contribution to the continuing integration of the Community';[75] while its press officer commented less blandly that 'we are convinced that the Federation will make Liberal policies more consistent and thus more credible . . . we are ready to take our place in the political arena'.[76] Similarly, the EPP lists as its objectives in Article 3 of the statutes:

The Party shall ensure close and permanent collaboration between its member parties and équipes in order to implement their common policy in the construction of a federal Europe. In particular

(a) it shall participate in the elections to the EP in accordance with the laws governing its direct election;
(b) it shall uphold pluralist democracy on the basis of a common programme;
(c) it shall participate in, and support the process of, European integration and co-operate in the transformation of Europe into a European Union with a view to achieving a Federal Union;
(d) it shall support, co-ordinate and organise the European activities of its member parties.

The Socialist Confederation was less definite in its 1974 rules of procedure (Article 2): 'The purpose of such co-operation is to strengthen inter-party relations and, in particular, to define joint, freely agreed positions on problems raised by the existence of the European Community.' However, its Political Declaration of 1978 did outline similar functions to the other federations: to strengthen co-operation between European Socialist parties; through permanent confrontation of ideas and meetings of party representatives to seek joint positions on the main problems raised by the existence of the EC; and to prepare for the coming elections to the EP by direct universal suffrage.[77]

How much did this really point towards a 'Europeanisation' of party politics, or did these officially declared political aims simply reflect the expected optimism of the federations over their avowed purpose? Direct elections did, in fact, give some reality to transnational party organisation by enhancing the need to differentiate between the various political forces, and this had implications for a possible 'Europeanisation'. A leading Italian Christian Democratic official enlarged on this point:

We see a danger in these European elections for Italy. A danger that the programmes of all parties – the political language, that the political discourse of the parties will be alike, the Socialists, we, the Liberals – say the same thing about Europe. Why is it a danger? Because the voters won't understand the differences. We want in Italy, as in Germany, etc., as Christian Democrats to emphasise the character of this our programme because otherwise ordinary people will not understand the difference between our vision of Europe and the vision of the Liberals, the Socialists and the Communists.[78]

The long process towards direct elections, indeed well before the official campaign opened, the need to define more clearly political positions within the European setting produced some of the party-political polemics which take place at the national level. This was a qualitative departure from the bland political standpoints which had previously characterised transnational activity. Notably, Mitterrand's assertion in 1977 that Europe had to be 'Socialist or it could not be' more than any other single statement provoked non-Socialist leaders in transnational meetings held throughout the EC, especially by Christian Democrats but also by Liberals and others.

Especially interesting for transnational activity were the party-political exchanges which took place directly between the federations themselves as a means of enhancing their visibility. They took various forms, such as assertions about which one was the first to be established and to produce a common programme; criticisms about 'disunity' within the other federations; some controversy about which federation was most akin to a genuine political party; and particularly attacks on proposals made in the rival common pro-grammes or policy declarations. So there developed some element of party-political competition between the different federations despite their own lack of real political weight. A significant aspect of this growing polemical dimension of transnational activity in the EC has been a visible trend arising from the habit of European-involved party leaders of speaking out on national political develop-ments in other Community countries, particularly when they hold their own elections. This has, for instance, developed through more regular expressions of fraternal solidarity between ideologically related parties, as a by-effect of closer transnational links, or warn-ings from different national leaders about 'Eurocommunism' in specific member states like Italy and France. The Italian election of 1976 was a powerful case in point of this trend, because of the prospective advance of the PCI and the central issue of its partici-pation in government; and, similarly, the 1978 French election with the greater impact of the Popular Front opposition. The West German election of 1976 also aroused comparable interest abroad, while the CDU itself maintained, in the words of one of its leaders, that the vote there would be 'not only a decision for Germany, but a decision for Europe'.[79] Equally, the enthusiasm of the CSU leader, Strauss, for the Conservative victory in Britain in 1979 reflected once again how much this trend, although indirectly relevant to the federations, still provided an important background feature to their development.

There remains the more significant area of the internal processes of the federations as the means of furthering the 'Europeanisation' of party politics, for this involved the integration of party activities both political and organisational and a consequent growth of 'European' attitudes within member parties. The essential condition for progress was the modification of the exclusive or predominant national orientation of the parties concerned. One national party Euro-expert had direct elections in mind when he said: 'National parties always live in an environment, and when the conditions of that environment change so the parties change because they are compelled to react to this new environment.' While such general conditions as politicisation in the EC formed the mainspring of new developments in transnational party co-operation, the actual mechanism it adopted could itself provide added momentum. In the spring of 1974, when the Confederation was inaugurated, Sicco Mansholt criticised the method of transnational party co-operation up until then:

> How often it happens that the parties meet after the national parties have already decided their positions. When there are no congruous ways of looking at things then one makes a compromise, which is always weak and cannot often be accomplished in reality. Our co-operation must therefore begin before the national parties have developed certain views. It is not a question of 'first of all national views, and then we can negotiate and come to a compromise'. Rather from the start we must develop in common our policies.[80]

Mansholt went on to argue that summits of national party leaders would create merely 'a new European oligarchy' and not suffice to bring about the necessary change, for effective transnational co-operation meant involving lower levels of the party hierarchies. Hence, he was talking about an all-embracing and active form of co-ordination by the federations.

Direct elections provided the crucial factor in galvanising transnational organisation and applying new pressures on national parties. First, they created according to the electoral deadline various concrete political tasks which not only, as already seen, had been a decisive factor in the establishment of the federations but also continued to exert demands on the member parties right up to the elections of 1979. With the main and obvious exception of those parties with no clear transnational links this continuous pressure promoted deeper involvement by parties in transnational organisation because of the institutional focal point of the EP. This was most evident with the Liberal parties for, as an official of the German FDP described this effect:

> The FDP as ELD party must carry out certain activities. Dele-

gates must be elected for the ELD, and that begins at the lowest level. There are motions on the theme of the ELD at party congresses, at the regional level as well as at district party congresses, *Land* party congresses and Federal party congresses. The FDP is called on within the ELD framework to carry out a number of items. Or the ELD delegates for the Brussels or the London congress are required to take up these or those positions. One can already see here a basic acquaintanceship with the process.[81]

Such an initiation into transnational activity was facilitated in the case of the Liberals by their lesser problems of individual identity and by the fact that, as small parties, they benefited in status terms from this co-operation, but direct elections produced analogous pressures with the other federations. The transnational involvement of activists below the party élite level was also here significant in breaking new ground.

Secondly, this closer co-operation through the federations could also acerbate political differences between ideologically linked member parties. While termed 'divisive' by some observers of transnational activity, it was a legitimate reflection of the fact that this co-operation had become politicised. This problem of homogeneity was not, however, due entirely to the existence of the federations. With the Socialists, in particular, their own greater ideological differences over European integration in the 1970s, compared with the earlier decade, could be explained by internal domestic changes in some parties (for example, the radicalisation inside the Dutch PvdA), the greater prominence of the issue of relations with Communist parties and the consequences of EC enlargement with the inclusion in transnational activity of sceptical Danish Social Democrats and the mistrustful British Labour Party. Therefore, when the Confederation was formed in 1974 its prospects for common political action were reduced by these new factors (as an extreme example the Labour Party boycotted its activities until early 1976). The process towards direct elections therefore contributed to, rather than created, the Socialists' difficulties of cohesion at the European level. With the other two ideological movements it was more the establishment of the federations which brought pre-existing internal divergences to the surface. The main controversial point arising when the EPP was founded was the selection of its name and the associated question of whether its membership should extend to Conservatives, which provoked conflict between progressive and conservative Christian Democrats. Similarly, a broad divide could be drawn between radical and conservative Liberals in the ELD, although this division occurred both between and within its national delegations.

Thirdly, policy debate within the federations was not confined to strictly Community common policies as a consequence of both the impact of direct elections and general politicisation in the EC, which helped to blur any clear distinction between (up until then limited) European and normal national affairs. The ELD programme recognised and encouraged this development:

> In recent years the member states have started co-operating outside the areas covered by the Treaties, particularly in the field of foreign policy. We welcome this as a step in the direction we advocate. We would like to see areas of policy not yet covered by the Treaties gradually brought within the Community's competence so as to become part eventually of the general competence of the European Union that we strive for.[82]

The ELD's statutes in fact allowed its congress to pronounce on 'all other matters' including national issues with the unanimous agreement of member parties, and it exercised this right notably in its regular digressions on the need for a voting system based on proportional representation in Britain. The Socialists also found it virtually impossible to confine their deliberations in the Confederation solely to EC concerns because of the wide application of their Socialist goals. The Confederation's Appeal to the European electorate of early 1979 stated this broader outlook: 'We do not see the EC as an end in itself. Neither can it be considered as the whole of Europe . . . We believe that in fighting for international Socialism we go beyond the confines of the Community.' This wide scope of policy interest was illustrated by *Euso*, the publicity organ for Confederation activities, which in the couple of years up to direct elections featured articles on such matters as human rights in Argentina, apartheid, arms and violence, the dictatorship in Chile, data protection and the political and economic situation in Austria. By the later 1970s, it had become clearly artificial to restrict policy discussion to what emanated directly from Brussels, although naturally specific policy action by the federations concentrated on the ongoing areas of Community harmonisation.

These three features of politicisation were present in the main political activity in which the federations engaged before the commencement of the direct elections campaign; namely the formulation of common programmes. Of course, much depended on how ambitious these programmes were and on their ultimate purpose. The key problem was pinpointed by the Liberal group chairman, who remarked that 'simply juxtaposing national policies will never lead to anything more than limited results'[83] from the programmes. At one stage, the ELD general-secretary commented modestly that 'the platforms drawn up by these federations as yet tend to serve as candidates' handbooks and to sound out one another's ideas rather than trace out political guidelines to be actually followed',[84] but they did in fact pretend to a higher purpose. Although the three federations adopted some different conceptual approaches to their programmes, they all involved a serious programmatic exercise rather than the production of US-style electoral platforms. Even though some of those responsible for drafting the programmes used the term 'electoral platform' (misleadingly), the actual process of formulation belied this as their exclusive function. In presenting the draft Confederation programme at a press conference in June 1977, Dröscher indicated:

> In this programme we want to say how we view the general development and what is possible in the five years that the directly elected European Parliament will have in its first period of office, and beyond that clarify the limits of future development – that is, longer-term aims will provide a direction.[85]

A decision was made in the Confederation to opt not for a programme of abstract principles but for one with concrete proposals (apart from its general preamble), and within this to attempt more than just a minimal basis of agreement. According to Dröscher:

> From the beginning we were in agreement that an electoral programme for the first election, if it was to be transnationally effective, had to achieve a highest possible common denominator. That is, we wanted to try and unite not on the smallest common denominator but on the highest common factor, and that this should occur not in a formless and disorganised discussion.[86]

The ELD rejected more explicitly the idea of a purely electoral declaration for, according to Martin Bangemann, 'the idea of a short electoral programme was rejected: the programme should contain all the important areas of policy, through this provide the basis for a future electoral appeal and at the same time be a means of self-identification for the Federation'.[87] In reporting on the work of his programme commission, Bangemann spelt out this point at the 1977 ELD congress:

> Like every committee, we are faced with a dilemma: should we provide the voter with four pages, knowing that he will read at least one and a half, or should we provide him with twenty-four, knowing that he will read none of them? We have opted for the second solution because we feel that the main purpose of this

programme is to bring the parties closer together through an objective debate and that we should give the different parties in our Federation a chance to state their position in the debate.[88]

The ELD programme was by far the longest in its final form (over sixty pages), whereas the EPP programme, as much shorter, seemed the closest to a US-style platform. In the latter case, the specific programmatic motivation was less strong and the electoral purpose more to the fore. The CDU general-secretary hinted at this when the EPP programme was published:

Apart from its content, the most important thing is that from Sicily to Flensburg these parties have agreed on a common programme. In this, for example, the Socialist parties in Europe have not succeeded. Thus, the integrative power of the Christian Democrats in Europe has been demonstrated by this programme.[89]

This implied a rather superficial definition of policy integration, although it illustrated the less pronounced programmatic inclinations commonly found among Christian Democrats – even if some of the EPP member parties took features of the draft more seriously than others. Moreover, it is possible to argue that the very failure of the Socialist Confederation to agree on a final version of its programme proved how seriously its members had taken the programmatic exercise, although in the end they had to content themselves with a generalised declaration and short electoral appeal.

The programmatic exercise was bound in one basic sense to be substantially different from that pursued by national parties because of the impact of nationality in transnational co-operation. Political homogeneity was therefore certain to be that much looser with the wide span of national outlooks represented in each federation, so that there was often considerable diversification within each ideological school. Comparative studies were in fact conducted of national party programmes to facilitate the formulation of common programmes,[90] but the obstacles to fully harmonised positions on a variety of issues were often insuperable, so that the necessary compromises weakened the meaningful content of final versions.

The resulting generalised wording of much of the programmes produced similarities between them, notably their common agreement on strengthening the EC institutions, the importance of human rights and the broad lines of foreign and defence policy.[91] Nevertheless, there were differences of emphasis and specifics which could be significant and discernible differences between the federations of general party-political terminology in places; for example, over the meaning of 'Europe' and especially in the field of economic policy.

On European institutions and integration in general, the ELD and EPP were the most positive, while the Socialists expressed reservations paying more attention to democratisation. On foreign questions, there were variations of emphasis over relations with the USA, with the Socialists more critical, while they showed a stronger interest in the EC's role towards the Third World and demanded that European integration should not be directed against Eastern Europe. The most marked divergences appeared over economic policy to which the Socialists paid full and detailed attention (stressing full employment, the importance of a structural policy and the need for economic policy), while the Christian Democrats adopted the concept of the social market economy and the ELD supported free enterprise.[92] Nevertheless, the three programmes were recognisable as respectively Socialist, Christian Democratic and Liberal, despite the many areas of mutual agreement and the bland phraseology.

Despite the strong element of compromise, the method of formulating the programmes was significant in illustrating whether this was treated centripetally rather than centrifugally by those concerned in the work of the federations. Furthermore, the process of programme formulation exemplified the differences of party-political behaviour and outlook between the Socialists, the Liberals and the Christian Democrats. The three cases of programme formulation will therefore be taken in turn before drawing some comparative conclusions about this unprecedented exercise in transnational party co-operation. In doing so, there are two relevant points of interest. Did the various member parties take this formulation and the attainment of compromise seriously? And, how much internal national party consultation was there over the draft programmes as an indicator of sub-élite involvement in transnational activity? The question of specific national demands and viewpoints in the programme formulation will be discussed later in this section.

In the Socialist Confederation, the main procedure for the formulation of the programme was as follows. Following the decision of the Socialist leaders at their Hague conference in November 1974 to accept the principle of a common programme for direct elections, a general working group was appointed in 1975 to begin initial consultations on the matter and this was supplemented by four special sub-working groups from the spring of 1976: democracy and institutions, foreign policy, the economy and social affairs. Each sub-working group had one representative from every national member party, and was assisted by a secretary, either from the Euro-parliamentary group or an equivalent expert employed by the European Commission and of Socialist affiliation. The combined draft programme was completed in the spring of 1977, submitted to the Confederation Bureau and then forwarded to the member national parties for discussion. The idea at this point was to incorporate amendments and then agree on a final version which was to be adopted at the next Confederation congress in late 1977 or in 1978. The programme was, however, never finalised because of the reluctance of several member parties to embrace it formally (especially the British Labour Party, the French PS and the Danish Social-demokratiet ['S']), so that the Bureau decided instead that the draft programme should form a basis for discussion and provide future guidelines for the member parties and that a shortened version should be produced for the purpose of the European campaign.[93] In some instances, the unfinalised draft was later incorporated in amended form in the national party programmes for direct elections (notably by the Dutch PvdA and, to some extent, the German SPD); but ultimately the members of the Confederation campaigned on the basis of separate national programmes while subscribing to the common Political Declaration of June 1978 and the Appeal of January 1979. It had been agreed that the Declaration would be applied flexibly to the national party programmes, or, in the words of the British Labour Party representative: 'Each party is free to do what it wants regarding its own election manifesto, but it will be under an obligation to write this manifesto within the framework of the Declaration agreed'.[94] This involved no great difficulty in view of the broad phraseology of this document. Similarly, the short Appeal was seen as the 'common basis' with which 'our parties will be able to direct their campaigns in each of the nine countries . . . having regard to the particular political situation obtaining in each country'.[95] These two documents represented the minimal programmatic consensus among the Confederation parties.

The Confederation had embarked on the formulation of a common programme rather ambitiously in the belief that common Socialist principles could be translated into programmatic terms in spite of national differences, but clearly the latter predominated. Furthermore, the new form of European party politics now being practised brought to the surface not only a fear of the erosion of party autonomy, but also a feature common to most Socialist parties whereby programme content becomes a matter of real, and often lively, debate. This was likely to create special problems in a European setting, as Bruno Friedrich, one of the Confederation's vice-presidents, pointed out in reference to work on its common programme:

I have been forced to appreciate that the democratic Socialist parties have encountered various statutory problems according to their traditions of internal party consultation. Namely, how can one allow the party base to form a judgement on this or that problem? In Holland the programme was examined in several hundred meetings, and there were hundreds of proposed amendments. But how can one include several hundred amendments from a small country in the formulation process of 11 parties?[96]

In fact, the process of internal party consultation did vary from party to party, with the Duch PvdA giving the draft programme the widest and most serious consideration – from the involvement of local branches to a special congress on the subject – and at the other extreme the British Labour Party, which objected to the programme from the outset and refused to consider it officially. In between, the other parties differed somewhat in procedure. The German SPD discussed different amendments at its own congress in November 1977, and then left the matter to the party executive.[97] Any wider consultation was informal, for the SPD press published the draft programme for the information of activists, as a result of which the party headquarters received many letters from the grass roots.[98] In the Italian PSI and the French PS the draft was sent to activists for information, but there was no elaborate consultation. In the French party discussion was conducted only at the national level by the executive and committee of directors, but this internal process was delayed by preoccupations with the French national election in early 1978, after which the party leadership decided to reject the draft.[99] Undoubtedly, pre-electoral tactics played a part in the reluctance of the PS to make a final judgement earlier. With the Belgian PSB there was no discussion in great depth in the party. A working group held several meetings to look at the draft, but it was not considered by the local branches.[100] The Danish Social Democratic Party, which had only sporadically participated in its formulation, found the draft unacceptable because it was 'far too integrationist' and was, in the words of one of its European experts, 'one of the parties which contributed to killing the platform'.[101]

Variations of attitude over the programme as a whole had been evident between the parties, with the problem of interlinkage between their different forms of internal consultation. In this sense, the British Labour Party, which received much of the public blame for the failure to produce a finalised programme, differed more from some other Confederation parties in the degree rather than the fact of its reluctance. The process of co-ordination between the member parties was therefore extended or postponed until their differences assumed proportionally more importance. According to one party international secretary and a close participant of the process, 'we were turning around the issues rather than trying to solve them . . . the entire problem for us was to try to gain time and to wait until we were more advanced on the views of the various parties'.[102] While the overall process of programme formulation had been generally taken seriously, the final compulsion to compromise was lacking.

The formulation of the ELD programme was just as elaborate with the main difference being that the willingness to compromise between the member parties was such that they succeeded in producing a unanimously adopted final version. The EC Liberals were less of a heterogeneous collection of parties than they had been in the 1960s, but this did not as such explain their compulsion to compromise as their ideological common ground was still somewhat disparate. The historical divide between radical and conservative Liberals surfaced at various stages in the programme discussion. What seemed to count in the process – in contrast with the Socialists – was the loose or often informal party structures making for procedural flexibility, that these parties had fewer distinct identity problems and, indeed, in most cases recognised domestic advantages in European co-operation being merely subordinate parties at home, and their absence of basic reservations over integration with the qualified exception of the Giscardians. The ELD general-secretary added the pressure of the electoral deadline: 'If the Liberals manage to present a united front for the direct elections, they will also be in a much stronger position than at present to act as an alternative large European political movement.'[103]

The programmatic procedure facilitated the success of this process, for it involved regular and sustained consultation between the parties which – with the exception of the Danish Radikal Venstre, which rejected the programme and left the ELD* – ultimately produced agreement. In 1976 seven working groups with national party representatives were formed on human rights, European institutions, agriculture, economic and monetary union, regional policy, foreign and defence policy and the environment (of which three were chaired by MEPs). These were accompanied by three further working groups (on social affairs, energy and middle-class interests) following an interim discussion of the prospective programme at the ELD congress in late 1976. The main work was carried out in eight sessions by the general programme commission with one representative from each party under Martin Bangemann, which edited the reports from the groups, negotiated various compromises and produced a reasonably cohesive draft by the spring of 1977.[104] The programme was finally consummated at the ELD con-

---

* According to a Radikal Venstre leader. the decisive reason for leaving the ELD was 'the very simple argument: we do not agree on the programme. If we had to dissociate ourselves from that programme (and on this there was unanimity). why then be a member? That's confusing. and that's no good to any of us' (interview no. 77).

gress in November 1977, which debated numerous amendments from the national parties and engaged in a line-by-line consideration of paragraphs in the draft.[105] Some of the amendments reflected particular national concerns, such as the FDP's on East-West relations and the key role of small businesses, those of the British Liberals on the right of EC citizens to vote in local elections where they lived and the one from the Dutch Liberal VVD on the role of women. The most controversial issue was that of energy, with a lively debate on nuclear power. Voting over the amendments did not always follow national lines – except with the French Giscardians – so that Gaston Thorn could remark at the end of the congress: 'We have often voted in different coalitions, often, indeed, across party lines and notwithstanding the constraints of party discipline.'[106] There were, therefore, divisions along ideological rather than strictly national lines within the pro-integration consensus. This was a significant example of genuine transnational activity.

The process of internal consultation within the member parties was thorough, though usually at the level of party executives and Euro-experts. The FDP, for instance, considered the draft programme in its specialist working groups in Bonn followed by a discussion of proposed amendments in its Federal committee before the 1977 ELD congress.[107] The British Liberals conducted an elaborate procedure during the latter half of 1977, beginning with initial consideration by their standing committee and advisory panels, the appointment of a subcommittee of the standing committee to consider amendments, discussion in the party council on the draft, a debate on the matter at the national conference in the autumn and the submission of proposed changes to the ELD.[108] The Dutch VVD went so far as involving their local branches in consultation over the draft, with their proposals being combined at district level for discussion at a special general meeting.[109] By contrast, the Danish Radikal Venstre rejected the programme outright because it was 'too unrealistic' and 'too federalistic', wrongly concentrating in its view on powers for the EC institutions rather than the political will to achieve common policies.[110] With this exception, the ELD Liberals may be said to have conducted the formulation of their programme in a centripetal, rather than centrifugal, way.

The EPP's process of formulating a common programme differed from the other two cases, for it succeeded in producing a final version, but this was based on less elaborate and intensive consultation. A small programme commission, chaired by the Belgian leader, Wilfried Martens, agreed on the original draft after commencing work in the summer of 1976. Following an interim examination by the Political Bureau in late 1976, the amended draft was ready in the spring of 1977 and, after further submission to the Bureau, was sent to the member parties before its final adoption at the EPP congress in March 1978. In producing the draft, the commission had drawn on the expertise of the Euro-parliamentary group for views on the general development of the EC, specialist advice on policy areas and assistance in the formulation of individual sections of the draft.[111] Problems arose over national differences of outlook, though these were usually handled with pragmatic flexibility for, as Egon Klepsch, the EP group chairman, explained:

> Attention has been paid to the fact that within the framework of the positions of principle of the national parties sufficient room remains for their pragmatic-political declarations. That relates not only to the shaping of merely national policies, but also to the scope for altercation during the course of the campaign for direct elections.[112]

This alluded to the strong electoral motivation of the EPP's programme.

Consultation over the draft within national member parties of the EPP involved predominantly national party executive organs and Euro-experts, but there were many amendments. In West Germany, the executives of the CDU and CSU discussed the draft with no formal consultation in the former case of its regional organisations for the CDU *Landesverbände* were 'not expressly involved – we thought through [the EPP programme] in the Federal Praesidium and the Federal Executive – for there was little to decide'.[113] The CDU did, however, send some 100,000 copies of the draft to its district branches, while in Belgium the Flemish CVP sent the same to all its 140,000 members.[114] The Dutch Christian Democratic Appeal (CDA) also provided its local branches with copies of the draft before it discussed it at the executive level;[115] while the Luxemburg Christian Democrats only considered the draft in their national council, and in Italy proper consultation within the DC was inhibited by difficulties in producing the Italian version of the text.

These three case studies illustrated significant differences of approach and conception concerning the quality of the transnational programmatic exercise. It is possible to generalise that the Socialists and Liberals (especially their radical progressives) were far more programmatically motivated than the Christian Democrats, but that the Socialists were less successful in their final outcome because they were as such more ideologically inclined (including over their integrationist reservations) and because their procedural methods were stricter with their more pronounced sense of national party autonomy. Despite these divergences and variations of national party consultation, the formulation of common programmes involved overall some degree of integrative activity because of the harmonisation of national party demands and viewpoints and the involvement, where this existed, of sub-élite levels of party structures.

The course followed by the Christian Democrats was in this sense the least integrative. This was partly because they started from a different standpoint of broad conceptual harmony on the importance of European integration and agreement on a vague category of Christian 'values' (as defined by the EUCD's Manifesto of European Christian Democracy, February 1976), so that their process was less precisely programmatic and consequently more élitist in its procedure. Also, this difference derived from the Christian Democrats' different way of conceiving the programmatic exercise. On the other hand, the centralist control over the process at the national party level which predominated in their case also marked the approach of the Liberals and most Socialist parties – if only because the dictates of European co-operation restricted the scope for internal party democracy. Therefore, behind the somewhat homogenised final versions of the common programmes or declarations there lay an interesting process of policy co-ordination. This was an important aspect of the new departure taken by transnational party co-operation.

One relevant feature of the general operation of the three federations must be its effect on the national member parties. It is feasible to ask whether membership of them and the politicisation of transnational links has not only been integrative but also possibly enhanced national awareness through closer contact. For what emerged, and was generally recognised by those involved, was that different national identities and historical backgrounds remained a very influential factor, despite the common ideological link. This was predictably emphasised by the Socialist Confederation in the preamble to its draft programme, but even the genially Europeanist Christian Democrats acknowledged this fundamental problem for, as Tindemans noted in his inaugural address at the EPP's 1979 congress: 'We had to base ourselves on our past. Each party had its own history and represented a national character which was not always readily understood by the other parties. We had our own traditions, customs and language, but also sometimes our own political jargon.' The national factor, which is the general theme of Chapter 4 in this study, will be discussed here only with reference to the federations' role concerning three specific questions: national demands and interests as presented in the formulation of the common programmes; general aspects of inter-party relationships within the transnational framework; and the specific problem of ideological compatibility in federation membership. Common to all three questions is the broad problem of the relationship between the two poles of the national political environment and the European-level ideological orientation of political parties in the context of politicisation in transnational activity.

First, the federation programmes seen overall could be described as a combination of declarations of commonly held ideological beliefs, values or *leitmotivs* (such as listed in the Liberals' Stuttgart Declaration of 1976) with a 'mixed grill' of national preferences especially over the specifics of policy areas. In some cases, however, national divergences could be categorised as ideological (for example, French reservations about European federalism), or as representing basic differences of policy outlook (such as the market-oriented Germans and the statist French or Italians in economic affairs). It is particularly in this context that the question arises as to whether the approach to policy co-ordination in the federations generally was a centripetal or a centrifugal one. We have already seen that, in the case of the Socialist Confederation, the centrifugal tendencies were sufficiently strong to prevent a finalisation of the programme. With the ELD, the Danish Radikal Venstre acted centrifugally to the extent of opting out of the federation altogether, although the federation otherwise acted centripetally. With the EPP no centrifugal tendency occurred, except for the mildly expressed federalist reservations of the small French Christian Democratic CDS, but it should not be forgotten that the EPP had no member parties from Britain and Denmark which, because of trends there of dislike for European integration, was fortunate for the general cohesion of the EPP.

In view of the preceding discussion of the formulation of the programmes, it is only necessary here to record a number of relevant points. The highest degree of basic policy divergences were found, as already seen, in the Socialist Confederation, especially as some of these divergences were ideological and proved unsurmountable. This was notably so with the British Labour Party, whose fundamental reservations about integration as a whole – reflected in its objections to the federalist tones in the draft programme – resulted in its refusal to participate in the programmatic process. The basic divergence between the German SPD and the French PS over the role of the state in the economy was overcome with a compromise formula.[116] The same occurred over the controversial issue of relations with the USA in the section on foreign policy, and again over agriculture, even though national interests here were obviously great.[117] In other instances, particular national proposals were included, such as from the Dutch PvdA on the control of multinationals on which it received support from the Italian PSI and the

French PS. This strong element of compromise with the merging or mixing of national policy proposals could be said to have weakened the homogeneity of the draft programme even before it was shelved. On the other hand, similar compromises are reached in national parties where there are marked divergences between ideological wings.

With the ELD, the policy differences were strong but more confined – in fact, mainly to the three areas of basic rights, European institutions and nuclear energy.[118] But, because of the general attraction of European co-operation for the Liberals, national divergences over these policy matters were treated centripetally with some signs of direct compulsion, such as in the decisive rejection of the French Giscardian amendments to reduce the commitment to human rights and stronger EC institutions.[119] In the EPP's case, there were some distinct divergences, such as between the Dutch CDA and the German CDU/CSU over the commitment to the Third World, nuclear energy and South Africa, in which the former favoured a strong responsibility towards the first and took a more critical line on the last two issues.[120] The Dutch were also concerned that the principles of the Christian approach were not stressed enough in the original draft, while they also had a specific interest in social affairs, industrial policy and employment,[121] although these did not necessarily cause friction with the other member parties. The most potentially centrifugal tendency among the EPP member parties was the French CDS's evident coolness about enlarging the EP's powers in particular and the principled commitment to European union in general. The prospect for European federalism was considered somewhat 'theoretical' and 'not realistic for the moment' by the CDS,[122] and clearly the French party was influenced by broad feeling in France about the national identity. The CDS was eventually outvoted in the EPP on this matter,[123] but, being a small member in a minority of one, it acceded to the will of the others. By and large, the generalised commitments of the EPP programme, together with the agreement to be flexible in the national context, allowed for national divergences to be de-emphasised. Also evident was a feature commonly found among Christian Democrats with their reserve about open programmatic conflict, so that for both reasons national demands and interests were contained in the process of programme formulation.

It is possible to trace national trends common to the different federations, thus perhaps indicating the limitation of transnational ideologies: the precise demands and often radical outlook of the Dutch (though less so with the conservative Liberal VVD), the French concern about national sovereignty (but with differences of emphasis between the various French parties), the Italian interest in agricultural interests and the German attention to East–West relations. But there were also exceptions to such generalisations – the British Labour insistence on national autonomy contrasted with the British Liberal espousal of European federalism – while these trends could also work in a positive direction, such as the pro-integrationist outlooks of the German and Italian parties. Where there were important national material interests at stake (for example, agricultural and industrial), then national conflicts were most likely to arise within the federations, although even here any direct antithesis could be modified by the different electoral structures of parties from the same country. The German SPD, for example, did not feel the same concern as the German FDP about the interests of domestic farmers.

The point arising from this discussion is that there was not always an automatic conflict between national demands and transnational ideological affiliation for a variety of reasons. Many national areas of policy were, in any case, open to ideological approaches or ideological differentiation between competing national parties, so that it was not so surprising when such competition repeated itself in a European setting. This could either involve a straightforward adjustment of ideological outlook to the European level or it could derive from a desire to seek European solidarity for buttressing a domestic political role. In some cases, there was evidence of mild pressure on individual national parties to conform to the general position taken by federations. However, there was much room for different policy interpretations within the ideological schools represented by the federations – indeed, distinctly more so than in the average national party – because of the broad ideological definitions adopted. Undoubtedly, such differences of interpretation owed much to the national factor in so far as they derived from deviating national experiences, but the relationship between the national environmental and the transnational ideological poles was often more complex than appeared at first sight. The national and the ideological factors could be transmitted through each other, or in some cases the ideological orientation (as both national and European) was more in evidence as it did not necessarily conflict with a party's role in domestic politics.

The second question of general inter-party relationships within the federations further illustrates the salience of the national factor and the fact that this cannot be viewed one-dimensionally. Two seemingly contradictory but somewhat complementary points underline the complexity of transnational links in the light of politicisation.

First, national consciousness has increased in some respects as a result of common federation membership, notably over the effective dominance of the German parties in all three cases. There are various reasons for this: numerical weight, organisational inclination and talent, financial resources as national parties and, not least, their European commitment as shown by the important role played by them in establishing the federations. The deputy secretary-general of the Socialist Confederation commented in these terms in the light of his experience:

> The Germans are very well-organised, they have a tremendous staff backing, they have never had problems with money, they never have problems with sending out people to meetings and they have also a very professional attitude in playing politics – so you can't do anything without their consent. But you can't do anything either without the consent of the other parties. It's not so simple as consent of the German party, the French party, etc. . . . We are really trying to obtain a general consensus.[124]

This dominance was particularly noticeable in the ELD because the relative strength of the FDP contrasted with the other parties' lack of facilities and because it enjoyed prestige as a governing party (unlike, say, the British Liberals as the other major member). The FDP played a crucial role in setting up the ELD, whose constituent congress in 1976 was organised in West Germany and where many of the party leaders' conferences prior to this had taken place. The German presence was often very visible, as one Dutch Liberal organiser remarked on the ELD meeting at Luxemburg in April 1979:

> The FDP was most significant there. For example, they came with three big buses and they were parked outside – all English double-decker buses, and they were completely blue with yellow 'F. D. P.'. Of course, it's very important for them that the ELD colours are the same as the FDP colours, so it's easy to promote them extra.[125]

Despite the general acknowledgement of the important Germans' role, their dominant weight could touch off political friction depending largely on the existence of anti-German feeling back home, especially in former occupied countries. The French Socialists, for example, felt at times constrained in their participation in the Confederation because their domestic ally, the PCF, publicly exploited anti-German feeling, claiming that the SPD was 'dominating' the PS. Since this was also a subjective problem, it could be conditioned by personalities for, whereas Willy Brandt's international popularity could be attractive for other Socialist parties, the almost universal aversion to Franz-Josef Strauss in other European countries was very marked, even among Christian Democrats involved in the EPP. Otherwise, such antagonism was conducted covertly within the federations, such as the determination in the Socialist Confederation to replace Dröscher by a non-German president in 1978.

On the other hand, the closer relations within the transnational framework could at the same time produce pressures to accommodate between member parties. German participants in the work of the federations have deliberately chosen to play their role low-key as far as possible for the aforementioned reason. There has been a certain unspoken rule of equality between federation members, so that even the two small Irish parties in the Socialist Confederation are certainly not ignored while, in the case of the EPP, the Irish Fine Gael has been influential. There can, in fact, be definite advantages in being a small party, for, as the general-secretary of the Luxemburg Socialists explained, 'we cannot be suspected of imperialism'.[126] It is also no coincidence that the presidents of two of the federations have come from small member countries – the Belgian Tindemans and the Luxemburger Thorn.* This accommodation could also reveal itself in exceptional cases over specific political issues of essentially national concern. A well-known case was over the West German policy of *Berufsverbot*, or exclusion from the public service of those regarded as political security risks. When the matter was first raised at the European party level relations between the SPD as governing party and its chief critics, the French PS and the Dutch PvdA, deteriorated for a time, but then German representatives in the Confederation took pains to explain the thinking behind this policy to foreign colleagues.[127] The friction subsided when the SPD began to change its own position on the issue, although this occurred primarily for domestic reasons, even if European pressure had some effect on the SPD, sensitive as it was to foreign opinion. Its own internal opponents of *Berufsverbot* had been strengthened as they 'found some allies outside the country'.[128] The Confederation's electoral Appeal of January 1979 did in fact 'reject exclusion from government service solely on the grounds of political beliefs', an inclusion that had been made at the request of the SPD itself after having announced an official change of position at its own European congress at the end of 1978.

There is one further interesting by-product of inter-party relationships within the federations. While ideological images might count

* According to Martin Bangemann of the German FDP, commenting on personal appointments in the new ELD: 'We will naturally proceed with great caution in personal decisions, especially we Germans ... we will in all probability when making personal appointments to the praesidium above all take into consideration those party friends from the smaller member countries, who have for some time been fighting very vehemently for Europe' (*Kommentarübersicht*, West German Federal Press Office, 2 December 1975).

with regard to individual party identities – for example, the SPD appeared 'right-wing' in the eyes of many of its co-members over the *Berufsverbot* – the experience of working in the Confederation began to unscramble such ideological labels with the realisation that various wings from separate national parties had ideological sympathies in common. Tony Benn, a relative newcomer to transnational party co-operation in the Confederation, emphasised this aspect:

> . . . many of them [the European Socialists] are more radical than the pro-Europeans [in the British Labour Party], who are their natural allies in terms of federalism. The [British] Social Democrats may be federalist like them, but by their standards they are quite right-wing . . . [European] Socialists have been very good on certain questions, which we would regard as items for the Left in Britain – nuclear power, and all that.[129]

With the other two federations this question of comparative ideological identities has been expressed less constantly, although it has nevertheless been present and surfaced most of all over the matter of ideological compatibility in federation membership.

This third question of ideological or party identity in joining a federation hardly arose in the case of the Confederation because all member parties were easily recognisable as Socialist/Social Democratic. At a mundane level, some linguistic juggling did allow for a flexible translation of the ideological title for the transnational organisation – 'Confederation of Socialist Parties of the EC' in English, 'Federation (*Bund*) of Social Democratic Parties' in German, and 'Union of Socialist Parties' in French and Italian, thus suiting the national party nomenclature in question and erasing any possible reservations on terminological or symbolical grounds.

With the EPP, the question of ideological compatibility in membership of the new party federation arose at the very beginning and caused some delay in its formation. A dispute broke out between its prospective member parties over the choice of the EPP's name and the associated question of the scope of its membership. At the beginning of 1976, there were two schools of thought, with the German CDU/CSU pressing strongly for the inclusion of Conservative parties to create a broad anti-Socialist bloc and an appropriate federation title omitting the term Christian as unacceptable by Conservatives for reasons of historical identity; and opposition to this line taken by the Italian, Belgian and Dutch parties, because of their own more pronounced confessional or social-Christian traditions (compared with the German parties) and their national alliances with parties of the left. For the sake of founding the EPP, a compromise formula was reached with the choice of the name 'European People's Party: Federation of Christian Democratic

Parties of the EC', while officially keeping open membership to other parties though, with regard to Conservatives, it was in effect shelved at least until after direct elections, if not permanently.[130] The problem of Christian Democratic links with Conservatives did, of course, reappear in another form with the establishment of the conservative European Democratic Union (EDU) in 1978 in which the CDU/CSU was involved (see below, Chapter 3, Section *d*, pp. 164–8). On related grounds, there were at the time of the EPP's birth some muted reservations among other nationals over the inclusion of the conservative Bavarian CSU as a member, but this never became a contentious matter because of the CSU's national link with the CDU and because of the credibility offered by the long-established role of its representatives in the Christian Democratic Euro-parliamentary group (one of whom had been its chairman for nearly six years). Perhaps a more interesting case of party identity was the Irish Fine Gael, whose historical tradition had never been called Christian Democratic (it had not belonged to the EUCD) but which felt sufficient policy affinity with (the more progressive) members of the EPP, not to mention their common Catholic cultural background. This pragmatic decision to ally for European purposes with the Christian Democrats had been prejudged by Fine Gael's opting for the Christian Democratic EP group on Irish entry to the EC several years beforehand.

The sharpest controversy over membership compatibility arose in the ELD, despite its compromise with the transnational heterogeneity of the European Liberals (not all of whom called themselves 'Liberals') in the title of the federation with 'Liberals and Democrats'. The main controversy over ELD membership erupted concerning a political party which could not claim any Liberal historical tradition – the French Giscardians, then called the Independent Republicans (FNRI). The FNRI had never, for instance, belonged to the Liberal International, but it had played a major role in the Liberal EP group (whose chairman had usually been a Giscardian). This Euro-parliamentary precedent unavoidably carried weight in clinching FNRI membership of the ELD during the course of 1976, but only after much bitter dispute on the part of certain Liberal parties who objected. The FNRI's membership was welcomed by the Belgian and Dutch Liberals, one of the Danish parties and the German FDP (though not unreservedly),[131] but there was expected opposition from the French Radicals because of national political incompatibility (who for this reason left the ELD after the FNRI joined) and vehement hostility from the British Liberals. The result was an interesting case study in the seriousness with which the new transnational organisational framework could be taken. The British objected on ideological grounds because the Giscardians were viewed as, in effect, a conservative party,[132] arguing the principle that federation co-membership involved a different kind of relationship from national party alliances (that is, with parties of different ideological affiliation):

> If we are meaning to be a political party – it's alright to work in a coalition with other people, but you cannot form a party with some sort of ideological programme together with people who are the same as the people you fight in your national elections. And the argument was also posed: how can we fight the European elections and make a point of our relations with other Liberals if every Conservative campaigner, if every Socialist campaigner, can turn round and say: 'But look, you are liaising in France with the French Conservatives'.[133]

The FNRI had in the past indeed had some links with Conservatives and Christian Democrats (as at the youth level), but the effective confinement of EPP membership to official Christian Democratic parties finally encouraged the FNRI to press for entry to the ELD after initial hesitation. Eventually, the British Liberals became reconciled to this favourable decision on FNRI membership because the latter did not enjoy the same weight in the federation as in the EP group and in their eyes came to be seen as a pragmatic party which could be 'stretched by being associated with a group of Liberals who had the bit between their teeth'.[134]

The variegated relationship between the national environmental and the European ideological poles and its importance in transnational activity revealed the beginnings of a 'Europeanisation' of party politics in the period up to the 1979 direct elections. In a number of different ways the existence and operation of the federations have challenged the customary outlook of their member parties by introducing the need for political choices at the European level and have sometimes applied secondary political pressures, as over specific policy areas. However, whatever progress towards 'Europeanisation' was made by the federations – and here they differed between themselves – this could not yet amount to any radical departure from the predominance of national politics in the views of the individual member parties. At best, the operation of the federations involved some minor modifications of this predominance, most evidently with the ELD, which was itself significant because, as smaller parties, the Liberals had less to lose from the merger of party identities at the European level. In the other two federations especially, the national orientation of individual parties persisted as their primary focus and was likely to remain the crucial determinant of their operation. As Bruno Friedrich, vice-president of the Socialist

Confederation, confirmed: 'We ourselves hold the view that the national parties will for long determine the development of the Confederation.'

The limited political role so far of the federations leads to one final question. What is their presence and can they be said to have any influence at the national level? Bruno Friedrich, as one federation leader, has on various occasions stressed the need for popular mobilisation on European questions and the relevance here of European parties as a channel of communication.[135] This was naturally an ambitious and long-term objective for the role of the federations and one not subscribed to by all party politicians involved in the federations as it entailed a likely rivalry with the national parties on their home ground.

Up to the 1979 elections, the impression made by the federations at the national level was not strong and primarily cosmetic. According to its deputy general-secretary, the Socialist Confederation had achieved some visibility, especially with its congress in January 1979, and 'we now receive letters from militants, not only because they want to have information [about the Confederation], but also because they want specific information [on policies]'.[136] Generally, the approach to direct elections was making the projection of the federations easier, although the Socialist Confederation did suffer here from not having a common programme, unlike the ELD and EPP. Among SPD activists it had at first made an 'unclear impression' but there had been a rise in interest during the year before European elections.[137] In the case of the Belgian Liberals, it was observed about the ELD that

> Very few people in the party have regular contacts with the federation. I believe that quite a number of people in the party itself have – I wouldn't say been totally unaware of the federation . . . although the party had organised a series of meetings with representatives from the various districts to inform them not only of the existence of the federation but also of the multi-party programme.[138]

Among the EPP member parties, the Dutch CDA was fairly assiduous in promoting its transnational organisational links. In the second half of 1978 it arranged educational programmes which were 'well accepted by activists', provided written explanations of the common programme and issued outline speeches in good time for the start of the European campaign. Even so, such national activity on behalf of transnational co-operation itself took time to have an effect, being 'a new thing for the ordinary man in the street'.[139]

It was essentially among the activist body of member parties that the federations gradually became better known, but here there were variations according to party-political tendency and country. The Socialist Confederation made the least use of visual techniques, having no convenient monogrammatic name like 'ELD' or 'EPP', although it had agreed on a common symbol of a thick-set arrow pointing upwards as representing 'progress, the future and dynamism',[140] while informally its members used the rose-in-fist symbol. The federation which was most regularly projected cosmetically at the national level was the ELD, its free publicity material being especially attractive for its small members with their limited resources. The EPP had its own flag and emblem (an 'E' in a circle of twelve stars with the party name, in green and white), which were generally used by its member parties.

There were, however, some distinct variations between EC countries in the readiness to cosmetise their transnational links, with the German parties noticeably active in this sense. Just as the CDU flew the EPP flag alongside its own party flag outside its headquarters in Bonn, and opened there a special 'Bonn office of the EPP' (in fact combined with its foreign department) which supplied federation material to CDU members and any interested members of the public; so, the SPD reproduced Confederation material as brochures in the German language with its own money[111] and reprinted Confederation documents in the party press.[112] Equally, the FDP was no less attentive in publishing frequent reports in its *Neue Bonner Depesche* as information for activists on anything to do with the ELD or fraternal Liberal parties, while its press service regularly boosted ELD activities.

The Italian parties also showed no inhibitions about publicising their transnational links, although actual promotion of them was less precise and systematic than in West Germany and more in vague terms of European (rather than specifically federation) relationships. The DC held a special day on 'Europe' at its national *Festa* at Pescara in September 1978, with a round-table discussion on the EP, including the EP group chairman, Egon Klepsch, and Emilio Colombo (the Parliament's President), a session on Christian Democratic youth and direct elections and a rally with Tindemans as guest speaker.[143] Local DC festivals sometimes advertised the EPP, typical of which was one visited by the authors at Pontassieve in Tuscany where the EPP flag was flown on the stands, EPP stickers were worn by orderlies and there was an extensive exhibition of posters depicting stages in the history of the EC. The DC newspaper *Il Popolo* reported only intermittently but then fully on its transnational activity, sometimes with headline treatment, as when the EPP programme was published in early 1978. The Italian PSI was less definite on the work of the Confederation, preferring often to project its 'Euro-socialist' connections with well-known Socialist leaders abroad like Brandt and Mitterand. However, the federations could suddenly receive full attention from such circles as the many European federalist associations in Italy.[144]

Examples of this publicity about the federations could also be drawn from the Benelux countries, although among the larger member states France and Britain were distinctly less enthusiastic in declaring or promoting transnational party relationships, partly because these were less uniformly applicable compared with such countries as West Germany, Holland and Belgium. Several major parties in France and Britain were not members of the three federations, and those that were did not necessarily see any advantage in advertising them either for reasons of domestic alliances or public disinterest.

The national projection of the federations and their activities was mainly confined to party activists also because the national press in member states did not pay much attention to them. If one excludes party newspapers, which might or might not have a vested interest in projecting transnational links, the national press up to the European campaign* showed an uninformed and, at best, a spasmodic interest in federation activities and then often with a national slant. Reporting was, in any case, primarily confined to the quality press, such as the *Frankfurter Allgemeine* in West Germany, the *Irish Times, La Stampa* in Italy and *The Times* in the UK (especially when the ELD pressed for proportional representation in Britain). This sparse coverage briefly expanded when a federation congress occurred, although in some countries the papers focused on this European 'event' not always mentioning or correctly using the title of the federation. In West Germany, the EPP congresses even enjoyed a passing mention in the regional or local press but, in the case of the 1978 one, with a marked tendency to dwell on Helmut Kohl's warning against 'Eurocommunism'. In Italy, the same congress was covered in all the party newspapers, including that of the Communists, although one secular daily did refer to the EPP somewhat provincially as the 'Euro-DC'.

It hardly needs saying that the federations' sub-European role, what there was of it, was not in any sense institutionalised and that for their cosmetic presence at the national level they were entirely dependent on the goodwill of member parties to promote their cause. During the later 1970s the federations did not make any impression at the grass roots as effective bodies, although they had only had a

---

* On the projection of the federations during the European campaign, see below, Chapter 5, Section (a).

few years to operate before the commencement of the European campaign. All this naturally served to confirm the obvious predominance of national party politics over the European dimension. It also emphasised that the 'Europeanisation' of party politics, so far as it had developed, was still much of an élite exercise. In other words, the federations' lack of a social-aggregative function meant that their incipient and minimal integrative capacity so far had been largely confined to national élites and individuals working at the European level.

(d) Other Forms of Transnational Co-operation and the Future of the Party Federations

This analysis of transnational party organisation in the European Community has been limited to a discussion of the three party federations – the European People's Party, the Socialist Confederation and the European Liberal and Democratic Federation – because these are qualitatively different both from their predecessor associations and also from other new contemporaneous party co-operative bodies, both in their institutional interlinkage in the EC and in their internal integrative purpose. Other forms of party co-operation of a multilateral or bilateral kind, which have developed in the same period from the mid-1970s, do not essentially fit this category. These other forms of co-operation in question were the conservative European Democratic Union (EDU), closer links between Communist parties in the EC and the appearance of a primitive form of links among fringe political forces like the extreme right and the new ecologists.

Yet, there are valid reasons for some consideration of them in this context of the party organisational dimension, although where relevant they will again be examined in the discussion of bilateral and multilateral links in Chapter 4 on the national party frameworks. Primarily, the development of other forms of co-operation was stimulated by the same source as the three party federations – the general politicisation in the EC, and especially the prospect of direct elections. Party co-operation in this context became a regular habit, spreading outside the federations to encompass other political forces, which for reasons of national political history were not geographically widespread or enjoyed a strong presence throughout the Community states, and therefore not in a viable position to form a federation. But they were also inspired by a sense of party-political competition at the European level, and did not wish to be excluded from the growth of party co-operation. While not integrative and only minimally institutionalised as party organisations, they did in varying degrees contain some transnational features and in the major cases related to Euro-parliamentary groups. Nevertheless, they were unlikely for the aforesaid reasons to develop in the same way as the federations in the future. As these other forms posed very divergent examples of European co-operation with different prospects as European party formations, they will be discussed in turn.

The EDU, established formally at Salzburg in April 1978, is more analogous structurally to the traditional Internationals than the new federations, although it has a comparable EC orientation and motivation within the framework of a broader European membership.* While it drew on a tradition of multilateral co-operation between Conservative and some Christian Democratic parties (notably, the CDU/CSU), it originated in the mid-1970s from alarm at the rise of 'Eurocommunism' and, more specifically, from the conception of an alliance of the centre-right. The latter motive, while applicable generally, referred in particular to the balance of forces in the EP, present and future, where the acquisition of majority status by the Socialist group in the summer of 1975 assumed a symbolic importance. The EDU was officially designated by the CDU, one of its principal founding members, as having among its functions that: 'It should prepare and facilitate the future formation of a coalition of all parties of the centre, only through which can a permanent non-Socialist majority in the European Parliament be guaranteed'.[145] Another express purpose was to 'prevent the relative isolation which the Conservative parties in Great Britain and Denmark face'. This was acknowledged by Douglas Hurd, British Conservative spokesman on Europe, who saw the formation of the EDU as 'strengthening the Tory dimension in European politics'.[146]

The EDU was therefore ideologically and politically inspired with reference to the Community, but from the point of view of transnational party co-operation it had neither a formal institutional interlinkage with the Community nor an integrative purpose and consequently differed substantially from the federations. First, the principle of restricting membership to Community member states was not recognised – indeed, the EDU made a virtue of its institutional links with countries outside the EC, and not merely with applicant states. Alois Mock, the second EDU chairman, emphasised in his statement on election in 1979 the organisation's membership from both EC and non-EC states and that it could 'serve as a bridge and as a link between these two parts of the free Europe'.[147] The EDU included parties from such other European countries as

* For a fuller discussion of the background and establishment of the EDU, see Geoffrey Pridham, 'Christian Democrats, Conservatives and transnational party co-operation in the European Community: centre-forward or centre-right?', in Z. Layton-Henry (ed.), *Conservative Politics in Western Europe* (1981).

Austria, Norway, Sweden and Finland as well as Greece, Spain and Portugal, and there was even a provision in Article I.2 of the 1978 Declaration of the EDU that 'non-European parties may also be invited to become observers'. The only criterion for membership was adherence to the principles of the EDU Declaration of 1978. The fact that the EDU's secretariat was housed in Vienna and that its first two chairmen were successive leaders of the Austrian People's Party underlined the non-EC scope of the organisation. There was consequently some ambiguity about the EDU's relationship with the EC: its geographical scope and political interest extended well beyond the Community, and yet it avowed a particular political purpose by offering itself as a framework for promoting an alliance factor in the EP.

Secondly, the EDU was not analogous to the federations because it could make no claim to have a party-political integrative purpose underlying its activities. Its very dual membership between Conservatives and Christian Democrats prevented an institutionalised relationship with any of the Euro-parliamentary groups along the model of the EPP, ELD or Socialist Confederation, although it apparently felt close to the European Conservative group (renamed European Democratic after direct elections in the summer of 1979). Furthermore, the unsystematic state of inter-group relations in the EP, at least up to the 1979 elections, precluded a serious application of the EDU's stated purpose, or at least made it premature. An integrative purpose was, in any case, impossible in view of its non-EC membership, and this was further confirmed by its limited structure. EDU leaders stressed at the time of its founding, and have repeated since, that the EDU made no pretence of becoming a 'party'. Its declaration refers to itself as a 'working association', and at its 1979 conference the retiring chairman, Josef Taus, reaffirmed that 'we all agreed that it should not become a bureaucratic body with a big central organisation'. Its institutional arrangements are strictly minimal with a chairman, treasurer (one of the national party treasurers acting as such), an executive secretary and the provision in Article III for an annual conference 'consisting of the chairmen or leaders of the member-parties and of the chairmen of the observers'. The EDU's main continuous function has been the deliberations of its subcommittees under different national chairmen, of which four were initially appointed concerned with the questions of European structures, Eurocommunism, employment policy and energy and the environment. At the 1979 EDU conference, the report on European structures confirmed the preference for minimal institutional provisions by noting the 'renunciation by the EDU of any further organisational consolidation, retention of a high degree of flexibility and repeated emphasis of its self-identity as a working group of parties and not as a European party'.[148] The EDU has developed none of the informal party-political articulation already apparent in the operation of the three federations, and offered no potential for sub-élite involvement in its operation.

It is necessary, however, to consider the relationship of the EDU to the federations, especially the EPP, because of the former's purpose in relation to the EC. The EDU's belated arrival on the European scene – its delay being due to differences among centre-right parties over its establishment – was controversial because it was regarded as divisive for the EPP's unity by those EPP member parties not involved or which had refused any association with it. The same line-up occurred as over the issue in early 1976 as to whether the new EPP should include Conservative parties (see above, Chapter 3, Section c, pp. 157–8) – that is, the German CDU/CSU supporting the EDU link (and being the only EPP member which joined the new formation), and the Dutch, Belgian and Italian parties decisively against it with the Irish Fine Gael now adding its weight to the second group. The latter's reasons were ideological, a matter of Christian Democratic identity and electoral, all of which were closely related. For those parties in the EPP which took seriously their 'Christian' vocation in politics (above all the Dutch CDA) and those which adhered to 'social Catholicism' (such as the Belgian party, and a section of the Italian DC), the Conservative ideological label was anathema, if only for historical reasons, with its fundamentally 'right-wing' connotations. On these same grounds, any formalised link with Conservatives was likely to be counter-productive in domestic electoral terms for those parties. It is significant that the internal EPP opposition presented the CDU/CSU with the principle of not dividing its transnational loyalty, another instance of ideological and party-political compatibility within the EC.

This controversy placed the German parties, and the CDU especially, in an awkward strategic situation. The problem for the CDU was that, apart from tactical considerations, such as behind-the-scenes pressure from the CSU and Strauss personally in favour of creating the EDU, it had itself for a long time fostered close links with the British Conservatives in particular which revealed a bond of *de facto* ideological sympathy between both sides in spite of their different historical identities. The issue came to a head during 1978 within the EPP, and there followed sharp exchanges at sessions of its Political Bureau. Granelli, the Italian DC representative, denounced the EDU in strong terms and repeated his attack in public when he said:

> The valuable state of unity will be defended with the support of all from every plot and every ambiguity, and for this reason . . . it is necessary to extol in the strongest way and with the greatest

clarity the basic ideas, the programme and the Christian Democratic image of the EPP, avoiding any move that could weaken such an indispensable formation.[149]

Various member parties of the EPP applied unremitting pressure on the CDU bilaterally, notably the Dutch Christian Democrats, who, according to one of their spokesmen:

> We have said: the EPP has been established in view of European elections. If you, Germans, are now going to start a new move with Christian Democrats of countries which are not members of the European Community, this cannot have anything to do with the European elections and European party form. Moreover, if you are going to try to get the Conservatives in the EDU, in this grouping which is European but has nothing to do with the European Parliament because Austria is in it and Norway I believe, we said: the door is closed so far as the EPP is concerned and you can do outside it what you want to but you are not a member.[150]

This insistence on loyalty to the EPP resulted in a compromise arrangement with a promise from the CDU leadership that, while remaining in the EDU, it would underplay the EDU at least until direct elections, in which the EDU would play no part, contrary to the original hopes of the British Conservatives.

Following the conclusion of direct elections, the EDU decided at its conference at London in July 1979 that, in the words of its outgoing chairman, Josef Taus, it

> will have to increase its public relations in order to get even better known as a political trade mark. I know that until the European elections in June of this year, EDU had to exercise self-constraint in view of the parties in the EPP. Henceforward, however, the solidarity between EDU parties should be shown at regular intervals to the full European public.[151]

The report on European structures specified further that 'it is of great importance to try to find a *modus vivendi* with the EPP, EUCD and the Christian Democratic parties – one form or the other of mutual links; thereby all possibilities should be kept open in order to make possible even closer links'.[152] Taus emphasised that 'concrete political steps' should be taken to overcome 'the prejudices of some Christian Democratic parties' against the Conservatives. The obstacles to a formal alliance between Conservative and Christian parties remain however decisive, because of unchanged objections among the latter, although some of their spokesmen have indicated a possible consideration of temporary arrangements 'on concrete problems', such as co-operation to prevent the election of a Socialist President of the EP despite their parties' ideological reservations about the EDU.[153] Notwithstanding plans by the EDU to make itself more visible, its potential as a European party formation remains restricted for a variety of reasons – structural and geographical as well as ideological.

Co-operation between Communist parties in EC member states has had a different motivation and assumed a different form from that of the federations and the EDU, although all reflect in common the stronger orientation towards the Community in party co-operation. Communist 'extra-parliamentary' co-operation is really more multi-lateral or bilateral than transnational, bearing in mind the loose form of links which have evolved under the banner of 'Euro-communism'. The Communist parties also make less of a clear-cut distinction than the other political forces between the EC area of policy action and that of wider Europe and beyond. Yet, they repre-sent one of the major political movements in the EC and their co-operation does have some transnational relevance, if only because they have formed a common group in the EP. The politicisation process in the Community has affected their common activity for three reasons. First, the Communist parties – and especially the PCI – have undergone in varying degrees an ideological revisionism with regard to the EC in accepting its importance. As such they have participated in the Community's 'system', and are viewed competi-tively by other political forces in the EC. Secondly, the overlap between domestic and European politics was emphasised in their case by the development, again especially on the part of the PCI, of complementary national and European strategies for political change. Thirdly, the move towards direct elections did, in the light of the preceding two factors, have a mobilising effect on the respective Communist parties, not only for reasons of national competition but out of a general desire to fight 'conservatism' in the EC.

These factors did not, however, produce an intensification of institutional links equivalent to those of the other political forces in the Community. There were a variety of reasons for this reluctance to increase their long-term transnational co-ordination. First, the Communist parties concerned have tended not to think in terms of the EC institutions *per se* as a basis for co-operation but to view them as a secondary matter in their analysis of the dynamics of Euro-pean integration,[154] not to mention that the PCF has been opposed to the principle of supranationality. Secondly, the Communist pre-ference for justifying political activity in ideological rather than functional terms has meant that, despite revisionism on European integration, transnational party co-operation as an institutionalised exercise is regarded in Communist eyes as 'artificial'. Early in 1977, Giorgio Amendola, chairman of the Communist Euro-parliamentary group, expressed his sceptical viewpoint on the matter:

> The time is still not ripe for the creation of European parties. Anyway, you have only to look at the differences between the British Labour Party and the German Social Democrats, between Strauss's Christian Democrats and the Italian Christian Democrats in order to understand the artificial character of certain alignments, that have purely an electioneering value.[155]

Communist leaders have at times waxed polemical against the trend of transnational co-operation, such as Napolitano's speech at the PCI national *L'Unità* festival in 1978 when he attacked other forces for papering over their political cracks 'behind a Europeanist rhetoric'.[156] Thirdly, the Communist parties are themselves basically divided over key EC issues, openly acknowledging this division, notably between the PCI and PCF over Community enlargement and strengthening the powers of the EP. Moreover, in the present EC context co-operation would essentially mean the bilateral axis between the PCI and the PCF in view of the fringe status of Communist parties in other member states. Fourthly, the Communists are distinctly aware of their autonomy as political parties. Giorgio Amendola emphasised this point in his speech to the PCI central committee on direct elections in December 1978, when he said that the formation of a 'European Communist party' would deny one of the basic principles of 'Eurocommunism' which was 'the requirement of each Communist party to determine in a sovereign way its own line of behaviour according to its own interpretation of the general interests of the nation'.[157] Fifthly, there was the special consideration that the Communists' European alliance strategy – notably that of the PCI – was not confined to co-operation with Communist parties, and therefore ran contrary to the whole principle behind transnational party co-operation in the EC.

The value of measuring Communist links against transnational party co-operation has been to emphasise the special characteristics of the latter. Nevertheless, there has been a trend towards closer multilateral and bilateral links between the main Communist parties. Following the general conferences of West European Communist parties in 1971 and 1974 there has developed a practice of regular meetings between the PCI and PCF leaders, the definition of common positions (as expressed by the declarations after these meetings), and a number of common activities including public rallies, conferences and colloquia on special themes. Apart from a mixed commission of Euro-experts from the two parties, there has, however, been no attempt to institutionalise these closer contacts. As Amendola remarked tersely, Eurocommunism 'does not exist as a unique operative and organisational centre',[158] while for the PCF Marchais has decidedly rejected any bureaucratisation of these links. No special common structures were introduced for the European campaign, so that, apart from their brief common declaration for the elections,[159] they campaigned with separate programmes (see below, Chapter 5, Section *a*, pp. 247–8).

The attempts to form closer multilateral links among the fringe political forces in the EC provides further evidence of the trend of party-political co-ordination for direct elections, although these revealed no significant institutional or integrative features in the period up to 1979. On the initiative of the Italian MSI, the extreme right began to gather its minority forces in the first part of 1978 in an effort to take advantage of the opportunity of publicity in the forthcoming European campaign. A meeting was held in Rome in April to inaugurate the 'Euro-right', a loose term used for co-ordination between the three parties of the Italian MSI, the French PFN and the Spanish Fuerza Nueva. It followed with a further meeting in Paris in the summer of 1978. The 'Euro-right' owed its existence very much to the individual efforts of the Italian party secretary, Giorgio Almirante, who in the preceding months had made a tour of the European capitals in a forlorn attempt to broaden co-operation to centre-right parties.[160] The decision to proceed with the 'Euro-right' clearly anticipated the eventual enlargement of the Community which would bring the inclusion of further parties of the far right. Seeing itself as an International, it declared its opposition to Euro-communism, its determination to prevent a 'Euro-socialist hegemony' in the EP and its adherence to a mixed set of aims under the vague rubric of the 'New European Man'.[161]

Other groupings showed a similar readiness to merge their efforts with direct elections in view. Regional nationalists and groups representing 'stateless nations' signed a declaration in 1976 asserting the right to 'equivalent representation' as member countries in the EP and spoke of the possibility of a common programme,[162] but nothing substantial came from this initiative. One main reason was the lack of resources, and this was equally true of the ecologists as a new political force which burst on the European scene during this period. Following their relative success in German regional and French local elections, they hoped to capitalise on the interest they aroused by co-ordinating activities for the European campaign. But, as the Paris-based Europe Ecologie movement complained, faced with the 'giants' which dominated the electoral scene 'we have no money, neither official nor hidden'.[163] Ecologist groups decided to discard the idea of a European party, and contented themselves with their common link through Ecoropa, an EC-wide association for the promotion of 'green thought'.[104] Despite the limited impact of these groupings, their efforts reflected the fact that European-level mobilisation for direct elections covered virtually the whole of the party-political spectrum.

In concluding, it is necessary to focus on the future development of this new departure in transnational party organisation in the European Community. Well before the 1979 elections, it became clear that the federations saw a long-term purpose in their existence, however much they were directly inspired by the prospect of European elections and whatever their own structural and political differences in their functioning. This is emphasised by the aims outlined in their formal statutory requirements, and is apparent in their long-term policy outlook. It is also guaranteed by the fact that the 1979 elections were the first of a permanent series of European campaigns at five-yearly intervals.

Yet, at the same time, the distinguishing characteristic of the new form of transnational party organisation is its orientation towards immediate or intermediate political tasks, unlike the traditional form of party co-operation. The preparations for, and the very exercise of, the European campaign fell into this category. The interest of the federations in the balance of European political forces, as represented in the EP, strengthened this focus on the immediate/intermediate. In this context, their decisive involvement in forming closer links with ideologically related political parties in the three applicant states of Greece, Portugal and Spain reflected the same concern, so that the new element of party-political competition in a European setting is unlikely to diminish after 1979.

The most important role of the federations in the post-European electoral future is, of course, their relationship with their respective Euro-parliamentary groups. Although in line with the classical European model of party development as extra-parliamentary bodies, this role of the federations has yet to be fully clarified in reference to the special exigencies of European integration, notably the predominance of the national factor. At the European level, the federations may occupy themselves less one-sidedly with their long-term role and more with the everyday politics being conducted in the EP, depending on the willingness of their member parties and the attitudes of the groups themselves. The possibility arises here as to whether the federations will be content to act primarily as agents defending the work of their respective EC groups or whether they will also seek to apply their own pressures on these groups, so that some institutional conflict between the organisational and parliamentary wings of the European Socialists, Liberals and Christian Democrats might ensue. One special feature of the future work of the federations will be their public role in mobilising support on European questions, but there is unlikely to be an advance in this respect without a significant new initiative, such as the introduction of a common electoral law, entailing further forms of European-level co-ordination.

Such speculation refers back to the schema presented above for the possible future progress of the federations towards party-political integration (see above, Chapter 3, Section *a*, pp. 115–6). Looking at the establishment and subsequent operation of the federations during the 1970s up to the first European elections, it may be concluded that they had already passed through the first stage of campaigning under a common banner (with the qualification that the Socialist Confederation was cosmetically less in evidence than the EPP and ELD). They also made progress in the second stage of formulating common programmes, with the major exception provided by the failure to finalise this effort in the case of the Socialist Confederation. At the same time, their organisational articulation represented a secondary continuum linking these different stages. The further three stages do, however, involve a significant reduction in, or modification of, the national-political orientation of individual member parties, as the essential precondition for the federations acquiring some measure of political authority and weight in electoral, organisational and power terms. All these further stages look to the long-term future and are fundamentally dependent on the future of the whole Community itself. In short, the federations are likely in the foreseeable future to remain as essentially a dependent variable of European integration, even though the new departure in transnational organisation which they represent could be described as a first modest step in the direction of their becoming active determinants of that general process. For this reason, the full historical importance of direct elections is uncertain, although they were decisive in providing an indispensable stimulus to the new form of transnational party co-operation.

Chapter 3: References

1 Wilhelm Dröscher, German federal press office. *Kommentarübersicht* (Bonn: 7 June 1977).
2 Norbert Gresch. *Transnationale Parteienzusammenarbeit in der EG* (1978), pp. 110–11.
3 ibid., p. 125.
4 The most advanced form of national parliamentary control was the Market Relations Committee in the Danish Folketing; see John Fitzmaurice, 'National parliaments and European policy-making: the case of Denmark', *Parliamentary Affairs,* vol. XXIX, no. 3 (Summer 1976).
5 FDP, *Leitlinien Liberaler Europa-Politik* (1975), p. 11.
6 Interview no. 1 (1979).
7 European People's Party. Josef Müller, 'Vorgeschichte und Gründung der Europäischen Volkspartei' (mimeograph) (1977), pp. 4–5.
8 On Belgian TV (8 July 1976).

9 Gresch, op. cit., pp. 113–14.
10 ibid., pp. 115–20.
11 Socialist Confederation, Helga Köhnen, *Co-operation between the Socialist parties of the European Community*, October 1976, p. 11.
12 Gresch, op. cit., p. 121.
13 Interview in *Das Parlament* (27 March 1976). According to its own publicity organ, the ELD was 'clearly founded with a view to the first direct elections to the European Parliament' (*Présence Liberale*, September 1978).
14 European People's Party, Müller, op. cit., p. 5.
15 Interview no. 97.
16 *Présence Liberale* (September 1978).
17 *Zusammenarbeit der Parteien in Westeuropa*, Bundeszentrale für Politische Bildung (Bonn, 1976). pp. 68–9.
18 Interview no. 21.
19 *Stuttgarter Zeitung* (28 February 1976).
20 See Geoffrey Pridham and Pippa Pridham, 'The new European party federations and direct elections', *The World Today*, vol. 35, no. 2 (February 1979), pp. 64–5.
21 Maurice Duverger, *Political Parties* (London: Methuen, 1964), p. xvi.
22 Interview no. 1 (1977).
23 Speech of November 1974, reprinted in *Europa-Union* (March 1975).
24 Interview no. 87.
25 *Frankfurter Rundschau* (10 April 1974).
26 Quoted in Gresch. op. cit., p. 168.
27 Interview no. 97.
28 Interview no. 2 (1979).
29 Interview no. 25.
30 Wolfgang Mischnick (ed.). *The Liberals for Europe* (1976), p. 17.
31 Interview no. 25.
32 Wilhelm Dröscher, 'Das europäische sozial-demokratische Programm', in T. Jansen and V. Kallenbach (eds). *Die europäischen Parteien* (1977), p. 28.
33 Interview no. 97.
34 Socialist Confederation press releases of 9 November 1977 and 19 January 1978.
35 *CD – Europe*, no. 4 (1978), p. 21.
36 See proceedings of meetings of EPP Political Bureau of 8 July 1976, published by EPP, 19 July 1976.
37 For example, the Political Bureau passed a statement on Mediterranean policy in January 1979, with the dissent of the CSU representatives. It was nevertheless published.
38 Interview no. 2 (1979).
39 Interview no. 25.
40 Interview no. 97.
41 Interview no. 2 (1979).
42 Interview no. 105.
43 F. Wijsenbeek, *Co-operation between Political Parties in Europe: A Practical Study*, paper to TEPSA conference, Amsterdam, April 1978, p. 33.
44 ibid., p. 29.
45 Lee *Présence Liberale* (April 1979), pp. 6–8.
46 Interview no. 26.
47 *CD – Europe* (February 1977), p. 10.
48 *Euso*, no. 10 (December 1978). p. 19.

49 ibid., pp. 16–18.
50 Interview no. 97.
51 *Euso*, no. 4 (1979), p. 2.
52 *Zusammenarbeit der Parteien in Westeuropa*, p. 67.
53 *Parlamentarisch-Politischer Pressedienst* (Bonn, 2 August 1976).
54 *Europäische Zeitung* (September 1977), p. 6.
55 Socialist Confederation, Köhnen, op. cit., p. 10.
56 ibid., p. 10.
57 Interview no. 96.
58 Interviews nos. 1 (1977) and 97.
59 Christian Democratic group, *Report on the Activities of the Christian Democratic Group of the European Parliament (Group of the European People's Party), 15.5.1977–15.5.1978* (May 1978), p. 8.
60 *Euso*, no. 1 (January 1978), editorial p. 1.
61 Interview no. 1 (1977). See also Gresch, op. cit., p. 155.
62 See proceedings of EPP Political Bureau meeting (8 July 1976), p. 3, statement by von Hassel.
63 Interview no. 2 (1977).
64 Socialist group, Ludwig Fellermaier, *The Work of the Socialist Group in the European Parliament*, Report to the 10th Congress of the Confederation of the Socialist Parties of the European Community (January 1979), pp. 1–2.
65 Interview no. 25.
66 Interview no. 2 (1979).
67 European Liberals and Democrats (ELD), *III. Congress, 2 and 3 December 1978, London*, proceedings, p. 35.
68 *European Parliament Report*, no. 32 (February 1977), p. 1.
69 Interview no. 25.
70 Interview no. 97.
71 European Liberals and Democrats (ELD), *Meeting Luxembourg, 7.4.79, Proceedings*, p. 9.
72 John Fitzmaurice, *The European Parliament* (1978), p. 93.
73 See Geoffrey Pridham, 'Christian Democrats, Conservatives and transnational party co-operation in the European Community: centre-forward or centre-right?', in Z. Layton-Henry (ed.), *Conservative Politics in Western Europe* (1981).
74 For example, see preambles to the federation programmes; also Section 2 of PCI programme for direct elections on 'changing the orientation of the Community'.
75 Mischnick, op. cit., foreword, p. 10.
76 *Présence Liberale* (September 1978), p. 12.
77 *Euso*, no. 10 (December 1978), p. 3.
78 Interview no. 68.
79 von Hassel in CDU. *24. Bundesparteitag der CDU, Mai 1976* (1976), p. 157.
80 *Frankfurter Rundschau* (Bonn: 10 April 1974).
81 Interview no. 22.
82 European Liberals and Democrats (ELD), *Programme for Europe* (English version), p. 17.
83 Jean-François Pintat, speech at ELD meeting at Luxemburg, 7 April 1979, proceedings, p. 7.
84 F. Wijsenbeek, paper at TEPSA conference, op. cit., p. 4.
85 Federal Press Office, Bonn, *Kommentarübersicht* (Bonn: 8 June 1977).
86 Dröscher in Jansen and Kallenbach, op. cit., p. 29.
87 Martin Bangemann, chapter on ELD programme in M. Bangemann,

R. Bieber, E. Klepsch and H. Seefeld, *Programme für Europa: die Programme der europäischen Parteibünde zur Europa-Wahl 1979* (1978), p. 101.

88 European Liberals and Democrats. *Congress Brussels 1977*, p. 19.
89 Interview with West German radio (7 March 1978).
90 Gresch. op. cit., pp. 169–70. 185–6.
91 See W. Dzieyk, 'Programme und Satzungen der Parteibünde in der Europäischen Gemeinschaft'. *Zeitschrift für Parlamentsfragen*, vol. 9, no. 2 (June 1978), pp. 183–4.
92 For fuller treatment of these policy differences between the three programmes, see Dzieyk, op. cit., pp. 182–6; R. Hrbek, 'Parteibünde in der Europäischen Gemeinschaft auf dem Weg zu programmatischem Profil', *Europa-Archiv* (10/1978), pp. 303–8; and R. Bieber in Bangemann. Bieber, Klepsch and Seefeld, op. cit., ch. 2, pp. 31–53.
93 H. Seefeld in *Programme für Europa*, p. 74.
94 *Guardian*, 24 June 1978.
95 *Euso*, no. 3 (1979), p. 23.
96 Interview no. 24.
97 Seefeld in *Programme für Europa*, p. 74.
98 Interview no. 23.
99 Interview no. 29.
100 Interview no. 96.
101 Interview no. 1 (1979).
102 Interview no. 96.
103 Quoted in Gresch, op. cit., p. 184.
104 On the work of the ELD programme commission. see articles by its chairman, Martin Bangemann in *Die europäischen Parteien*, pp. 97–104, and *Programme für Europa*, pp. 96–118.
105 Peter Knowlson, British Liberal, memorandum on 1977 Congress, 'European Liberals adopt a more radical manifesto'. undated.
106 European Liberals and Democrats, *Congress Brussels 1977*, p. 45.
107 *Programme für Europa*, p. 105.
108 Interview no. 16 (1978).
109 Interview no. 90.
110 Interview no. 77.
111 E. Klepsch in *Programme für Europa*, pp. 81–2.
112 ibid., p. 83.
113 Interview no. 21.
114 Interview no. 2 (1979).
115 Interview no. 87.
116 *Programme für Europa*, p. 69.
117 ibid., pp. 67–8.
118 *Programme für Europa*, pp. 106–16.
119 Knowlson, op. cit., p. 3.
120 Interviews nos. 81 and 82.
121 Interview no. 84.
122 Interview no. 64.
123 *The Economist* (3 March 1979). p. 51.
124 Interview no. 97.
125 Interview no. 90.
126 Interview no. 99.
127 *Frankfurter Allgemeine* (12 June 1976).
128 Interview no. 96.
129 Interview no. 101.
130 See Geoffrey Pridham in Layton-Henry, op. cit.

131   *The Economist* (13 November 1976).
132   See Michael Steed. *The French Threat* (January 1976).
133   Margarethe Holmstedt, former member of British Liberal international liaison office, paper at conference on British Political Parties and the EEC, University Association for Contemporary European Studies, at Preston Polytechnic, November 1978.
134   Interview no. 16.
135   Interview no. 24. See also article by B. Friedrich. 'Parteien als Vermittler zwischen dem europäischen Wähler und der Europäischen Gemeinschaft', *Transnational 8: Europa wählen – der Bund der Sozialdemokratischen Parteien der EG stellt sich vor* (1978). pp. 3–7.
136   Interview no. 97.
137   Interview no. 23.
138   Interview no. 27.
139   Interview no. 87.
140   SPD, *Sozialdemokrat-Magazin* (August 1978).
141   Interview no. 23.
142   For example, the entire Confederation draft programme was reprinted in *Vorwärts* (16 June 1977).
143   *Il Popolo* (3 September 1978).
144   For example. *Comuni d'Europa* (February 1979). monthly of Associazione Unitaria di Comuni. Province, Regioni, reprinted the preambles to the federation programmes. the Socialist Declaration and a declaration by the PCI and PCF.
145   *CDU – Dokumentation,* no. 33 (5 October 1978). p. 5.
146   Talk at Chatham House, London. 17 May 1978.
147   Alois Mock, speech to EDU conference, London. July 1979.
148   EDU conference, July 1979, resolution on European structures. p. 4.
149   *Il Popolo* (30 June 1978).
150   Interview no. 87.
151   Report of Josef Taus, EDU conference, London, July 1979, p. 2.
152   EDU resolution on European structures, July 1979, p. 5.
153   Interviews nos. 64 and 68.
154   Carole Webb, 'Eurocommunism and the European Communities', *Journal of Common Market Studies,* vol. XVII, no. 3 (March 1979), p. 251.
155   Interview in *The Times* (1 February 1977).
156   *L'Unità* (11 September 1978).
157   Giorgio Amendola, *I Comunisti italiani e le elezioni europee* (1978), p. 31.
158   *Panorama* (24 October 1978).
159   Published in *L'Unità* (18 December 1978) and *L'Humanité* (18 December 1978).
160   *Panorama* (19 December 1978).
161   *Corriere della Sera* (28 June 1978).
162   Bureau of Unrepresented European Nations, June 1976.
163   Europe Ecologie, *Souscription nationale pour les elections au Parlement Européen* (1979).
164   *The Economist* (26 May 1979).

4

The National Party Frameworks
and Transnational Party Co-operation

The subject of this chapter is the final, and so far the most important, dimension in the triangular construction of transnational party
co-operation – the individual national parties of the nine Community member states; and how they conditioned the Euro-parliamentary and transnational party-organisational dimensions during
the process of politicisation in the period 1974–9. The distinctive
feature of this period was the growth of the interlinkage between
these three dimensions, which previously had been extremely minimal and, in any case, had not been properly triangular in the
absence of a viable transnational organisational element related
specifically to the EC. This change resulted at the national level
from a more serious attention to transnational links, a greater
readiness to intensify and to institutionalise them and a recognition
of the need to develop them with a more political content in the
light of direct elections and the wider context of politicisation in
the EC, with its stronger recognition that many problems could
only be solved Community-wide.

In other words, this chapter focuses essentially on the 'upward'
vertical transaction of this interlinkage between national and European levels of activity, as distinct from its 'downward' vertical
transaction as represented by the effects of transnational co-operation on the national parties. Since the examination of the latter
aspect in the preceding chapter confirmed the obvious predominance
of the national orientation of political parties over their increasing
European-level activity, with some secondary or minor modifications during the 1974–9 period, the inclusion of the former aspect is
very necessary for completing this study of transnational party
co-operation.

This discussion of the national party frameworks will therefore
consider, as in the preceding chapters, the 'Europeanisation' of party
politics and the party-political 'internalisation' of European politics
as the two broader contextual sides of the same coin of transnational
party co-operation. In doing so, it will consequently draw together

many of the influential features which have conditioned such co-operation, but this time from the national viewpoint. The domestic handling of legislation providing for direct elections as well as national-level preparations in the extenuated pre-campaign period, for instance, occasioned a wider debate about European integration in varying degrees in the member countries, with important implications for the development of party co-operation. Moreover, an examination of the national arena of party politics allows for closer attention to be paid such relevant aspects as the impact of individual party traditions and ideologies, the domestic effects of formulating European programmes, the importance of government or opposition roles, the influence on transnational activity of national inter-party relationships, the relevance of internal party matters and national party organisational structures and the problem of national publics and how far these impinge on party co-operation.

Common to these aspects is the general question of the possible modification of the predominant national orientation of political parties in the member states, on which discussion must again focus in order to complete the picture introduced in the foregoing chapters; although the principal interest in looking at the national party frameworks is to determine specifically and illustrate the ways in which they have influenced or conditioned the development of a more politicised form of transnational co-operation.

There are various methodological difficulties in making a comparative analysis of the national party frameworks in this respect. These all relate to the requirement that any meaningful discussion of transnational co-operation, together with the process towards direct elections and the evolution of party European policies in general (with their increasing overlap into areas of domestic political concern), involves some incursion into wider problems of the national party systems, as indicated by the aspects listed in the previous paragraph. While this itself reflects the politicisation in transnational links, it does present analytical difficulties and could make an examination of the national party frameworks unmanageable. However, this politicisation was still at a relatively early stage during 1974–9 so that it is possible to confine discussion strictly to those categories of determinants of transnational activity issuing from the national party frameworks, and which were introduced as the analytical basis of this study in Chapter 1: the party-traditional factor, the political-functional factor and the socio-political factor (see above, Chapter 1, Section *b*, p. 17 ff.).

Whereas these categories were used in looking at the history of party European policies during the first two decades of European integration up to the 1970s, they will now be applied to the third decade, and particularly to the period of 1974–9, in order to estimate the precise influence of national determinants for progress in European-level party co-operation and thereby estimate how they may have both inhibited and promoted it. At the same time, it is essential not to forget that transnational involvement has usually represented a somewhat peripheral or at best secondary channel of activity for national political parties – so alluding to the limits of politicisation with the absence of a strong power focus in the EP – although this chapter seeks also to spotlight any trends or signs that transnational co-operation has not been easily compartmentalised and has begun to engage wider party interest outside the restricted circles of party leaders and European specialists, especially with the new priority accorded EC policy positions. At a later stage, the study of the national party frameworks will, of course, become increasingly difficult according to the further politicisation of transnational co-operation and its greater scope for broader domestic party involvement in the period following direct elections in 1979.

(a)   The Party-Traditional Factor: Consistency or Readaptation?

It was concluded in the survey of European policies in the 1950s and 1960s that party traditions provided a regular and fundamental determinant of these policies, although only a general indication of reactions by individual parties to particular issues of European integration.* This generalisation was equally true of the period of 1974–9 leading to the first direct elections of the EP, so that the advantage of looking closely at such a period is to identify the salience and intensity of individual party traditions and to note the different manner with which they came to bear. The special relevance of these elections for the present study was that it promoted a greater association of transnational party co-operation in particular with party European policies in general, and thereby compelled political parties in Community states to declare more cogently than before their positions on both.

This consequence of the 1974–9 period was inevitable because direct elections came to be regarded by virtually all parties without exception as an overt political question. Unlike many other EC policy areas, which featured a high technical content (so presenting an intellectual obstacle to sub-élite party involvement), the issue of elections to the EP was from the beginning recognised as a clear and straightforward political matter, whether by pro-integrationist

---

* See above, Chapter 1. Section *b*, p. 17. Party-traditional features include ideology with respect to European integration, long-term policies and party outlooks and internationalist traditions.

parties, who hailed its historical importance for EC development, or by anti-integrationist parties, who implicitly, if not explicitly, did the same by the degree to which they opposed them. Even the most technical aspect of this process – that is, the need to agree on electoral laws for direct elections – aroused controversy in so far as any departure from conventional practice immediately touched on traditional party interests. This was hardly surprising as the question of electoral reform had always occasioned such a reaction (as in West Germany in the late 1960s, and Britain in the mid-1970s). Above all, the issue of direct elections was political – and in some member countries such as France and Britain a hot one – because it acquired a symbolic importance in the eyes of many parties. Thus, the issue of direct elections affected party-traditional outlooks and, in turn, became linked with the exercise of transnational party co-operation. This cause-and-effect situation was only qualified where particular parties did not possess a clear transnational link.

The question of direct elections was treated as symbolic, despite the generally acknowledged institutional weakness of the EP, because it reopened the debate about the future of the European Community as a whole. This fundamental viewpoint provoked the strongest ideological responses and revealed a consistency of traditional party outlooks over the opposing concepts of national sovereignty as against European federalism or supranationality, which, as mentioned in Chapter 1, had throughout the history of European integration been a basic point of reference in distinguishing the pro- and anti-integrationist parties from each other (see above, Chapter 1, Section *b*, pp. 19–20). These concepts were now revived as a matter of political debate with the further issue of extending the official powers of the EP, which became linked with direct elections politically, although constitutionally it was strictly a separate question. Predictably, the Christian Democratic parties displayed the most positive and uncomplicated response. The West German CDU reaffirmed its adherence to the idea of constructing a European federal system, as stated in its Berlin programme of 1971 and its European manifesto of 1976, just as in its *Grundsatzprogramm* of 1978 it spoke of the need to 'complete the historic work of European unification' initiated by Adenauer, Schuman and De Gasperi.[1] The French CDS, the only Christian Democratic party which voiced any federalist reservations, nevertheless showed evidence of a distinctly pro-integrationist outlook consistent with its lineage from the MRP, as in a survey published early in 1979 which revealed overwhelming support among its activists for strengthening the EP's powers, a common European foreign policy and abandoning the unanimity rule in the Council of Ministers.[2]

The relevance of this distinction between pro- and anti-integrationist parties for transnational activity was that there emerged in the course of the 1970s a marked correspondence between their readiness to engage in the latter and their ideological positions on the future of the EC as a 'political system'. Generally, the prospect of direct elections had the effect of reinforcing or intensifying traditional party outlooks on European federalism, in so far as these were essentially ideological, rather than changing them. For example, the German SPD, which had already moved to a pro-integrationist position under Brandt's leadership well before direct elections were seriously anticipated, demonstrated a greater interest in the EP as an institution from the early 1970s because of steps towards EC self-financement and enlargement[3] and proved to be the most active of the Socialist parties in transnational co-operation. In its declaration on direct elections of April 1978, the SPD executive went so far as referring to these as 'an overdue historic event' and recalling the demand in its 1925 Heidelberg Programme for a United States of Europe.[4]

The same correspondence between positions on transnational co-operation and those on integrationist ideology is underlined at the opposite extremity by the attitudes of parties which were basically anti-integrationist. The best example was the British Labour Party because it showed a strong consistency of outlook and, unlike the other anti-integrationist forces (the French Gaullists and Communists and the Danish People's Movement against the EC), it possessed an obvious transnational link in the Socialist Confederation. While the British Labour Party had reversed its negative official policy on Common Market entry under the impact of governmental responsibility in the 1960s, there was still a profound anti-integrationist pattern in the party itself which could be traced back to the 1950s. This trend, which could be described as ideological because integration was viewed widely in the party as being motivated by capitalist considerations and as presenting a potential obstacle to the effecting of socialist policies in Britain, was strengthened with the increased influence of the left in the party after defeat in the 1970 British election. After re-election in 1974, the new Labour government found itself under more consistent pressure than ever before from the party organisation to assume anti-integrationist positions. Such was the ideological motivation behind this line that even the clear confirmation of EC membership in the British referendum of 1975 did not substantially reduce anti-integrationist attitudes throughout the Labour Party, although the lack of public enthusiasm for membership in the following years made the party line more viable. The persistent objections to continued British membership of the EC, let alone further projects for integration (such as the European Monetary System as proposed in 1978), were expressed regularly in the anti-integrationist motions submitted by the national executive to party conferences throughout the 1970s, whereas in the preceding decade the EC had appeared only intermittently as an issue at conferences.[5] Support for this anti-integrationist approach received a powerful new impetus from the introduction of direct elections, against the idea of which the party, as represented by its national executive, struggled determinedly and only eventually agreed to participate in while still rejecting the principle of the elections. The continuous leitmotiv of Labour criticisms of direct elections, of the party's unequivocal rejection of further powers for the EP and of its fundamental objections to the Socialist draft programme alike was the argument that all favoured a move towards European federalism. This fundamental attitude was expressed forcefully in the conference resolution of 1976 (approved by a majority of almost two to one):

> This conference opposes the introduction to Britain of direct elections to the EEC Assembly, for which no mandate was given by the electorate at the time of the referendum. Direct elections are intended as a major step towards the merging of this country in a new super-state, which would further weaken the British people's democratic control over their own affairs and in which the possibility of carrying out the British Labour Party's basic programmes would be increasingly remote.[6]

The British Labour Party was a clear instance of where reluctance to participate in transnational co-operation – it boycotted membership of the Socialist Confederation until 1976, and even then continued to refuse collaboration in drafting the common programme – was a logical result of its anti-integrationist ideology and was followed in a manner somewhat exclusive of other considerations. With other comparable examples, the connection between transnational and European policy positions was present, though clouded by ambiguity because of the influence of political-functional determinants. The Danish Social Democratic Party basically opposed the idea of 'European union' (meaning federalism), although the particular position it took over direct elections was a cautious one choosing to emphasise the need for maintaining democratic control over EC decisions through the Folketing.[7] Its principled opposition to federalism did, however, appear in its reluctance to agree with relevant passages in the Confederation draft programme, although this was less publicly aired than in the case of the British Labour Party since the Danish 'S' leadership was less affected by anti-integrationist attitudes than its broad membership.

With the French Gaullists and Communists, the principle of

national sovereignty was upheld flamboyantly for different ideological reasons, but it had no important impact on their transnational co-operation since in neither case was a viable transnational link available. The PCF, like the pro-integrationist PCI, had no intentions of institutionalising their co-operation outside the EP (see above, Chapter 3, Section *d*, pp. 168–70), while the Gaullist RPR showed no interest in extending organisationally its Euro-parliamentary group membership with the Irish Fianna Fail, which had, in any case, no convincing ideological basis. However, it is instructive to mention these two cases because they underline once more the consistency of ideological attitudes on European integration as these reappeared over the issue of direct elections, all the more as domestic controversy over it in France recalled the political debate over the European Defence Community (EDC) in 1954.[8]

The traditional factor was underlined in the RPR's case by its explicit adherence to General de Gaulle's conception of European unity as in its manifesto for direct elections, which under the electoral banner of 'Defence of the Interests of France in Europe' (DIFE – the name adopted by the RPR for direct elections) stressed French national independence in a 'really European' Europe, attacked the bureaucratic 'mechanisms' of the EC and signs of US influence and asserted in an accompanying document that 'our attitude with regard to Europe is inscribed in the tradition of Gaullism'.[9] This traditionalist ideology on integration (it formed the conceptual basis of the RPR's European policy and represented widely held beliefs throughout the party) was not reflected in an outright hostility to direct elections, partly because of the constraints of its governmental relationship with the Giscardians but also with its own internal divisions over the issue it had to take a mildly ambiguous position – it did not reject direct elections as such, but continued to proclaim the threat to national sovereignty from a stronger EP. In its purest form, this traditionalist outlook was articulated by Michel Debré, de Gaulle's first Prime Minister, who became prominent in campaigning on the issue of protection of national sovereignty, arguing that direct elections were incompatible with the 1958 French constitution and that an upgraded EP would amount to 'a crime against the nation' and he formed a 'Committee for the Independence and Unity of France' to promote his ideas.[10]

The anti-integrationist ideology of the PCF was reflected in the hostile stand it took, for most of the period under discussion, on direct elections, although its position was modified by the need to compromise with the PS in the Union of the Left (once European elections became a firm likelihood) and by its own decision not to boycott them. Following its official opposition to the principle of direct elections announced in 1974, the PCF had continued to trumpet an emotive line on the issue, arguing that a directly elected EP would be, in the words of Marchais, a 'betrayal of France' and become an 'instrument' of German–US dominance in Europe. Despite Marchais's modified position in his declaration of April 1977 that he 'might contemplate' supporting direct elections (if there were an undertaking they would not entail strengthening the EP), the PCF did not refrain from taking an anti-integrationist line in the assertion of its national parliamentary group that 'there is no democracy where there is supranationality' (December 1978) and in attacking the European Commission's information campaign as 'an inadmissible interference by a foreign institution in French politics' (November 1978).[11] At the same time, the PCF stressed the importance of direct elections in providing an occasion for mobilising its activists against the proposed enlargement of the EC which was 'contrary to the interests of workers and the nation' (declaration of PCF political bureau, July 1978).[12]

In other words, there was evidence that the politicisation effects of direct elections on individual parties, while reflecting their general ideological positions on integration, resulted in certain ambiguities among those which were anti-integrationist when it came to participating in them. Hardly any of the latter, including fringe parties, chose specifically to ignore the European elections – the anti-integrationist Dutch, Irish and West German Communist parties (none of which had any prospect at all of a seat in the EP) all decided to use this event to expose the 'reactionary character' of the EC.[13] It was interesting, therefore, to record how the main anti-integrationist parties justified their decision to participate in direct elections and press for strong representation in the EP. The British Labour Party reiterated in its 1977 conference resolution its opposition to direct elections but, in the light of their taking place, argued that 'we do not wish to let the mounting feeling of dissatisfaction with the EEC go unrepresented at the Strasbourg Assembly',[14] and decided to campaign on a programme of radical change in the EC. The PCF stated more specifically that whether direct elections would be the 'springboard' for 'the Europe of austerity, unemployment and supranationality' or a 'fulcrum for the struggle of workers and peoples' depended on the result and especially on the size of Communist votes.[15] In the eyes of the Gaullists, their participation in direct elections was on the grounds that successful candidates would not be European deputies but 'representatives of each country at the European Assembly' and that those of the RPR would be 'charged with defending the interests of France in Europe'.[16] As a final example, the Danish People's Movement against the EC had decided after much internal debate over the matter to campaign because, in the words of one spokesman, 'we had to demonstrate the resistance in Denmark, and create an obstacle to too many pro-EC people in the European Parliament'.[17] While couched in different party-political terminology, all forms of justification had in common a protest role which they sought to play from within the EP. If carried into effect, this was likely to contribute to political conflict there.

By comparison, pro-integrationist parties – the major parties in Italy can be included in addition to those already mentioned – found no basic problem in confronting the issue and participating in arrangements for direct elections, unlike the anti-integrationist parties, which were torn between their ideological opposition to further integration (direct elections being seen as another stage in this direction) and their compelling need to respond to this event. These patterns of behaviour were repeated in their participation, or lack of it, in transnational co-operation (as shown in Chapter 3, notably over the formulation of common programmes), and were a basic determinant of the latter because such co-operation could not be detached from the symbolic importance of direct elections.

Having concentrated on those cases where ideological positions on integration, whether positive or negative were strongly held, this discussion, however, cannot avoid the fact that ideology is not always easily distinguishable from other shades of party attitudes and traditions (such as the looser form of party 'belief systems' and long-term policy lines), that many parties cannot be described as holding an ideological position on European integration as such, and that where parties are ideological towards integration their actual positions assumed over direct elections and transnational activity were not a straightforward reflection of their ideology on integration because of internal divisions over this. These three aspects will now be examined.

Taking the first two aspects together, it becomes apparent that, while applying essentially to parties which were ideologically or pragmatically pro-integrationist, these aspects help to explain their differences of attitude and behaviour in the area of European policy with evident implications for their transnational activity. Thus, the Christian Democratic parties were ideologically pro-integrationist, as for them European unity had from their early postwar years been one of their principal common beliefs, but the intensity of their conviction here was limited by their not being ideologically based parties in the sense that Socialist or Communist parties, in espousing systematic doctrinal beliefs, were. Consequently, their blanket approval of integration, shared as it was by their whole parties, tended not to stimulate real internal party debate as opposed to parties which were ideologically anti-integrationist but also divided; and, equally, participation in transnational co-operation posed no problems of conscience for Christian Democrats and was readily adopted by their 'belief systems'. Specific policy outlooks – such as the CDU's antagonism towards popular fronts, and the CSU's over-whelming priority to European security matters – did, of course, reappear within the transnational context. Such differentiation was even more apparent among non-Christian Democratic but pro-integrationist parties. The German SPD has been categorised as ideologically pro-integrationist, but this should not be simply stated without noting that such a position resulted from its change of basic policy course from the end of the 1950s: the SPD even asserted in the report of 1975 from its European policy commission that a more democratic EC structure would provide an outlet for 'the aim of achieving democratic Socialism through reforms in the sense of the Godesberg Programme'.[18]

Other parties could be described as pragmatically pro-integra-tionist, as they clearly did not favour European federalism and had adopted a positive position in European policy following a long-term policy preference by their leaders in government. An obvious case was the British Conservative policy since 1961, which came to see itself as 'European' despite party traditions of patriotism and an attachment to national sovereignty. *The Right Approach*, a state-ment of Conservative aims published in 1976, indicated in its section on the European Community:

> Our view is that those who want it to succeed would do well to concentrate on what is practical and what is attainable. But, while it is not sensible to set Utopian and unreal targets, we do need to recognise that there are many problems, beyond the range of national governments, which can best be dealt with on a Euro-pean level.[19]

This was, if anything, a pragmatic statement, but it was often dif-ficult to disentangle pragmatic lines of policy from ideological motivation if noting at the same time the Conservatives' distinct anti-Socialist interest as reflected in their transnational activity and their pursuit of a centre-right alliance. The French Giscardian Parti Républicain may be considered similarly as pragmatic in that, while broadly pro-integrationist from the time of its founding as the FNRI in 1966 (though supporting a looser European confederation rather than federation), its line of European policy followed that of its leader, Giscard d'Estaing. It did not, for example, formulate any position on direct elections until the new French President made his initiative on that issue in 1974, while its approach to transnational party co-operation was marked by a certain pragmatic flexibility *vis-à-vis* the strong pro-integrationist line of its fellow Liberal parties in the ELD.

Looking at the third aspect of internal party divisions over European policy, it followed from the earlier discussion that these were most likely to appear in the case of parties which had ideological reservations about integration. As a stronger determinant than the first two aspects in affecting the actual progress of transnational co-operation as well as to some extent in promoting internal party involvement over it, internal divisions will be treated more fully. From the mid-1970s, these divisions as ideological ones became more pronounced with the need to prepare for direct elections, whether at the level of transnational co-operation (on which they had direct repercussions) or domestically over legislation on the principle of these elections or implementing arrangements for them. The chief examples were, apart from the Gaullist RPR, among the Socialist parties, which provides a further explanation of the difficulties encountered by the Socialist Confederation in trying to harmonise the activities of its member parties for European elections (see above, Chapter 3, Section *c*, pp. 145–8). With the French PCF, the operative principle of democratic centralism did not allow for ideological divisions over integration to appear, if they existed at all.

Among those Socialist parties divided over integration, the main line of internal conflict was along traditional left/right cleavages, as had been so before the 1970s (see above, Chapter 1, Section *b*, pp. 11, 20). This was markedly so in the British Labour Party and also evident in the Danish 'S' among those mentioned earlier as examples; but also true of other national parties like the French PS, constituted as a new party in 1971 with a strong left-wing (especially the CERES, the Centre for Study, Research and Socialist Education, an internal pressure group, which took an anti-integrationist line comparable to that of the PCF), and the Dutch PvdA, whose traditional pro-integrationist outlook was modified by the growing internal influence of a critical younger generation of leaders originating from the New Left of the late 1960s. These examples taken in turn all illustrate that, while these divisions derived essentially from the national political environment, they were accentuated by the new priority given to European policy in the 1974–9 period and accordingly influenced the behaviour of individual parties in the transnational framework.

British Labour's traditional left/right divisions over the EC from the leadership downwards were again reflected in the voting patterns of the party's MPs during the 1976–8 parliamentary sessions over direct elections legislation (for example, they split 132 for and 124 against in the second reading in July 1977). This deep division, together with the pervasive influence of the anti-integrationists and

the habitual concern of the party leader (from Gaitskell to Callaghan) for maintaining party unity at the cost of European initiatives,
meant that any involvement in the (for Labour) new transnational
activity was regarded unenthusiastically, if not with suspicion. Hence,
Labour boycotted the EP from 1973 to 1975 as well as the Socialist
Confederation, although it changed its position on both after the
1975 referendum. By the late 1970s, the growing power of the left
in the party organisation had begun to show in its greater interest
in transnational activity as an additional channel for controlling
party policy lines, as illustrated by Tony Benn's own participation
in Confederation activities from 1978, the dominant NEC role in
determining Labour's direct elections manifesto and in preparing
and organising the campaign and in the NEC's nagging concern
that the provision of European finance for research facilities for its
MEPs 'might lead to a competitive bureaucracy in Brussels which
might formulate different policies from those in London'.[20]

While less pronouncedly ideological, a similar divisiveness over
integration occurred along clear left/right lines in the Danish 'S',
where internal differences over prospective EC entry had begun to
appear from 1968 encouraged by activist mobilisation over the
separate Vietnam issue, so that at the time of the 1972 referendum
on Denmark's membership this question became hotly contested
within the party. Unlike the British party, where division over integration was present from top to bottom in the party structure, the
main division in the S over this question was between its pragmatic
leadership which dominated in government and the left-wing among
the activist body. In this particular respect, the division had a left/
right perspective, as a party European specialist noted:

> Some people like to be considered as Left-wing, and in doing so
> they automatically accept that they have to have a particular
> attitude towards the European Community. It's not the other way
> round . . . you have to find something to distinguish yourself from
> the others, and this EC/anti-EC issue has been used for that, and
> that to a certain extent maintains that issue.[21]

Despite this lack of profundity among anti-EC activists in the 'S',
the pressure of this attitude helped to constrain the role of the
party leadership in its transnational activity – all the more as the
former had the backdrop of public scepticism over the EC. Membership of the Confederation was not itself disputed in the 'S', but,
according to the same interviewee, 'we do stress that the Confederation of course is not a European party . . . just an organisation where
independent parties collaborate with each other – so it hasn't been
an issue at all.[22]

With the French and Dutch Socialist parties, the left/right internal divide over integration proved a significant, if not powerful, determinant of their transnational behaviour, although their own differences here did reflect divergent party traditions as a whole over the EC. The French PS has since its founding followed a distinctly different course on the EC from its predecessor, the strongly pro-integrationist SFIO, which had declined in the 1960s from a position of prominence under the Fourth Republic. Its departure from this traditional stand related to the composition of the new party with its merger of old SFIO elements and left-Liberal and especially Socialist groups in addition to the need following its alliance with the PCF to establish fresh policy positions. The PS from the beginning supported direct elections and never contested membership of the Confederation, but its own lack of internal cohesion has inevitably affected its positions taken on integration, with the Rocard–Mauroy wing pro-integrationist (Rocard himself chairing one of the Confederation's four working groups on the draft programme), the CERES anti-integrationist and Mitterrand with the remainder of the party verbally pro-integrationist but ambiguous in practice.[23] This internal conflict, which surfaced, for instance, with pressure from the CERES to make the party's manifesto for direct elections less 'Social Democratic',[24] inevitably rebounded on the PS's role within the Confederation. According to one of the party's active figures in that organisation, transnational co-operation

> is becoming a very important issue in our internal debate, both because this co-operation is becoming more instrumental and because the PS itself has developed a more nationalist position over the last few years... As a result, we are seeing Europe becoming an essential issue within the party debate. The CERES has refused to vote our European programme, has refused to vote the Confederation texts – the Declaration of Brussels and the Appeal...[25]

The Dutch PvdA witnessed, like the Danish 'S', the rise of a younger-generational activist left within its ranks which similarly challenged the traditional pro-integrationist line of the party (as in its repeated demands in the past for direct elections). There was hardly any real discussion of integration within the party until the earlier 1970s, when a new generation of party activists politicised by the student movement of the late 1960s began to make its presence felt, voicing criticism of Holland's membership of NATO and of the EC, as well as proposing more strongly Socialist solutions on a variety of socio-economic issues. At the 1974 party congress traditional positions on NATO and the EC were for the first time called into question by a strong minority, while from the mid-1970s integration acquired growing attention within the party.[26] What is significant is that domestic policy concerns intermixed very definitely with attitudes towards the EC on the part of the new left-wing, in that integration was viewed within the wider scope of Holland's role in the capitalist system and therefore from a distinct ideological standpoint. At the party congress in early 1977, the motion was put (but not carried) that the PvdA should not participate in direct elections, although once these elections became certain the attentions of the left-wing groups turned to the content of the Socialist Confederation's draft programme. Objections were made on a variety of items, such as nuclear energy, the environment, aid to developing countries and the problem of democracy in the EC. On the last point, the idea of more power for the Community institutions aroused hostility because, in the words of one of the left-wing activist leaders

> we want to defend the possibility of our own parliament, our own government, to regulate things; because we have no confidence in what kind of politics or policy will follow when the European institutions get more power; because we think that a more Conservative, more Liberal, more capitalistic view will win; and that the grip of the powers that are against such a development are weaker on the European level than on a national level.[27]

While this viewpoint shared common ground with the left of the British Labour Party, the critical line in the PvdA did not, however, make an issue of national sovereignty, nor did it stress national interests chauvinistically.

It was significant, too, for the impact of transnational activity on the national parties that energies critical of the EC in the PvdA were channelled through increased participation of the membership to an extent greater than in any of the other Socialist parties in Community states. This, of course, reflected the more open state of internal party democracy in the Dutch case, although evidently the process towards direct elections helped to reinforce this. By 1977, there had crystallised three differentiated groups within the PvdA: long-standing or traditional pro-integrationists, including both older-generational leaders (like the ex-Prime Minister, Joop den Uyl, and the parliamentary president, Anne Vondeling) and younger pro-integrationist parliamentarians like the active MEP, Schelto Patijn; sceptics who were not convinced by pro-integrationist answers to the demand for democracy in the EC; and anti-integrationist or sceptical groups who voiced opposition on Socialist ideological grounds.[28] It was the third group which had been active proponents of the new critical line, which, while remaining a minority, was nevertheless influential enough to help modify the party position on European policy. This process of internal party involvement in the PvdA revolved round the discussion of the Confederation's draft programme, and culminated in a special congress on the subject in February 1978. The draft was debated widely among 500–600 local branches and, although only about a quarter of them proposed amendments, this was the first time that European policy had become a matter of active concern at the grass roots.[29] A special congress discussed and debated many of the amendments collated from those submitted to the party executive by the branches, and the modified version of the Confederation's draft eventually became the official programme of the PvdA for European elections.

The internal divisions in the Gaullist RPR posed a different case because its anti-integrationist ideology was personalistic, involving loyalty to the policy concepts of the party's historical father figure rather than being related to doctrinal beliefs in other policy areas. For the party as a whole, the term 'federalism' had provocative implications, but there emerged internal differences over the specific issue of direct elections with a small minority favouring these (including older leaders like Chaban-Delmas and Olivier Guichard, not to mention various Gaullist MEPs) in line with a 'Liberal' interpretation of Gaullism which drew them to the European policy of Giscard. Diametrically opposed in sympathy were the ultra-traditionalists led by Debré who, aroused to anger by the Tindemans report on European Union of 1976, virtually rejected direct elections, but they were also a minority in that they represented a rigid interpretation of Gaullist traditions. These internal differences over the issue threatened party unity at times, so that Chirac was forced to try and maintain cohesion by pressing for postponement of French ratification of the EC agreement on direct elections while voicing traditionalist Gaullist rhetoric in warning about supranational tendencies.[30] As a consequence, the exclusive preoccupation of the RPR leadership became the maintenance of party unity on this issue, not to mention their competitive prestige *vis-à-vis* Giscard d'Estaing, so that the very subject of transnational links seemed from their point of view an irrelevant diversion.

Looking overall at party ideology as it has been interpreted over integration – especially concerning the opposing concepts of European federalism and national sovereignty, which tended to flush out distinct basic attitudes where they existed – and at the three ways just discussed in which such ideology could be qualified, it becomes clear that the issue of direct elections with its accompanying galvanising effects on transnational party co-operation forced individual parties to define their positions on the EC more concretely or more elaborately than ever before. This new priority given to their European policies by parties was, of course, most evident in the need to formulate programmes or manifestoes for direct elections, which has already been discussed with regard to the common programmes of the European party federations in Chapter 3 but deserves further mention in the national context.

The main point worth emphasising is that political parties were required in the vast majority of cases to formulate proper European programmes for the first time in their histories. Few parties had done so before direct elections became a serious proposition in the 1970s (see above, Chapter 1, Section *b*, p. 16). This necessity of defining their European policies in the form of special programmes on the EC was also true of parties outside the federations, as it was of those operating within them, including the member parties of the Socialist Confederation which, in the absence of a finalised common programme, produced their own individual programmes for direct elections. The German FDP outlined its European policy for the first time in a document arising from its congress at Mainz in October 1975[31] – where the Community had been the main subject with statements being issued on specific EC issues, as distinct from the dutiful and vague discourses on Europe which had characterised previous party congresses[32] – even before it participated in formulating the common programme of the ELD.

This general absence previously of separate European policy programmes was equally applicable to parties ideologically pro-integrationist as much as others. The West German CDU, as an example of the former, never attempted to formulate its overall policy on the EC as such before the 1970s. In January 1972, the CDU/CSU *Fraktion* issued a short action programme on the EC inspired by a desire to promote further progress in integration;[33] then in 1976 the CDU published its European Manifesto as part of the proceedings of its congress held at Hanover in May of that year.[34] Among the Socialist parties, the SPD showed a strong increase in policy interest in the EC during this period, particularly with the long report of its European policy commission of 1975, which was introduced as a contribution by the party to the formulation of a common programme in the Confederation.[35] All other Socialist parties eventually followed with their own individual programmes for direct elections: the French PS in October 1978, the Irish Labour Party at its special conference in December 1978 and the British Labour Party in February 1979, to mention a few. The general-secretary of the Luxemburg Socialist Workers' Party (POSL) summarised this change when he said that his party had for the occasion of direct elections adopted a specific European programme for the very first time, although it had always had a section on foreign policy (including the EC) in its general programmes.[36]

Just as there was a certain overlap between European and domestic issues in the work on the federation programmes (see above, Chapter 3, Section *c*, p. 142), so this tendency was even more marked in the individual national programmes. The Deniau Report published in February 1979 as the programme of the Union for French Democracy (UDF) (the alliance of the Republican Party, the CDS and the Radical Socialist Party in support of President Giscard d'Estaing) included sections on the family, consumers, health, protection of the environment and youth and sport in a European setting, as well as such EC concerns as monetary policy, energy and agriculture.[37] More precisely, the Irish Labour Party opened its programme with the assertion that the Community 'is now a part of the normal life of any citizen of any of the nine member states',[38] while even the campaign handbook of the British Labour Party commented similarly: 'As membership of the EEC increasingly affects our lives in Britain, it becomes more difficult to talk about "Common Market policy" in isolation.'[39]

What this exercise in European policy formulation in particular, and direct elections in general, illustrated was the need to redefine, re-examine or merely confirm as well as declare basic positions with reference to the Community institutional framework, and this in turn conditioned the readiness of parties to engage in transnational activity. This process invariably touched on some aspect of individual party identity, as all basic policy reappraisals tend to do. Party identity is, of course, central to the question of the party-traditional factor, and may be examined most relevantly in this context by looking at the general internationalist traditions of parties concerned. This feature applies to most political parties, except where they are unique to a particular country or so new as not to have developed such a tradition (as with the Danish Progress Party, the French Giscardians and regionalist parties), and is an important addition to applying the ideological test to party positions on integration. Notably, activity geared to direct elections involved a narrowing of focus on the EC with respect to international relations in the broad sense, and therefore provided a pointer to the readiness by individual parties to engage seriously in transnational party activity.

It was noted at the beginning of this study that, whereas Christian Democratic parties tended as new postwar formations to be more Euro-centric, parties of the left – both Socialist and Communist – with their longer-standing traditions embraced a wider internationalism because of their identity as party of world-wide international movements (see above, Chapter 1, Section *b*, p. 13). Despite the growth over the preceding two decades of a broad party-political consensus about the basic value of European integration, this difference of orientation did reappear somewhat as a result of the politicisation during the period 1974–9. The Communist parties had evidenced the greatest difficulty in redefining their international activity within the EC context, although the PCI did so most successfully and found no problems in espousing direct elections. The PCF, on the other hand, found it virtually impossible to marry its internationalist traditions with full and unreserved participation in integration activity. Just before direct elections, it declared that it had been 'since its first steps soaked in internationalism' which above all arose from its 'active support for the young and fragile October Revolution', that it was 'anchored to the history of the European working-class movement', and that it had a 'legitimate pride' in its role in the International Brigades during the Spanish Civil War and in the anti-Nazi Resistance during the German occupation of France.[40] In short, although much of the PCF's internationalist tradition related to European history, this was, as the basis of its identity, expressed in negative tones towards the EC for ideological reasons. The smaller Communist parties in EC member states were similar to the French party in their reluctance to commit themselves specifically to the EC framework. The British Communist Party, for example, drew a distinction between 'real' internationalism and the '*supra*-nationalism' designed by the Community.[41]

Among the Socialist parties, their wide internationalist outlook was reflected in *Euso*, the publicity organ of their Euro-parliamentary group, with its inclusion of international issues of a global concern (see above, Chapter 3, Section *c*, p. 142); however, the adaptation by many of these parties to the EC framework well before direct elections, specifically from the original six member states, did mean they had no major problems in developing their transnational activity in the Community once it became more politicised from 1974. The Irish Labour Party was a further example, from one of the new member states, of a party which fully participated in its federation once national entry to the EC was assured, having reversed its previous critical position following the Irish referendum. Its earlier objections had been expressed in its conference resolution of 1971 that, although 'internationalist in its outlook', it held deep reservations about 'the philosophy, *modus operandi* and institutions of the EC', while indicating an interest in the possibility that a further enlarged EC and one moving 'in the direction of a united democratic Europe' would be 'of immense significance in East/West relations, especially in a European détente'.[42]

The most difficult case of marrying its internationalist position with the new emphasis on European policy was the British Labour Party, which in its own words is an internationalist party, and sincerely believes in greater co-operation and unity of action between Socialist forces throughout the world – and not just in part of Western Europe. But a belief in internationalism does not in any way imply an acceptance of the supra-nationalism of the EEC, nor does it imply a subjugation of the legitimate national interests of individual states.[43]

This strong insistence on broad internationalism was reflected, for instance, in the special attention accorded the Third World in the Labour Party's programme for direct elections, and, so far as trans-national activity was concerned, in the comment of one of its anti-integrationist leaders that the Socialist Confederation was 'a form of blockism, of regional nationalism'.[44] In other words, Labour's ideological reservations about the EC were buttressed by its parti-cular internationalist outlook.

With the other political movements in member states there were far fewer problems of according internationalist outlook with EC-oriented transnational activity, because the former was less speci-fically geared to the wider world and also less expressed in an organised form. The Christian Democrats, for the aforementioned reason of their Euro-centricity, encountered no basic difficulty here because their own internationalist position was rooted in the concept of European unity, although there were some variations within this approach. In the case of three Dutch parties, the Catholic People's Party (KVP) had a stronger background of Euro-pean confessional links than the Protestant ARP (Anti-Revolu-tionary Party) and CHU (Christian Historical Union) because, of course, the Dutch Protestant Churches were national, unlike the Catholic Church, although all three retained some wider inter-nationalist outlook deriving from Holland's historical commercial relationships outside Europe.[45] With other parties of the centre-right the adaptation to the EC framework presented no conflict with their internationalist traditions. For the two Danish parties – the Con-servative People's Party and the Centre Democrats – EC member-ship had from the beginning been seen in the same light as Denmark's participation in NATO with the priority given to main-taining 'a free Denmark' in their position on integration.[46] The Liberal parties in the EC countries had less coherent internationalist traditions compared with other political movements, which made it easier for them to adapt to transnational activity, especially as their enhanced prestige and visibility deriving from this more than counterbalanced any reservations they might have held. Only the British Liberal Party had, despite its pro-integrationist position, expressed reservations about the idea of establishing a party federa-tion when the idea was first muted, but this merely revealed a concern at being excluded at a time when British membership of the EC was not yet secured.[47]

A special feature of the international side of party traditions was the development over time of bilateral or multilateral relations with other individual parties, for they provided some indication of party identity in relation to other national forces of the same ideology. Such relations differed qualitatively from transnational activity, because they involved not integrative but loose or *ad hoc* co-operation between two (bilateral) or more than two (multilateral) parties, but they provided an important though subsidiary addition to the former. These relations had traditionally taken the form of mutual visits between different national party leaders for purposes of information, socialisation and solidarity (for example, invitations to speak at the other party's congress), but had rarely attracted much attention. In the 1970s they came to have a more relevant, though indirect, bearing on transnational party co-operation, because they also were subject to the politicisation of party links: they became more regular and less *ad hoc*, were broadened to include party officials and not just the top leadership, as had normally been the case, and they began to attract more publicity. In looking at the closer interlinkage between such contacts as a background factor and transnational activity, various questions are relevant. What were the effects of the politicisation of bilateral/multilateral relations on transnational co-operation? Did they help to solidify this co-operation or produce divisiveness within it? And did these relations represent more ideological or national points of sympathy relations represent more ideological or national points of sympathy or convergence? These questions overlap and may be answered together with regard to four characteristics of bilateral/multilateral links.

The first characteristic of the 1974–9 period is that the practice of bilateral/multilateral contacts was adopted more widely, becoming thereby less 'spontaneous' and more functional. In the past, only some of the parties in EC states had sought to foster this ancillary activity, notably larger parties in line with their internationalist traditions so far as these applied to the European context. Now smaller parties, those new to the transnational scene and also new parties followed suit. Sometimes contacts remained sparse, based essentially on the Euro-parliamentary link, although they could refer to a common tradition, such as those between British and Danish Conservatives (not to mention other Scandinavian parties), going back to the 1950s, but which became more regular because of their sharing a common group in the EP from 1973, although largely confined to exchange visits between MEPs from both countries.[48] The British Conservative Party under Margaret Thatcher was assiduous in cultivating bilateral party links from 1975 in conjunction with its policy of seeking a centre-right alliance which eventually bore fruit in the EDU. For the first time, the motive behind party links was discussed seriously at a Conservative conference in October 1975, when the party spokesman on foreign affairs, Reginald Maudling, emphasised the need 'to defend ourselves against the power of the Socialists within the European Parliament'.[49] There followed a series of party visits abroad by Margaret Thatcher, such as to Germany in 1976 to address the CDU congress in Hanover, to Rome in 1977 to promote relations with the DC, and to speak at the Spanish UCD congress at Madrid in October 1978. Closer contacts were furthered with the French Gaullists but above all with the West German CDU, which, following Helmut Kohl's visit to London in July 1976, led to a formal agreement between the two parties on a regular exchange between party administrators.[50] According to a British Conservative official involved in these inter-party relations,

> there is a closeness between ourselves and the CDU . . . the levels of thinking and co-operation, interchange of personnel. A lot of people have gone in recent months from this country over to conferences and meetings organised by the CDU; and certain people from CDU headquarters are regular visitors here. So, the interchange between people as well as ideas had been very considerable.[51]

This intensification of the bilateral link between the British party and the CDU was an important background factor in the moves towards founding the EDU (see above, Chapter 3, Section *d*, pp. 164–8).

The second characteristic of bilateral/multilateral links is that they were influenced by general politicisation in the EC during the same period. This emerged over the growing attention to 'Eurocommunism', of which one smaller feature was the attempt by the PCI to cultivate bilateral contacts with parties of the moderate left, notably the British Labour Party and the SPD. In Britain the PCI had for long maintained informed links with Marxist groups, but contacts began to develop slowly with the Labour Party at the informal personal level so that PCI representatives were invited to attend the party conferences in 1977 and 1978. Relations between the PCI and the SPD had begun at the end of the 1960s and became more regular but informal exchanges of views between party representatives, but were not made official because of the need for discretion on the German side and the likelihood of domestic anti-Communist repercussions.[52] These contacts hardly had any immediate bearing on transnational activity, although they were viewed by the PCI as in line with its aim of a united European left.

In one other way politicisation in the Community had a more direct effect on bilateral/multilateral links and, in turn, on transnational co-operation – the prospect, which became definite during this period, of further EC enlargement to include Greece, Spain and Portugal, with the encouragement this gave to party co-operation. Links with ideological partners in the applicant countries developed apace after the end of dictatorships in all three cases during 1974–5, anticipating and preparing for the eventual inclusion of new member parties in the federations from the early 1980s. The West German parties played the key role here with their superior organisational and financial resources. Uppermost in their thinking was their particular emphasis on the need to promote and strengthen democracy throughout Western Europe, a primary motive of theirs in their unreserved commitment to direct elections and involvement in transnational activity.

During the latter half of the 1970s these links became most firmly established between the respective Socialist parties of Spain and Portugal (contacts with Greece were complicated by a dispute about with which of the two Socialist parties to ally) and the SPD and, to some lesser extent, the French PS and Italian PSI. Regular visits took place bilaterally between Brandt, who was the leading SPD figure in this respect, Felipe Gonzalez of the Spanish Socialist PSOE and Mario Soares of the Portuguese PSP. These personal relations became very close and had from the beginning been supplemented by SPD financial assistance for both parties including, in the PSOE's case, help in training party functionaries and arrangements for holding meetings on German soil even before Franco's death opened the way for its full participation in Spanish domestic politics.[53] In the 1977 Spanish elections the SPD provided the PSOE with much campaign material, and early the following year some common working groups on the role of parliaments and bilateral aid were set up between the two parties.[54] On the Portuguese side, the PSP was originally founded with support from the SPD and given further encouragement by a committee chaired by Brandt and set up in autumn 1975 under the auspices of the Socialist International to promote democracy and socialism in Portugal through solidarity meetings and fund-raising.[55] One unspoken motive of the SPD was to strengthen the Socialist parties *vis-à-vis* the Communists in both countries; while by contrast the interest taken by the French PS in the subject was coloured by its desire to seek international credibility for the model of its own alliance with a strong Communist party (the same problem arising in both applicant countries). A similar interest was shown by the West German CDU/CSU in links with fraternal parties in Spain and Portugal[56] and exchange visits were arranged between party representatives, but there was less systematic progress than with the Socialists because their common ideological bond was complicated by the existence of a variety of possible partner parties – some more conservative, others more Christian Democratic – and a consequent dispute between the CDU and CSU over which were the more appropriate allies.[57] Among the EC Liberals there was much less activity in this direction for the problem of locating the relevant ideological partner proved more difficult.[58] In general, the promotion of these links in southern Europe, especially among the Socialists, prepared the way for the geographical broadening of transnational co-operation.

The third characteristic of bilateral/multilateral links was that in the 1974–9 period they began to dovetail more closely with transnational activity itself. This appeared in the work of the party federations as these promoted closer association between individual parties. An important illustration of this was the relationship between the German SPD and the French PS, which had some background of bilateral contacts with these becoming more regular during the mid-1970s, especially through mutual visits between Brandt and Mitterrand. However, among the member parties of the Socialist Confederation these two were virtually at opposite ends of its internal ideological span. This ideological difference started to express itself more pointedly during 1975–6 over the issue of relations with Communist parties and came to a head with the *Berufsverbot* question (see above, Chapter 3, Section *c*, pp. 156, 157, leading to bitter relations for a time. Undoubtedly, their closer partnership in the Confederation helped to bring this conflict to the surface, but this equally demanded an amicable solution. A turning-point in their bilateral relations came in the spring of 1976 when their own differences were openly discussed at the leadership level and the initiative was taken to form three common working groups on the Third World, socio-economic questions and the future of European integration, composed of senior party representatives and Euro-experts.[59] The problem of relations with Communist parties was essentially side-stepped and discussed only 'insofar as it is an important subject in French politics'. The collapse of the French Union of the Left later in the following year in any case reduced that as an area of conflict, so that since then SPD/PS relations steadily became more cordial and provided one of the mainstays of general co-operation within the Confederation. This case study showed how the transnational framework could both induce bilateral friction and require a necessary solution to such differences.

While, therefore, bilateral or multilateral relations could provide additional cement to transnational party co-operation, there was another phenomenon within it of subgroup relations, especially among smaller parties. This began to appear as a trend with their desire to assert their common interests *vis-à-vis* the larger parties within the federations. There was, of course, some tradition of informal consultation between parties from the Benelux states, mostly developed by the relevant socialist parties but also present in a more casual way among the Christian Democrats. With the former, these trilateral contacts even went back to the prewar years, while during the postwar period they had been continued, though at times intermittently.[60] Usually they had taken place at the level of party leaders, but during the later 1970s they began to involve lower levels of the party structures, including common meetings between local branches and weekend colloquia for interested representatives from the respective parties.[61] There was also the idea of enlarging the Benelux group of Socialist parties to include those from other smaller EC states, such as Denmark and Ireland.[62] The reason for this was the greater commitment to political action within the Confederation, as one Danish Socialist representative explained:

> There is more interest in developing contacts with other parties in order to decrease your degree of isolation in the Confederation . . . within the Confederation, you can easily see that some parties because they are bigger have better opportunities of having contacts with other parties. The smaller parties if they didn't do enough for themselves would be relatively more isolated than the bigger parties; so the smaller parties certainly try to develop their mutual contacts. Of course, the big ones are doing it all the time – at least, the Germans and the French.[63]

The leader of the Dutch PvdA similarly emphasised that such co-operation between Socialist parties from smaller countries was being organised 'so that we are not dominated in an absolute way by the parties from the greater countries', and that such co-operation was new but had already led on the initiative of the PvdA to preparatory consultations before executive meetings of the Confederation bringing 'representatives from those parties together to organise our attitude in the meetings'.[64]

The fourth and final characteristic of bilateral/multilateral links during this time is that the element of ideological sympathy which underlay them was often reinforced by national motives, in the sense that traditional relations between different countries affected such links. The ideological and national factors were not necessarily exclusive of each other, and in some cases helped to complement each other. The co-operation between Benelux parties clearly reflected the special relationship between these three countries since the Second World War; similarly, the Franco-German relationship as the main axis within the development of the EC had been a further aspect urging reconciliation between the PS and SPD, although this relationship was less evident among the Christian Democrats because of the fringe role of the French CDS compared with the German CDU/CSU. Among the Christian Democratic parties in the EPP there were different examples illustrating the intermixture of both factors. The Luxemburg party felt close to the Belgian Christian Democrats on ideological grounds, but nevertheless cultivated more extensive personal relations with the CDU because of the organisational ability and active interest of the latter, not to mention the imprint of German culture in Luxemburg.[65] The French CDS was closest to the Belgians on ideological grounds through their common attachment to a social Christian outlook, but this link was also fortified by cultural and especially linguistic links, notably with the Walloons.[66] Relations between the Dutch and German Christian Democrats were restricted in their warmth for both ideological reasons and national ones in that, on the Dutch side, progressive attitudes were sometimes accompanied by anti-German feelings.[67]

What often emerges is the strong trace of national cultural traditions, such as the persistence of Nordic links outside the EC by the Danish parties despite their membership of party federations and in the special case where the Walloon and Flemish Socialists have developed separately links with the French PS and the German SPD, as well as the Dutch PvdA, respectively. Linguistic ability clearly plays a part in the pursuit of bilateral contacts, such as in facilitating closer relations by the Dutch PvdA with the British Labour Party rather than the French PS. So far as these links have generally affected transnational activity, what seems to have counted most is when the ideological and national factors have reinforced each other and promoted co-operation within the federations; that these bilateral/multilateral contacts have acted as a useful filter for individual differences, a requirement made more necessary by common transnational membership; and that as a whole these contacts tend to reflect the mosaic of relationships within the federations. Where such links appeared to be divisive as in a subgroup form, they were in fact contained within the federations. In other words, these bilateral/multilateral links have helped to condition the work of the federations, just as in turn the existence of the latter stimulated the further development of such links.

In conclusion, this discussion of the party-traditional factor has shown that overall individual party traditions have played a crucial role in motivating, conditioning and restricting or encouraging participation in transnational co-operation. Whereas before the 1970s party traditions had been a basic determinant of party European policies in general, although only as a vague guide, the specific activity of transnational party co-operation in its politicised form during the 1974–9 period involved a more direct interpretation of party-traditional aspects – whether ideology, party outlooks and beliefs, long-term policy lines, forms of party identity and inter-nationalism – in relation to the EC and a consequent growth of complexity in this activity. In so far as positions on transnational co-operation related integrally to general positions on European integration on the part of individual parties, then there was a consistency with their previous patterns of behaviour over EC affairs.

On the other hand, there were various signs of some re-adaptation in the party-traditional area. Direct elections required political parties, whether participants in the federations or not, to give a new and sustained priority to European policy both in terms of particular issues and of the future of integration itself, a trend sustained by the growing political impact of the EC as a whole. Parties were thereby relating more concretely than before to the EC framework, which made their transnational activity correspondingly more important, a process which caused the greatest difficulties to the anti-integrationist parties as reflected in their ambiguous positions. In other cases, this process strengthened previous trends of adaptation to the Communiy framework. It cannot, however, be argued that the move towards direct elections and the dictates of transnational co-operation produced any 'conversion' by anti-integrationist parties to this framework.

In short, features of party tradition were generally reinforced and sometimes modified but not radically changed. As party traditions had evolved essentially out of the matrix of national politics, the outcome of the 1974–9 period was accordingly only a mild alteration of the predominant national orientation of political parties. Even where parties were by tradition strongly pro-integrationist, their involvement in transnational co-operation could be restrained by domestic political pressures; indeed, the previous discussion has alluded to cases where political-functional aspects have modified ideological or other party-traditional approaches. Here the limits of the discussion of the party-traditional factor are reached for it cannot be considered further without reference to the political-functional factor.

(b)   The Political-Functional Factor: the Interlinkage between National and Transnational Party Roles

The same basic problems arise when looking at this factor – that is, the specific influence of national determinants of transnational party co-operation, and the possible modification of the predominant national orientation of political parties in EC member states – but they are viewed here in the context of short or intermediate rather than long-term (that is, party-traditional) aspects. These determinants include, as introduced in Chapter 1 (see above, Chapter 1, Section *b*, pp. 21–2), the different roles of parties in their national political systems, the relevance of national party alliances and rivalries, the question of power structures within parties and the involvement of party organisations in transnational activity and, not least, the relationship of MEPs with their national parties. The political-functional factor, as combining these interrelated features, therefore focuses on the intermeshing between national and transnational party activity and introduces the discussion of how the progressive erosion of the traditional distinction between European and domestic politics may have benefited transnational co-operation.

The first point of interest must certainly be the domestic political roles of parties during the period of 1974–9 as an obvious determinant of, or constraint on, the positions they take transnationally, because the latter cannot be divorced from their European policy options and priorities. The different roles of member parties of the various European party federations occurred simply because of the autonomy of national political trends, as indicated by the results of domestic elections. This underlined the difficulties of isolating and analysing the effects of any 'Europeanisation' of party politics, since it is virtually impossible to claim that, or assess how, electoral trends in one EC state may have affected those in another, even though political élites may seek to argue otherwise. For example, among the member parties of the Socialist Confederation those in West Germany, Britain and Denmark were in government during the said period, and the Dutch party for some of the time; while those in France and Italy were in opposition. Of the EPP members, those in Italy, Belgium and Holland were in government, with the Irish member part of the time; while those in West Germany and Luxemburg were in opposition. Similarly, the different roles played by Liberal parties, usually as junior partners with other parties, was exemplified by the ELD members which held governmental positions in France, West Germany and Luxemburg, and for part of the time in Belgium; and performed an opposition role in Italy for most of the time, in Britain (though modified by the Lib-Lab pact of 1977–8) and mainly so in Denmark and Holland. It should also be added that the government/opposition dimension did vary between member states of the EC with the tradition of a clear divide between the main forces in Britain and West Germany in particular, and the more predominant habits of coalitional politics blurring such clear distinctions elsewhere, whether this was the practice of 'accommodation' in the Netherlands or the ambiguous course of 'converging parallels' in Italy.

What effects did this variegated party-political scene have on transnational party co-operation, and how much did the politicisation of this activity bring these different roles more into play? This question is all the more pertinent during the 1970s as direct elections made European politics less of a purely long-term concern for the purpose of national parties.

Parties in government invariably had to correlate their transnational positions with the European policies conducted by their leaders in office, with which they were, of course, identified, although this requirement could be modified where parties took an independent line from their own governments. The governmental role could act therefore as a constraint on the freedom of such parties in their transnational relationships, depending on whether there was much potential for divergent policy lines between both respects. Unqualified support for the official line over the EC was shown, for instance, by the French Giscardian Parti Républicain, especially since the President's and the government's standing became directly linked to its European positions not only because of Giscard d'Estaing's personal commitment to direct elections, but also because French ratification became an object of party-political controversy at home with Gaullist as well as opposition attacks on presidential European policy. This strong correlation meant that the Parti Républicain could not sympathise with the pro-integrationist aspirations of the ELD, although in practice it chose not to highlight this difference being in a minority of one there. In several cases, the strongly pro-integrationist lines of governmental European policy (especially with Christian Democratic parties) presented no substantial difficulties of co-ordination for their respective parties at the transnational level. Among the Socialists two interesting and different cases were the parties from Britain and West Germany. In the former instance, there surfaced a conflict between most Labour leaders in government (except the significant minority who were anti-integrationist) committed to implementing the EC decision on direct elections, and a sizeable group of their MPs taking an opposing line and backed by the negative line of the party organisation. The party's challenge to the government over the issue rebounded on Labour's transnational activity because the party organisation controlled relations with the Confederation. With the SPD there was not so much a conflict between party and government as some difference of policy emphasis reflected in the former's transnational involvement. The difference of tone between party and government was indicated by the inclusion of more radical proposals in the former's direct elections programme than were typical of the SPD's national programmes (for example, thirty-five-hour week, control of investment by multinationals).[68] Another example of a mild policy divergence was the FDP's acceptance of a more critical position on nuclear energy in the ELD programme than its government leaders in Bonn. Such differences were not regarded too seriously as the prospect for effecting transnational policies was restricted by the weak institutional role of the EP.

Another obvious consequence of the governmental role for parties transnationally arises from their preoccupation with performance in office, with the mere burden of everyday politics and with other policy demands apart from the EC. Apart from the lower priority which these preoccupations generally forced on party co-operation, they could have different effects on the ability of such parties to pay attention to their transnational engagements. The reluctant attitude of the British Labour Party towards direct elections, ministers and party organisation alike, was in part conditioned by the assumption that Labour would suffer in its European vote from an anti-government swing and from differential voting, because Labour voters were less enthusiastic about the EC than Conservative ones, so that there would be, in the words of Ian Mikardo, 'a massacre of the Labour candidates and a substantial addition from Britain to the already considerable built-in anti-Socialist majority in the European Parliament'.[69] This made the Labour Party even less enthusiastic about the work of the Socialist Confederation. The political standing of a governmental party at a particular time could therefore colour its transnational participation. From another angle, the involvement of parties in office with routine policy-making and the overwhelming demands of governmental action meant that trans-national co-operation was left in the hands of a few Euro-specialists, who enjoyed a certain freedom from control by party leaders.

The issue of direct elections was itself, of course, one of the policy problems facing national governments simultaneously from the mid-1970s, with consequent demands on their own parties organisationally and politically; but its phasing into domestic political business was not always a straightforward case of compelling a new priority to European activity. In Britain the implementation of direct elections legislation ran concurrently with the more pressing question of devolution, where internal parliamentary party problems over the one issue affected behaviour over the other. In Belgium a firmly pro-integrationist government led by the Christian Democrat, Tindemans, found its direct elections arrangements complicated and delayed by their interrelating over the electoral law with the long-term unsolved issue of the linguistic communities.[70] Finally, the low-profile role played by the Italian DC, not to mention other Italian parties, in transnational co-operation owed much to an excessive preoccupation with national politics and its regular vulnerability to government crises.

There is one further aspect of government roles with regard to transnational party co-operation which relates to the politicisation of the latter and provides a pointer to future complexity in transnational relationships. This is the problem of apparent or potential contradiction between intergovernmental relations within the Community and transnational party activity, a problem raised tentatively before the 1979 European elections by some party representatives involved in party co-operation. The implication was that party-political differences between governments were ignored pragmatically in EC policy-making, whereas transnational party co-operation aimed at promoting ideological approaches in this respect. The chairwoman of the Dutch Labour Party emphasised this matter over the general question of party-political accountability by government leaders at the European executive level:

> It's ridiculous what's going on now. The ministers in the several Socialist governments are defending the things we don't have in our programmes or are rejecting in our programmes, and they are in those Councils of Ministers. So we have to find the opportunity to bring together the ministers from the Socialist parties, the parliamentarians from the Socialist parties and the representatives from the parties. Just to discuss matters at least, and maybe come to a common attitude at several points. I think that is very necessary.[71]

This hinted at a possibly stronger role of co-ordination for the party federations. A French Socialist Euro-specialist remarked more placidly that 'there have obviously been contradictions and tensions in-between bilateral relations between parties on the one hand and bilateral presidential relations between Schmidt and Giscard on the other, and that is a conflict to add to the others.'[72] The problem has been fundamentally insoluble because the national-governmental and the transnational-party areas have been mutually exclusive and separate, seeing that national leaders in the Council of Ministers have to compromise with other national leaders from ideologically different parties. Furthermore, socialisation among governmental leaders, as at Community summits, has tended to reinforce their own relationships irrespective of political leanings. In fact, party-political differences have hardly appeared at this level for they have been 'so far submerged by mutual and tacit consent'.[73]

Yet the question of this possible contradiction received some exposure in the light of direct elections, showing an awareness of the party-political side of EC relationships. Helmut Schmidt made play with it shortly after the British general election in May 1979, when he commented in response to Margaret Thatcher's claim that they both believed in free enterprise and tax cuts: 'Don't go too far; you will spoil the relations between me and my own party.'[74] This touched on the problem of the identical value of ideological labels between EC member states which was a necessary basis for transnational party cohesion. Schmidt himself remarked at the special SPD congress for direct elections in December 1978: 'The CDU and CSU should consider why we Social Democrats can work together with Christian Democrats in other European countries so well and so much more than with this CDU.'[75] The Chancellor was, of course, making a domestic partisan point and something of a virtue out of the intergovernmental relationship in emphasising the looseness of transnational labels. But the same thought was also voiced by party organisers. A speaker at the meeting of the national council of the Giscardian Parti Républicain in February 1979 reacted as follows to the possibility that his party could ally with the French Socialists on matters of European integration because of their broadly positive positions here:

Why don't we underline this convergence? We must also under-line the ambiguities, especially concerning economic affairs . . . The [French] Socialists want to create Europe for 'promoting an answer to the crisis of capitalism'. But the other European Socialist parties do not question the market economy and make it responsible for the crisis. Everywhere where they are in power the European Social Democrats follow a policy similar to that of M. Barre, for which the PS only has hard words . . . We will oppose a Socialist Europe with a social Europe, and in doing so are closer to the ideas of M. Schmidt and M. Callaghan than are the French Socialists . . .[76]

The question for the future was whether European ideological solidarity would have greater claims over such pragmatic assertions of policy affinity between government leaders from different political backgrounds.

This problem of party-political contradiction between governmental and transnational roles did, of course, lend emphasis to various limitations of the latter: above all, the fact that transnational roles were very subordinate to governmental roles in importance; that the two areas were conceived separately because of the original institutional isolation of the EP, and the tendency of transnational activity to concentrate on the long and intermediate term while the principal focus of government action is on the short and intermediate term; and the relative lack of seriousness with which governmental leaders have in general regarded the Parliament in view of its marginal role in EC policy-making and their own absence of direct contact with transnational activity (with few exceptions like Tindemans of Belgium and Thorn of Luxemburg). The pressures of national office, increased substantially by the growing demands of ministerial activity at the European executive level, make the problem of direct accountability to a transnational party authority very difficult despite the new convention of more regular appearances of governmental leaders before the EP.

With opposition roles in member states many of the converse conclusions may be drawn with regard to transnational party activity, especially where there is a clear-cut distinction along the government/opposition divide. Opposition parties enjoy more time which they may among other things devote to party co-operation, and for the same reason they are freer to adjust to the longer-term perspective of this activity and in doing so are less immediately concerned with both emphasising national interests and being considerate towards other national governments. Furthermore, opposition parties are especially conscious of their profile, so that European party co-operation provides a welcome international stage with their own lack of official level contacts and the advantages of prestige and publicity acquired by government parties. This attraction of transnational activity has been particularly apparent with West German and British opposition leaders, despite the very limited publicity for this at home (though there is rather more attention to this in West Germany than in Britain). Thus, the CDU/CSU began to assume a far more active part in transnational co-operation after its role in opposition was decisively confirmed by its electoral defeat of 1972.[77] The British Liberals are a classic case of where a small opposition party striving to enhance its profile has engaged full-heartedly in the ELD for, in the words of one of their international specialists: 'The European area is the one area – inside the federation – where we can actually be the size we are, and therefore Europe is important for us.'[78] One pertinent question is whether the British Labour Party, having been defeated in the 1979 national election, might participate less reservedly in transnational activity. This possibility was voiced by the authors of a Fabian pamphlet published in 1977: 'It has also to be borne in mind that, should Labour become the Opposition party at Westminster, the Confederation will be the only main avenue through which British Labour policies can be pursued in the Community.'[79]

In other EC states, where government and opposition roles are less clear-cut or more subject to frequent interchange, these points about opposition parties may apply less explicitly. Here, the discussion of the effects of national political roles on transnational co-operation must include domestic alliances and party inter-relationships. The best examples are provided by Italy and France, where this aspect was the most controversial during the 1970s and had some repercussions on transnational activity. It has emerged during the period as an important background variable of party co-operation, and offers some measure of how it has become politicised.

In the case of Italy, the greater conceptual readiness of party élites than in many other EC states to introduce a European dimension into their own politics has facilitated this development. For instance, the ideological but polemical dispute about Marxist-Leninism initiated by Bettino Craxi, the PSI general-secretary, in the late summer of 1978[80] was quickly understood to be aimed partly at European elections. It related to Craxi's strategy of re-launching the PSI's active involvement in international party politics, as demonstrated by his regular and much-publicised meet-ings with other European Socialist leaders, and suited his domestic calculations about electoral dividends for his party at the cost of the PCI. His attacks on the ambiguities of 'Eurocommunism' and promotion of 'Eurosocialism' were obviously intended to strengthen the credibility of the PSI,[81] and they showed a deliberate attempt to mix European with domestic party politics.

The main issue of controversy which surfaced at the transnational level was the 'historic compromise' relationship between the DC and the PCI during 1976–9 following the latter's electoral advances of the mid-1970s. This caused serious friction between the German and Italian Christian Democrats both within the EPP and bilater-ally, and was exacerbated by their closer transnational co-operation. The basic issue at stake was the different national strategies of Christian Democratic parties, ranging from the determined centre-right position of the CDU/CSU in sole opposition to the SPD/FDP government through the tradition of co-operation with Socialist parties in Belgium and Holland to the Italian DC and its govern-mental agreement with the Communists. Arguments about these differences – specifically between the CDU/CSU and DC – acquired ideological tones in the light of the general concern with 'Euro-communism'. Luigi Granelli, the DC spokesman in the EPP, noted that the Italian and German parties differed 'in their positions towards "Eurocommunism" because of the different historical and political contexts in which they operate'; and that this difference covered also their attitudes towards socialism for the DC felt 'there is no room for an anti-Socialist policy in Europe'.[82]

At the same time, Granelli saw the EPP as a helpful channel for explaining the Italian situation fully to other member parties: 'Internal discussion within the EPP will be fruitful because it can lead, through common loyalty to the values which unite us, to greater understanding of our different historical experiences.'[83] The question of the Italian 'historic compromise' (a term not in fact recognised by Christian Democrats) was raised directly on several occasions in the EPP's Bureau meetings under the regular item on its agenda concerning national situations. The line that has come to be adopted is one of autonomy of member parties in their national affairs (which accords with the principle contained in Article 2 of the EPP statutes), as Granelli explained: 'We are not bound to obtain the consensus of the other parties [in the EPP] for doing what we have to do in Italy, and *vice versa* ... this is an agreement: the maximum of autonomy on the national level and the maximum of agreement on the European level for European questions.'[84]

The problem in practical politics is that such fine distinctions are not always easy to apply for, as shown by the work of the federations, there occurred some overlap between the two levels of politics (see above, Chapter 3, Section *c*, p. 142). This was the basic reason why friction ensued. Relations between the CDU/CSU and the DC became quite acerbic at times during 1976–8 and this appeared in sessions of the EPP Bureau, where generally the habit on national matters was the exchange of mutual information and the sharing of opinions. Fear about the growing credibility of 'Euro-communist' parties on the part of the West Germans combined with sensitivity on this issue among the Italians to bring the matter to a head. In the spring of 1977 there were bilateral contacts when Helmut Kohl visited the DC in Rome in an attempt to improve relations, but these did not become so cordial and were not helped, for instance, by Kohl's warning against 'Eurocommunism' at the EPP congress in March 1978. On the German side, attitudes oscillated between expressions of admiration for Andreotti's deft tactics *vis-à-vis* the PCI[85] with promises 'not to leave the DC in the lurch'[86] and adamant statements that for the CDU/CSU the main political enemy in Europe was the left. Other Christian Democratic parties in the EPP took a less intransigent line than the CDU/CSU, flexibly accepting the special Italian situation but with no desire to envisage any similar arrangement with their own Communist parties.[87] The issue did, in any case, lessen in importance once the PCI began to lose voting support locally and then later in the Italian national election of 1979. This example has been worth lengthy treatment not only because it was one of the principal cases of conflict between transnational partners over domestic alliances, but especially as it illustrated well the limits of transnational party loyalty and of the scope for involvement by the federations in matters outside EC concern.

The example of France offered the second main example of the difficulty of keeping domestic alliances and transnational loyalties strictly apart. An interesting case of transnational contradiction was presented by the Giscardian Union for French Democracy (UDF), an alliance of pro-governmental parties – the Republican Party, the Christian Democratic CDS and the Radical Socialist Party – formed before the 1978 French legislative elections with no special consideration of transnational arrangements.[88] The UDF continued to operate for European elections even though the CDS belonged to the EPP and was likely to elect its MEPs to the Christian Democratic group in the EP, while the other two parties had joined the ELD and belonged to the Liberal group. The UDF itself did not, of course, have any transnational link, but this alliance, which chose to fight the European campaign on its own Deniau Report rather than the ELD or EPP programmes (though each party adhered to its respective federation programme), involved some contradiction with transnational loyalties. However, this contradiction was not emphasised by the French parties concerned and this domestic alliance was not carried to the extent of breaking with the consistency rule whereby member parties have to belong to the Europarliamentary group of their federation.[89]

The more controversial case of a domestic alliance in France arose at the transnational level over the PS's domestic Union of the Left with the PCF of 1972–7. This had two consecutive stages. First, the PS's alliance made well before the Confederation was formed required some compromise with the PCF on European positions. The section on the EC in their common policy programme of 1972 had been one of the most difficult to formulate because of basic divergences between the two French parties in this area,[90] but it nevertheless required a commitment by the PS to implement a radical socio-economic programme in government with the PCF emphasising their 'freedom of action' within the EC and to press for the 'liberation' of the Community from the dominance of 'big capital'. The Union of the Left naturally affected the PS's behaviour inside the Confederation, whereby it took a divergent line from most of the other members over issues like CAP, energy, foreign affairs and employment and acted reservedly or defensively because of PCF disapproval of its transnational relationship with Social Democratic parties.[91] The Union of the Left became a direct point of tension within the Confederation because the very issue of relations with Communist parties became controversial in the context of the general debate about 'Eurocommunism' from 1975. During the following year, Mitterrand made efforts to sell his alliance model abroad by arranging multilateral meetings between southern European Socialist leaders on the grounds that countries such as France,

Italy, Spain and Portugal had relatively strong Communist parties in common, entailing a need for accommodation with them.[92] This caused ill feeling among other Confederation members, notably the German SPD and also the British Labour Party. However, improved relations between the SPD and PS from 1976 helped to reduce tension, while from 1977 the effective collapse of the French Union of the Left virtually removed the issue.

Secondly, this appearance of a domestic rift between the PS and PCF had direct repercussions on the former's transnational links because the PCF chose to exploit them for propaganda reasons. The Communist organ, *L'Humanité*, featured regular articles attacking interference by 'foreign parties' (meaning the federations) in French politics in quite violent terms, such as its denunciation of the rally of European Socialist leaders at Lille in November 1978[93] and its reference to the EPP as 'heir of the German Reich' presided over by a 'foreign' prime minister[94] (who was in fact a Belgian!). This pre-direct-elections domestic controversy continued to place a public constraint on the PS about its membership of the Confederation, because it feared the PCF might arouse general French suspicions of foreign links, although now freed of the Union of the Left it participated less reservedly in the actual work of the Confederation.

The question of national coalitions or alliances was therefore broached during the 1970s with regard to transnational party co-operation with, consequently, the general 'agreement to differ' in all three federations. Martin Bangemann of the ELD had raised the matter as early as 1975 when, referring to the long-term 'coalition question' in the EC, he said that a solution was only possible if one accepted the principle that European-level coalitions did not have to accord with those at the national level.[95] This problem, specifically relations with Communist parties, was reluctantly touched on within the Socialist Confederation, although it became 'a sort of unspoken tradition that, when this is necessary in the national framework of politics, it is accepted by the other parties'.[96] Socialist leaders tended to play down the importance of the issue, as when Wilhelm Dröscher argued that it was strictly a national matter since an alliance with the Communists in the EC was out of the question as there was no prospect of a 'European government' emerging from direct elections,[97] and Bruno Friedrich asserted that the Communists were not, in any case, such a large force within the Community.[98] However, as the EPP had shown, it was sometimes impossible to distinguish between domestic and European politics, particularly as direct elections aimed at mobilising together the national electorates of the different EC states. The 'agreement to differ' was indeed the only viable solution but, while serving to underplay the consequences of the growing interlinkage between the European and national levels of party activity, it could not erase that development. Needless to say, there were also other cases where national alliances were not so controversial or hardly affected transnational party co-operation. This was another possible pointer to future complexity in transnational activity in the event of further politicisation in the 1980s. But there seemed no realistic prospect for solving any contradictions between national alliances and transnational loyalties, given that the individual party systems in member states were differently structured with regard to the balance of political forces.

Before turning to a discussion of structural and organisational aspects of the political-functional factor, it is worth noting that the extended process of preparatory arrangements for the first ever European elections and of gradual mobilisation for the campaign broadened or opened up the possibility for the 'internalisation' of European affairs and transnational activity within parties. The preceding examination of national political roles and their effects on party co-operation has already indicated some interlocking of transnational activity with domestic strategic and tactical considerations. This inclusion of the European dimension in routine party politics of course depended for its extent on individual party as well as national conditions, but generally it was promoted by two features.

First, party interests were in many cases directly affected by national preparatory arrangements, especially over the electoral laws to be adopted for European elections. In West Germany, this question reactivated the intermittent controversy over a 'fourth party' in the form of a nation-wide CSU, because of the original proposal for federal party lists of candidates, until a compromise formula was reached allowing for both combined and individual Land lists.[99] In Britain, the thorny matter of proportional representation was reintroduced at the prodding of the Liberals through their pact with Labour in the face of intransigent hostility towards the idea from the Labour Party organisation as well as basic opposition from the Conservatives. It led to a vote in the House of Commons where PR was finally defeated. Elsewhere, as in France and Italy – not to mention the special Belgian case with the linguistic communities – party interests were brought into play, although any conflict was eventually solved by agreement on some version of PR.

Secondly, the interest of parties in European elections was promoted by the over-spilling of inter-party rivalries into preparations for this event. This occurred particularly in those EC states where direct elections were themselves disputed, notably France and Britain and, to some extent, Denmark. In France competition between the parties of government and opposition and internal rivalries within both camps dominated party calculations during this period;[100] while in Britain the anti-Conservative motive was decisive in spurring the Labour Party into action for, as Ron Hayward, its general-secretary, proclaimed, his party could not 'stand on the sidelines' and 'hand victory on a plate to the Tories'.[101]

The question here is whether such mobilisation by political parties produced any relevant changes in party structures with regard to European affairs in the sense of broadening involvement in decision-making, requiring organisational readjustment and generally solidifying or underpinning their transnational activity. It has already been established in discussing the party federations that the national level of transnational involvement within member parties has essentially been the preserve of élites and even individuals rather than party activists as a whole (see above, Chapter 3, Section *b*, pp. 126–7, and Section *c*, p. 163); and also that a high degree of centralisation at the national level is necessary to make European co-ordination a practicable possibility (see above, Chapter 3, Section *c*, pp. 146–7 and 149–50). Notwithstanding this, the question merits further examination in the context of the national parties themselves for a more specific discussion of how far relative changes might have begun to occur within party structures compared with earlier years and whether these provide any interesting pointers to further development. One European party federation official commented in 1979 on the importance of member party structures:

> The best thing that has happened in the last two years is the fact that they have been forced by the coming of European elections really to deal with European problems, with European policy. They have never done so before. There was no urgency, there was no pressure – neither for the militants. Europe had always been the small working field of the international élite of the parties.[102]

How much did this view from the transnational level accord with a closer look at individual national parties?

Various particular conclusions can be drawn from earlier discussion of individual party involvement in the formulation of common programmes of the federations – extensive in a few cases, spasmodic in most – about the nature of party power structures so far as transnational decisions were concerned. From this and earlier analysis in the present chapter two points may be made about the political aspect of party structures. First, there was a clear difference between smaller parties with minimal bureaucracies and large parties with more elaborate structures. In the former instance, it was much easier for individual party leaders to dominate personally their parties' transnational links, as with some of the Danish parties whose chairmen had been or aimed to be MEPs. Secondly, in so far as party structures relate to the power factor, which may not be static, the transnational dimension has been affected by the current political situation in which the party leadership in question may find itself. For example, Craxi of the Italian PSI was using his association with the Confederation and European Socialist leaders to buttress his consolidation of his internal position after assuming the party secretaryship in 1976, as well as for promoting PSI's profile against the PCI. From another angle, the British Labour Party organisation chose to focus its mounting challenge to the dominant policy control of its governmental leaders among other things on transnational activity, as a new area it could control by taking advantage of the party's somewhat disparate internal coalition of different institutional entities like the parliamentary party, Transport House and the constituencies. This showed how national political determinants could impinge temporarily on transnational activity, but this general problem of party structures with regard to European affairs must be viewed further in the light of specific party organisational matters.

The pattern of national party structural involvement in transnational activity during the period 1974–9 by and large confirmed the central role played by party international secretaries or European specialists as before that time. But the more regular work involved, the more institutionalised relationship with other parties in the EC and the practical arrangements for direct elections did mean, in many cases, that these restricted circles acted less autonomously in their own separate area and more as a filter for an enlarged group of party Euro-élites. There was, however, much variation between individual parties, just as their differences of organisational weight was itself one variable in determining the respective influence of member parties in the federations.

One major obstacle to widening the circle of those directly concerned with transnational activity was the specialist nature of the work. The expertise possessed by party international secretaries and European experts through from their background and experience – the technical know-how of European affairs, the cultivation of personal contacts in other countries, a versatile linguistic ability – was not readily acquired by normal party officials or activists. A European specialist of the Danish Social Democrats had this problem in mind when he remarked: 'Very few people are well-informed about these things; you have to start from scratch in explaining them.'[103] He went on to suggest that this produced an unavoidable élitism, although noting that the élite concerned could be constrained by this very problem:

The problem is the higher you go up in the political pyramid, the more interest you will find in international affairs and European affairs; whereas lower down it's very hard to get people interested. This means that people lower down are very reluctant ... On the other hand, people higher up realise we are very dependent on other countries – but they have to take decisions from one policy to another because people lower down wouldn't really understand if there were a complete European ideology ... we have to be very pragmatic about it.[104]

The customary isolation of international and European experts within their own parties was not merely a matter of specialism, but derived also from the fact that they operated in a conceptual world apart from the general body of activists. In the small Luxemburg Socialist Workers' Party the general-secretary himself was responsible for transnational links, but this was not only because of the party's limited bureaucratic structure but particularly the prevalent attitude whereby 'European policy is still considered by many people in the party as a domain reserved to certain wise people who know about things'.[105] Both problems of expertise and attitude were explained in full by one Dutch Christian Democrat commenting from personal experience on

The isolation of people who work in the foreign field within their own parties, when you talk with people who are mainly concerned with internal affairs. Working in the foreign field you tend to take much more into account the [different] national influences on party politics, and then we realise that a lot of parties are bound by this. In Holland, people look at the German Christian Democrats and judge them by their own national circumstances ... then the judgement is easy: the German Christian Democrats are very conservative groups that would be even to the Right of our Liberal Party in the Netherlands, and people say how can you co-operate with them on the international level? – 'We can't understand it'. We as people working in the foreign field realise the German background – they have been in Opposition for so long, there is quite a bit of heterogeneity within their own party, the differences between the CDU and the CSU. We take all this into account, and we come to a somewhat milder conclusion. We still say they are rather conservative, it's dangerous and we must watch it and all that, but we say we can co-operate with them on the European level. We come to a different conclusion, but it's very hard to sell this to the national parties ... it's not only better knowledge, but another way of looking at things – perspective.[106]

Despite these basic problems there were ways in which an awareness of transnational activity was beginning to percolate slowly downwards through party structures. The growing visibility of the federations, the greater awareness by European specialists of their own isolation as a problem and the relative need to bear the (uninformed) attitudes of the activist element in mind as an indirect influence on policy formulation all contributed to such a process. Furthermore, the trend during the 1970s where many prominent party leaders increasingly played a direct role in the transnational activity of their parties – notably, Brandt of the SPD, Mitterrand of the PS, the two federation presidents, Tindemans and Thorn, and the chairmen of several small parties – meant they lent their name and prestige to party co-operation, which accordingly strengthened the potential interest among their own party activists in this exercise. In addition, the need to gear the party organisation to direct elections automatically broadened the area of those involved in European affairs, on the organisational rather than policy-making side, even though this was being conducted essentially at the domestic level. For the first time, party organisations were therefore being activated for a European purpose, excepting those national cases where referenda on the EC had been held in the first half of the 1970s (see above, Chapter 1, Section *b*, pp. 25–6). The European campaign did differ from those referenda in being the first stage of a permanent future task, although many individual party arrangements for it were somewhat *ad hoc*. This was especially true of smaller parties, like the Liberal ones, which did not enjoy the bureaucratic facilities and financial resources to man their transnational links systematically, and also of parties from smaller countries. The Irish parties, for instance, established special committees for preparing direct elections composed of parliamentarians and national organisers – although one of them, Fine Gael, was content to rely on the European reputation and expertise of its leader, Garret Fitzgerald, for advice.[107]

Among the larger national parties in the EC states the crucial variable with regard to organisational readjustment to, or involvement in, European elections was the combination or not of a clear pro-integrationist ideology or outlook in the party, together with a strong sense of organisational efficiency and accompanying resources. The outstanding example of this positive combination were the West German parties benefiting, as they did, from the advantages of generous state finance. Above all, so widespread were pro-integrationist values among party activists at all levels[108] that no ideological obstacles were placed in the way of a full-hearted commitment of the party machines to transnational activity leading to direct elections, as evidenced by their ready adoption of European-style cosmetics and invitations to foreign speakers. As a result, those involved in European affairs in their respective parties have relatively gained in estimation 'because they are engaged in an area which now has a future ... has become much more concrete, and who have an advantage of information, of knowledge and that is played up'.[109] It should be added that the preparation of federal lists of European candidates at the district and Land level in the SPD and FDP engendered an interest among party activists at the grass roots; while the procedure of the CDU/CSU was less elaborate. In other national cases, there was less ready organisational readjustment, although the degree of this was determined by the strength of the combination of pro-integrationist ideology and party-machine efficiency.

The absence or weakness of one or both created a serious problem for party mobilisation for direct elections. Reservations about the EC among party activists caused some concern to the Danish Social Democrats:

> The problem is that some of our party workers are against the EC, and they haven't worked out those problems of for and against and what this election is about. For instance, in the region of Aarhus, in Jutland, where there was a big majority against [in the 1972 referendum], I've heard several people saying it might be difficult to mobilise party workers because of their attitudes ... We have been very careful the whole time not to re-open this issue [of EC membership] by stressing that the campaign is not about being for or against ... but it is below the surface and will remain for quite some time, and it threatens to re-open every time there is a major issue like direct elections.[110]

The best example of a party which was broadly anti-integrationist in its transnational relationship and also weak in its own organisation was the British Labour Party, which was accordingly inhibited in its preparations. The official Labour position of opposition to the principle of direct elections and decision not until April 1978 to fight them only encouraged strong reservations among the party rank and file, for whom anti-EC views were common currency. The preoccupation among Labour activists with the party's fortunes in the forthcoming national election, the dubious state of party finances and the threadbare nature of much local constituency organisation, the dominance of left-wing activists in many areas and a certain attitude of giving a priority to local over European elections all produced a situation where 'there will, no doubt, be an inclination for many stalwart party members who have turned out for every past election and party crisis to wonder whether they should, after all, give European elections a miss'.[111] This state of affairs contrasted significantly with the British Conservatives, who held no serious ideological reservations about the EC and who had been dutifully preparing for direct elections since the spring of 1976, when their national union had set out a framework for Euro-constituency organisation and candidate selection.[112] They had also a decided advantage over Labour with a well-oiled and efficient party machine.

There was one further special way in which party activists became involved in European contacts, namely the growth of local branch twinning, a practice much more developed between some EC states than others, especially in Germany, France and Benelux. It reflected the same factors of organisational sense and pro-integrationist values, and grew out of the more intensive bilateral and multilateral contacts which accompanied transnational co-operation during the years before direct elections. The main West German parties took this additional exercise seriously and pursued it more systematically than other national cases. The CDU even issued formal instructions for its local branches on how to make twinning arrangements.[113] These emphasised that such 'partnerships' should be long-term and involve the active co-operation of members with somebody specifically responsible, be financed by the local party and generally accord with the international contacts of the Federal CDU. The envisaged activities included the exchange of views on cultural and sporting matters and common events like seminars and tourist visits. The national CDU headquarters offered to help arrange contacts which invariably, as with other parties, tended to follow the pattern of traditional town twinning as to the choice of partners. So the CDU developed such arrangements with regional as well as local branches of Christian Democratic parties in other EC states, such as Holland and Belgium, although it also took these up with branches of the British Conservatives. The latter demonstrated considerable interest in the subject, as when their European spokesman reported at the party conference in October 1977 that 'there is now a new dimension in the life and work of our party: area by area, constituency by constituency, section by section, Conservatives of their own initiative are forming links and friendships with like-minded parties on the Continent',[114] although these were predominantly with the CDU.

Branch twinning also became something of a convention among some Socialist parties with the SPD taking the lead. The German party had the most frequent arrangements with the Dutch, Belgian and French parties (the last being based to some degree on local connections through the Franco-German youth exchange scheme), though not with the British Labour Party, which showed little interest in the subject. Successful arrangements were advertised in the party members' magazine 'like marriage announcements'. Difficulties emerged with the Italians because of the language problem on both sides, all the more so in the case of party activists than national Euro-specialists.[115] The FDP, on the other hand, had made less progress because of the practical problem of costs, underlining here its limitations as a smaller party, although there was some loose contact with the British Liberals at the regional rather than local level.[116] This problem was particularly true of smaller parties in other EC states. The Danish Centre Democrats expressed an interest in local twinning, but simply did not have the organisation to make it possible.[117] Another variation of local branch contacts was some growth in border co-operation, such as common meetings and policy discussions (for example, on tourism), where linguistic ability was less of a problem among local activists who, for instance, in parts of eastern France spoke German. A similar phenomenon occurred among Danish Socialist branches in south Jutland and SPD activists in Schleswig-Holstein where many people were bilingual.[118]

This grass-roots involvement in European contacts contributed indirectly to transnational activity, although as a subsidiary form of socialisation it tended to reinforce rather than create anew any European consciousness. It did not, of course, involve party activists in European policy-making. That continued to be dominated by party *Europapolitiker* or those leaders and parliamentarians who took a special interest in EC affairs, with the participation or support of party Euro-experts from the national party bureaucracies. Here, MEPs invariably played a crucial part because of their own experience at the European level so it is relevant to look finally at their role in the party structures and particularly their institutional links with their own parties as a political-functional determinant of transnational activity, an aspect which is likely to develop more in the 1980s after direct elections than it has done in the 1970s.

The main reason why little thought was given to the national party links of MEPs during the period of this study was simply the fact that up to the 1979 European elections all MEPs were dual-mandated. Their link with their national parties was transmitted through their domestic role as national parliamentarians. The concern here is not with MEPs' past or future relationship with their home parliaments as institutions, and with this the wider question of possible conflict between a directly elected EP and the various national parliaments, but strictly with the party aspect.

During the 1974–9 period there was in fact little forward thinking about the future national party links of future members of the directly elected Parliament. Partly this was due to the lack of time where party organisational energies so far as they were concentrated

on the European dimension were absorbed by the business of preparing for the direct-elections campaign. There was also less urgency
in most countries other than Britain, which chose to operate the
system of constituency-based MEPs unlike the other states which,
using various forms of proportional representation, automatically
established a means of control by national parties over MEPs
through the party lists. This did not, however, institutionalise any
regular basis of consultation during the five years of the future
European parliamentary period.

The most immediate problem lay in Britain, where any links would
have to start afresh with special arrangements at the national level
as well as the need to take account of the newly created Euro-
constituencies. Concern about this problem was rather late in
developing. In the summer of 1978, the Conservative European
spokesman, Douglas Hurd, wrote:

> It is essential that they [the MEPs] and their staffs should be
> meshed into their political parties at home at all levels, from the
> leadership through the parliamentary party, the voluntary organ-
> isations, to the constituencies. Indeed, it will be in their own
> interests to keep this close connection. They will rely upon it for
> their election, for their constituency operations after the election,
> and for their re-election later . . . Thus, the immediate responsi-
> bility lies with the political parties . . . on the Continent as well as
> in Britain, the political parties must take the lead. They are now
> recruiting a new regiment of elected representatives to their
> ranks.[119]

However, nothing concrete was decided before the 1979 elections,
when the British Conservative manifesto merely stated that 'Conservatives here at home, in Government and Parliament, and in Europe
will be part of the same team'[120] and an accompanying booklet
noted: 'We shall have to find ways of involving MEPs in the work of
the party at Westminster; we shall of course make available to them
briefing and other assistance from official sources'.[121] In the Labour
Party, where instrumental accountability by parliamentarians is
taken more seriously, there was more specific thinking on the subject
though little progress before direct elections. In September 1977, a
Fabian pamphlet touched on it in a general discussion of the party's
organisational crisis.[122] It argued that 'big problems' awaited the
party after direct elections, 'in particular, as to how Labour MEPs
are going to develop and maintain their ties with the party', and that
in the event of Euro-constituencies 'the party will need to develop
new structures' for building a relationship between MEPs and the
party. There were, however, considerable financial obstacles to such

structures in addition to practical problems of maintaining a viable link over the vast areas covered by the new constituencies.[123] Nearer the elections there were attempts by the party organisation to impose political strings on prospective Labour MEPs, such as a promise not to observe the EP's rule against placing mandates on members to take a particular line and strong pressures to carry out radical proposals contained in the party's European programme.[124]

In other EC states, the most definite (and unusual) idea was that adopted by the French Gaullists for their MEPs to be replaced after only one year by others further down the party list. This strengthened the possibility for party control, especially personally on the part of Chirac, the national motive behind which was revealed in the RPR brochure for direct elections: 'This system will allow avoiding the creation of a caste of European parliamentarians cut off from the people and locked up in preoccupations foreign to the real problems and interests of the French.'[125] There would be regular meetings of the 'Group of 81' (that is, all the RPR's European candidates on its list) at Paris, and it saw itself as a 'permanent counterweight to the threats that technocrats of Brussels make to our economy with their excessive regulations'.[126] This was a unique case and unlikely to be imitated by other parties, which were more inclined to concentrate on functional links between their MEPs and national parliamentary parties.

There are various possible institutional links that may develop as partial practical solutions, as when future MEPs hold national, regional or local offices in their own parties back home, although this would not be with respect to direct accountability over European affairs. More significant from the transnational point of view is the probable extension of a procedure already evident before the 1979 elections whereby MEPs may be delegated to represent their own parties on the executive organs or other bodies of the European party federations, thus involving a personal embodiment of the triangular construction of party co-operation. In general, much will depend on the interest or motive of the respective national parties as to whether links with their MEPs are envisaged as primarily a source of information, a means of control, a channel for expressing views at the European level or merely as a way of maintaining contact *per se*.

There is one other link for MEPs and that is where they retain membership of their national parliamentary parties. As shown by the situation up to the 1979 elections, individual MEPs acted as a personal bridge between the national and Euro-parliamentary levels, their effectiveness in view of the burdens of the dual-mandate depending on distance from the national capital, national arrangements facilitating their work in the EP and the general regard shown

European activity in their own national parties. In the directly elected Parliament of 1979 there would continue to be 126 out of 410 MEPs (or 30·7 per cent) holding dual-mandates, but there was much variation between member states, as illustrated by Table 4.1.

Table 4.1 *Numbers of directly elected MEPs holding dual-mandates, 1979*

Member State	Total MEPs	Dual-Mandates
Belgium	24	19
Denmark	16	6
France	81	22
West Germany	81	28
Ireland	15	13
Italy	81	25
Luxemburg	6	6
Netherlands	25	2
UK	81	5

Source: European Parliament, Directorate-General for Information, *Elections '79: Voting figures in the Nine and composition of the new Parliament* (July 1979), p. 4.

This disparity between countries – all or almost all MEPs from Luxemburg, Ireland and Belgium holding dual-mandates, almost none from Holland and Britain and roughly a third or a quarter in West Germany, Denmark, Italy and France – meant that some countries had a ready-made forum for their MEPs' links and others less so. Altogether, as a result of short-term thinking, the situation as to the national party bases for directly elected MEPs was still largely an open question subject to special arrangements, both parliamentary and organisational, being worked out after the 1979 elections.

Ultimately, what would count was not only the form of domestic party links but also the political standing of MEPs which would affect their relationship with their national parties. Here, there had been marked variation from country to country – a higher value accorded the MEP's role in the Netherlands and, to some extent, in the Federal Republic, a lower one in the UK and Denmark – but also from party to party according to each's ideology or outlook on the EC. Thus, party-traditional aspects could influence various political-functional aspects, as already noticed in the case of parties' comparative ability to prepare for direct elections and in their readiness to introduce new institutional arrangements or practices in their structures. In party-political development, organisational matters can never be divorced as such from political considerations.

This refers back to the general problem raised at the start of this section whether the increased and more regular tasks of transnational activity in the 1970s themselves brought about changes in the national orientation of political parties in EC countries. Was the politicisation of party co-operation essentially a European-level phenomenon, or did it also, through the pressures stemming from direct elections and the experience of membership of the federations (not to mention the Euro-parliamentary groups), affect the functional operation of individual parties?

As shown by the preceding discussion of political-functional determinants, the predominance of the national party frameworks was confirmed in general terms, such as political roles and inter-party relationships in national systems having a decisive effect on transnational behaviour. The limits of transnational party loyalty were clearly encountered over such questions as intergovernmental relations between national leaders of different political persuasions (because of the relative weakness of European-level ideological attachments) and over the contradiction with national party alliances (arising from the basic autonomy of national politics). All these aspects acted as powerful constraints on the development and acceleration of transnational party relations and the ability and readiness of individual parties to devote time to them and participate in them. There were at the same time many signs that a growing awareness, recognition and application of European considerations were becoming part of national party activity as an additional area, a development promoted by the instinct of party interests – electoral and political – and by the competition of party rivalries.

This amounted to an 'internalisation' of European politics, but how much had there also emerged a 'Europeanisation' of national party politics which would be favourable to the broader impact of transnational party co-operation? Here it was difficult to generalise because of much variation between individual national parties, where their pro- or anti-integrationist positions tended to be confirmed or reinforced rather than substantially altered under pressure from transnational or European-electoral commitments. Among the pro-integrationist parties the widening of internal involvement in the business of European affairs was most evident and, although incremental rather than qualitative (it still remained an élite activity), it represented a relative change from before; while their encouragement of grass-roots European contacts created some mild potential for European-style socialisation. 'Europeanisation' did not have to entail a wholescale change of orientation, but the inclusion of a 'European' dimension as a central part of individual parties' modes of operating and thinking. As a result of the closer interlinkage between national and European politics up to 1979, there were various pointers in this direction and possible areas for future development, but any broader 'Europeanisation' beyond the tentative and small steps taken depended on more favourable circumstances in the EC as a whole and was, in any case, likely to be a slow development.

(c) The Socio-Political Factor: Towards a European Dimension?

This factor was introduced above as consisting of a variety of heterogeneous aspects such as public-political constraints on political activity, major structural changes in national party systems and different influences of a 'political-cultural' nature (see above, Chapter 1, Section *b*, p. 25). The fundamental question underlying discussion of the socio-political factor is whether, or how much, the politicisation of transnational party co-operation, motivated, as it strongly was, towards the direct election of the EP by the various EC member electorates, had any impact on the wider national political environments, and in what ways influences emanating from them facilitated or hindered its progress. In the broad sense, did transnational party developments during the 1970s involve some growth of 'European consciousness' or movement towards identifying a 'political community' in the EC, which would naturally strengthen the potential for transnational activity at a deeper level?

An initial answer to these questions, based on the preceding discussion in this book, would be with due scepticism to suggest a minimal basis for any development of a European dimension in the national environments. That is, transnational activity was a very élite exercise and any 'Europeanisation' of behaviour or outlook occurred within very restricted circles; and, although there was significant variation between different parties in their attachment to transnational activity, national interests and priorities generally played a considerable part in its operation. However, since the above-mentioned aspects provided some basic constraints on European-level party co-operation, if only indirectly, it is important to look more closely at the 1974–9 period from the point of view of the socio-political factor.

National parties were, for instance, affected in their approach to transnational activity, so far as it was now more political, by the kind of consensus on the EC in their own countries, whether this evidenced a positive or negative pattern, the division of opinion or even public apathy. It is possible to generalise by noting the different public responses in member states to the prospect of direct elections which from the mid-1970s became a regular subject of the Eurobarometer opinion surveys conducted on behalf of the European Commission and were a key test of opinion towards the EC. For example, there was a broad public concensus favourable to these elections in Italy, Ireland, Holland and West Germany, which meant that the principle of holding them was not contested domestically. This made it easier for parties concerned to engage more freely in transnational activity because it was unlikely to offend public attitudes if publicised. In the Federal Republic much was made of the need to promote democracy in the Community[127] – not surprising in a country which from historical experience did not take democracy for granted. On the other hand, public opinion over direct elections in Britain and Denmark was either more reserved or it was divided. In Denmark, the controversy over EC membership had never completely subsided since entry in 1973 and it was refuelled by the direct-elections issue and exploited by the People's Movement against the EC which had last been very active during the referendum campaign of 1972.[128] Consequently, pro-integrationist parties like the centre-right Venstre and the Conservatives were cautious in emphasising their attachment to the Community and in using 'European' slogans and, where these applied, chose to play down their transnational links.[129] In Britain, the continuing problem of public apathy or hostility over the EC despite the positive outcome of the 1975 referendum restricted severely the scope for any impact by party co-operation.

Political parties had, of course, to operate against the background of trends of public outlook in their own countries which they could only partly help to determine, although over European integration there were particular problems here because it was not an area of policy which easily mobilised opinion, not least because of the EC's 'distance' from the national publics. The integral link between the EC in general and the particular problems of direct elections and of transnational activity emerged in parties' thinking and response to public moods; but how much did these latter questions attract public attention? What really mattered was the intensity or not of national interest in direct elections as well as integration generally, which would, in turn, affect the potential for party co-operation.

The period leading up to European elections in 1979 showed in fact that transnational party co-operation achieved very little public salience in EC member states, a feature commonly acknowledged by interviewees sympathetic to the Community or not. One party federation official referring to co-operation between the German SPD and Communist MEPs in the EP said: 'It isn't dangerous, it isn't being brought back to the home countries – because there are so few journalists . . . it can't play an emotional role.'[130] This low profile of transnational activity was seconded by the Gaullist international secretary, who underlined the public ignorance, for 'they don't know we are linked with the Fianna Fail, they don't even know what is the Fianna Fail: "Mr. Lynch", "Fianna Fail" – that is Chinese'.[131] This problem of the national projection of party co-operation indicated the fundamental limits of its politicisation and was revealed in the uninformed, spasmodic or nationally oriented interest shown in the operation of the European party federations by the mass media (see above, Chapter 3, Section *c*, p. 162), an aspect which will be further treated in the following discussion of the European campaign.

The low intensity of public interest in direct elections was underlined by the fact that in those countries where the issue became controversial – France and Britain – the debate was essentially confined to party élites and had very little mobilising effect on the respective national publics.[132] What is interesting is that the party-political controversy in France occurred despite the existence of fairly strong public approval for direct elections during the years preceding 1979: 51 per cent approving them against 21 per cent not in late 1976, rising to a three-quarters approval the following year.[133] In 1976 already 46 per cent supported enlarging the EP's powers, but perhaps more significant is that one-third could not express any opinion on direct elections.[134] The juristic debate among party élites in France tended in fact to strengthen the feeling among the public that European affairs were the concern of specialists in that area.[135]

In general, the potential impact of transnational activity suffered therefore from the overall problem of how to project the European Community to the national publics or simply the reluctance to do so in some cases. As of the summer of 1977 more than half of the EC publics taken together had heard or read nothing about the EP, although direct elections made a relative difference because those informed had heard about it in connection with these elections.[136] Parties were accordingly inhibited in their promotion of transnational links because of the wider problem of having to start from basics in informing the public about the EC. Many of them tried to overcome this information deficiency. The British Conservative European campaign guide was modelled on the national election handbooks but with one major difference, as it was thought 'desirable to devote a good part of the book to detailed descriptions of the European institutions and the European background whose counterpart would be unnecessary in a guide designed for the familiar British political scene'.[137] It included a short section on European political parties with only minimal reference to transnational links. Many other parties in EC states issued basic question-and-answer information on the EC generally in their pre-campaign publicity with little attention to the specifics of party co-operation. The limited receptivity of the national publics to EC matters circumscribed the ability of parties to perform as educative agents in this respect.

Given this problem and the lax interest of the mass media in transnational activity, it was only through the means of the national parties that this activity could depend securely for its promotion at the sub-European level. However, the very willingness of individual parties to do so was conditioned – apart from party-traditional aspects already discussed in this chapter – by their own political positions at home and their fortunes within their national party systems. This provided an important background variable for their participation in transnational co-operation in so far as this was now included in their general range of activities. It should not be forgotten that seven of the nine EC states underwent major structural changes in their party systems during the course of the 1970s, the two exceptions being West Germany and Ireland.[138] In several cases long-established larger parties began to lose their predominance with the rise of new parties or internal splits, a development which owed much to a combination of long-term socio-structural changes and the difficulties of governmental performance in the face of the world economic crisis of this decade. These parties – such as British Labour, the Danish Social Democrats, the Italian DC and the major Belgian parties (following the persistent challenge from the linguistic community parties) – felt under added pressure because direct elections involved, in effect, the whole of their national electorates with probable repercussions on their national standing.

The effect of national party development on transnational co-operation depended much on the existence or not of a firm public consensus on the EC, but also on the nature of the change in question. For instance, the merger of the three Dutch Christian Democratic parties into the Christian Democratic Appeal (CDA), which arose from the de-confessionalisation of Dutch life and the weakening of traditional religious subcultures, only helped their closer co-operation at the transnational level.[139] On the other hand, the increased vulnerability and temporary decline of the Danish Social Democrats' electoral strength in the 1970s made them even more reluctant to engage in European activities which could be divisive among their own supporters. A different case was offered in West Germany, where the more open rivalry between the CDU and CSU – both strongly pro-integrationist parties – since the 1976 national election, overflowed into their transnational links as an additional element of complexity, as over the founding of the EDU. Although this particular problem was instigated by political leaders, the rivalry which ensued became related to the electoral potential of both parties. It should be emphasised that in all such cases the transnational side of party activity was a very secondary consideration.

Any reduction or increase in the electoral fortunes of the larger parties in particular could, of course, affect the political weight carried by such parties in European party co-operation and, indeed, the priority they gave it. A connected feature was the nature of individual party electorates, such as their attitude towards European affairs, and how this might influence transnational activity. Thus, the British Labour Party's line as a reluctant member of the Socialist Confederation cannot be fully explained without reference to the predominantly anti-integrationist values among its own voters, as indicated by opinion research. A parallel example is offered by the Danish Social Democratic Party, of whose voters apparently half had voted against EC entry in the 1972 referendum, and this pattern remained during the years before direct elections.[140] An interesting exception to the logic behind this kind of connection occurred with the French Gaullists, whose voters (as with those of the other French parties, but not the PCF) clearly supported direct elections (58 per cent in favour as of late 1976) and even included a slight majority (51 per cent) for enlarging the powers of the EP.[141] This suggested a miscalculation on the part of the RPR leadership, concerned as it was with the party's anti-integrationist traditions as well as its own unity, although the question of transnational links was not affected as the RPR did not possess a viable one. The trend of views among party electorates acted as a constraint on leaders in their willingness over transnational involvements, even though the low public salience of these helped to neutralise this problem. Interviews with party officials did indicate that in many cases transnational links were taken into account in their thinking about party identity and electoral appeal – in other words, they *thought* the public might be concerned about such links. For instance, a British Conservative official commented as follows on a possible link with Christian Democratic parties which represented a different historical tradition:

Think if a Conservative candidate went on the hustings in this country, and said: 'I am being supported by the EPP' – it would be as difficult for him in the rural bits of Sussex as it would be for an Italian Christian Democrat in Perugia to say: 'I am linked with the Conservative Party'.[142]

A summary of the preceding discussion of the socio-political factor would underline that it has been a question during 1974–9 of the national political environments influencing the course of transnational party co-operation rather than vice versa, but that the precise impact of socio-political determinants is difficult to identify and measure because they are themselves vague or broad. There were visible and significant divergences between EC member states as to signs of a 'European consciousness', but, as the socio-political factor concerns the question of national consciousness rather than merely the national orientation of party politics, it is far less tangible as an area of analysis. This difficulty also reflects the limited or negligible importance of transnational party politicisation at a deeper level. Generally, there was no apparent evidence that transnational party co-operation had begun to modify national attitudes outside party élites or that it benefited from some 'political-cultural' underpinning, except that national publics favourably disposed towards the EC could potentially transfer these attitudes to the specific area of party co-operation. That, however, referred to the long-term future of this relatively new activity.

While the process towards direct elections added relatively greater visibility to the European Parliament and did much to convince national parties to take their transnational links more seriously than ever before, it was not accompanied by any significant changes leading towards a sense of 'political community' as a basis for the EC's system of policy-making. The socio-political factor was therefore the least important of the three in determining the course of transnational activity. This emphasised the limited scope for the politicisation of transnational party co-operation, although in the short historical period of its new development in the 1970s such change could hardly have been expected. In so far as this activity affected national parties, then it concerned party leaders and élites, activists and voters in a swift descending order of importance with the latter two distinctly marginal. The outcome of this development did not amount to any substantial 'Europeanisation' of national party politics, for such changes which did occur through transnational experience were élite-confined and were, in any case, very secondary to the overall operation of individual parties.

Nevertheless, transnational party co-operation had become during the 1974–9 period relatively less peripheral to general national party activity in that previously it had been of intermittent occurrence and an exclusive concern of a few Euro-specialists without reference or accountability to wider groups in the party structures. Although the principal conclusion of this chapter is that the national party frameworks are of overriding importance, as illustrated by the impact of the various national determinants on transnational activity rather than vice versa, the very influence of the former was proof of the closer interlinkage between the two levels of party politics. In this respect, a basic difference emerges between the two main factors of the three discussed in this chapter. Whereas the party-traditional one had always motivated party European policies, it was now not only specifically geared to transnational co-operation but also subject in this context to cross-influences from the newly emerging impact of political-functional determinants. The latter were therefore a more direct reflection of the degree of politicisation that had begun to mark transnational activity.

All three factors are likely to have a continuing and fundamental influence in the further development of party co-operation in the EC during the decade of the 1980s and beyond, when the socio-political one may come more into its own with a deeper level of such politicisation. However, any future projections must remain cautious in view of the fact that vertical influences moved predominantly in an 'upward' rather than 'downward' direction during the 1970s and that by the nature of the exercise involvement in transnational co-operation was qualitatively more élitist than national party politics.

Chapter 4: References

1 CDU, *Grundsatzprogramm* (Bonn: 1978), p. 53.
2 CDS, *Démocratie moderne* (1 February 1979), p. 12.
3 Juliet Lodge, *The European Policy of the SPD* (1976), p. 58.
4 Published in SPD, *Dokumente zur Europapolitik* (1978), p. 5.
5 See Stuart Hercock, 'The Labour Party and the Common Market', in Peter Ebsworth (ed.), *Europe: A Socialist Strategy* (1979), pp. 17–33.
6 See British Labour Party, *The EEC and Britain: A Socialist Perspective* (1977), p. 67.
7 See section on the EC in the party programme adopted by the Danish Social Democrats at their conference in September 1977, reprinted in *Euso* (26 October 1977). pp. 7–9.
8 J. C. Hollick, 'Direct elections to the European Parliament: the French debate', *The World Today*, vol. 33. no. 12 (December 1977), p. 472.
9 From European manifesto of the DIFE and *Les Gaullistes et l'Europe*, material supplied by the RPR headquarters, Paris.
10 Interview with Debré in *Stuttgarter Zeitung* (22 December 1978); Debré speeches reported in *The Times* (21 January 1977 and 16 June 1977).
11 *Les Communistes Français et l'Europe*, bulletin of PCF members of European Parliament, no. 3 (January 1979). pp. 16–17.
12 ibid., p. 27.
13 See statements published in *Eurored*, journal of West European committee of British Communist Party, no. 8.
14 British Labour Party, *Labour and Europe: Recent Statements of Policy* (1978). p. 10.
15 Report of Charles Fiterman in PCF. *Dossier Comité Central 27/28 septembre 1978*, p. 7.
16 RPR, *Europe 10 juin 1979: les questions que se posent les français?*, p. 4.
17 Interview no. 79.
18 SPD, *Dokumente zur Europapolitik*, p. 58.
19 British Conservative Party. *The Right Approach: A Statement of Conservative Aims* (1976). p. 68.
20 *Guardian* (29 March 1979).
21 Interview no. 1 (1979).
22 ibid.
23 Report on French parties by Ilsa Koch in *Das Parlament* (3 March 1979). p. 9.
24 *Le Figaro* (23 October 1978).
25 Interview no. 29.

232 *Transnational Party Co-operation and European Integration*

26 The following information in this paragraph draws heavily on interview no. 89.
27 ibid.
28 Theo Timman, 'Niederlande: Wahlkampf in europafreundlichem Klima', *Europa-Archiv* (25 December 1978). pp. 815–16.
29 Interviews nos. 84 and 89.
30 See Hollick. op. cit., pp. 476–7.
31 Published by FDP as *Leitlinien liberaler Europa-Politik* (1975).
32 Report in *Europa-Union* (November 1975).
33 Published in *Union in Deutschland* (20 January 1972).
34 CDU, *24. Bundesparteitag, Hannover, 1976* (1976). pp. 159–63.
35 See SPD. *Dokumente zur Europapolitik*, pp. 41–75. for the full text of this report of its European policy commission.
36 Interview no. 99.
37 UDF, *Rapport de la Commission Européenne présidée par Jean-François Deniau* (Paris: 1979).
38 Irish Labour Party. *Ireland and the European Community* (Dublin: 1978). p. 6.
39 British Labour Party. *Campaign Handbook: The EEC* (London: 1979). p. 1.
40 D. Debatisse *et al.*, *Europe: La France en jeu* (1979). pp. 228–30.
41 Gerry Pocock, *The Common Market Fraud: A Communist Party Pamphlet*.
42 See Irish Labour Party. *Ireland and the European Community*, pp. 8–9.
43 British Labour Party, *Campaign Handbook: The EEC*, pp. 6–7.
44 Interview no. 101.
45 Interview no. 87.
46 Preamble to direct elections programme of Danish Conservative People's Party. *A Free Denmark in a Free Europe* (Copenhagen: 1979); also Interviews nos. 75 and 76.
47 Norbert Gresch. *Transnationale Parteienzusammenarbeit in der EG* (1978). p. 139.
48 Interview no. 75.
49 *The Times* (10 October 1975).
50 *Frankfurter Allgemeine* (10 July 1976).
51 Interview no. 19.
52 Interview no. 23.
53 *Süddeutsche Zeitung* (14 May 1975).
54 *Frankfurter Allgemeine* (19 January 1978).
55 *The Times* (6 September 1975).
56 See Henning Wegener, 'Christdemokratische Zusammenarbeit', *Europäische Zeitung* (February 1979).
57 *Süddeutsche Zeitung* (23 January 1976).
58 Gresch. op. cit.. pp. 199–200.
59 *New York Times* (8 April 1976); *Frankfurter Allgemeine* (30 September 1977); *Neue Zürcher Zeitung* (5/6 February 1978).
60 Interview no. 99.
61 ibid.
62 Interview no. 96.
63 Interview no. 1 (1979).
64 Interview no. 84.
65 Interview no. 100.
66 Interview no. 64.
67 Interview no. 87.
68 *Die Zeit* (15 December 1978).

69 *The Times* (30 September 1976).
70 Jacques Vandamme, 'Belgien: Beschleunigung des inneren Wandels', *Europa-Archiv* (25 December 1978), pp. 819 ff.
71 Interview no. 84.
72 Interview no. 29.
73 H. Wallace, 'Direct elections and the political dynamics of the European Communities'. *Journal of Common Market Studies*, vol. XVII. no. 4 (June 1979). p. 296.
74 *Guardian* (12 May 1979).
75 SPD, *Ausserordentlicher Parteitag, Köln, 9–10.12.78* (Bonn: 1978), p. 72.
76 *Conseil National du Parti Républicain, 3.2.79*, report by Philippe Pontet, pp. 8–9.
77 Gresch, op. cit., p. 157.
78 Margarethe Holmstedt. former member of Liberal Party international liaison office, paper at UACES conference. Preston, November 1978.
79 R. Northawl and R. Corbett, *Electing Europe's First Parliament*, Fabian Tract no. 449 (1977), p. 24.
80 See Craxi's article. 'Il vangelo socialista'. *L'Espresso* (27 August 1978).
81 Emanuele Gazzo, 'Italien: mögliche Änderungen in der Parteienkonstellation', *Europa-Archiv* (25 December 1978), p. 810.
82 *Il Popolo* (20 May 1977).
83 Interview with Granelli in *La Discussione* (13 March 1978).
84 Interview no. 71.
85 Interview no. 9; interview with H. Geissler. CDU general-secretary. on West German radio (7 March 1978).
86 Interview with von Hassel, president of EUCD. on West German radio (29 June 1977).
87 Interviews nos. 87 and 100.
88 Interview no. 91.
89 Interview no. 94.
90 Interview no. 61.
91 Interview no. 97.
92 *Le Monde* (24 May 1975); *The Times* (26 January 1976).
93 *The Times* (8 November 1978).
94 For example, *L'Humanité* (8 March 1978).
95 Interview with Bangemann in *Europa-Union* (August 1975).
96 Interview no. 97.
97 *Frankfurter Allgemeine* (11 June 1977).
98 Interview with West German radio (24 June 1978).
99 See Rudolf Hrbek, 'Das deutsche Wahlgesetz zum Europäischen Parlament in der Parteienkontroverse', *Zeitschrift für Parlamentsfragen*, vol. 9, no. 2 (June 1978), pp. 168–79.
100 See Hollick, op. cit.
101 *The Times* (3 December 1977).
102 Interview no. 97.
103 Interview no. 1 (1979).
104 ibid.
105 Interview no. 99.
106 Interview no. 81.
107 Mary Robinson, 'Preparations for direct elections in Ireland'. *Common Market Law Review*, vol. 15 (May 1978). pp. 196–8.
108 This was illustrated, for instance, by local and regional party interviews in Hesse (interviews nos. 32–6); as well as Geoffrey Pridham's own local and regional research on German parties, especially the CDU/CSU, during earlier years.

109 Interview no. 22.
110 Interview no. 1 (1979).
111 Northawl and Corbett, op. cit., p. 21.
112 *New Statesman* (1 June 1979); The Economist (11 December 1976).
113 Published in *Union in Deutschland* (19 October 1978).
114 Douglas Hurd in Conservative Party, *Annual Conference, Blackpool, October 1977* (London: 1977). p. 128.
115 Interview no. 23.
116 Interviews nos. 16 and 22.
117 Interview no. 75.
118 Interview no. 1 (1979).
119 Douglas Hurd. 'Can the political parties rise to the European challenge?', *The Times* (25 July 1978).
120 *Conservative Manifesto for Europe 1979* (London: 1979), p. 5.
121 Conservative Research Department, *European Questions and Answers* (London: 1979), p. 9.
122 Dianne Hayter, *The Labour Party: Crisis and Prospects*, Fabian Tract no. 451 (London. 1977). pp. 10–11.
123 Interview no. 14 (1978).
124 *Daily Telegraph* (13 March 1979).
125 RPR. *Europe 10 juin 1979: les questions que se posent les français?*, p. 7.
126 ibid., p. 9.
127 Wolfgang Wagner. 'Deutschland: spät erkannte Detailprobleme'. *Europa-Archiv* (25 December 1978), p. 832.
128 Peter Reichel, 'Politisierung und Demokratisierung der EG? Zur ersten Direktwahl des Europäischen Parlaments', *Aus Politik und Zeitgeschichte* (26 May 1979). p. 11.
129 Interview no. 74; N. J. Haagerup. 'Dänemark und die Wahlen zum Europa-Parlament', *Dokumente, Zeitschrift für internationale Zusammenarbeit* (March 1977). p. 57.
130 Interview no. 97.
131 Interview no. 63.
132 D. Allen and R. Morgan, 'Grossbritannien: Vorrang der nationalen Probleme'. *Europa-Archiv* (25 December 1978). p. 798.
133 *Europäische Zeitung* (July 1977); Gerard Tardy, 'Französische Hindernisse', *Dokumente, Zeitschrift für internationale Zusammenarbeit* (March 1977), p. 50.
134 Tardy. op. cit., p. 50.
135 ibid.
136 *Europäische Zeitung* (July 1977).
137 Conservative Party, *Campaign Guide for Europe 1979* (London, 1979). p. ii.
138 Stanley Henig (ed.), *Political Parties in the European Community* (1979). p. 300.
139 Interviews nos. 80 and 87.
140 Haagerup, op. cit., p. 56; ibid. 'Dänemark: Direktwahlen im Schatten wirtschaftlicher und sozialer Probleme'. *Europa-Archiv* (25 December 1978), p. 826.
141 *Europa-Union* (February 1977).
142 Interview no. 19.

5

The Direct Elections Campaign and Transnational Party Co-operation

This chapter seeks to determine the extent to which the campaign for the first direct elections to the European Parliament in June 1979 gave a further stimulus to the development of transnational party co-operation. It will analyse how the campaign reflected and illustrated the politicisation of this activity during the 1974–9 period and the extent to which it could be regarded as the culmination of this development. It is important to emphasise that this chapter is not an attempt to give a comprehensive view of the whole European election campaign in all nine member states, but rather an analysis of its implications for transnational party activity.

However, a broad question which arises immediately is how far the campaign could be considered 'European' and, hence, providing a favourable context for party co-operation. The common orientation of all election campaigns in the nine member states was obviously towards the EC, just as the common objective of all the parties involved was to achieve as much representation as possible in the EP. As a consequence, all parties were for the first time simultaneously focusing on and debating their European policies and activities. There were, however, two major factors which contributed to the lack of a 'European' dynamism in the campaign. The first is best seen in comparison with national elections in member states, where the objective of national parties is to gain access to executive power. This objective serves to mobilise the parties intensively in terms of stimulating the élites and galvanising their activities. By contrast, the direct-elections campaign lacked an obvious governmental-power focus and, hence, the fundamental stimulus for a European-wide mobilisation and any closely concentrated European party-political conflict.

The second major contributory factor to this lack of dynamism was the necessity of conducting a preliminary information campaign on the EC itself and its basic features both for activists and voters. As one party organiser in Holland, an original member state and one with a traditionally strong pro-integrationist consensus, said:

'The trouble for the parties in the campaign is the first thing you have to do now is to promote the election itself, and the second step is . . . "Look, you have to vote for us, and not for the Socialists" . . .'[1] Similarly, the chairman of the Socialist Confederation electoral committee made the same point more colourfully that in direct elections 'one must build a locomotive, lay down lines and then put steam in the locomotive; normally, in election campaigns on the national level it is only a question of the steam'.[2] Not only was it necesary to inform people about the election but also about the EC in general and, above all, the EP in particular. As two British politicians observed after the election:

> . . . the real difficulty was that we were having to say to people, look here's this European Parliament which you probably only heard of for the first time a few months ago. From now on, it is going to be more important in your lives than it has been up to now . . .[3]

but at the same time:

> none of us . . . was able to describe in very precise detail what the European Assembly was about. I remember David Steel in a party political broadcast saying that it's a body with no power but immense influence, and going round this country asking people to exert themselves for this rather amorphous institution with rather strange and ill-defined powers is just not likely to set people alight . . . not likely to set the campaign on fire.[4]

This problem was not confined to new member states, for even in Luxemburg, one of the seats of the EP, according to a party general-secretary:

> . . . the majority of the Luxembourg people, they see the Parliament exists but they don't see the use of it. A lot of people when we have meetings ask but why? Why that Parliament? Why those elections? . . . The main question which has arisen when you have a meeting is, Europe yes, but what is the use of it? At the borders you still have to pass the customs and so on. And that is the main question that has always arisen.[5]

Thus, even those parties which regarded the promotion of their transnational links as an important element of their European activity were inhibited in giving them much priority. However, the direct elections campaign of 1979 was the first of a five-yearly cycle and, as in future the necessity for basic information may decrease, greater emphasis can be given to the projection of transnational party aspects.

In order to discuss the importance of the European campaign for the theme of this book, the first section of the chapter will focus on how and to what extent European policy positions and transnational links were promoted by political parties with reference to the party federations. The second section will consider the stimulus given to the more *ad hoc* multilateral and bilateral links, which had developed as a subsidiary and contributory factor to transnational co-operation but played a special role in the campaign. The third section will examine how in the light of this campaign national determinants of transnational party activity were again in evidence.

(a) The Transnational Party Organisational Dimension and its Electoral Activity

As discussed in Chapter 3, the prospect of direct elections stimulated the three major political tendencies in the Community's nine member states to develop formal transnational organisational links. It is therefore very pertinent to see how the federations actually came into operation once direct elections took place, and with what effects. How far did national parties project themselves ideologically and organisationally as part of a wider European tendency, and to what extent was this envisaged as the basis for future European party development? In this connection, were the federations and the party groups stressed as interrelated units within the triangular construction of transnational party co-operation, or was the emphasis on individual party autonomy in a European setting?

So far as the 1979 elections were concerned, the answers to these questions will inevitably be modified by two considerations: first, the embryonic state of the federations as Euro-party formations, and, secondly, the novelty of the organisational practice of using their limited facilities by the various national parties. Although the federations and party groups, politically speaking, offered little more than a frame of reference for the purpose of electioneering, they also provided a variety of cosmetic facilities, such as the production and circulation of stickers, badges, posters, common slogans and symbols; organisational facilities with the holding of common meetings, the arranging for the exchange of national speakers between countries, a contribution towards the financing of the various national party campaigns and the printing of material; and, last but not least, the opportunity for using common programmes or declarations.

Nearly all the member parties of the Socialist Confederation mentioned during the course of their campaigns their nebulous desire to promote socialism in Europe or create a more Socialist Europe, the main exception being British Labour. A relevant extension of this is how far the unity of all EC Socialist parties was considered to be an important precondition in the achievement of this. Here there was a noticeable reluctance among the Socialist parties to take the step from projecting the need for European socialism towards promoting an integrated party structure to achieve this end, so that the Confederation was not elevated to this level.

The Italian Socialist Party was one of the most vociferous and uninhibited of all Confederation members in its emphasis on its Socialist connections in the EC, with its main slogan for the contemporaneous national and European campaigns 'If you speak Socialism, you will be understood all over Europe', which was written in all languages of the Community including Dutch.[6] The Dutch Labour Party, too, stressed the need for a more Socialist Europe, but had to play a generally low-key campaign with regard to transnational links due to emerging divisions over integration within the party and attacks by national party rivals on divisions within the Confederation.[7] The Belgian Socialists similarly took as their theme 'how we can reinforce the Socialist views and the Socialist solutions within the European Community', but went further in emphasising the need for a party-political follow-up:

> We feel that we can rely on the strength of the Socialist parties in the other countries. Well, to disclose the main slogan on the Flemish side: 'Together, we are the strongest in Europe'. So, we are constantly linking our movement to the other parties. To give you another idea, the figure of the chairman of our party will be presented together with the figure of Willy Brandt and Joop den Uyl, slightly in the background, but nevertheless this idea of combining our strength with the other parties will be very much used.[8]

The West German Social Democrats, on the other hand, placed their main emphasis on their country's role in the EC, summarised in the poster with a picture of Helmut Schmidt and Willy Brandt and the slogan, 'Our Word Counts in Europe', with correspondingly less attention to transnational party aspects despite their active interest in the Confederation. So it can be seen that generally during the campaign it was the smaller parties and the opposition parties which most of all emphasised a Socialist Europe and extended this to a discussion of links with other EC Socialist parties. This arose from their desire to prove that they were not 'isolated' in the European sphere and that they had a supportive framework of international links, where domestic motives of prestige played a part.

The larger and governing parties tended more to emphasise their role and influence in the Community in general.

Thus, in the Socialist campaign there was no attempt to project any form of 'European Socialist party'. This possibility was only raised as a point of contention, although it did not become an issue, in the campaign in Denmark, so that the Social Democrats there had to emphasise that the Confederation was not a European party, an 'accusation' made by its opponents, particularly the People's Movement against the EC and by some of the more left-wing parties.[9] Nevertheless, the Confederation and the party group did feature as organisational entities in the campaign, although the low-key cosmetic role of the Confederation reflected the lack of emphasis on its potential role. While all the member parties of the Confederation used the red *flèche* symbol on their election material, it was not necessarily explained or promoted as a European Socialist emblem.

The extent to which the Confederation's common statements were used varied from country to country. The Appeal to the Electorate of January 1979 formed the basis of the line of the French Socialist Party with, for instance, Jacques Delors, member of the PS's *comité directeur*, emphasising the points of agreement which existed between the European Socialist parties leading to the formulation of the Appeal.[10] In Italy, the small PSDI took an even more transnational line: 'The Appeal to the Electorate was our basic campaign document, our electoral platform and programme. In our view, the appeal should reflect a common desire for action on the part of all the member parties of the Confederation.'[11] By contrast, despite its pro-integrationist position, the German SPD, which supported the Appeal of the Confederation, attempted to play it down during the campaign as it advocated policies to the left of some of those followed by the Schmidt government at the national level. The CDU/CSU nevertheless attempted to make an issue of this, on the one hand vilifying the European Socialists for having no common programme and, on the other, emphasising the SPD's association with the 'left-wing' Appeal. The SPD's national coalition partners, the FDP, also attacked it in similar terms for its 'left-wing' European programme.[12] In Britain, copies of the Appeal were supplied to candidates and delegates to members' meetings, but it was not distributed to the electors in any large numbers; although its use was not forbidden, it was not viewed with much enthusiasm by the party organisation.[13]

Despite its generally low-profile cosmetic projection, the Socialist Confederation financed and co-ordinated a comprehensive series of specialised conferences and joint rallies in most member states. As the deputy secretary-general of the Socialist Confederation argued:

We say that we have a lot of things in common, but we are not completely unanimous on various things; that we have a unanimous attitude in let us say the basic outlines, but we do have differences of opinion on the implementation. So we try to regard the electorate as [those] who can crystallise for themselves whether we are a serious party and whether we make a serious effort to overcome problems. And for that reason we have organised a series of specialised conferences in the member countries on issues which we find are very important for the forthcoming elections and also for the forthcoming European Socialist group.[14]

Each meeting involved relevant experts from member parties and normally three people to make an introductory statement – an area specialist, a political leader and a representative from the trade unions with the objective of attracting a delegation from each country of six to eight people.[15] The British Labour Party was the major exception in that it did not hold its scheduled conference on development aid after its international officer attended the first meeting in Holland, for even though 'the Confederation would have met the cost . . . the British Labour Party felt that the effort of providing, for example, six languages would not have justified it'.[16] These meetings culminated in a grand finale in Paris, which was attended by all the major European Socialist leaders, including James Callaghan as well as Mario Soares, with a major press conference followed by fireworks and a concert by the London Symphony Orchestra in the Jardins du Trocadero.[17]

The Confederation did not directly arrange the interchange of national speakers between countries due to shortage of staff and facilities for this, although they assisted with contacts when requested.[18] The Confederation did help with the financing of the various national party campaigns, either supplementing the not insubstantial funds available to state-aided parties, such as in Germany, or as an essential source of finance for other parties, such as British Labour. The latter, for example, financed the printing of 25 million copies of the national election address, *Labour and Europe,* out of the £300,000 Confederation grant, without which 'many parts of the country would not have had election addresses.[19]

A feature of the Socialist campaigns was the lack of prominence of the party group in the EP, either as a unit in which Socialist parties had been co-operating for some time in an effort to further a Socialist Community, or as the parliamentary arm of the Confederation. This, as will be seen, was somewhat in contrast to the Christian Democrats. When the party group was mentioned it tended to be in terms of the Socialist group being the largest in the Parliament and hence the most effective one to be aligned with in the protection of national, regional, local and specific interests. As one of its two principal themes, the Irish Labour Party stressed that 'Irish national interests within the Community would be best served by strong representation in the Socialist Group within the European Parliament; the Socialist Group is the largest group and the only group with members from all nine member states'.[20] The Danish Social Democratic Party also projected its membership of the Socialist group by saying 'that belonging to the largest political configuration in Europe people will be better able to look to them to support Danish interests if they vote for us rather than some of the smaller parties'.[21] Similarly, the British Labour Party in an election broadcast emphasised that the Socialist group was the largest political group in the EP, but in terms of having defended British interests with help from the British government in the Council of Ministers. Furthermore, John Prescott introduced a national partisan aspect into it:

The Tory party have criticised us as anti-European. In fact they are the lepers of Europe. They are considered too politically extreme for all other European conservative parties. With the exception of one extreme Danish party, they have all refused to join the Tories in an alliance in the European Assembly. And the reason's clear. It is their right-wing policies in the Assembly . . . The British Tory party is far too conservative even for the European right-wing parties.[22]

Therefore, parties which were both strongly and reservedly inte-grationist tended alike to emphasise the group, when it was men-tioned at all, as a vehicle for defending specific interests.

One feature which all the Socialist campaigns had in common, with British Labour less emphatically so, was the use of politically 'safe' slogans pronouncing a broad commitment to the furtherance of socialism in the EC, but remaining on the level of mutually uncontroversial generalities. There was a noticeable absence of concrete reference to specific transnational party as opposed to national party means to achieve this aim. Nevertheless, in most of the national parties the existence of the Confederation became that much better known to the activists through the campaign; while the voters were introduced to the idea of European Socialist solidarity at a cosmetic level. In practice, the Confederation played a very minimal co-ordinating role for the conduct of the nine national campaigns.

The seven Christian Democratic parties tended not so much to refer to European-wide Christian Democracy as such, as to con-centrate on the specific presentation of the European People's Party

(EPP) as an organisational unit, thus reflecting their more pragmatic approach to party co-operation. This less reserved projection of the EPP was illustrated by its strong cosmetic role. The EPP flag flew at every major meeting and many minor ones, while stickers with the emblem of the EPP and the slogan 'Together Towards a Europe of Free People' underneath were widely distributed at all meetings. There were also produced T-shirts, neck-scarves, key-rings (all with the EPP emblem) and an EPP 'European Passport'. Thus, the existence of the EPP gained salience during the campaign.

When it came to the practicalities of actively promoting the EPP, there were noticeable differences between the various countries. In some, such as Italy and Holland, the existence of the EPP was acknowledged but not carried further, while in others, such as Germany and Belgium, the membership of the EPP was a visible feature of the campaign, as it was in Ireland. The Italian Christian Democrats were less inclined to promote the EPP, reference to its symbol and slogans being conspicuously absent from DC newspaper advertisements.[23] Some individuals did choose to include references to the EPP, such as the advertisement of Senator Luigi Noè who had been a member of the EP.[24] This general omission stemmed partly from their reluctance to emphasise their links with the German CDU/CSU,[25] and partly their preference to stress their influence as a governing party in the EC. The Dutch Christian Democrats were reluctant to promote the EPP, but this lay in the technical reason that the national CDA (the confederation of their three confessional parties) was only a few years old and at too early a stage to promote yet the further new idea of the EPP.[26] Nevertheless, green-and-white stickers were available in Holland with the EPP symbol and CDA initials side by side.

More active and enthusiastic attention to the EPP was given by the German and Belgian parties. The EPP symbol featured on much, though not all, of CDU advertising, and the party held five major European festivals with much EPP publicity in large cities which attracted more than 10,000 people in total. A major European congress was held in Kiel and documents and speeches from it were reproduced, including that of Leo Tindemans as president of the EPP, with each district branch receiving 100 copies for distribution to opinion formers.[27] The Belgian CVP fought under the banner of the EPP, and attracted between 1,200 and 1,500 people a time to a four-hour road show which toured across Flanders.[28] The Irish Fine Gael also emphasised their links with other European Christian Democrats through the catchphrase 'Strongly together in the European People's Party'.[29]

In addition to the cosmetic projection of the EPP, it was implied, if not openly stressed, that the Christian Democratic group in the

EP was the parliamentary arm of the European People's Party. In Ireland, Euro-parliamentary links became something of a contentious issue centring around whether Ireland's interests could best be served by being a large part of a smaller group, as Fianna Fail in the DEP, or a small part of a larger group, as with Fine Gael and the Labour Party in the CD and Socialist groups respectively: 'The European election was enlivened by a last-minute allegation that the Fianna Fail has been exploring the possibility of joining the Liberal group in the European Parliament, which was . . . denied by the FF Senator Michael Yeats.'[30] In Germany, as more representative of the other Christian Democratic parties, membership of the party groups did not feature as an issue between the national parties or as a major part of the CDU/CSU campaign. The CDU, however, circulated to its activists a bulletin called *CDU-Europawahl*, in which the party groups were presented together and the broader aspects of the EP discussed.[31]

The use of the EPP programme varied from country to country and flexibly according to national circumstances. The promotion of the programme was generally limited to circulation of the shortened and glossy version, primarily to activists but also available emblazoned with the EPP symbol at Christian Democratic meetings. The Dutch, for example, circulated 300,000 copies of this to party members and campaign teams, while an issue of *CDU-Europawahl* was devoted to the election platform of the EPP.

The EPP did not play an obvious co-ordinating or organisational role in the election campaign. In July 1977, the election commission of the EPP first met 'to draw up concrete guidelines for the conduct of the election campaign',[32] but ultimately the role of the EPP involved a limited number of minimal tasks, such as the distribution of its programme. Unlike the Socialist Confederation, the EPP did not specifically supervise the organisation of common meetings, but rather national parties organised mass meetings or rallies under the auspices of the EPP and many of these included prominent speakers from other European countries, such as at the five CDU European festivals mentioned, and that held by the Christian Democrats in Luxemburg on 6 May which was attended by Helmut Kohl and Leo Tindemans. The authors asked themselves if one of the songs sung by the dancing group – 'I'll Do It My Way' – was significant! In fact, the interchange of speakers between EPP member parties was a special feature of their campaign with the EPP president, Leo Tindemans, particularly active in this: 'My campaign has taken me all over Belgium. I have also spoken in Holland, in Germany, in Italy, in France, in Luxembourg, and in Ireland. In Denmark and Britain, I have been interviewed on Radio and TV.'[33] Generally, the EPP relied heavily on its national parties during the campaign for their moral and organisational support.

By contrast with the Socialist parties, which promoted the concept of European socialism but avoided too specific a reference to a European Socialist party formation, the Christian Democrats declared their open association with an EC-wide political party. This reflected the different approach and attachment to the idea of 'party' between the two ideological tendencies. The EPP was not seen as a potential threat to existing national parties in the same way that a European party might be seen by the Socialists. On the other hand, the EPP's projection by its members was distinctly cosmetic rather than policy-oriented. In this sense, the co-operation of parties within the EPP was undoubtedly projected through its publicity not simply among party activists, but also externally to the general public.

The campaign of the Liberal ELD was the most co-ordinative in organisational terms of the three federations in the first European elections, with the readiness of member parties to use its limited facilities. Cosmetically, the role of the ELD was comparable to that of the EPP, and there was also present a general attachment to Liberal principles and the value of European integration.

There was no equivalent to the symbol of the EPP, but the common slogan 'Liberals United for a United Europe' or 'Liberal Democrats United for a United Europe' was used by all parties except the French Giscardians, due to their combined UDF list with other national parties. The common colours of the ELD – yellow and blue – featured widely, particularly in the German FDP campaign, since they coincided with that party's own colours. The initials 'ELD/LDE' and the name of the federation also were prominent on the widely circulated publicity material, such as its colourful car stickers. The extent to which the publicity of the ELD made an impact locally varied from country to country. It was particularly appreciated during the campaign at the local level among British Liberal activists, due to their party's almost complete dependence on the ELD for publicity material. As one Liberal agent expressed it: 'We have had a lot of publicity material sent us from the European Liberals and really good stuff that we are getting out to the public.'[34]

The Liberal group in the EP when it featured in the campaign tended to be linked to other themes, such as underlining the governmental links of the various national Liberal parties. As the British leader, David Steel, said in a party-political broadcast:

Liberals elected from Britain won't be joining a small minority, as we are in the House of Commons, but a substantial group of fellow Liberals elected from the other countries. For Liberalism is a powerful force in Europe. Most of our neighbours enjoy strong coalition governments, where members of more than one party pull together for the benefit of their country. And Liberals, therefore, participate in government in most of Europe. In fact, in five of the nine member states today the foreign ministers are Liberals.[35]

Occasionally, the federation and the group were mentioned together, as, for example, in an advertisement for the Italian PRI, which declared: 'The Republicans in the Federation of the 12 Liberal and Democratic Parties of the European Community: the third group of the European Parliament.'[36] Similarly, an election address from Plymouth, England, made no mention of the ELD, but emphasised the party group in terms of defence of specific interests:

... the Liberal party will be working with the European Liberals and Democrats who are already a well-established group in the European Parliament. Their policy is to look after the interests of the individuals as the Community develops. Individuals as consumers, as producers, as business people, as inhabitants of particular regions with particular needs.[37]

The promotion of the ELD programme formed an important part of the campaign, but its distribution depended on national parties. There were in fact conditions on the member parties of the ELD to do so: 'After we had agreed the programme, we were obliged to use it. It was not a case of being able to use it or not. Although there are some items of the programme which are stressed more heavily in one country than they are in other countries, we use the same points.'[38] Some parties issued additional qualifying statements such as the British, and others like the Dutch who also produced their own glossy summary of the programme. A hundred thousand copies of the ELD programme were printed and distributed by April 1979. However, much more widely circulated were the 10 million copies of the ELD brochure *Strong Points*, which was regarded by all party campaign managers as the most successful campaign publication.[39]

Although it would be too optimistic to conclude that 'the twelve parties united in the European Liberal Democrats' Federation are fighting this campaign, not as twelve campaigns, but as one campaign',[40] as the secretary-general of the German FDP did a month before the election date, the ELD played an acknowledged organisational role in co-ordinating the activities of the twelve different member parties. Its main centralised activity was the printing of publicity material for all member parties, but it also played an important role in facilitating the reciprocation of information between parties, aiding the exchange of national speakers between countries and assisting with the organisation of meetings. The ELD campaign committee comprising representatives from each member party played an important part, if not in co-ordinating their efforts, at least in exchanging organisational notes on the way in which each national party was approaching the campaign. The election managers met every six weeks to two months from June 1978:

> At every meeting of the campaign managers' committee we allowed about half an hour to explain what they were planning to do nationally. And then other parties said that is a good idea, we will do the same. The Germans, they are of course richer than anybody else, have for example installed three double decker buses complete with bar, films, electrical equipment, to show films, speeches, etc. . . . all the parties have done the same, like the Luxembourgers and the Dutch and the British.[47]

When the campaign managers were not in session, the ELD headquarters in Brussels provided a central focus or information 'switchboard' for the member parties. All parties except the French and the Italians had telexes installed, and most were in almost daily contact with Brussels towards the end of the campaign.

The ELD office was often involved with the exchange of major speakers between countries, with the initiatives and specific requests coming from the individual national parties. The ELD established the initial contact and arrangements were then made bilaterally. It also helped to ensure that at every major national meeting representatives from other parties were present. Each country was asked to stage a Euro-congress between the beginning of 1979 and the election. The British Liberals initiated this series with the London ELD congress in December 1978, while another highlight was an election rally in Luxemburg at the beginning of April attended by leading European Liberals as well as representatives from Liberal parties in Spain, Portugal and Greece. This 'demonstration congress' to show the unity of European Liberals included speakers from the major Liberal parties.

From the preceding discussion it can be seen that the predominant role of the ELD was the co-ordination of publicity and information. Although the broad principles of Liberalism were projected in the campaigns of all the parties – the rights of the individual, a pluralist Europe and cultural diversity – these were not presented as a European Liberal ideology comparable to the ideological orientation of the Socialists. However, the Liberal parties stressed their common support for the furtherance of European integration. Following their mutual co-operation during the campaign, the party election managers had future plans to meet regularly every three months and maintain their contacts. This was important as the ELD, like the other federations, was ultimately dependent on the willing co-operation of its member parties: 'Although there are some functions that we have to do ourselves, we are dependent for anything which is on a more practical level on the national parties.'[42]

The Communist parties are considered under this section both because they represent a major European-wide ideological tendency, with particular application to Italy and France, and as they have formed a transnational group in the EP; even though their campaign at the European level was essentially bilateral or multilateral. Individual national Communist parties did not as a whole project themselves during the campaign as exponents of a European ideology. However, in an interview Maxime Gremetz of the PCF central committee underlined the importance of the international activity of the Communists in the course of the European election campaign, emphasising the common struggle with the Italian Communists towards a Europe of the workers. Generally little attention was given to the activities of Communist parties in their EP group, although it was reported that 'Communist leaders have stressed that their links with leftist parties in other countries of the nine will make them a more effective force in Strasbourg'.[43]

In practice, the predominant international activity of the Communist parties tended to be on a bilateral basis. French representatives met all the Communist parties from the other Community states and those from countries concerned with EC enlargement. Joint declarations were issued on specific policy areas, but were sufficiently vague as to allow agreement. The French and Belgian Communists met in Brussels at the end of May 1979, and issued an indictment of multinationals, reaffirmed their support for the workers, determined to develop a true co-operation between sovereign nations and to progress beyond the politics of 'blocs'.[44] Similar mutual interests between the French and German Communist parties were proclaimed at a large meeting in Munich about the same time.[45] The Italian and Belgian parties issued a joint declaration for the European elections, which were described as 'an important political event' and an 'opportunity for change'. Both parties gave their support to 'a workers' Europe', a 'democratic' and peaceful Europe and the need for greater agreement between democratic forces, including the Socialists, Social Democrats, Communists, Christian Democrats and the lay parties.[46]

The culmination of this bilateral activity was the mass rallies in Marseilles and Turin in May 1979, which were intended as a demonstration of solidarity between the Italian and French Communist parties. The theme pursued by Berlinguer in Marseilles was the unity of the French and Italian workers, but his main preoccupation was the problems at home with a final reference to the opportunities afforded by the EC. In Turin, a few days later, at a European rally which was reported as the biggest ever to be held on the Continent[47] Berlinguer and Marchais were the main speakers, although there were twenty-four Euro-candidates also on the platform. Marchais continued what he had been saying in Marseilles, underlining the struggle for employment and development, defence of democracy and the need for peace.[48] Despite the pledges between the parties to increase their co-operation in Europe and their agreement on the need to transform the Community, they were open about their specific differences such as over enlargement. In this sense, of all the national parties outside the federations the Communists developed the most active European-level approach to their campaign.

As this discussion of the European campaign from the transnational angle has shown, there were several common features to the parts played by the different federations. These were mainly functional, and included to a greater or lesser extent the use of common programmes or declarations, the exchange of speakers between countries, the holding of common meetings and the distribution of common publicity or information material. In carrying out these tasks, the federations alike were basically dependent on the efforts of member parties at the national level. When viewing the electoral role of the federations in a more political light, interesting and basic differences emerged between them and reflected their divergent approaches to the idea of European party co-operation. It is possible to summarise the broad distinctions between the three cases with respect to the ideological, organisational and cosmetic aspects of their part in the campaign. The Socialist Confederation, while the strongest in projecting a sense of European-wide ideology, was the most reluctant through its members to promote its transnational implications for party activity. The Christian Democratic EPP, on the other hand, revealed a less emphatic ideological identity in European terms, but was more insistent on using the campaign to further its importance as a European 'party', although this took a largely cosmetic form – thus underlining the Christian Democrats' pronounced electoral orientation as such. The Liberal ELD, while equally vague as to its European ideological identity, gave substance to its transnational electoral role by applying its own co-operation to the organisational level.

These broad distinctions between the three federations confirmed those already identified in the discussion in Chapter 3 of the transnational-organisational dimension from the mid-1970s. However, in assessing the impact of transnational roles in the direct-elections campaign it is important not to forget that the latter comprised in reality nine individual national campaigns, although they were simultaneous and operating under the same European rubric. The common, if limited, experience of party co-operation in the first European elections undoubtedly benefited the party federations, but the full consequences of this and their earlier activity depends on the future course of the European Parliament's role in the Community.

(b) Bilateral and Multilateral Electoral Co-operation

Bilateral and multilateral contacts, which had been a significant background factor in transnational activity, achieved a special salience in the shape of electoral co-operation during the European campaign. The first part of this discussion will consider this co-operation between those parties which are members of the federations, and in addition those outside them but which belong to Euro-parliamentary groups (except the Communists already discussed). The second part will consider bilateral and multilateral campaign activities of those parties with no transnational basis.

Such co-operation, stimulated by the direct elections campaign, took two major forms: the most visible was speeches by leading politicians at rallies in other EC countries; while, on a less spectacular level, there was the presence of representatives from other national parties at regional or local meetings. Due to logistic problems the latter was not possible on a wide scale, but was most highly developed at a cross-border level. This bilateral/multilateral activity was significant in its contribution to party co-operation in view of the undeveloped electoral role of the federations. According to the Socialist Confederation, in reference to the exchange of national politicians between countries: 'We are not co-ordinating that. We have been thinking about it, but we can't because I would have to engage one or two people to do it. It is being done bilaterally. That is to say, that we do assist because we do have contacts.'[49]

What emerges is that the regularity of electoral contact of this kind depended on the country in question, and the party within it. Generally, the two countries most involved here were Italy and West Germany. In both cases, the themes of the campaign were strongly pro-integrationist across parties with their rivalry to prove their 'Europeanness'. The German Social Democrats held a 'Europe Day' attended by 25,000 on 20 May in Nuremberg, which was attended by many foreign party representatives – including a speech by Karl Van Miert, the Flemish Socialist party leader. The SPD was equally involved to varying degrees in the campaigns of its neighbour parties along the borders of Belgium, the Netherlands and Denmark. The CDU/CSU held major rallies which were attended by foreign representatives and foreign speakers, including John Kelly from the Irish Fine Gael, who gave six major addresses in German in two days, and Tom Normanton, a British Conservative, who spoke at rallies in Hamburg, Stuttgart and Munich. There was also some border activity between the German Christian Democrats and the Dutch CDA.

The Italian parties were also anxious to establish their European credentials electorally. The PSI was reported as 'adorning' itself with references to links with the German Social Democratic party.[50] Willy Brandt spoke in Italian at the inaugural meeting of the Socialist Party in Turin and appeared regularly on PSI electoral broadcasts, urging people to vote Socialist in both Italian and European elections to build a 'truly European Socialist dimension'.[51] Brandt's support was also claimed by the Italian PSDI (which caused some friction between the two Socialist parties), and a letter from him to that party was published as part of its publicity campaign.[52] Although the Italian Christian Democrats were reserved about their links with the German CDU/CSU, they stressed their association with the 'Europeans' Konrad Adenauer and Robert Schuman but more commonly they stressed their governing role rather than their party-political links in the EC. The Italian Liberals and Republicans sought to attract as many foreign speakers to their meetings as possible.

The Benelux countries featured various multilateral and bilateral contacts during the campaign. The Dutch parties were somewhat hesitant about their respective links with the German political parties due to the articulation of anti-German feeling among the Socialists and, in the case of the Christian Democrats, following a particularly unsuccessful interview with Helmut Kohl on Dutch television a few months before the campaign. However, Leo Tindemans, nicknamed 'Mr Europe', was described as being 'integrated' into the CDA campaign[53] and he spoke at three major rallies. The parties in Luxemburg tended to concentrate on their own national legislative elections, which took place on the same day. Nevertheless the Socialist party received more requests than it could handle from the French, Italian and German Socialists to speak abroad, partly because of the Luxemburgers' linguistic ability. The POSL itself presented other European speakers at major meetings such as at the Socialist Euro-candidates' rally in Luxemburg on 26–27 April attended, among others, by Willy Brandt, François Mitterrand and Barbara Castle.

In France, the Socialists were the only party to participate actively in multilateral or bilateral activities of the kind outlined. This culminated with the meeting at the end of May in Paris attended by all the Socialist leaders. Some foreign speakers supported candidates on the Giscardian UDF list, but this was not a widespread feature of the campaign. In Britain the exchange of foreign speakers was with all parties on a rather arbitrary basis. One or two foreign speakers came to Labour Party meetings for, according to the national agent, 'there has been no opposition to them: if people have wanted to have them then they could have had them; but most of the candidates realised that the most important thing was how we were going to enthuse our people'.[54] German Christian Democrats attended meetings in Sussex, Cheshire and north-west London as a result of private contacts with Conservative MPs.[55] Some British Liberals went abroad in direct request from other Liberal parties, though no such requests were received from France. Liberals who came to Britain included Ove Guldberg, former Danish Foreign Minister, who did a tour of the south coast and participated in a local television programme; Florus Wijsenbeek, secretary-general of the ELD and Willy de Clercq from the Belgian PVV, as well as two German Liberals. One of them, Gunter Verheugen, declared support for Russell Johnston in a press conference in Britain:

> Russell Johnston has been a very distinguished and successful Member of the Liberal Group in the European Parliament for six years, and let me tell you quite openly how desperately we are hoping to see him and some more British Liberals back in the European Parliament. The leader of my Party, Foreign Minister Hans-Dietrich Genscher, together with Prime Minister Gaston Thorn of Luxembourg and the other Liberal foreign ministers in Europe have therefore sent a message to Russell Johnston pledging their support to him and his colleagues in the present campaign. We want them and the British public to know that they are not standing alone in this fight, but that the hopes and the expectations and the support of all European Liberals are on their side.[56]

In Ireland, 'if the issues have been mainly though not exclusively domestic, the participants have been totally so – no Willy Brandt in Liberty Hall, no Franz-Josef Strauss at the chapel gates, and positively no Jacques Chirac anywhere'.[57]

From the discussion it can be seen that such multilateral and bilateral co-operation tended to be unstructured, *ad hoc*, informal and dependent on personal contacts as well as those between various national party headquarters. In addition, the availability of foreign speakers was in part determined by the nature of their own electoral systems, where the existence of a party list and a secure place on it allowed them freedom to travel, not to mention their general linguistic ability. Judging by the 1979 campaign, these bilateral/

multilateral contacts were complementary to, and not competitive with, the transnational element in it.

Similar though sparser contacts developed also among parties with no transnational membership, notably among those on the fringe. The new ecologist parties, which campaigned in most EC countries, made no attempt to project themselves as a part of a European ideological stream. The principal point of convergence between them and their 292 candidates was their opposition to nuclear energy. Also, no attempt was made to project Ecoropa, the EC-wide association of ecologist parties, as a potential party organisational structure, and even its existence was not stressed. However, it did produce a manifesto[58] with contributions from individuals in Edam, Paris, Bordeaux, Oslo, Bonn and Berlin, but this was dismissed by the British Ecology Party.[59] There was also a meeting on 21–22 April at Saint-Germain-en-Laye (Yvelines) of the German, Belgian and British ecologist parties which included the Italian and Dutch Radical parties 'to focus on the methods of their campaign'.[60] The German ecologist list was launched before the press in Brussels, and representatives from the 'green movements' from other countries gave their support.[61] Primarily, any contacts between the various ecologist parties were of an *ad hoc* nature, and their campaigns were really national. Apart from specific environmental issues concerning their respective countries, the French, German and Dutch ecologists were concerned with trying to abolish, or at least publicise, the unfairness of the 5 per cent requisite minimal vote (4 per cent in Holland).

Although some of the smaller anti-integrationist parties made tentative overtures of a bilateral kind, these were also of a weak and *ad hoc* nature, because of their different national motives. The Danish People's Movement against the EC (Folkebevaegelsen mod EF) tried to establish contact with British, Irish, Welsh and Scottish opponents of the EC to form 'a group' with them. These overtures were not received well by the British Labour Party, which felt that party loyalty should be the primary consideration:

As a matter of fact, we were very concerned that two or three of our candidates had lent their support to the anti-Danish campaign by putting their names to a declaration . . . on the grounds that we would take a very poor view if any Socialist party in another country supported here, say, the anti-Common Market candidates in a parliamentary election . . . on the basis that no one should give support to somebody who is fighting official Danish Labour party candidates.[62]

Thus, the campaigns of the parties opposed to the Community, including small parties in Italy and Belgium, fought national campaigns with no emphasis given to associations with allied parties in other countries.

Similar nationally based differences were to be found among the extreme-left parties which attempted to form an international platform for the campaign in January 1979. About twenty such groups from Community countries (including the PSU [United Socialist Party] in France, the Sinn Fein in Ireland, Lotta Continua in Italy) held a meeting at Saint Gérard near Namur. Although they agreed on their denunciation of the Community as a haven for multinationals and 'the ambitious attempt at hegemony in the EC on the part of Social-Democrat parties, led by the German SPD', there was disagreement over the course to be followed. The Sinn Fein proposed that the elections be boycotted; the Danes called on Denmark to leave the Community; and the Belgians, French and Italians were in favour of taking part in the elections.[63]

Despite such lack of agreement, what emerges from looking at these smaller and disparate parties is that the direct elections campaign stimulated even among them the search for bilateral/multilateral partners. These were necessarily *ad hoc*, tenuous and full of differences, but it will be interesting to see how much the activities of the EP during the subsequent five years convince them of the need to organise their common efforts more systematically for the second European election.

(c)   The Relevance of the National Party Frameworks

So far the role in the campaign of the three federations has been treated somewhat in isolation. The intention here, following the discussion in Chapter 4 of the national party frameworks, is to identify the ways in which national determinants constrained this transnational electoral element. In one obvious sense the role of the federations was made very relative by the fact that the first campaign was essentially a combination of national events, but it is important again to focus specifically on the interlinkage between transnational and national party activity. At the national level, the European campaign cannot be so isolated from the overall political context of each national party, while the campaign for direct elections was treated primarily as an additional political and organisational hurdle to be overcome in the national party-political game.

The overall national political situation determined the general focus of the separate campaigns and set the party battle lines: the general problems facing the country in question; its and the parties' broad attitude to the EC; and the time-differential between the national and the European elections, as well as the interrelationship of these three aspects. In Italy, for example, there was much pre-occupation with terrorism, inflation and, of course, the parliamentary election, which was held the weekend before the European elections. There was some element of truth in the observation: 'The European election was built up by all parties as a kind of return match for the national election of 3 June.'[64] In Ireland, it was generally acknow-ledged that direct elections would be interpreted as a mid-term test of the government which faced 10 per cent unemployment, a sixteen-week long postal strike, three-hour petrol queues and high inflation. In Denmark, by comparison, the focus of the campaign was on the merits and demerits of membership of the EC. There was some tendency to regard it as a re-run of the referendum over entry in 1972, according to the People's Movement against the EC, although 'in a sense it is equivalent to a referendum, because we can demon-strate how strong the resistance against membership is, it is not a referendum and can't be argued that way'.[65] In Britain, the some-what reserved attitude of the country towards the EC combined with post-electoral fatigue following the national election a month before to reduce the impact of the European campaign. In Luxem-burg, the coincidence of national and European elections on the same day highlighted the priority accorded the former. According to the POSL, 'the national elections were the centre of attention throughout the entire election campaign; some parties did not fight the European elections at all'.[66] In France too, the European elec-tions were treated in effect as a preliminary skirmish for the presi-dential contest of 1981, though the debate was to a surprising extent centred on European issues.

Having established the national political contexts, this examina-tion of national determinants of transnational electoral activity will follow the outline used earlier in this book where applicable to the European campaign, notably aspects of the party-traditional and political-functional factors.

To what extent was the European aspect of a party's ideology projected at the national level? The German case illustrated that, even though all three major parties were clearly pro-integrationist, their self-presentation tended to be national-political in the first instance extrapolated into the European sphere. While the EC Socialist parties promoted the concept of European socialism, the SPD found that: 'Because it is clear from opinion polls that most voters will vote in the same way as in other elections, so it is a question of mobilising people used to voting for the "SPD".'[67] Similarly, the CDU/CSU drew on themes of national election cam-paigns as: 'Germans: vote for a free and socially-conscious Europe – against a Socialist Europe.' On films and TV commercials, it emphasised the threat of abandoning Europe to a class-struggle, showing Mitterrand dressed as a scarecrow and pictures of Willy Brandt and Brezhnev in Red Square before a Russian military march-past. They stressed the 'left-wing' links of the SPD with the 'anti-German' Dutch Socialists, and with the Italian Socialist and Communist parties. As a secondary feature, the CDU/CSU touched on their transnational link through the EPP alongside references to its European father figure of Konrad Adenauer.

In other countries, there was less concern with European ideological or transnational questions as much as the need to explain to the electorate the position of each party first on integration and then on specific EC issues. In the countries which were broadly pro-integrationist, it was difficult to distinguish party political profiles in this area since there was general agreement on a united Europe to prevent war and promote peace between its component nations, as well as for the purpose of tackling the common problems of unemployment, inflation and the energy shortage. On specific policies such as the CAP for Britain and the regional policy for Ireland and Italy, there was overall agreement between national parties on the need to reform them.

As a feature of the political-functional factor, the position of individual parties, whether in government or opposition, had the greatest influence on their projection of the transnational element in the campaign. Those in government tended to stress their performance on behalf of their country in the EC. This was particularly true of the large governing parties such as the German Social Democrats and the Italian Christian Democrats. The Danish Social Democrats argued that their policy must be carried out in all the EC institutions whereby the EP was not envisaged as acting contrarily to the Council of Ministers. Reg Underhill of the British Labour Party said that his line was:

Whether you like it or not there are elections and there are Tories to clout, and we have got to do something about it. The first thing is that we have lost the Government and therefore the pressure we could bring on the Council of Ministers has been reduced. It could only then be [applied] through the Parliament, and therefore added representation to the European Assembly will give us another avenue for pushing our case and getting support from other countries.[68]

The opposition parties showed a divergence of behaviour between the larger and smaller. The larger ones invariably attacked their rival governing parties along familiar national lines, but with an element of European spice. This was particularly so with the German

Christian Democratic Party and the Italian Communists, who pointed to the difficulties Italy suffered from under the government of the Christian Democrats, causing that country to become 'isolated' from the other stronger EC member states. The British Labour Party, having just lost power, emphasised the role it *had* played at the European level and particularly in the EP in defence of British interests. The Dutch Socialist PvdA called on voters to decide whether they wanted a Europe of (the Christian Democratic Prime Minister) van Agt.[69] The smaller parties in opposition, on the other hand, preferred to spotlight their transnational links in order to capitalise on their association with a wider European framework. Thus, the Irish Fine Gael stressed its membership of the EPP and position in the second largest group in the EP in comparison with the Fianna Fail's membership of a smaller EP group, which might 'have little or no say in the new European Parliament'.[70] As already mentioned, the Italian Socialists laid great stress on their transnational links, though this was regarded as part of their national strategy to be included in a coalition with the Christian Democrats to the exclusion of the Communists.[71] The Liberal parties generally straddled the two approaches of government and opposition parties because of their secondary status in the national context. They both stressed their overall influence in the EC through their inclusion in six out of nine national governments as coalition partners and also underlined their transnational party links.

It can be seen from this discussion that an overriding problem posed for national political parties was the absence of a concrete focus of attention for their campaigns – above all they were not aiming to achieve a governmental position. This vacuum was somewhat uncomfortably filled by injecting into the European elections some of the elements of national political rivalry. However, because the lines of battle and the rules of the game were not clearly defined, since it was the first time that any such election had taken place, there was often a feeling that at the national level the parties were sparring in different dimensions.

A discussion of the impact of individual leaders during the campaign introduces the extent to which national politicians were involved in mobilising support for their parties and giving credence to the European dimension. Some prominent individuals, such as Leo Tindemans and Willy Brandt, could be said to have actively promoted transnational party co-operation by being involved in campaigns in other EC countries. In Britain, the involvement of Edward Heath, a well known 'European' and ex-Prime Minister, stressed the European dimension of the elections, with his 7,000-mile campaign, thirty-five major speeches and probably twice as many minor ones. According to one press observer:

Not since Mr. Gladstone barnstormed Midlothian has a single individual so dominated an election campaign in this country . . . After making twice as many public speeches as any other politician during the general election, he is now making three times as many in the European elections. Meanwhile Tory ministers burrow deeper into their departments . . .[72]

This involvement of some leading politicians who were not standing and also national leaders who headed their party lists, such as François Mitterrand of the French PS, Georges Marchais of the PCF and Enrico Berlinguer, the Italian Communist leader, indicated the importance of the European elections for national party politics. However, the examples cited are the outstanding ones, for often party leaders, especially those in national office, played a relatively minor role, and in several countries party activists complained that the absence of influential politicians on the European lists was a major contributory factor in the widespread problem of mobilising the vote.

The related question of party-organisational mobilisation is relevant to transnational behaviour simply because the federations had to rely here on their member parties. As one party international secretary expressed it:

For organising an election you are relying on the existing organisation, which means that you fall back on the traditional means you have been using for other elections which will also be used here. This means that you will be relying on an apparatus which has been geared to national elections.[73]

From the transnational point of view, the matter arises as to how much activists were aware of and promoted the European dimension of the campaign and fraternal links with other national parties. In general it could be said that the wider European dimension of the campaign was stronger than the transnational party-political aspect of it. For example, local branches of the German political parties organised social evenings with a European flavour, such as a 'Dutch' party of the Frankfurt branch of the FDP, and a similar 'French' event organised by a local branch of the German CDU. These tended to be most common in Germany but also took place in other countries. In the Benelux countries, the European together with the transnational party-political aspect were more prominent than elsewhere because of the general proximity of the EC to these countries and because of the relatively small size of their parties. In general, it should be remembered, as discussed earlier, that the presence of the transnational element varied from federation to federation, with generally the greatest awareness of a European 'party' among the

EPP member party activists and that of transnational party links among the Liberals. However, the actual projection of these links to voters by the activists was necessarily limited, because they found the most important priority was to inform generally about the EC and mobilise voters, thus reducing the dynamism which could be injected into the European party-political aspect of the campaign.

There was a similar tendency in the case of the media to concentrate on the broader European, rather than the specific transnational party, aspect of the campaign. It is outside the capacity of this book to discuss the overall role of the media in this campaign.[74] However, the European dimension of the direct election campaigns was particularly dependent on media interest and treatment, and hence the latter had a potentially powerful capacity for emphasising or not the existence of transnational links and the state of transnational party activity. In addition to independent media coverage, a second possible aspect was the use made by the individual parties themselves of the media to emphasise the same.

Although leading newspapers in most countries ran information articles about the EC, there was a noticeable lack of attention given to transnational party activity. Even the quality press, which in many countries featured national case studies of the campaign elsewhere, made very little reference to this activity and only usually in connection with the appearance of prominent foreign speakers. As to television, the pre-eminent medium on which voters rely most heavily, there was some variety of interest between countries, but generally only vague references to the party groups in the context of the EP as an institution and rarely, or not at all, to the party federations.

With regard to the parties' use of the media to project their transnational links, the same problem of having to inform their voters about the EC and their habitual national focus reduced this possibility to the minimum. Party advertisements in the national press were more common in some EC states than others – such as West Germany, Italy and Ireland – but even in these pro-integrationist countries transnational party links were not specially emphasised and, if at all mentioned, it was in the small print. Party television commercials were also distinctly nationally rather than transnationally oriented, and where more specific on EC matters reference tended to be made to the EP and, to some extent, its component party groups rather than to transnational-organisational links. This incidental transnational party-political treatment underlined how little the party federations had in their few years of existence affected the consciousness of party organisers at the national level, and this in turn hardly encouraged much interest by the media themselves in transnational party behaviour.

While illustrating further some of the national determinants and constraints of transnational party co-operation, the European campaign itself showed how subsidiary the latter was to general party activity when it came to the 'hot phase' of the election. Although in the extenuated pre-campaign period political parties had begun to take their transnational links more seriously and pursue them more systematically, it was difficult to argue that the campaign did much to stimulate their further promotion at the national level.

Any assessment of the importance for transnational party co-operation of the campaign in the 'European' sense must necessarily be constricted by the pronounced national autonomy of the simultaneous campaigns for the EP and the elementary problems of projecting the European Community for the first time in an electoral manner. The European campaign was, of course, the culmination of the process of politicisation of transnational activity from the mid-1970s, in which the deadline of direct elections had been a major catalyst. For the federations in particular the campaign was the first electoral 'blooding', although as shown there was distinct variation in the nature and extent of the roles they played. Generally, the experience of the campaign underlined once again the élite tendency of transnational party relations, just as it reaffirmed different characteristics of the federations as party-political entities, as discussed in looking at their development during their formative years.

The European election of 1979 was unique in that it was the first of a new ongoing series, where the term 'direct' can no longer be applicable because this five-yearly cycle will become a natural part of the Community's future. Each consecutive election should be a progressively more rigorous test of the progress of transnational activity, especially with regard to the role of the federations and also the importance accorded the Euro-parliamentary groups as a channel for political influence. This will be all the more so if, according to the EC timetable, the second and subsequent elections are conducted under a uniform electoral system. With such a system, a comparison between the national campaigns from a transnational angle can be more stringent. In the event of these developments, it will be possible to speak of a further historical phase in transnational party co-operation.

Chapter 5: References

1   Interview no. 82.
2   Interview no. 24.
3   Douglas Hurd, Minister of State at the Foreign Office and former Conservative European spokesman. on Radio 4 (8 June 1979).
4   Roy Hattersley. Labour MP. ibid.
5   Interview no. 99.

6   *Financial Times* (23 May 1979).
7   Report by Dutch PvdA on its European Campaign (Luxemburg: 24 September 1979).
8   Interview no. 96.
9   Interview no. 1 (1979).
10 *Le Monde* (2 June 1979).
11 Report by PSDI on its European Campaign (Luxemburg: 8 August 1979).
12 *Frankfurter Allgemeine Zeitung* (9 June 1979).
13 Interviews no. 14 (1979) and 105.
14 Interview no. 97. The meetings included those on the following subjects held in:
    Holland, 'Employment in Europe' (December 1978).
    Germany, 'European humanity and cultural democracy' (March 1979).
    Luxemburg, 'Equality of women' (March 1979).
    Italy (PSDI), 'Social Europe' (March 1979).
    France, 'Europe and the new industrial revolution' (April 1979).
    Denmark, 'Economic democracy' (April 1979).
    France, 'Europe and the new industrial revolution' (April 1979).
    Northern Ireland, 'Regional policy' (April 1979).
    Luxemburg, Candidates meeting (April 1979).
    Italy (PSI), 'Economic, monetary and employment policies' (May 1979).
    Ireland, Electoral meeting (May 1979).
    France, Final rally (May 1979).
15 Interviews nos. 97 and 14 (1979).
16 ibid. Interview no. 14 (1979).
17 *Irish Times* (26 May 1979).
18 Interview no. 97.
19 Interview no. 14 (1979).
20 Report by Irish Labour Party on its European Campaign (Luxemburg: 25 September 1979).
21 Interview no. 1 (1979).
22 Labour Party political broadcast (4 June 1979).
23 See, for example, *Corriere della Sera* (9 June 1979).
24 ibid. (7 June 1979).
25 *Frankfurter Allgemeine Zeitung* (9 June 1979).
26 Interview no. 82.
27 CDU, *Informationen für den Europa-Wahlkampf 1979*, no. 12 (25 May 1979).
28 *Observer* (3 June 1979).
29 *Irish Times* (5 June 1979).
30 *Irish Times* (7 June 1979).
31 *CDU – Europawahl*, nos. 14 and 6 (14–15 April and 6–8 February 1979).
32 *CD – Europe* (June 1977), p. 10.
33 *Irish Times* (21 May 1979). Tindemans spoke at public meetings of all EPP member parties, including ten times in Germany, at least six times in Holland and twice in Italy. (Letter from Josef Müller, EPP deputy general-secretary, to authors, 22 November 1979).
34 Len Wilkinson, Liberal agent in a mixed urban and rural constituency in north-east England, on Radio 4 (2 June 1979).
35 British Liberal Party political broadcast (3 June 1979).
36 *Corriere della Sera* (8 June 1979).
37 George Spring, Plymouth, election address.
38 Interview no. 90.
39 ELD post-electoral report of meeting of election campaign managers, Luxemburg (23 July 1979).

40 Gunter Verheugen, at press conference of British Liberal Party (16 May 1979).
41 Interview no. 25.
42 Interview no. 25.
43 *Daily Telegraph* (8 June 1979).
44 French Communist Party publication (1 June 1979). Material supplied by PCF.
45 ibid. (31 May 1979).
46 *Europe*, Agence Internationale d'Information pour la Presse, no. 38 (22 May 1979).
47 *Irish Times* (26 May 1979).
48 *L'Unità* (22 May 1979).
49 Interview no. 97.
50 *Frankfurter Allgemeine Zeitung* (9 June 1979).
51 *Financial Times* (23 May 1979).
52 It was headed by 'Appeal of Willy Brandt to the Italian People' and underneath, 'Why Vote Social Democrat – Message from the President of the Socialist International and the President of the German Social Democrats to Saragat and Longo' (*Corriere della Sera*, 24 May 1979).
53 Interview no. 87.
54 Interview no. 14 (1979).
55 *Daily Telegraph* (11 May 1979).
56 Verheugen, op. cit.
57 *Irish Times* (6 June 1979).
58 Ecological Manifesto for a Different Europe (January 1979).
59 Jonathan Porritt, Chairman Ecology Party, in a letter to the authors (26 August 1979).
60 *Le Monde* (14 April 1979).
61 *Europe*, op. cit. no. 23 (5 April 1979).
62 Interview no. 14 (1979).
63 *Europe*, no. 3 (25 January 1979).
64 *Irish Times* (13 June 1979).
65 Interview no. 79.
66 Report by Luxemburg Socialist Party on its European Campaign (Luxemburg: 24 September 1979).
67 Interview no. 24.
68 Interview no. 14 (1979).
69 *Neue Zürcher Zeitung* (24 May 1979).
70 *Irish Times* (5 June 1979).
71 *Financial Times* (23 May 1979).
72 Ferdinand Mount in the *Spectator* (2 June 1979).
73 Interview no. 96.
74 See J. G. Blumler and A. D. Fox, 'Communication in the European elections: the case of British broadcasting', *Government and Opposition* (Autumn 1979), pp. 508–30; as well as J. G. Blumler and A. D. Fox, *The European Voter* (1980).

6

The Results of Direct Elections: A Transnational Party Perspective

In general, the value here of looking at the results of the European elections on 7–10 June 1979 is to establish their relevance to the development of transnational party co-operation as the subject of this book. It is therefore not the intention to provide a full-scale psephological analysis of the outcome of these elections, but rather to identify various particular features which have implications for, and possible effects on, this activity.

Direct elections were the culminating event of the fourth historical phase of transnational activity in the 1970s and the results offer some basis for its further development in the first half of the 1980s. They may be said to provide an intermediate judgement on the progress of party co-operation. However, these elections were the first of their kind, there was no immediate political consequence of them in the sense of a government formation, while long-term projections about the stability of European political forces depended heavily on trends in the different national party systems, so that firm conclusions of a political nature are difficult to draw. The main such feature which arose after direct elections was that of majorities in the EP as a result of the voting. While the Socialist group as before emerged as the strongest single one, despite the setbacks for the British Labour and the Danish Social Democratic parties, the centre-right as represented by the three main groups of the Christian Democrats, Conservatives and Liberals emerged with an overall 'majority'. Compared with the old Parliament this centre-right formation now held 52 per cent of the total seats (212 out of 410) as against 47 per cent of the seats (93 out of 198) before the elections; although the long-term significance of this particular result must take into account the limited strength, duration and cohesion of Euro-parliamentary majorities, as discussed above in Chapter 2 (Section *b*, ii, pp. 45–50). Its importance was further reduced by the impossibility of speaking of a clear or uniform 'swing to the right' for, if this occurred in several member states, national factors were predominant in explaining it. Furthermore, the Conservative 'victory' in the British case was exaggerated by the constituency-based electoral system. This predominance of individual national factors as against possible uniform patterns of EC-wide voting is likely to continue even with a common European electoral law from the second elections in 1984.

The main relevance of the 1979 direct elections for the present purpose lies in a number of specific features based on the results themselves, and for this reason this chapter concentrates on providing some comparative data. First, the turnout on 7–10 June was markedly lower than that for the general average for national elections, as a measure of the cognitive and affective attitudes of the national electorates to the European Community in the light of problems of projecting it publicly. But there were strong variations between member states, with, for instance, three of them showing little divergence from the national level of turnout – Belgium and Luxemburg because of compulsory voting, and Italy with its strong obligations to vote. These different patterns are illustrated by Table 6.1:

Table 6.1 *Turnout in European Elections, 1979*

Member state	European turnout (%)	Turnout in preceding national election (%)
Belgium	91·4	94·6 (December 1978)
Denmark	47·8	88·9 (February 1977)
France	60·7	82·8 (March 1978)
West Germany	65·7	90·7 (October 1976)
Ireland	63·6	76·9 (June 1977)
Italy	85·5	89·9 (June 1979)
Luxemburg	88·9	90·1 (June 1979)
Netherlands	57·8	87·5 (May 1977)
United Kingdom	32·4	76·0 (May 1979)

Source: European Parliament, directorate-general for information, *Elections '79: The Results* (July 1979), p. 3.

It must be added, however, that turnout itself, although reflecting on the limited potential for wider impact by transnational activity, will not directly condition the further operation and development of party co-operation especially in the EP, for, as Roy Jenkins, President of the European Commission, noted at the time of direct elections:

... I don't think that the turnout invalidates the results or detracts from the effectiveness of the European Parliament. What counts in the future is how effective the newly-elected members are in the Parliament. The new Parliament will have more influence and an increased moral authority by virtue of being directly elected. The elections also give the Parliament an opportunity to use its powers more effectively and make the Council and the Commission more sensitive to parliamentarian opinion. They open a new chapter in the development of the European Community.[1]

Secondly, while the EP contained a 'multi-party system' as before the elections, the relative strengths of individual groups had changed (see Table 6.2).

Table 6.2 *Comparative Strengths of Euro-parliamentary Groups*

	Before direct elections		After direct elections	
	% of seats	No. of seats out of 198	% of seats	No. of seats out of 410
Socialists	33·3	66	27·3	112
Christian Democrats	26·3	52	26·3	108
Liberals	11·6	23	9·8	40
Conservatives	9·1	18	15·4	63
Communists	9·1	18	10·7	44
DEP	8·6	17	5·4	22

The main differences in the strengths of individual groups were the rise in representation for the Conservatives essentially as a result of the British vote and especially electoral system, the decline of the Progressive Democrats (DEP) owing to substantial loss of support both by the Irish Fianna Fail and, to a lesser extent, the French Gaullists, and the lower proportion of seats held by the Socialist group primarily because of the unfavourable results for its parties in Denmark and Britain. All these changes underlined the dependence of the groups ultimately on national political trends. Notwithstanding this, the transnational significance of party group strengths was highlighted by the critical attitudes among other Socialists towards the British Labour Party's performance during the election. Claude Cheysson, a French Socialist and European Commissioner, launched a bitter attack on the British party the day after the election:

Well, as a Socialist I am disappointed to find a weakened Socialist group in the Assembly. It is weaker than I expected. I think that the main responsibility lies with the British Labour Party. The Labour Party did not show any interest for this election. Now I would like to understand what the British are doing in the Community at present. Do they belong to it or don't they? If they belong to it, are they interested in this democratic concern or not? If they are against the Community, then fair enough. But the fact that they should be against the democratisation of the Community would seem to me to be completely absurd. And particularly in Britain, the Labour Party has really made a ridiculously low effort . . . Their campaign was perfectly confused and you see the results show this. There has been an enormous drop in votes in their favour. This is going to reduce the force of the Socialist group in the Assembly.[2]

Despite such importance being attached to the results in this respect, what really will count in the work of the Euro-parliamentary groups will be their respective states of internal cohesion, where the Socialists have traditionally been the most united and might indeed benefit from lower representation for British Labour anti-integrationists (who comprise eleven out of seventeen British Socialist MEPs).[3]

Thirdly, it is interesting in this context to indicate the relative weight of national component elements within the various party groups in the EP with reference to the discussion in Chapter 2, Section *c*, i and ii, pp. 75–82. The most significant feature here, following earlier discussion in Chapter 2 of national subgroup influences in the Euro-parliamentary groups, is the increased proportional representation of West German MEPs in the two largest ones, the Socialists and the Christian Democrats. In the Socialist group their proportion of seats rose from 22·7 per cent to 31·3 per cent, and in the Christian Democratic group from 34·6 per cent to 38·9 per cent. Altogether, national representation within the groups after direct elections was as shown in Table 6.3.

Table 6.3   *Nationalities within Party Groups*

	Soc.	CD	Lib.	Con.	Comm.	DEP
Belgium	7	10	4	0	0	0
Denmark	4	0	3	3	1	1
France	21	9	17	0	19	15
West Germany	35	42	4	0	0	0
Ireland	4	4	1	0	0	5
Italy	13	30	5	0	24	0
Luxemburg	1	3	2	0	0	0
Netherlands	9	10	4	0	0	0
UK	18	0	0	60	0	1
Total	112	108	40	63	44	22

Fourthly, the socio-economic background of MEPs is a relevant feature in view of the tentative appearance earlier and the potential growth in the new Parliament of interest-oriented behaviour by MEPs in a cross-group fashion. Table 6.4 on p. 267 provides such background on the 410 MEPs elected in June 1979.

Finally, it is useful as information on member political parties involved in transnational activity to include comparative data on the results for European elections from the different countries of the Community (Tables 6.5 to 6.13).[4]

Chapter 6: References

1   *Europe*, Agence Internationale d'Information pour la Presse (11/12 June 1979).
2   BBC television report (11 June 1979).
3   *The Economist* (16 June 1979), p. 29.
4   The following data are taken from European Parliament, directorate-general for information, *Elections '79: The Results* (July 1979), pp. 5–13. They have been amended where necessary.

Table 6.4 Profile of MEPs' Professional Background

Occupation	Total %	Total No.	UK	France	West Germany	Italy	Belgium	Denmark	Netherlands	Ireland	Luxemburg
Businessman	13	53	26	12	4	4	1	1	2	3	0
Civil servant or Eurocrat	8	34	9	8	5	2	3	1	4	2	0
Doctor	1	3	1	0	0	1	0	0	0	1	0
Farmer	5	22	6	5	2	1	0	0	3	5	0
Housewife	2	9	2	0	1	2	1	0	2	0	1
Journalist/author	10	43	8	6	9	15	0	4	1	0	0
Lawyer	12	54	6	8	15	8	10	0	2	2	3
Politician	15	63	6	17	6	20	3	3	5	2	1
Teacher	6	23	2	7	8	1	0	3	1	0	1
Scientist/engineer	3	11	2	4	4	1	0	0	0	0	0
Lecturer/professor	6	26	7	4	2	10	0	2	1	0	0
Other white-collar	2	9	2	0	7	0	0	0	0	0	0
Manual worker/trade unionist	7	27	2	9	9	2	4	0	1	0	0
Others	8	33	2	1	9	14	2	2	3	0	0

Source: European Parliament Digest (November 1979), p. 4.

Table 6.5   Belgium

| | Electorate (European Elections): 6,800,584 | | | Electorate (General Election): 5,478,080 | | |
| | European Elections June 1979 (24 seats) | | | General Election December 1978 (212 seats) | | |
Party	Votes	%	Seats in EP	Votes	%	National seats
Socialist Party (Walloon)	575,886	} 37·6	7	1,451,733	27·10	57
Socialist Party (Flemish)	698,892		3	488,182	9·11	25
Liberal (Flemish)	512,355	} 23·3	4	523,740	11·64	32
Liberal (Walloon)	372,857		3	580,521	12·70	26
Christian People's Party (Flemish)	1,607,927	} 16·2	2	582,426	10·87	37
Christian People's Party (Walloon)	445,940		2			
FDR Rassemblement Walloon	414,412	7·6	2	—	—	—
Flemish People's Union	324,569	5·9	1	383,455	7·15	14
Ecologists	185,821	3.42	—	—	—	—
Communist	145,804	2·62	—	—	—	4
Others	138,404	—	—	984,792	18·38	17
% Turnout	5,422,867 91·4		24	4,994,849 94·6		212

Table 6.6 Denmark

| Party | Electorate (European Elections): 3,725,235 | | | Electorate (General Election): 3,542,843 | | |
| | European Elections June 1979 (16 seats) | | | General Election February 1977 (158 seats) | | National seats |
	Votes	%	Seats in EP	Votes	%	
Social Democrats	382,487	21·9	3	1,150,355	37·0	65
Social Liberals	56,944	3·3	—	113,330	3·6	15
Conservatives	245,309	14·1	2	263,262	8·5	15
Retsforbundet (Single tax party)	59,379	3·4	—	102,149	3·3	—
Social People's Party	81,991	4·7	1	120,357	3·9	7
Centre Democrats	107,790	6·2	1	200,347	6·4	11
Communists	—	—	—	114,022	3·7	7
Folkebevaegelsen (Anti-Market Movement)	365,760	21·0	4	—	—	—
Christian People's Party	30,985	1·8	—	106,082	3·4	6
Liberals	252,767	14·5	3	371,728	12·0	21
Left Socialists	60,694	3·5	—	83,667	2·7	—
Progress Party	100,702	5·8	1	453,792	14·6	26
Siumut (Greenland)	5,118	—	1	—	—	4
Others (including Atassut)	4,654	—	—	27,206	0·9	—
	1,754,850		16	3,106,297		158
% Turnout	47·8			88·9		

Table 6.7 France

Party	Electorate (European Elections): 35,180,531 European Elections June 1979 (81 seats)			Electorate (General Election): 35,179,654 General Election March 1978 (491 seats)		National seats
	Votes	%	Seats in EP	Votes	%	
Socialists and Radicals of the Left	4,763,026	23·4	21	7,054,066	24·7	114
French Communist Party	4,153,710	20·4	19	5,870,340	20·5	86
Union for French Democracy (UDF)	5,666,984	27·9	26	6,122,180	21·4	122
Defence of interests of France in Europe (DIFE)	3,301,980	16·2	15	6,451,454	22·6	155
Rally for the Republic RPR						
Others	2,445,740	12·0	—	3,083,022	10·8	14
	20,331,440		81	28,581,062		491
% Turnout	60·7			82·8		

Table 6.8 *Germany*

Party	European Elections June 1979 (81 seats)			General Election October 1976 (518 seats)		
	Votes	*%*	*Seats in EP*	*Votes*	*%*	*Bundestag seats*
	Electorate (European Elections): 42,751,940			Electorate (General Election): 42,058,015		
CDU (Christian Democratic Union)	10,883,085	49·2 }	34	14,367,302	48·6 }	254
CSU (Christian Social Union)	2,817,120		8	4,027,499		224
SPD (Social Democrats)	11,370,045	40·8	35	16,099,019	42·6	224
FDP (Liberals)	1,662,621	6·0	4	2,995,085	7·9	40
DKP (Communists)	112,055	0·4	—	118,581	0·3	—
Die Grünen (Ecologists)	893,683	3·2	—	—	—	—
Others	108,500	0·4	—	215,014	0·6	—
	27,847,109		81	37,822,500		518
% Turnout	65·7			90·7		

Note: There are 3 MEPs for Berlin.

Table 6.9 *Ireland*

| Party | *Electorate (European Elections):* 2,188,798 *European Elections June 1979* (15 seats) | | | *Electorate (General Election):* 2,118,606 *General Election June 1977* (148 seats) | | |
	Votes	*%*	*Seats in EP*	*Votes*	*%*	*National seats*
Fianna Fail	464,450	34·68	5	811,615	50·63	84
Fine Gael	443,652	33·13	4	488,767	30·49	43
Labour Party	193,898	14·48	4	186,410	11·63	17
Independent	189,499	14·15	2	116,235	7·27	4
Sinn Fein	43,943	3·28	—	27,209	1·7	—
Others	3,630	0·27	—	—	—	—
	1,339,072		15	1,630,236		148
% Turnout	63·6			76·9		

Table 6.10 *Italy*

| Party | Electorate (European Elections): 42,193,369 | | | Electorate (General Election): 42,213,962 | | |
| | European Elections June 1979 (81 seats) | | | General Election June 1979 (630 seats) | | |
	Votes	*%*	*Seats in EP*	*Votes*	*%*	*National seats*
Christian Democracy (DC)	12,752,602	36·5	29	14,007,594	38·3	262
Italian Communist Party (PCI)	10,343,101	29·6	24	11,107,883	30·4	201
Italian Socialist Party (PSI)	3,857,436	11·0	9	3,586,256	9·8	62
Italian Social Movement (MSI)	1,907,452	5·4	4	1,924,251	5·3	30
Italian Social Democratic Party (PSDI)	1,511,320	4·3	4	1,403,873	3·8	20
Radical Party (PR)	1,282,728	3·7	3	1,259,362	3·4	18
Italian Republican Party (PRI)	895,083	2·6	2	1,106,766	3·0	16
Italian Liberal Party (PLI)	1,269,560	3·6	3	708,022	1·9	9
Democratic Party for Proletarian Unity (PDUP)	404,794	1·1	1	501,431	1·4	6
Proletarian Democracy (DP)	250,414	0·7	1	293,443	0.8	—
National Democracy Party (DN)	141,350	0·4	—	228,340	0·6	—
South Tyrol People's Party (SVP)	196,189	0·6	1	206,264	0·6	4
Aosta Valley Union (UV)	165,260	0·5	—	33,250	0·1	1
Others	—	—	—	135,124	0·4	1
	34,977,289		81	36,501,859		630
% Turnout	85·5			89·9		

Table 6.11 Luxemburg

Party	Electorate (European Elections): 212,740 — European Elections June 1979 (6 seats)			Electorate (General Election): 212,740 — General Election June 1979 (59 seats)		
	Votes	%	Seats in EP	Votes	%	National seats
Socialist Worker Party	211,097	21·7	1	737,931	22·51	14
Independent Socialists	—	—	—	66,907	—	1
Communist Party	48,738	5·0	—	177,269	4·86	2
Democratic Party	274,345	28·1	2	648,693	21·90	15
Wiert lech	—	—	—	30,271	—	—
Christian Social Party	351,942	36·0	3	1,049,393	36·38	24
Revolutionary Communist League	5,027	0·5	—	6,984	—	—
Liberal Party	5,596	0·5	—	6,143	—	—
Enrôles de force	—	—	—	135,356	—	1
Socialist Democrat Party	68,310	7·0	—	181,931	6·37	2
Club of Independents	—	—	—	849	—	—
	965,054a		6	3,041,727		
% Turnout	88·9			90·1		

a In Luxemburg, voters had 6 votes each in the European election and a number equal to the seats to be filled in the national election (24 votes in the Southern constituency, 20 in the Centre, 6 in the West and 9 in the North).

Table 6.12 Netherlands

| Party | Electorate (European Elections): 9,799,761 | | | Electorate (General Election): 9,497,991 | | |
| | European Elections June 1979 (25 seats) | | | General Election May 1977 (150 seats) | | |
	Votes	%	Seats in EP	Votes	%	National seats
PvdA (Labour)	1,722,240	30·39	9	2,813,795	33·83	53
CDA (Christian Democrats)	2,017,743	35·61	10	2,652,280	31·89	49
VVD (Liberals)	914,787	16·14	4	1,492,691	17·95	28
D'66 (Independents)	511,967	9·03	2	452,423	5·43	8
Others	500,566	8·83	—	906,422	10·90	12
	5,667,303		25	8,317,611		150
% Turnout	57·8			87·5		

Table 6.13   *United Kingdom*

Party	European Elections June 1979 (81 seats)			General Election May 1979 (635 seats)		
	Electorate (European Elections): 41,559,460			*Electorate (General Election): 41,093,264*		
	Votes	*%*	*Seats in EP*	*Votes*	*%*	*Commons seats*
Conservative Party	6,508,481	48·4	60	13,697,753	43·9	337
Labour Party	4,253,210	31·6	17	11,509,524	36·9	267
Liberal Party	1,690,600	12·6	—	4,313,931	13·8	11
Scottish National Party	247,836	1·9	1	504,259	1·6	2
Plaid Cymru	83,399	0·6	—	132,544	0·4	2
Ulster Unionists	125,169	0·9	1	175,171	0·6	5
Democratic Unionist Party	170,688	1·3	1	61,625	0·2	3
Social Democratic and Labour Party	140,622	1·0	1	16,480	0·05	1
Others	226,071	1·7	—	306,938	0·8	7
	13,446,076		81	30,718,225		635
% Turnout	32·4			76·0		

Conclusion: Towards a European Community Party System?

Speaking of the possibility of a 'European Community party system' must seem presumptuous taking into account the present limited reality of the EC as a political and institutional entity, and bearing in mind that even though transnational party co-operation has undergone a qualitative change during the course of the 1970s it is far from approximating to any viable party system. The European Community has during this decade acquired several overt political features following the period of stagnation in the 1960s. This has been evident with its broader and more open-ended policy discussion and the growing intrusion of European considerations in the domestic politics of the member states, but many questions about its need to adapt as a structural 'system' to this evolving situation have remained unanswered. While positive, rather than negative, integration has become the order of the day, the fact that the EC has outgrown the framework of the Treaty of Rome in institutional as well as policy terms has not brought any serious effort to strengthen constitutionally its decision-making processes at the European level in a direction analogous to that of a *bona fide* 'political system'. Only in one respect did the Rome Treaty anticipate a major EC institutional change – in its provision for the direct election of the European Parliament – which initiative was taken and implemented during the 1970s, although there were signs that the heads of government in their decision did not fully expect the politicising impact of this prospective event. Whatever the positive consequences of direct elections for the EP as an institution by way of enhanced status and political influence, it is unlikely by present patterns to break the mould of an EC 'system' which is disparate and somewhat fragmented.

Transnational party activity has, of course, been bound by the institutional limitations and weaknesses of the European Community itself. Just as it has a history almost as long as that of European integration, though essentially only at the Euro-parliamentary level, so it has been conditioned by the framework within which it has operated. In a political sense, this has meant that party co-operation has encountered the predominant multinational orientation of politics in the EC as much as its other forms of activity, even with the differences of 'Europeanness' between member states. It is significant, however, that both these institutional and political limitations have only consistently become a widely recognised factor with

regard to transnational party activity during the 1970s, thus underlining its emergence then as an area of some political importance,
albeit of a very secondary kind, in the development of European
integration. Here, the 'chemical' or galvanising effects of the inter-
connection between the broad policy area of European affairs (with
its increasing political content), the link issue of direct elections and
the previously peripheral or isolated activity of transnational co-
ordination between political parties provided the crucial explanation.
In particular, this involved a more distinct reorientation of general
international co-operation between relevant parties to EC policies
and the EC institutional structure.

The qualitative change this amounted to in transnational party
co-operation has been described in this book as a process of 'politicisation' in this activity, but what exactly has been the form of this
politicisation and to what extent has it occurred? Briefly, it involved
the common acceptance by parties and political leaders in the EC
that there was a European party-political framework for the interpretation of Community issues, the provision of more comprehensive and meaningful channels for the pursuit of this activity and its
acquiring some relevance as well as bearing some resemblance to
party politics in general as this is practised in member states. Above
all, it was the closer interlinkage between the three dimensions of
transnational activity – the Euro-parliamentary, the transnational
party-organisational and the national party frameworks – which
promoted this process within the wider context of politicisation in
the EC as a whole. In other words, party-political differentiation
and pressures began to emerge more into the open within the broad
consensus over the values of European integration, though even in
the latter respect there remained some divergent tendencies on the
part of individual national parties.

It is difficult, nevertheless, to claim that the outcome of this
process in the 1970s has already produced the basis and outline of a
future EC-wide party system, let alone the party-political ground-
work for some form of European socio-political community. So
far as transnational co-operation evolved during this decade, it was
related to the institutional structure of the EC as it was and within
that aimed to promote a more overt political approach to policy-
making rather than seeking to establish anew any alternative framework. While transnational party formations achieved more salience
than ever before, they were hardly in a position to instigate radical
institutional and political change in the EC seeing that at best their
potential was one of influence as opposed to direct power.

Yet despite these fundamental reservations about transnational
party activity's prospects, it is still worthwhile to stand back and
look at its development during the 1970s in the light of a possible

EC party system emerging in the long-term future. This does at least offer some means of judging its overall significance and an analytical perspective for assessing its further growth and performance. In doing so, a variety of broad questions which have surfaced in this book at different stages furnish some guidance. To what degree has in fact European-level party-political ideology or identity come to the forefront in place of a general attachment or otherwise to pro-integrationist standpoints? With a view to the discussion of the 'Europeanisation' of party politics in the various member states and the contemporaneous party-political 'internalisation' there of European affairs as complementary features of the progress of transnational co-operation, can it be said that this activity has gained any dynamism of its own and, if so, does it amount to party co-operation becoming in any way an active determinant of European integration rather than merely its dependent variable? If this process appears to follow some continuum, what are its constants and where is it leading – does it indicate the pre-history of any EC party system, and what sort of system might this eventually become? All these questions are not totally separate from each other and will receive direct comment at the end. The method meanwhile is, keeping them in mind to revert to the two analytical approaches presented at the beginning of this study – the comparative-political and the integrative-proper. These approaches are discussed in turn by way of summarising further conclusions from the book.

The comparative-political approach is useful in highlighting characteristics of transnational party co-operation with reference to familiar criteria of party-political behaviour, although as noted earlier on several occasions these can only be applied to a restricted extent owing to the uniqueness of European integration as a form of politics. It does, however, provide some measure of the way in which party co-operation has become more political, and hence an additional and interesting element in European party development. Two aspects may immediately be recorded. First, the transnational scene is clearly a case of a 'multi-party system', which is obvious from the composition of political forces in the European Parliament both before and after direct elections and an inevitable consequence of the fact that individual national party systems in the nine EC member states are not uniformly similar in the sense of the existence of different political forces and the balance of strength between them. For example, the Socialists are represented in all EC states in differing degrees of strength, the Liberals in eight of them and the Christian Democrats in seven, while the Communists are a major force in only two states so that at the Community level they have appeared as a smaller group. No one transnational party formation has enjoyed an absolute or overwhelming majority in the EP, nor is this ever likely unless there were an unforeseeable electoral landslide favouring the same force in many EC states at the same time.

Secondly, as shown by the afore-mentioned forces at the EC level ideological labels and identities are, of course, recognisable to observers of European party development. The formation of the European Progressive Democrats (DEP), as a combined representation of two different national parties in France and Ireland, illustrates on the other hand that original transnational forces are possible, if seemingly artificial, while other familiar forces such as the Conservatives have adopted transnational names. Moreover, it is significant that several characteristics commonly associated with the principal forces in particular have been reproduced at the European level. That is, general differences between Socialists, Christian Democrats and Liberals as witnessed by their history as national parties have been apparent in the nature and conduct of their transnational activity, notably in the articulation of their own structural relationships, their methods of pursuing the programmatic exercise in the formulation of common policies and programmes and altogether in their concept and practice of what entails a 'political party' as evident from the longer-term development of the Euro-parliamentary groups as well as especially their projection of the federations as EC-wide party organisations. Thus, the Socialists demonstrated the strictest sense of structural relationships, took the content of programmatic formulation very seriously and were the most ideologically conscious of the three, and were consequently the most sceptical about their own possibility of forming a 'European party'. Somewhat by contrast, the other two forces faced less intrinsic inhibitions in their efforts to harmonise their activities transnationally judged by their own standards. The Christian Democrats were much looser in their structural relationships, blander in their taste for common programmes and very electorally oriented and cosmetically conscious in their idea of a party formation. The Liberals were the least structured in their own internal relationships, the least ideologically conscious and for both reasons were able to concentrate with less difficulty on the practicalities of transnational activity, although this achievement was rather stronger in the case of their federation than their group.

At the same time, transnational party co-operation has featured forms of behaviour and organisational characteristics typical of European party development which are common to the various political forces. Among the Euro-parliamentary groups these would include the greater importance attributed to internal cohesion and comprehensive policy formulation and the growing interest in

majority formation, though here differences have emerged be
tween the three major groups (the Socialists, Christian Democrats
and Liberals) on the one side and the others in their ability to
perform in these respects. This dual distinction is furthermore evident in that the former three have established EC party federations
as extra-parliamentary organisations linked to their respective Euro-
parliamentary groups according to the classic European model of
party structural relationships. The federations have additionally
developed internal organisational arrangements which are a direct
reproduction of those usually found among national parties in
member states.

There are, however, limitations to this line of comparison not
only because of the inapplicability beyond a certain point of the
European model of party development, but simply as the transnational party formations are not fully-fledged party-political entities. For instance, many functions normally attributed to political
parties in EC states – such as organisational work among their grass-
roots activists, interest representation and patronage, policy implementation and above all the means of access to governmental office
– are not applicable to transnational activity. In other words, the
transnational party formations are not in the EC the principal form
of linkage or the 'gatekeepers' between the institutions and the
wider political system, as political parties are in the national states
of the Community. It is here that the limits of the comparative-
political approach are realised, and the integrative-proper approach
becomes relevant.

The basis of this integrative-proper approach is that the EC while
evidencing some similarities with traditional European institutional
methods and political habits is nevertheless unique as a form of
'political system', sufficiently so at least to be judged on its own
merits. In comparison with its component member states, the EC
is notably deficient if measured by the criteria of a 'representative
democracy'; however, as this criticism concerns the potential role
of the EP as an influential institution and a possible controlling
agent of the EC executive bodies in the long term, the importance
of transnational party activity, for which the EP is the institutional
focal point, comes into play. What contribution may party co-
operation offer as a democratising force in the EC, given the latter's
inadequate and incohesive structures? Here comparisons of the EP
with itself are useful, for contrasted with its own 'platonic' role in
the 1950s and 1960s (rather than with the national parliaments) the
the EP has *relatively* enhanced its visibility and influence as an
institution. In conjunction with this, transnational party co-operation
through its own politicisation process in the 1970s has in a relative
sense become less peripheral as a channel of activity in the EC, just

as national parties have clearly begun to take it more seriously.

While noting this significant though modest change, several aspects of the integrative-proper approach as a method of evaluating transnational party co-operation require recapitulation and overall assessment. First, what really is 'integrative' about this activity? The answer must be that this basic function lies more in the potential than the actual performance of the Euro-parliamentary groups and their respective party federations, depending naturally on the future political and institutional development of the EC as a whole. In the 1970s, however, some features have been asserted as a probable basis for this potential integrative role of the transnational party formations. EC-wide ideological identities have been defined and established through the medium of organisational units, while party co-operation in the full sense (embracing its three dimensions acting more closely together) has been strictly geared to the EC institutional framework and within this has engaged in an active version of policy commitment. These are the main achievements of transnational party activity in this decade. At the same time, the limits of this politicisation process are underlined by the situation where the party formations have no direct means of promoting or implementing their policy commitments and hence no ultimate binding force.

Secondly, the fundamental aspect of transnational co-operation is the interaction between the European and national levels of activity and in particular the prospects for two-way effects between them. This book has shown that there has been some advance in both party-political 'Europeanisation' and 'internalisation' of European standpoints, although the main conclusion confirms the predominance of national political considerations. National and individual party-political pressures have increasingly surfaced in the operation of the Euro-parliamentary groups as an indicator of the closer relationship between the two levels of party activity, while in the federations national influences have been present from the beginning. However, the merger of different national considerations within the common transnational framework has produced some evidence of inter-national compromises here and some degree of better mutual knowledge if not understanding between member parties, not to mention a certain greater involvement within individual national parties over European questions. If there has been any 'Europeanisation' of party politics, this has nevertheless been largely élitist in kind whether at the national or European level. It is possible therefore to speak of a mild modification of the overriding national orientation of political parties as a consequence of their transnational co-operation, with some perceptible variations between the different ideological tendencies, but this has to be fully explained in the light of the gradual erosion of the traditional distinction between external and domestic politics as a result of Community membership.

Thirdly, the triangular relationship between the three dimensions of party co-operation – the horizontal interaction between the two transnational areas of the Euro-parliamentary and the Euro-organisational, and their respective relationships with the national member parties – raises the general question as to whether the potential role of the transnational party formations is more superstructural with reference to national member parties or infrastructural with reference to the EC institutions, or to a greater or lesser extent a combination of them both. Essentially this question remains an open one as it points to very long-term possibilities, even though in their activity during the 1970s the transnational formations tended to concentrate on promoting their superstructural functions without this entailing necessarily a basic restriction on national party sovereignty as the term 'superstructure' would suggest. Thus, while the Euro-parliamentary groups and party federations have made some progress in aspects internal to themselves, their wider relationship or political location within the EC system as a whole remains unclarified apart from their institutional home or reference point in the EP. As a result of this study, it is however possible to make various projections based on an examination of the three dimensions of transnational party co-operation during the 1970s.

In the case of the Euro-parliamentary groups, with their institutional location in the EP, much depends on the latter's general impact following direct elections which, while not according this institution any new formal powers, granted it a new legitimacy and boosted its self-confidence. Greater constitutional powers for the Parliament would, of course, in turn provide the groups with more political muscle within the wider institutional structure of the EC, but failing these it is not beyond the capability of the groups to exploit fully the limited powers of the EP and seek ways in which both to give the EP more 'bite' and enhance their own political profiles as has indeed occurred during the 1970s. This was apparent in their determination to maintain group dominance in the working of the upgraded Parliament and in their readiness to introduce new areas for policy discussion. It should be added that the more full-time status of MEPs and their greater commitment to European-level careers are likely to encourage the same trend of an 'informal' growth in the effective influence of the EP and its component groups. On specifics, the role of MEPs could vary according to their priority in representing alternatively their broad national interests, individual national party loyalties or regional and sectional interests as competitive influences within their transnational party formations or possibly in conflict with them, although the stronger value placed by groups, especially the larger ones, on internal cohesion and common policy formulation is likely to remain. The increasing intrusion of national and individual party-political pressures has in fact revealed that they are not a one-dimensional or continuous factor contradicting transnational party loyalties necessarily, for they are rarely united or durable and may be subsumed or absorbed into the latter. Further enlargement of the Community in the first half of the 1980s will introduce new political blood into the groups, while moderately altering their relative balance of strength and adding some further diversification to the party-political spectrum in the EP. In general, judging by developments during the 1970s in comparison with previous decades the established Euro-parliamentary groups have created ideological, political and organisational precedents which will be hard to reverse.

The party federations are newer entities with less secure roots within the EC institutional structure, although in their few formative years from the mid-1970s they demonstrated an interesting concern to promote themselves as *communautaire* agents of party-political harmonisation. Their clearest external relationship is with their respective Euro-parliamentary groups, and probably their first priority after direct elections will be to elaborate and strengthen this extra-parliamentary relationship in both a supportive and controlling manner. The one area where some breakthrough could occur in their acquisition of a more political role at the European level would be in the event of a uniform electoral law throughout the EC, necessitating greater European co-ordination in the next elections for the EP. Meanwhile, until then their activity in the inter-electoral period should produce more evidence of their ability to pursue their ultimate goal of mobilising political and public support on European questions, though here the experience of the latter half of the 1970s must induce a note of scepticism. As less established and less institutionally based units of transnational party co-operation, the federations have a more incalculable future than the Euro-parliamentary groups. Many unresolved aspects of their role remain, notably with regard to their political relationship with their national member parties.

The third and most important dimension of transnational party co-operation, the national party frameworks, is equally the most difficult to project because, as shown in this book, it is less subject uniformly to certain promotive and restrictive constants as is European-level party activity and more to the vagaries of national political trends. In the long run the closer interlinkage between national and European levels of party activity will develop further, bearing in mind the growing importance of EC policies for member states internally and the new practice of relating transnational activity to the national party structures. One specific feature to watch will be the creation of effective national party links by those primarily active in European party politics as an aspect very undeveloped up to direct elections. On the other hand, in so far as these elections and the prospect of them had been a crucial factor in promoting the national/transnational interlinkage, there might be in the immediate post-European electoral years some relapse of interest in their transnational links on the part of individual parties in view of the necessary priority they give to national political demands and the pressures of national electoral deadlines before the second round of European elections appears on the horizon. One uncertainty is the possible effects of direct elections on individual party European policies, a question encouraged by the generally superior voting performance of the pro-integrationist over the anti-integrationist parties in these elections, for this again depends more on events in the national rather than European arena of politics. The increasingly successful impact of the European Parliament in the five years before new elections in 1984 could, of course, rub off on the national parties, convincing them of the need to develop their own transnational activity with more vigour as the obvious means to keep ahead with any such growth of Euro-parliamentary institutional influence. Whatever the outcome of all these various possible developments, the one vital constant of the national party dimension of transnational party co-operation is that the latter depends heavily on the former for its sub-European existence.

From the foregoing analysis of transnational party co-operation during the decade of the 1970s, various broad tentative conclusions may be drawn – tentative, that is, because this activity is relatively new as a viable branch of European integration and consequently somewhat open-ended in its future development. These may be made in direct answer to the three basic and partly futuristic questions presented earlier on p. 279.

First, European-level party-political ideologies and identities have progressively replaced overall pro-integrationist positions so far as transnational party activity specifically has been concerned, the main exception being those few individual national parties which have persisted in holding to an anti-integrationist course occasioning conflict with transnational party requirements where such links have existed. In a broader sense, the growth of transnational party positions has not been much in evidence, most notably at the EC executive level.

Secondly, the possibility of transnational party co-operation acquiring some dynamism of its own and becoming more of an active determinant of European integration is no longer such an unrealistic proposition, seeing that the Euro-parliamentary groups have already become in a mild way active determinants within the limiting confines of the EP as an institution. Undoubtedly, their main potential in this respect depends on the EP obtaining further constitutional powers and informal political influence in the years following direct elections, while the process of formulating common programmes or policies by the federations is a possible area indicating future scope for a determining role, if not directly *vis-à-vis* the EC as a whole then at least with regard to their national member parties.

Thirdly, the question of the shape of the EC party system to be, if it should come to deserve this description, is the most futuristic one to answer. All the signs of the 1970s would suggest that, while similar in many respects to European party development in general, transnational party co-operation will continue to be characterised increasingly by the *sui generis* nature of European integration. Aside from a qualitative jump in party co-operation arising from the unlikely event of the European Parliament acquiring major new powers, this activity will continue to progress in an evolutionary fashion and hence slowly, being ultimately dependent on the general course and direction of the European Community. Since the EC has not itself progressed very coherently as a 'political system'. transnational party co-operation could equally become an uneven development. This means that transnational activity of the 1970s as the party-political beneficiary of politicisation in the Community formed a pre-history, without using this term too optimistically, but that its end result in some kind of EC party system was unclear and in any case a very long-term prospect.

List of Interviews

1 Bent Wigotski, deputy secretary-general of Socialist Confederation, Brussels, April 1977; as official of Danish Social Democrats, Copenhagen, April 1979.
2 Josef Müller, executive secretary of UECD, Brussels, April 1976 and April 1977; as deputy general-secretary of EPP, Brussels, January 1979.
3 David Cross, *The Times* correspondent in Brussels, Brussels, April 1977.
4 Vivion Mulcahy, member of Christian Democratic group secretariat, Brussels, April 1977.
5 Richard Moore, assistant secretary-general of Liberal group, Strasbourg, April 1977, and Luxemburg, February 1979.
6 Geoffrey Harris, Socialist group secretariat, Strasbourg, April 1977.
7 Timothy Bainbridge, Conservative group secretariat, Strasbourg, April 1977, and Brussels, January 1979.
8 Winifred Ewing, SNP independent member of EP, Strasbourg, April 1977.
9 Egon Klepsch, vice-chairman of Christian Democratic group, Strasbourg, April 1977.
10 Martin Bangemann, vice-chairman of Liberal group, Strasbourg, April 1977.
11 Michael Yeats, vice-president of EP and DEP member, Strasbourg, April 1977.
12 Carlo Galluzzi, Communist member of EP, Strasbourg, April 1977.
13 Michael Stewart, former deputy chairman of Socialist group, London, May 1977.
14 Reginald Underhill, Labour Party national agent, London, February 1978 and June 1979.
15 John Holmes, Liberal Party national agent, London, February 1978.
16 Peter Knowlson, head of policy division of British Liberal Party, London, February 1978 and June 1979.
17 Ian Mikardo, Labour MP and representative on bureau of Socialist Confederation, London, February 1978.
18 Douglas Hurd, Conservative spokesman on Europe, London, February 1978 and June 1979.
19 Roger Boaden, British Conservative direct elections officer, London, July 1978.
20 Nicholas Ashford, former secretary-general of European Democratic Students (EDS), Bristol, January 1979.
21 Henning Wegener, head of external relations office of CDU, Bonn, January 1979.
22 Peter Jeutter, head of Europa-Büro FDP Fraktion, Bonn, January 1979.
23 Veronika Isenberg, foreign department of SPD, Bonn, January 1979.

24 Bruno Friedrich, vice-president of Socialist Confederation and head of its electoral committee, member of SPD praesidium, Bonn, January 1979.

25 Florus Wijsenbeek, secretary-general of European Liberal Federation (ELD), Brussels, January 1979 and April 1979.

26 Margarete Steinfort, press spokesman of European Liberal Federation (ELD), Brussels, January 1979.

27 Jan Engels, parliamentary secretary to Flemish Liberals (PVV) in Belgian House of Representatives, Brussels, January 1979.

28 Oest Erling Nielsen, secretariat of EP Communist group and collaborator of central committee of Danish Communist Party, Brussels, January 1979.

29 Jean-Pierre Cot, national delegate of French Socialist Party for European Community, Brussels, January 1979.

30 Hans-August Lücker, chairman of Christian Democratic group in EP 1969–75, Brussels, January 1979.

31 Arnaldo Mellone, PSI federation at Brussels and Inter-Socialiste group there, Brussels, January 1979.

32 Raphael Lewenthal, chairman of working group on European policy of Young Democrats (FDP) and vice-chairman of Liberal youth movement of EC, Frankfurt/Main, January 1979.

33 Dieter Hildebrand, head of organisation CDU Landesverband Hesse, Wiesbaden, January 1979.

34 Franz Volkers, SPD business manager Frankfurt, and responsible for party European campaign in South Hesse, Frankfurt/Main, January 1979.

35 Michael Opoczynski, press spokesman of Frankfurt SPD, Frankfurt/Main, January 1979.

36 Ulrich Keitel, CDU town councillor Frankfurt and chairman of Europa-Union Frankfurt, Frankfurt/Main, January 1979.

37 Dick Gupwell, Socialist group secretariat, Luxemburg, February 1979.

38 Anders Torbøl, European Conservative group secretariat, Luxemburg, February 1979.

39 Thomas Earlie, deputy secretary-general of the group of European Progressive Democrats, Luxemburg, February 1979.

40 Massimo Silvestro, secretary-general of the Liberal and Democratic group, Luxemburg, February 1979.

41 Mario Pasqualotto, Communist group secretariat, Luxemburg, February 1979.

42 Altiero Spinelli, member of the Communist group, Italian left independent, Luxemburg, February 1979.

43 Alan Reid, European Conservative group secretariat, Luxemburg, February 1979.

44 Pieter Dankert, Dutch member of the Socialist group, Luxemburg, February 1979.

45 Raymond Forni, French member of the Socialist group, Luxemburg, February 1979.

46 Geoffrey Rippon, chairman of European Conservative group 1977–79.

Luxemburg, February 1979.
47 John Prescott, British member of the Socialist group, Luxemburg, February 1979.
48 Sir Derek Walker-Smith, British member of the European Conservative group, Luxemburg, February 1979.
49 Schelto Patijn, Dutch member of the Socialist group, Luxemburg, February 1979.
50 André Soury and Jacques Eberhard, French members of the Communist group, with Jean-Claude Thomas, Communist group secretariat, Luxemburg, February 1979.
51 Hanna Walz, West German member of the Christian Democratic group, Luxemburg, February 1979.
52 Jean-Pierre Haber, economic adviser of the group of European Progressive Democrats secretariat, Luxemburg, February 1979.
53 Bob Mitchell, British member of the Socialist group, Luxemburg, February 1979.
54 Michael Palmer, EP, Directorate-General II, Director of Directorate C, Luxemburg, February 1979.
55 David Millar, EP, Directorate-General V, Luxemburg, February 1979.
56 Jean Laleure, Socialist group secretariat, Luxemburg, February 1979.
57 Paolo Falconi, deputy secretary-general of the Socialist group, Luxemburg, February 1979.
58 Manfred Michel, secretary-general of the Socialist group, secretary-general of the Socialist Confederation, Luxemburg, February 1979.
59 Daniel Debatisse, foreign policy section, French Communist Party, Paris, February 1979.
60 Sylvain Dreyfus, secretariat of Communist group of EP, Paris, February 1979.
61 Gerard Fuchs, responsible for European institutional links in French Socialist Party, Paris, February 1979.
62 Michel Thauvin, assistant to Robert Pontillon, secretary-general for international affairs of French Socialist Party, Paris, February 1979.
63 Jean de Lipkowski, international secretary of French Gaullist Party (RPR), Paris, February 1979.
64 Jacques Mallet, international secretary of French Christian Democrats (CDS), Paris, February 1979.
65 Jan de Koning, Dutch minister of economic development and former chairman of Anti-Revolutionary Party (ARP) and Christian Democratic MEP, Brussels, February 1979.
66 Giampaolo Bettamio, secretary-general of the Christian Democratic group of EP, Brussels, February 1979.
67 Garret Fitzgerald, leader of the Irish Fine Gael Party, Brussels, February 1979.
68 Angelo Bernassola, deputy director of international office of Italian DC, Brussels, February 1979.
69 Charles McDonald, Irish Fine Gael MEP in Christian Democratic group, Brussels, February 1979.

70 Carlo Russo, chairman of foreign affairs committee of Italian Chamber of Deputies and former minister of foreign commerce, Brussels, February 1979.

71 Luigi Granelli, MEP in Christian Democratic group of EP and director of international office of the Italian DC, Brussels, February 1979.

72 Lars Meyer, Danish Socialist People's Party (SF) parliamentary group, Copenhagen, April 1979.

73 Jørgen Junior, Progress Party member of Danish Parliament, Copenhagen, April 1979.

74 Niels Thygesen, Danish Venstre candidate for direct elections, Copenhagen, April 1979.

75 Niels Bollmann, Centre Democrat member of Danish Parliament, Copenhagen, April 1979.

76 Erhard Jakobsen, chairman of Danish Centre Democrats and European Conservative MEP, Copenhagen, April 1979.

77 Niels Petersen, leader of Danish Radikal Venstre parliamentary group, Copenhagen, April 1979.

78 Bjørn Hansen, secretary of Danish Radikal Venstre, Copenhagen, April 1979.

79 Poul Overgaard Nielsen, member of board of Danish People's Movement against the EC, Copenhagen, April 1979.

80 Gerard van Leyenhorst, CDA member of Dutch Parliament, The Hague, April 1979.

81 Maarten van Eden, assistant to Gerard van Leyenhorst and leading functionary in Dutch Christian Democratic Youth, The Hague, April 1979.

82 Jan Lohmann, secretary of Dutch CDA European campaign committee, The Hague, April 1979.

83 Len Berghoef, assistant to Schelto Patijn, Dutch Socialist MEP, The Hague, April 1979.

84 Ien van den Heuvel, chairwoman of Dutch Labour Party (PvdA), The Hague, April 1979.

85 Anneke Vrylandt-Krynen, VVD member of Dutch Parliament, The Hague, April 1979.

86 Cornelis Berkhouwer, head of Dutch VVD list for direct elections, and former President of EP, The Hague, April 1979.

87 Joost van Ierssel, member of executive board of Dutch CDA, The Hague, April 1979.

88 Anne Vondeling, Speaker of Dutch Parliament and head of PvdA list for direct elections, The Hague, April 1979.

89 Walter Etty, Dutch PvdA local councillor at Amsterdam and direct elections candidate, Amsterdam, April 1979.

90 Hugo Dittmar, head of organisation and publicity for Dutch VVD, The Hague, April 1979.

91 François-Michel Gonnot, head of French UDF publicity for direct elections, Paris, April 1979.

92 Daniel Le Conte, head of organisation and publicity of French Gaullist RPR, Paris, April 1979.

93 Laurence Cossé, organiser of French Socialists for direct elections, Paris, April 1979.

94 Bernard Pomel, chef de cabinet to Jacques Blanc, secretary-general of French Parti Républicain (PR), Paris, April 1979.

95 Ode Dugué, international office of French Parti Républicain (PR), Paris, April 1979.

96 Oscar Debunne, international secretary of Belgian Socialist Party, Brussels, April 1979.

97 Dick Toornstra, deputy secretary-general of Socialist Confederation, Brussels, April 1979.

98 Michael Barbeaux, official of Belgian Christian Democratic Party (Walloon), Brussels, April 1979.

99 Robert Goebbels, general-secretary of Luxemburg Socialist Workers' Party, Luxemburg, May 1979.

100 Jean-Pierre Kraemer, general-secretary of Luxemburg Christian Social Party, Luxemburg, May 1979.

101 Tony Benn, chairman of British Labour Party European campaign committee, Bristol, June 1979.

102 Gerard Mansell, managing director of BBC external services, London, June 1979.

103 David Wood, European correspondent of *The Times*, London, June 1979.

104 George Clark, parliamentary correspondent of *The Times*, London, June 1979.

105 Jenny Little, international secretary of British Labour Party, London, June 1979.

106 Bernard Tait, BBC radio European campaign coverage, London, June 1979.

107 Tom Dale, British Liberal Party international liaison officer, London, June 1979.

108 John Morrell, BBC television European election results coverage, London, June 1979.

109 Reginald Dale, European editor of *Financial Times*, London, June 1979.

110 Lord Bessborough, European Conservative MEP, London, June 1979.

Bibliography

This list is not intended to be comprehensive, for we have preferred to include only those references from the individual chapter source lists which have been of general use as well as indicate further possibilities for reading on the subject (as part of the first section).

1 Books and Articles

Arthur Aughey, *Conservative Party Attitudes towards the Common Market*, Hull Papers in Politics, no. 2 (Hull: November 1978).

Aus Politik und Zeitgeschichte, B14/79, 7 April 1979: Hubertus Dessloch, 'Die Europäische Volkspartei EVP'; Guntram von Schenck, 'Die sozialdemokratischen Parteien der EG vor den Direktwahlen'; Volkmar Kallenbach, 'Die Föderation der Europäischen Liberalen Demokraten'.

M. Bangemann, 'Preparations for direct elections in the Federal Republic of Germany', *Common Market Law Review*, vol. 15 (August 1978).

M. Bangemann and R. Bieber, *Die Direktwahl: Sackgasse oder Chance für Europa?* (Baden-Baden: Nomos Verlagsgesellschaft, 1976).

M. Bangemann, R. Bieber, E. Klepsch and H. Seefeld, *Programme für Europa: die Programme der europäischen Parteibünde zur Europa-Wahl 1979* (Bonn: Europa Union Verlag, 1978).

F. S. Baviera, 'Preparations for direct elections in Italy', *Common Market Law Review*, vol. 15 (May 1978).

D. Bell, 'The Parti Socialiste in France', *Journal of Common Market Studies*, vol. XIII, no. 4 (June 1975).

R. Bieber, 'Funktion und Grundlagen direkter Wahlen zum Europäischen Parlament im Jahre 1978', *Zeitschrift für Parlamentsfragen*, vol. VII (1976).

R. Bilski, 'The Common Market and the growing strength of Labour's left wing', *Government and Opposition*, vol. 12, no. 3 (Summer 1977).

J. G. Blumler, 'Communication in the European elections: the case of British broadcasting', *Government and Opposition*, vol. 14, no. 4 (Autumn 1979).

J. G. Blumler and A. D. Fox, *The European Voter* (London: Policy Studies Institute, 1980).

G. Bonvicini, 'The future role of Parliament in the EEC: interaction between the European Parliament and political forces', *Lo Spettatore Internazionale* (October/December 1973).

G. Bonvicini, 'Interaction between parliamentary institutions and political forces', in European Parliament, *European Integration and the Future of Parliaments in Europe* (Luxemburg: 1975), papers of symposium at Luxemburg, May 1974.

G. Bonvicini and S. Solari, *I partiti e le elezioni del Parlamento europeo* (Bologna: Il Mulino, 1979).

F. Borella, *Les Partis politiques dans l'Europe des Neuf* (Paris: Editions du Seuil, 1979).

K.-H. Buck, 'Die Haltung von KPI und KPF gegenüber Direktwahl und Funktionen des Europa-Parlaments', *Zeitschrift für Parlamentsfragen,* vol. VII (July 1976).

J. L. Burban, 'Les Anglais et l'élection du Parlement européen au suffrage universel direct', *Revue du Marché Commun,* no. 151 (1972).

P.-H. Claeys and N. Loeb-Mayer, 'Trans-European party groupings: emergence of new and alignment of old parties in the light of the direct elections to the European Parliament', *Government and Opposition,* vol. 14, no. 4 (Autumn 1979).

D. Coombes, *The Future of the European Parliament,* Studies in European Politics, No. 1 (London: Policy Studies Institute, May 1979).

D. Coombes, assisted by I. Wiebecke, *The Power of the Purse in the European Communities* (London: Chatham House/PEP, 1972).

B. Criddle, *Socialists and European Integration: A Study of the French Socialist Party* (London: Routledge & Kegan Paul, 1969).

D. Debatisse, S. Dreyfus, G. Laprat, G. Streiff and J.-C. Thomas, *Europe: La France en jeu* (Paris: Editions Sociales: Notre Temps/Tribune, 1979).

M. dell'Omodarme, 'Ruolo e azione del Parlamento europeo per l'elezione a suffragio universale diretto dei suoi membri', *Politico,* vol. XXXVI (1971).

H. Dessloch, 'Europäische Wahlen 1978?', *Politische Studien,* no. 232 (1977).

W. Dettling, *Die Christliche Demokratie vor den Europawahlen* (Hanover: Niedersächsische Landeszentrale für Politische Bildung, 1978).

K. Deutsch *et al., France, Germany and the Western Alliance: A Study of Élite Attitudes on European Integration and World Politics* (New York: Scribner's, 1967).

Dokumente, special edition 'Direktwahl in Europa – mehr Demokratie' (Cologne: Verlag der Dokumente, March 1977).

W. Dzieyk, 'Programme und Satzungen der Parteibünde in der Europäischen Gemeinschaft', *Zeitschrift für Parlamentsfragen,* vol. 9, no. 2 (June 1978).

P. Ebsworth (ed.) *Europe: A Socialist Strategy* (Edinburgh: EUSPB, 1979).

R. Edwards, 'Experiences of a Labour Member of the European Parliament', *Government and Opposition* (Spring 1979).

Europa Archiv, vol. 14, no. 2 (December 1978), special edition on direct elections (Bonn: Verlag für Internationale Politik).

W. J. Feld (ed.), *The Foreign Policies of West European Socialist Parties* (New York: Praeger, 1978).

J. Fitzmaurice, *The Party Groups in the European Parliament* (Farnborough, Hants: Saxon House, 1975).

J. Fitzmaurice, 'National parliaments and European policy-making: the case of Denmark', *Parliamentary Affairs,* vol. XXIX, no. 3 (Summer 1976).

J. Fitzmaurice, *The European Parliament* (Farnborough, Hants: Saxon House, 1978).

J. Forman, 'Preparations for direct elections in the United Kingdom',

Common Market Law Review, vol. 15 (August 1978).

J. R. Frears, 'The French Parliament and the European Community', *Journal of Common Market Studies*, vol. 12 (1975).

Government and Opposition, special edition entitled 'After the European Elections', vol. 14, no. 4 (Autumn 1979).

N. Gresch, 'Die supranationalen Fraktionen im Europäischen Parlament', *Zeitschrift für Parlamentsfragen*, vol. 7, no. 2 (July 1976).

N. Gresch, *Transnationale Parteienzusammenarbeit in der EG* (Baden-Baden: Nomos Verlagsgesellschaft, 1978).

E. B. Haas, *The Uniting of Europe: Political, Social and Economic Forces, 1950–1957* (Stanford, Cal.: Stanford University Press, 1958).

R. J. Harrison, *Europe in Question: Theories of Regional International Integration* (London: Allen & Unwin, 1974).

S. Henig (ed.), *Political Parties in the European Community* (London: Policy Studies Institute and Allen & Unwin, 1979).

S. Henig and J. Pinder (eds), *European Political Parties* (London: Allen & Unwin, 1969).

V. Herman and J. Lodge, *The European Parliament and the European Community* (London: Macmillan, 1978).

V. Herman and J. Lodge, 'Is the European Parliament a Parliament?', *European Journal of Political Research*, vol. 6 (1978).

V. Herman and R. van Schendelen (eds), *The European Parliament and the National Parliaments* (Farnborough, Hants: Saxon House, 1979).

J. C. Hollick, 'Direct elections to the European Parliament: the French debate', *The World Today*, vol. 33, no. 12 (December 1977).

R. Hrbek, *Die SPD — Deutschland und Europa: die Haltung der Sozialdemokratie zum Verhältnis von Deutschland-Politik und West-Integration, 1945–1957* (Bonn, Europa Union Verlag, 1972).

R. Hrbek, 'Parteibünde: Unterbau der EP-Fraktionen und unverzichtbares Element einer funktionsfähigen Infrastruktur der EG: Entwicklungsstand, Probleme und Perspektiven', *Zeitschrift für Parlamentsfragen*, vol. 7 (July 1976).

R. Hrbek, 'Parteibünde in der Europäischen Gemeinschaft auf dem Weg zu programmatischem Profil', *Europa-Archiv* (10/1978).

R. Inglehart, 'Public opinion and regional integration', in M. Hodges (ed.), *European Integration: Selected Readings* (Harmondsworth: Penguin, 1972).

R. E. M. Irving, *Christian Democracy in France* (London: Allen & Unwin, 1973).

R. E. M. Irving, 'Italy's Christian Democrats and European integration', *International Affairs*, vol. 52, no. 3 (July 1976).

R. E. M. Irving, 'The European policy of the French and Italian Communists', *International Affairs*, vol. 53, no. 3 (July 1977).

R. E. M. Irving, *The Christian Democractic Parties of Western Europe* (London: Allen & Unwin, 1979).

R. Jackson and J. Fitzmaurice, *The European Parliament: A Guide to Direct Elections* (Harmondsworth: Penguin, 1979).

T. Jansen and V. Kallenbach, *Die europäischen Parteien* (Bonn: Europa Union Verlag, 1977).

A. Jüttner and H.-J. Liese, *Taschenbuch der Europäischen Parteien und Wahlen* (Munich: Günter Olzog Verlag, 1977).

H. H. Kerr, 'Changing attitudes through international participation: European parliamentarians and integration', *International Organisation*, vol. 27 (1973).

P. Kirk, 'A team for Europe', *Spectator* (21 August 1976).

P. Kirk, 'Britain's imprint on Europe', *Spectator* (4 September 1976).

E. Klepsch and E. Reister, *Der Europäische Abgeordnete* (Baden-Baden: Nomos Verlagsgesellschaft, 1978).

M. Kolinsky, 'Parliamentary scrutiny of European legislation', *Government and Opposition*, vol. 10, no. 1 (Winter 1975).

Konrad-Adenauer-Stiftung, *Die Europäischen Parteien der Mitte*, Handbücher der Politischen Akademie Eichholz (Bonn: Eichholz-Verlag, 1978).

E. Lakeman, *Nine Democracies: Electoral Systems of the Countries of the European Economic Community* (London: Arthur McDougall Fund, 1973).

T. Läufer, *Begründungen und Stellungnahmen zur Direktwahl des Europäischen Parlaments* (Bonn: Institut für Europäische Politik, 1977).

T. Läufer, *22 Fragen zur Direktwahl* (Bonn: Institut für Europäische Politik and Europa Union Verlag, 1978).

J. F. Leich, 'The Italian Communists and the European Parliament', *Journal of Common Market Studies*, vol. 9 (1971).

R. J. Lieber, *British Politics and European Unity: Parties, Élites and Pressure Groups* (Berkeley, Cal.: University of California Press, 1970).

J. Lodge, *The European Policy of the SPD* (Beverly Hills, Cal. and London: Sage Publications, 1976).

G. Marchal-van Belle, *Les Socialistes belges et l'integration européenne* (Brussels: Editions de l'Institut de Sociologie, 1968).

D. Marquand, *Parliament for Europe* (London: Cape, 1979).

R. Morgan, 'New tasks for the European Parliament', *The World Today*, vol. 35, no. 10 (October 1979).

R. Morgan and D. Allen, 'The European Parliament: direct elections in national and Community perspective', *The World Today*, vol. 34, no. 8 (August 1978).

L. A. M. Mulders, conference report on 'Direct elections and the future of the European Parliament' held in London in June 1977, in *Common Market Law Review*, vol. 15 (February 1978).

P.-C. Müller-Graff, *Die Direktwahl des Europäischen Parlaments* (Tübingen: J. C. B. Mohr (Paul Siebeck), 1977).

L. Neels, 'Preparations for direct elections in Belgium', *Common Market Law Review*, vol. 15 (August 1978).

R. Northawl and Richard Corbett, *Electing Europe's First Parliament*, Fabian Tract No. 449 (London: Fabian Society, May 1977).

G. van Oudenhove, *The Political Parties in the European Parliament* (Leyden: A. W. Sijthoff, 1965).

M. Palmer, 'The role of a directly elected European Parliament', *The World Today*, vol. 33, no. 4 (April 1977).

A. Papisca, 'I partiti politici europei, ovvero: il "Fronte dell'Europa'",

Il Mulino, no. 254 (November–December 1977).

W. E. Paterson, *The SPD and European Integration* (Farnborough, Hants: Saxon House, 1974).

W. E. Paterson and A. Thomas (eds), 'Social Democratic parties of the European Community', special supplement in *Journal of Common Market Studies*, vol. XIII, no. 4 (June 1975).

A. Pilati, 'Italian political parties and the international scene', *Lo Spettatore Internazionale*, no. 4 (October–December 1977).

G. Pridham, 'Transnational party groups in the European Parliament', *Journal of Common Market Studies*, vol. 13, no. 3 (March 1975).

G. Pridham, 'Christian Democrats, Conservatives and transnational party co-operation in the European Community: centre-forward or centre-right?', in Z. Layton-Henry (ed.), *Conservative Politics in Western Europe* (London: Macmillan, 1981).

G. Pridham and P. Pridham, 'The new European party federations and direct elections', *The World Today*, vol. 35, no. 2 (February 1979).

G. Pridham and P. Pridham, 'Towards transnational parties in the European Community', *Studies in European Politics 2* (London: Policy Studies Institute, May 1979).

G. Pridham and P. Pridham, 'Transnational parties in the European Community I: the party groups in the European Parliament' and 'Transnational parties in the European Community II: the development of European party federations', in S. Henig (ed.), *Political Parties in the European Community* (London: Policy Studies Institute and Allen & Unwin, 1979).

J. Raschke (ed.), *Die Politischen Parteien in Westeuropa* (Hamburg: Rowohlt, 1978).

H. Rattinger, M. Zängle and R. Zintl, 'The distribution of seats in the European Parliament after direct elections: a simulation study', *European Journal of Political Research*, vol. 5 (1977).

P. Reichel, 'Politisierung und Demokratisierung der EG? Zur ersten Direktwahl des Europäischen Parlaments', *Aus Politik und Zeitgeschichte* (26 May 1979).

M. Robinson, 'Preparations for direct elections in Ireland', *Common Market Law Review*, vol. 15 (May 1978).

D. Sassoon, 'The Italian Communist Party's European strategy', *Political Quarterly*, vol. 47 (July 1976).

C. Schöndube (ed.) *Parlamentarismus und Europäische Integration* (Bonn: Bundeszentrale für politische Bildung, 1975).

C. Schöndube (ed.), *Die Direktwahl des Europäischen Parlaments* (Bonn: Europa Union Verlag, 1977).

R. J. Shepherd, *Public Opinion and European Integration* (Farnborough, Hants: Saxon House, 1975).

A. Shlaim, 'The Vedel Report and the reform of the European Parliament', *Parliamentary Affairs*, vol. 27 (1974).

T. Stammen, *Parteien in Europa* (Munich: C. H. Beck, 1978).

M. Steed, 'The European Parliament: the significance of direct election', *Government and Opposition*, vol. 6, no. 4 (Autumn 1971).

M. Stewart, 'Direct elections to the European Parliament', *Common*

Market Law Review, vol. 13 (1976).

P. Vannicelli, *Italy, NATO and the European Community* (Cambridge, Mass.: Center for International Affairs and Harvard University Press, 1974).

W. J. Veenstra, 'De Partij van de Arbeid en Europa', *Internationale Spectator* (April 1977).

Vers les elections européennes, Etudes et Perspectives Européennes, colloque organisé by L'Association Française d'Etude pour l'Union Européenne, Le Centre Culturel Allemand Goethe Institut Paris, Le Centre Universitaire d'Etudes des Communautés Européennes de Paris, 29–30 September 1977, Paris.

H. Vredeling, 'The Common Market of political parties', *Government and Opposition*, vol. 6, no. 4 (Autumn 1971).

R. Walker, *Dal confronto al consenso: i partiti politici italiani e l'integrazione europea* (Bologna: Il Mulino, 1976).

H. Wallace, 'The impact of the European Communities on national policy-making', *Government and Opposition*, vol. 6, no. 4 (Autumn 1971).

H. Wallace, 'Direct elections and the political dynamics of the European Communities', *Journal of Common Market Studies*, vol. 17, no. 4 (June 1979).

C. Webb, 'Eurocommunism and the European Communities', *Journal of Common Market Studies*, vol. XVII, no. 3 (March 1979).

M. Wheaton, 'The Labour Party and Europe 1950–1971', in G. Ionescu (ed.), *The New Politics of European Integration* (London: Macmillan, 1972).

B. Wigotski, 'Sozialdemokratische Plattform für die Europäischen Wahlen – Zum Stand der Diskussion' *Die Neue Gesellschaft*, 4/77.

F. R. Willis, *France, Germany and the New Europe 1945–1967* (London: Oxford University Press, 1969).

G. Zellentin, 'Form and function of the opposition in the European Communities', *Government and Opposition*, vol. 2, no. 3 (April–July 1967).

Zusammenarbeit der Parteien in Westeuropa (Bonn: Schriftenreihe der Bundeszentrale für Politische Bildung, 1976).

2 Documentary Material

G. Amendola, *I Comunisti italiani e le elezioni europee, Relazione al Comitato Centrale del PCI del 4/5/6 dicembre 1978.* Supplemento a *I Comunisti italiani e l'Europa* a cura del segretariato del gruppo comunista e apparentati, Luxemburg.

Campaign Guide for Europe 1979 (London: Conservative Central Office, 1979.

Christian Democratic Group (Group of the European People's Party, *CD–Europe* bulletin (1976 onwards).

————, *European Digest*, Christian Democratic group of the European Parliament (ed.), vol. 1 onwards (Luxemburg).

——————, *I DC Italiani al Parlamento Europeo* (Luxemburg: July 1978).

——————, *Relazione di attività del gruppo Democratico Cristiano (Gruppo del Partito Popolare Europeo) del Parlamento Europeo per il periodo intercorrente tra il 1° e il 11° Congresso del Partito Popolare Europeo, marzo 1978-febbraio 1979* (Luxemburg: February 1979).

——————, *Report on the Activities of the Christian Democratic Group of the European Parliament (Group of the European People's Party), 15.5.1977-15.5.1978* (Luxemburg, May 1978).

——————, *The Contribution of the Christian Democrats to the Construction of Europe* (Luxemburg: January 1979), Doc/1128/79/GB/tg.

——————, F. Fugmann (ed.), *The 1979 Direct Elections – A Background to European Policy as Seen by the Christian Democratic Group (Group of the European People's Party) of the European Parliament* (Luxemburg: 1979).

——————, *Twenty-Five Years: Christian Democratic Group 1953–1978* (1978).

Christlich-Demokratische Union (CDU), *CDU-Dokumentation.*

——————, *CDU – Europawahl*, no. 1/2, 11 January 1979–no. 22, 31 May 1979 (Bonn).

——————, *Europa*, CDU – Bundesgeschäftsstelle Abt. Information/Dokumentation, nos 1–21 (Bonn, 17 January 1979–6 June 1979).

——————, *Europaparteitag der CDU, Kiel, 26 und 27 März, 1979 – Reden, Dokumente, Beschlüsse* (Bonn: 1979).

——————, *Informationen für den Europa-Wahlkampf 1979*, no. 1, 11 April 1979–no. 15, 5 June 1979 (Bonn).

——————, *Presseschau*, Bundesgeschäftsstelle Abt. Information/Dokumentation, miscellaneous issues (Bonn).

——————, *Redner-Handbuch für den Europa-Wahlkampf* (Bonn: 1979).

Communist group, *I Comunisti al Parlamento europeo: interventi dei parlamentari italiani del gruppo comunista e apparentati nelle sedute del Parlamento europeo 1978* (various issues).

——————, *I Comunisti italiani al Parlamento Europeo: interventi dei Parlamentari della delegazione PCI-PSIUP-Ind. Sinistra nelle sedute del P.E. dal marzo 1969 all octobre 1972*, numero speciale di 'Note – Informazioni – Documentazione' (Luxemburg: December 1972).

——————, *I Comunisti italiani e l'Europa: dichiarzioni, documenti, interventi, 1973–1976* (Luxemburg).

——————, *I Comunisti italiani e l'Europa: dichiarazioni, documenti, interventi, 1977–1978* (Luxemburg).

——————, *Les Communistes au Parlement européen: interventions des parlementaires du Group Communiste et Apparentés (Ind. Sin. – SF) de septembre 1976 à décembre 1976*, numéro special 'Les Communistes au Parlement européen' (Luxemburg).

Deutsche Gruppe der Liberalen Internationale und Liberale Bewegung für ein Vereintes Europa e.V., *Programmatische Aussagen der Liberalen Parteien in der EG* (Bonn: 1978).

Europe (Brussels: Agence Internationale d'Information pour la Presse, April–July 1979).

European Conservative group, *Conservatives in Europe* (Luxemburg: 1979).

———, *European Conservative*, issue no. 1 onwards (Luxemburg: 1978 onwards).

European Liberals and Democrats (ELD/LDE), *Congress Brussels 1977: 18/19/20 November* (Brussels).

———, *Congress London 2/3 December 1978* (Brussels).

———, *Constitution* (Stuttgart: 26–27 March 1976).

———, *Meeting Luxembourg 1979: Saturday, 7 April 1979* (Brussels).

———, *Programme for Europe* (Brussels).

European Parliament, *Debates: Reports of Proceedings* (Luxemburg).

———, *Elections to the European Parliament by Direct Universal Suffrage* (Luxemburg: July 1977).

———, *Electoral Laws of Parliaments of the Member States of the European Communities* (Luxemburg: August 1977).

———, *European Elections Briefing*, nos. 1–6 (London: January 1977–September 1978).

———, *European Parliament Digest*, no. 1 onwards (London: November 1979 onwards).

———, *European Parliament – EP News*, vol. 1, no. 1 onwards (Luxemburg: July 1979 onwards).

———, *European Parliament Report*, nos. 6–58 (London: November 1974–July/August 1979).

———, *Information: The Sittings*, January 1977 onwards (gave way to *EP News*) (Luxemburg).

———, *List of Members of the Bureau, Parliament, Political Groups and Committees* (Luxemburg: July 1975 onwards).

———, *Minutes of Proceedings of the Sittings* (Luxemburg).

———, *The Week* (Luxemburg: February 1977 onwards).

European People's Party (PPE/EVP), J. Müller, 'Vorgeschichte und Gründung der Europäischen Volkspartei Föderation der Christlich-Demokratischen Parteien der Europäischen Gemeinschaft', mimeograph (Brussels: January 1977).

———, Programme of the European People's Party (1978).

———, Statutes (8 July 1976).

Freie Demokratische Partei (FDP), *Leitlinien liberaler Europa-Politik* (Bonn: 1975).

———, *Liberale Argumente zu Europa-Wahl und ELD Programm* (Bonn: October 1978).

Labour Party (British), *Labour and Europe: Recent Statements of Policy* (London: 1978).

———, *Parliamentary Labour Party – Delegation to the European Parliament – Report 1975/1977* (London: April 1977).

———, *Parliamentary Labour Party – Delegation to the European Parliament – Report March 1977 – March 1978* (London: July 1978).

———, *The EEC and Britain: A Socialist Perspective* (London: October 1977).

Liberal group, *Présence Liberale* (Luxemburg: 1977 onwards).

————————, *Speeches and Initiatives by Members of the Liberal and Democratic Group of the European Parliament* (Luxemburg).

————————, *Twenty-Five years, 20.6.1953–20.6.1978* (Luxemburg: 1978).

W. Mischnick (ed.), *The Liberals for Europe* (Bonn: FDP-Fraktion im Deutschen Bundestag, 1976).

Le Monde, Dossiers et Documents – 'Les Premières Elections euro-péennes, juin 1979 – la campagne et les résultats, les institutions et le bilan de la CEE' (Paris: June 1979).

J. Müller, 'Bedeutung und Notwendigkeit der Integration der politischen Parteien auf der Europäischen Ebene und ihres Zusammenwirkens' (mimeograph) (Brussels: May 1974).

Parti Communiste Français, *Les Communistes Français et l'Europe*, no. 1 onwards.

Partito Comunista Italiano, *The Italian Communists*, PCI Information Service for Abroad, bi-monthly bulletin of the PCI in French, Spanish and English (Rome, PCI).

Socialist Confederation, *Appeal to the Electorate – Europa 79* (Brussels: 1979).

————————, *Conference 23/24 June 1978, Brussels – Political Declaration* (Brussels: 1978).

————————, H. Köhnen, *Co-operation between the Socialist Parties of the European Community*, background document, adapted from an article in *Neue Gesellschaft*, vol. 6/76 (Brussels: October 1976).

————————, *European Socialists on the Eve of Direct Elections* (Brussels, June 1978).

————————. *Rules of Procedure of the Congress of the Confederation of the Socialist Parties of the European Community* (Brussels: November 1978).

————————, *Rules of Procedure of the Confederation of Socialist Parties of the European Community* (Luxemburg: 27 September 1974).

Socialist group, *Euso*, monthly review (Luxemburg). See the following articles in particular: 'Socialist Group 1953–1978', no. 5 (June 1978); 'Confederation of the Socialist Parties of the European Community', no. 10 (December 1978); '10th Congress of the Confederation of Socialist Parties of the European Community', no. 3 (1979).

————————, L. Fellermaier, *The Work of the Socialist Group in the European Parliament*, report to the 10th Congress of the Confederation of the Socialist Parties of the European Community (Brussels: January 1979).

Socialist Community, journal of Young European Left (London).

Sozialdemokratische Partei Deutschlands (SPD), Bundes-Delegierten-Konferenz und Ausserordentlicher Parteitag Köln, Mess-Kongress-Zentrum Ost 9–10.12.1978, Unkorrigiertes Protokoll 9 and 10 (Bonn).

————————, *Dokumente zur Europapolitik* (Bonn: 1978).

————————, *Parteiarbeit*, Handbuch für die Arbeit in sozialdemokratischen Ortsvereinen–Europa 79 Daten, Dokumente, Materialien (Bonn: 1978).

————————, *Soziale Demokratie für Europa: Programm der Sozial-demokratischen Partei Deutschlands für die erste Europäische Direkt-wahl 1979* (Bonn: 1978).

M. Steed, *The French Threat* (Wells: New Outlook, January 1976).

M. Steed, *Who's a Liberal in Europe?* (booklet published by Community Newspapers Ltd, Manchester, undated).

W. Stephens and T. Llewellyn, *A Parliament Is Born: The European Parliament After Direct Elections* (London: Bow Publications, February 1979).

Transnational 8: Europa wählen, Der Bund der Sozialdemokratischen Parteien der Europäischen Gemeinschaft stellt sich vor (Bonn: Europa Union Verlag, 1978).

Transnational 9: Europa wählen, Die Föderation der Europäischen Liberalen Demokraten stellt sich vor (Bonn: Europa Union Verlag, 1978).

3 Newspapers Consulted

Algemeen Dagblad (Rotterdam).
Corriere della Sera (Milan).
Daily Telegraph (London).
The Economist (London).
Europäische Zeitung (Bonn).
Financial Times (London).
Frankfurter Allgemeine Zeitung (Frankfurt/Main).
Frankfurter Rundschau (Frankfurt/Main).
The German Tribune (Hamburg).
Guardian (London).
L'Humanité (Paris).
The Irish Times (Dublin).
Luxemburger-Wort (Luxemburg).
Le Monde (Paris).

Neue Zürcher Zeitung (Zürich).
Observer (London).
Panorama (Milan).
Das Parlament (Bonn).
Politiken (Copenhagen).
Il Popolo (Rome).
Le Soir (Brussels).
Spectator (London).
Der Spiegel (Hamburg).
Stuttgarter Zeitung (Stuttgart).
Sunday Times (London).
The Times (London).
l'Unità (Rome).
Die Welt (Hamburg).
Western Mail (Cardiff).
Die Zeit (Hamburg).

Index

For Product Safety Concerns and Information please contact our EU
representative GPSR@taylorandfrancis.com
Taylor & Francis Verlag GmbH, Kaufingerstraße 24, 80331 München, Germany

www.ingramcontent.com/pod-product-compliance
Lightning Source LLC
Chambersburg PA
CBHW071838270326
41929CB00013B/2031